PSYCHOLOGY
OF INDUSTRIAL
BEHAVIOR

Third Edition

PSYCHOLOGY OF INDUSTRIAL BEHAVIOR

HENRY CLAY SMITH, Ph.D.

Professor of Psychology
Michigan State University

JOHN H. WAKELEY, Ph.D.

Associate Professor of Psychology
Michigan State University

McGRAW-HILL BOOK COMPANY

New York   St. Louis   San Francisco   Düsseldorf
Johannesburg   Kualu Lumpur   London   Mexico
Montreal   New Delhi   Panama   Rio de Janeiro
Singapore   Sydney   Toronto

This book was set in Univers by Allen-Wayne,
and printed and bound by Kingsport Press, Inc.
The designer was Allen-Wayne.
The editor was Walter Maytham.
Sally Ellyson supervised production.

PSYCHOLOGY OF INDUSTRIAL BEHAVIOR

Library of Congress Catalog Card Number 72-172264

07-058900-3

1234567890KPKP798765432

To Our Wives

CONTENTS

PREFACE

This revision, like the first two editions, is designed as a text for courses in business psychology, personnel psychology, and industrial psychology. The education, experiences, and interests of students in these courses differ widely. Most of the students are undergraduates who have had only one other course in psychology, but some are graduate students with a broad background in psychology. Many of these are planning careers as business administrators, some are considering careers as industrial psychologists, and some have not yet made career decisions. However, all share an interest in understanding the human problems of modern business and industrial organizations.

Executives, managers, and supervisors have day-to-day responsibilities and experiences which make them especially aware of the importance of these problems. They, too, should find this book a useful part of their personal reading and training.

Since the second edition, there have been many new developments in the field, among them the techniques of organization development, comparatively unknown in 1964. These new developments are discussed and old problems re-examined in the light of new facts (more than one quarter of the references used in the present edition were published since the last revision). New facts lead to reexamination of old premises; in the past it seemed appropriate to accept the form of the organization as a given and the goals of productivity and job satisfaction as its basic aims. New facts reveal that the individual's satisfaction with conditions surrounding his work differs from his satisfaction with the work itself. Consequently the aims of the organization are no longer two, but three: productivity, integration (satisfaction with the work environment), and morale (satisfaction with the work itself). These findings indicate that the form of the organization is not a given but a variable which plays a major role in the psychology of industrial behavior.

This edition is organized in four parts. Part 1 examines how organizations are structured, what goals they pursue, and how they go about measuring progress toward their goals. Part 2 is concerned with how people relate to the various aspects of their jobs. Why do people work at all? How do they relate to their tools and equipment, to co-workers, to leaders and supervisors? Part 3 discusses how organizations can improve through selection, training and appraisal of personnel, as well as through changes in basic systems and structures. Part 4 provides two summaries of the book: one from the perspective of the psychologist and the other from the perspective of the executive.

Throughout this edition three broad principles guide the search for solutions to specific problems. The first is the principle of common goals: "The more common goals a company and its workers can develop, the more fully will the potentialities of the organization and its members be realized." The second is the principle of supportive relationships: "The leadership and other processes of the organization must be such as to ensure a maximum probability that in all interactions each member will view the experience as one which builds and maintains his sense of personal worth and importance." The third is the principle of responsibility: "The processes of the company must be such as to ensure a maximum probability that each member will seek and accept more responsibility for his own work and for the work of the organization."

Our thanks are due the students and teachers who evaluated and commented on the earlier editions. Their advice has led to changes that, we hope, make the book more readable and useful. We are grateful to our wives for what they did with typing and details and for who they are.

Henry Clay Smith
John H. Wakeley

1

ORGANIZATIONS
AND THEIR GOALS

In 1970 several hundred psychologists in the United States were working with governmental agencies or private companies. The typical industrial psychologist makes over $24,000 per year (Vincent, 1969). He
earns his salary by helping an organization to select, place, train, appraise, and counsel its employees at all levels. He also helps the organization to develop more effective relations between men and machines,
between individuals and groups, and between the organization and the
larger community. The major purpose of this book is to explain the
work of an industrial psychologist. To do this, it is necessary to know
what an organization is, what its goals are, and what role the psychologist plays in relation to these goals.

1

THE ORGANIZATION

An organization is a group of people brought together to achieve human goals. A human invention to meet human needs, its success depends upon how it is deliberately structured, how it deals with the structure that arises without deliberation, and how it defines and works toward its goals. These basic problems face every organization whether family or church, orchestra or art gallery, football team or bridge club, army or corporation. The primary concern of the industrial psychologist, however, is with the business and industrial organizations in which most people work in our modern society.

FORMAL STRUCTURE

The most obvious need of an organization is for rules and customs to specify how individuals should relate to each other. If people behave randomly toward each other, then the chance of accomplishing a specific goal is small.

Rules about how to act and react help remove some of the uncertainty from relationships and increase the likelihood of cooperation. If a rule says that the small man shall hold the chisel and the big man shall swing the sledge, they can go immediately to the task. If there is a custom in a council that the oldest man speaks first, then when the men gather about the council fire no time is wasted in deciding who the first speaker is to be. The major difference between an organization and a crowd is the presence of rules which specify how people are to act toward each other.

Human organizations have faced the problem of rules from the beginning. The Egyptians building pyramids 6,000 years ago and the Egyptians building dams on the Nile in modern times need to answer the same kinds of questions. How shall the work which needs to be done be divided among the people who are available to do it? Who shall divide up the work? How shall workers be recruited, selected, and trained? What rules shall govern them? What should workers receive for their efforts? How can "superior" workers be differentiated from "inferior" workers? How can the organization survive until the job is done? Though the answers change, the questions remain the same.

The answers vary because of changes in technology, communication, and the education level of the population. Above all, they are different because research has changed our thinking about what motivates human beings in organizations. In the first decades of this century people were thought to be motivated almost exclusively by economic considerations. Organizations thus sought to control people by manipulating economic incentives. Any activity which did not seem to be an attempt by the worker to maximize his economic return was considered irrational. Therefore the organization had to use rules which prevented men from working against their "own best interests." These views of man and organization were not restricted to "ignorant robber barons," "evil captains of industry," or "grasping paternalists." They were the ones accepted by almost every one, including ministers, professors, and often the working man himself.

Now in place of "economic man," we speak of "complex man" (Schein, 1965). Man is not motivated exclusively by economic considerations. Money is important, but the social and personal aspects of organizations are also important. Each person brings to the job a different mixture of motivations, skills, and traits. Since people want more than economic returns from the organizations in which they work and since people vary in how important they consider these other returns to be, organizations need rules of compensation and relation more complex than they were fifty or sixty years ago.

ORGANIZATIONAL CHARTS

Frequently the mention of formal organization brings to mind a chart such as that shown in Figure 1-1. Such charts are a useful shorthand method for presenting the complexity and dynamic quality of human organizations. Behind the shorthand, however, is a network of policies, procedures, precedents, traditions, customs, laws, and rules which relate people to their work, people to each other, and the various functions of the organization to one another.

This total masterplan of the *formal* organization tries to specify how several things should be (Tannenbaum, 1966, Chapter 1). Among these are the work to be done, the specialized groups and individuals who will do it, the order in which the events of the organization will proceed and how all these activities are to be coordinated. In addition, the system of authority as well as the methods and kinds of compensation must be made explicit. All of this can be done at an abstract level and specific people need not be taken into account. People, for purposes of establishing the formal organization, may be considered interchangeable and replaceable. For example, in Figure 1-1 the vice-president for production may be Bill Jones or Mary Jones or any other person you may think of. In any case the vice-president will "report" to the president, "consult" with other vice-presidents, and "receive reports" from directors and plant managers.

All of these specifications produce a complicated organization when they apply to large numbers of people. On the other hand even small work groups need a formal organization. For example, we may specify that the organization will have a foreman and six workmen. The foreman will assign all work and be responsible for its completion. He will check each workman every thirty minutes to see if his work is satisfactory. Each workman will receive three pounds of wheat, or one pound of salt, or one jug of wine for each eight hours he works. The foreman will receive any two of the above plus an occasional gold coin. The work unit is to build a wall three feet high and twelve feet long during each eight-hour period using the materials at hand.

BUREAUCRACY

The ideas of Max Weber (1952) about formal organization are widely known and have generated considerable research and controversy. He gave us the term *bureaucracy*. His idea was to construct a rational, impersonal system for relating people to each other and to their work. The main goal of this

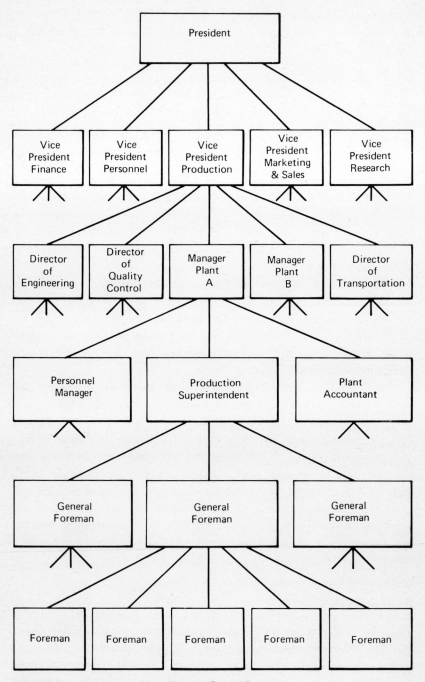

FIGURE 1-1 Organization Chart Showing Formal Structure.

system is to complete all the tasks of the organization with maximum efficiency by removing human error, favoritism, paternalism and idiosyncratic human behavior. To accomplish this each job is defined completely and carefully supervised, and no deviation from the job description is permitted. In its extreme form a bureaucracy operates like a machine for accomplishing tasks. People would be interchangeable and each person in the bureaucracy would fit himself or be fitted to the job description for his particular job.

There are no pure bureaucracies. Nevertheless, the idea of an organization in which everyone knows his job and does it in a completely rational way is appealing to some people. Others, however, feel that bureaucracy stifles human abilities and creative urges and is not necessary to control "human errors, favoritism, paternalism or idiosyncratic behaviors." Still others seem to believe that while *they* would be stifled by bureaucracy, most *other people* do require careful job descriptions and close control. Later chapters will deal with the basic problem of freedom versus control on the job. Despite the general dislike for the word "bureaucracy," the ideas of Weber continue to be important to those who try to understand organizations and the behavior of those who work in them.

INFORMAL STRUCTURE

Formal organization is important. The psychologist or anyone else studying or working in an organization needs to know how things ought to be. What has become increasingly clear, however, is that formal organization is not the whole story. People do have personal motives and peculiar ways and do not always behave as they are expected to. They are rarely interchangeable parts. The person who holds a particular job does make a difference. Whether two friends work together or two enemies work together makes a difference. The psychologist needs to know the *formal* organization but it is equally important for him to know the *informal* organization.

The informal organization is made up of the groups formed by workers, which are not recognized by the formal organization. In spite of their lack of recognition these groups are very powerful influences on the way people perform their jobs. In any particular company the psychologist will want to know about the formal organization—how people are expected to behave—and about the informal organization—how people do behave. He will also be alert to any differences between how they should and how they do behave.

THE HAWTHORNE STUDIES

In 1924 at the Hawthorne Works of the Western Electric Company a group of researchers began a series of studies concerned with the effects of illumination on the productivity of workers. The results shed little light on the effects of illumination, but they did challenge the basic ideas of how organizations operate (Roethlisberger and Dickson, 1939). The most important finding was that within the organization there exists a powerful *informal* organization.

Descriptions, discussions and criticisms of these studies are readily available and no attempt is made here to provide a complete or systematic review of the research (Roethlisberger and Dickson, 1939; Dickson and Roethlisberger, 1966; Landsberger, 1958). Some of the results are, however, worth noting.

In one set of experiments people produced efficiently under a light intensity of only three foot candles. Another group of volunteers were highly productive under conditions as dim as moonlight. Productivity was maintained under almost all light conditions without complaints of eyestrain, injury to health, or fatigue.

In another set of experiments a group of workers were isolated from other work units and formal supervision was greatly reduced. The experimenters observed that the "human relations" developed by the group permitted them to maintain high and efficient productivity over a wide range of working conditions.

The results suggested several hypotheses which have continued to be sources of interest and research for almost fifty years. The hypothesis of most interest to the discussion of informal organization is that *people in organizations do not act as isolated individuals*. Workers form small groups which are not officially recognized by the formal organization, but which affect the activities of the organization. They may improve efficiency and productivity as in the Hawthorne studies or they may restrict production. The informal organization—the way people actually behave—is one which holds power.

THE FORMAL AND INFORMAL ORGANIZATIONS TOGETHER

The difference between formal and informal organization causes problems for those interested in research about organizations as well as for leaders within organizations, because this difference makes prediction and control of behavior much more difficult. Suppose the rule says that the big man should swing the hammer and the small man should hold the chisel, but in practice two particular men work out an informal arrangement and decide to take turns. Then neither the foreman nor the researcher knows who is holding the chisel unless he is there watching.

The difference also leads to some erroneous beliefs. One of these is that the informal organization makes a company less efficient and less productive. Even though the opposite was found to be the case in the original Hawthorne studies, the belief still exists. The informal organization can, in fact, hold a company together. In one case, for example, the formal organization of a company was in a state of great flux. The top group of executives was engaged over a period of months in a heated controversy about how things should be organized and run. The staff groups working most closely with the top executives, e.g., engineering and accounting, were reduced to a state of almost complete inactivity. However, the informal organization of the company kept things going and even managed to improve some production processes.

A second misconception is that informal organization is restricted to the lower levels of the company. Informal organization has to do with how people behave and since vice-presidents as well as machine operators are people, informal organization exists at the top as well as the bottom. A group of vice-presidents may agree "informally" that certain information should not be transmitted to the president. A group of supervisors may agree that certain decisions are to be accepted without argument, but see to it that they are implemented very, very slowly.

The psychologist needs to know about the informal organization in the particular company where he may be working and to know some general hypotheses about how informal organizations come about and how they operate.

Some investigators are primarily interested in the formal *structure* of organizations, i.e., formal organization. These people explore questions of who should report to whom, how many people should report to one boss, what is the relationship between line activities and staff activities. They want to know how the pieces of a company should fit together. Sometimes students and researchers with this type of interest give the impression that people in organizations are at best a nuisance. Other investigators are primarily interested in how people *behave* in organizations. To them the important questions are why and how informal organizations come into being, what is the effect of people's attitudes on their performance, how do leaders behave, and whether people behave differently in work groups than they do in other kinds of groups. These investigators sometimes give the impression that formal structure, rules and policies are a nuisance.

The structural approach and the behavioral approach are complementary, not contradictory (Bass, 1968; Leavitt, 1962; Pugh, 1966). More and more psychologists agree that how people act in organizations depends both on the particular skills, abilities and personalities they have *and* on the kind of organization in which they work.

GOALS OF ORGANIZATIONS

What is a goal? This simple question is hard to answer. It is somewhat easier to answer for an individual, but it becomes more and more difficult as we go from the goals of one person to two people to a small group to a large organization.

An individual's goal may be defined as a statement of what he hopes will be true at some time in the future. The student may say, "My goal is to get a bachelor's degree in four years." This can be expressed in a way more consistent with the definition as, "Four years from now I hope that this is a true statement: I have a bachelors degree." This way of thinking about goals raises several problems even at the individual level. Two major ones are: How far into the future do you need to go before the statement is true? How general or how specific is the statement? Right now your goal may be to read the next sentence within one second. That is a specific and short-range goal. On the other hand, one of your goals may be to devote your life to productive service to your fellow man. That is a very broad and general goal and a very long-range one. A third major problem is how to measure progress toward a goal. The more specific and short-range the goal, the easier it is to know if you are making progress; the more general and long-range the goal, the harder.

If we try to define a goal for an organization, we still have the three problems of range, specificity and measurement. We also have an additional problem, for an organization is a group of people. "It is difficult to introduce the concept of organizational goals without reifying the organization— treating it as something more than a system of interacting individuals." (Simon, 1964, p. 2). If the organization is a small one, the goals of one especially powerful person may be the goals of the group or the members may talk until there is complete consensus about the goals. If all the members of the group share a very powerful belief, e.g., there is only one true God, then the goals of the members and the goals of the organization will quite likely correspond to a high degree.

How does a group of people go about making statements about the future when it disagrees not only about what the future should be but about what the present is? How great a variety of statements, over how great a time span, with how much generality or specificity, can an organization permit and still be an organization? Even if an organization can reach consensus or wide agreement on its goals at one time, how can the goals be changed as individuals within the group change or as the environment in which the organization exists changes?

Despite the problems and unanswered questions associated with defining goals, measuring progress toward goals, and finding ways of making statements of goals, organizations do have goals. They even try to state them explicitly. Some people leave organizations because their personal goals are incompatible with those of the organization. Others join the organization because they like its goals. In the end, whether the organization thrives or dies is based on whether there are enough people who will join and stay with the organization and whether the physical and social environment surrounding the organization is compatible with its goals.

CATEGORIES OF GOALS

All organizations have three different categories of goals. In one category are the *production* goals. Organizations form to do something, and that something must be done efficiently and effectively. The army must win battles, the church must win converts, the hospital must provide aid and comfort, and the automobile company must produce cars and trucks.

In a second category are the *integration* goals. The organization must stay together long enough to get the jobs done and must remain intact to accomplish future jobs. Even if the rules which define the organization change, or particular jobs change, or particular people leave and others join the organization, the chances of continued existence must remain high. State University is still State University but the rules by which students and faculty relate to each other have changed greatly in the last thirty years. Chrysler Corporation no longer makes 1929 Plymouths and does not make DeSoto automobiles at all but it is still Chrysler Corporation. The United States Army of 1812 and the United States Army of 1972 are recognizeable as the same organization.

In a third category are the *morale* goals. The people in the company must find the jobs to be done interesting, engaging, stimulating, or at least worth doing. If the job is not or does not seem worth doing, then eventually it is not done and the *production* and *integration* goals are threatened.

Psychologists working with organizations need to know the goals of the company. They are aware of the three general categories of goals, but for each company they need to know the specific goals in each category. From knowledge of the specific goals psychologists attempt to develop criteria for

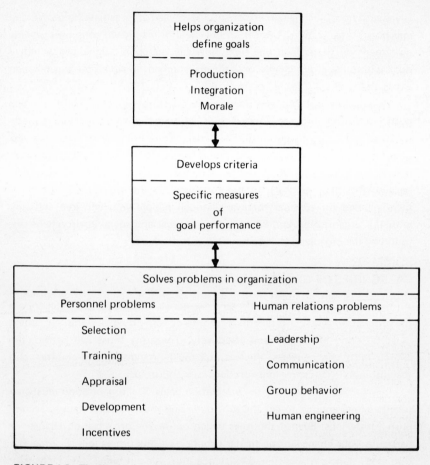

FIGURE 1-2 The Work of the Industrial Psychologist.

measuring goal performance and thereby make their major contribution to the company.

THE WORK OF THE PSYCHOLOGIST

The diagram in Figure 1-2 gives an overview of the work of the psychologist in industry and business. It also shows how this book is organized. The theme of Figure 1-2 and the theme of this book is that the major concern of the psychologist working in industry is to determine how the activities of people in the organization contribute to the attainment of organizational goals.

As the middle box in the figure shows the psychologist works to develop *criteria*—measures of goal performance—which can be used to evaluate the progress of organizations toward their goals. This is the most important and the most difficult task of the industrial psychologist. The nature of criteria, how the psychologist uses them, and ways of developing better ones are the concerns of the next chapter.

The box at the bottom of the figure indicates that psychologists have special skills and training to deal with problems involving people which occur frequently in organizations. Part 2 of this book deals with the physical and social environment of the organization, with leadership and communication. Part 3 shows how the psychologist deals with personnel problems such as selection, training, appraisal, development, and work incentives. In all of his work the psychologist wants to be sure that the solutions to the immediate problems help to move the organization closer to its goals.

SUMMARY

Organizations are attempts to get groups of people together to accomplish something. They are social inventions made by specifying how individuals are expected to relate to each other and the work tasks. The master plan which specifies how things should be is called the *formal organization*. Formal organization attempts to make the structure, policies, and procedures explicit in as rational a way as possible. While the formal organization is an abstraction of how people should behave, the *informal organization* refers to the ways in which people do behave and to the groupings of people which actually occur but are not always recognized in the formal plan. Organizations are nothing more or less than groups of people acting toward each other in accordance with certain rules, customs, and regulations. Thus people may behave in accordance with the formal or in accordance with the informal rules. And since people are people, they may behave in accordance with one set of rules at one time and another set of rules at another time; they may behave in accordance with both sets of rules at the same time; and they may, of course, not follow either set of rules. The presence of informal organizations in companies does not necessarily create conflict or make it harder to accomplish organizational goals.

All organizations have three general goals, *production* goals, *integration* goals, and *morale* goals.

The psychologist working with an organization must be aware of the formal and informal organizations. He must be particularly aware of the goals of the organization. His most important job is to try to develop criteria in order to measure progress towards the goals of the organization.

The psychologist works with a variety of personnel and human relations problems and consistently tries to measure the effects of employees' activities on the goals of the organization.

2

MEASUREMENT OF GOAL PERFORMANCE

Production, integration, morale—these are the goals of every company. All three are essential, and all are interrelated. The determination of the efficiency of an organization and of the causes for its successes and failures requires measurement of progress toward all three.

Each organization will develop its own measures of goal performance. These measures are called *criteria*. The development of useful criteria is the most important and difficult task of the industrial psychologist. In the next several pages are examples of the kinds of criteria used in business and industrial organizations and illustrations of how psychologists translate the general goals into specific measures for a particular organization.

PRODUCTIVITY

The production of a company is its output of goods or services. *Productivity is output per unit of labor input.* Productivity is so central a goal in many enterprises that it is often seen as the only goal.

The measurement of productivity is relatively easy in companies that produce raw materials like oil or coal or such material products as cars or planes. Production under these circumstances is the quantity and quality of output; productivity, the output divided by the number of man-hours required to produce it. Measurement is more difficult in a bank or a restaurant, where services rather than goods are produced. The bank, however, can count the number of checks processed by its clerks per hour and the restaurant can count the number and size of checks handled by different waitresses per evening. In any case, service organizations have profit and loss statements that provide valuable information about productivity. In churches, government bureaus, universities or other non-profit organizations, development of adequate measures of productivity becomes very difficult indeed.

Even where good measures of productivity are available, they may be of little value to the manager. He wants help in making decisions: How should we go about hiring men? Who should we hire? What kind of training should we give them? How should we evaluate their performance? How should we pay them? How should their work be organized, and what kind of work leaders should we be looking for?

Figures on last month's profits or productivity are seldom of much help to the manager in answering such questions, for a particular case of low or high productivity is usually the result of so many possible causes that it is impossible to identify the specific one with confidence. Consequently, a manager is most interested in productivity figures that *can* be related to a particular cause. The following examples use work music and rest periods to show how the psychologist is able to provide managers with such figures. The same general procedures would be followed with other possibly more important, and certainly more difficult to measure variables, such as leadership style.

PRODUCTIVITY AND WORK MUSIC

The central personnel management of a large manufacturing company wanted to know what to do about playing music during working hours. Many employees in different divisions of the company had requested permission to bring their radios to work and play them. Some divisional managers had granted permission; some had refused. The central management, feeling a consistent policy would be desirable, appointed a music committee composed of personnel representatives from the various branches to recommend a policy. The members of the committee could not agree. Most felt music would be an expensive headache because it would decrease productivity. The company had no facts about the relation between music and productivity in its plants, and the committee members could find no decisive information in the published literature. The committee recommended, therefore, that a staff psychologist at one of the branches be asked to study the relation between productivity and music (H. C. Smith, 1947).

Figure 2-1 shows the results of his study. Compared to the shifts during which music was *not* played, the music shifts were over 10 percent more productive. Half the 42 women involved in the study worked on the day shift, half on the night shift. All were on a production line manufacturing small rubber-sealed terminals for radios, and all had highly repetitive tasks. Studies of production trends showed no decline in the effectiveness of music over the eight weeks of study. Interviews with the women during the last week of the study revealed a continued high enthusiasm for the music.

The psychologist reported that music would improve productivity on most repetitive jobs and was extremely unlikely to have any adverse effect. He explained its beneficial influence by the fact that it directs employee attention away from such activities as brooding, talking, or finding excuses for leaving the job. On the basis of these conclusions, the company adopted a policy encouraging the management of branches to use music. The publication of the results of the study encouraged other companies to adopt a similar

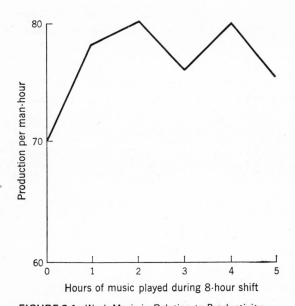

FIGURE 2-1 Work Music in Relation to Productivity.

policy. Between 1947 and 1957, the number of companies providing music for employees increased from 23 to 35 percent (Scott et al., 1961). Today companies such as Muzak take a leading role in researching the effects of music in work situations and selling music systems to a wide variety of companies. Many banks, insurance companies and retail stores as well as business and industrial organizations include music as a part of the work environment.

PRODUCTIVITY AND REST PERIODS

The management of a large office wanted to introduce regular rest periods for the clerical workers but was uncertain about the effects upon productivity. McGehee and Owen (1940) determined the effects upon a group of 16 female comptometer operators who were processing applications for loans. The office manager kept a record of the number of applications processed by each worker each day, so that the productivity of a worker could be readily determined by dividing the number of loans processed by the number of hours worked. The psychologist first computed the average productivity of the women for two weeks during which the only authorized rest period was the 45-minute lunch period. Then the office manager announced to the girls that beginning the following Monday, an additional morning rest period from 10:22 to 10:30 and an afternoon rest period from 2:23 to 2:30 would be introduced. He also announced that the 15 minutes of rest would be added to the length of the working day. The psychologist computed the productivity for the next two weeks.

The right-hand column of Table 2-1 gives the results. The figure 100 represents the average productivity per hour before the introduction of the authorized rest period (the average number of applications actually processed per hour was 20). Compared to productivity without authorized rest periods, the productivity with rest periods was 28 percent higher.

One of the psychologists conducting the investigation had his desk in the

TABLE 2-1 **Productivity and actual rest with and without authorized rest periods**

Authorized rest period?	Minutes of actual rest per hour	Productivity
No	3.0	100
Yes	3.3	128

SOURCE: Adapted from McGehee and Owen (1940).

room with the operators prior to and during the study. Consequently, he was able to keep a record of the *un*authorized rest periods taken by each worker both when there was and when there was not any authorized rest. He recorded on a chart the number of minutes each woman was out of the workroom on an unauthorized rest period. As Table 2-1 shows, the women who had no authorized rest periods actually averaged 3 minutes of unauthorized rest each hour. The women who had an authorized rest period took only a little over a minute of unauthorized rest each hour. When the authorized and unauthorized rest for the latter group was averaged, it was only slightly more than the 3 minutes of unauthorized rest taken by the former group. That is, the office manager thought he was deciding whether to give the workers rest time. Actually, he was deciding whether or not to authorize the rest time they took anyway.

INTEGRATION

Productivity cannot be the only goal of a company, for a business not only must be productive now, but must continue to be so. In order to maintain its productivity, it must at least maintain and at best increase its integration. *The integration of a company is its ability to maintain its structure and function.* If a company is losing its workers and losing its ability to function effectively, its integration is declining. If it is keeping its workers and its effectiveness, it is maintaining its integration. If it is improving its ability to keep its workers and improving its organizational effectiveness, its integration is increasing.

Executives may feel they are forced to be concerned with immediate productivity at the expense of integration. Often, for example, a man is placed in charge of a department or plant knowing that the more he increases productivity, the better are his chances for advancement. Sometimes he can show a phony improvement by juggling the inventory or by failing to maintain the plant. That is, he can increase productivity in the short run by liquidating the physical resources of his organization. The reward system of the company may also encourage him to liquidate the human resources. He pressures his subordinates to push production up so that at the end of the year the figures show him to be a "fine manager." He is promoted to another job and repeats the performance. Meanwhile, back at the first plant, his high-pressure methods show up in decreased loyalty to the company, lack of motivation to do a job, labor turnover, slowdowns, scrap loss, and inability to meet emergencies effectively. His replacement, who finds the organization falling apart, may be handicapped for years by the deep-seated distrust and hostility generated by the "fine manager."

Integration or the lack of it is easier to see in small than in large groups. It is easier, for example, to observe in a football team than in a corporation. The degree of integration and its value are also easier to observe in a crisis than in normal times. At a critical point in a difficult game, the coach can sometimes almost see his team falling apart.

Companies are larger than teams and operate in a routine rather than a crisis atmosphere. It is not surprising, therefore, that company executives are often too little aware of the importance of company integration or of the actions that raise or lower it. Whether an executive is aware of it or not, however, the level of integration in his organization is determining his and his organization's success. Integration is, in other words, an essential company goal.

Although integration determines productivity, it does so in indirect and long-range ways. Therefore, it is best viewed as relatively independent of immediate productivity—as a goal to be sought for its own sake.

Can differences between the integration of organizations or changes in the integration within organizations be measured? They can, but the measures are harder to get and harder to interpret than measures of productivity. Companies long ago learned the danger of trusting the measurement of their economic state to the untrained. They are now learning that it is more dangerous to trust the measurement of integration to them.

The most obvious, serious, and objective signs of disintegration are increasing labor turnover and grievances. More sensitive signs are increasing dissatisfactions—with company policies, with company administration and supervision, with working conditions, and with interpersonal relationships on the job. Obtaining criteria of integration and evaluating possible executive actions in the light of them are tasks that the industrial psychologist is being increasingly called upon to perform.

INTEGRATION AND JOB ORIENTATION

A worker who is hired for a job that he knows about is more likely to stay with a company than one who does not have a clear idea of what he will be doing. Weitz (1956) tested this principle for an insurance company. He sent a booklet describing the job of insurance agent to one group of applicants and did not send the booklet to a control group of applicants.

Table 2-2 shows the percentage of agents hired in each month who had left the company by the end of the experiment. For every month, the turnover for the booklet group was lower than for the no-booklet group. (Of course, the percentage drops for both groups in the later months because

TABLE 2-2 The effect of an orientation booklet on agent turnover in an insurance company

	Percent who had left the company by November		
Month that agents were hired	Among the group who did NOT receive the booklet	Among the group who DID receive the booklet	Difference
May	47	32	15
June	49	34	15
July	31	25	6
August	22	18	4
September	10	5	5
October	9	3	6
Total	27	19	8

SOURCE: Weitz (1956).

agents hired then had had less time to quit.) In all, 8 percent fewer agents had terminated from the experimental group. Giving prospective agents a realistic concept of the job is one way to reduce termination.

The rate at which workers quit is a measure of company integration. It is, however, an extreme one. Workers may show many signs of poor integration without quitting; they may feel rejected by their coworkers, lack any sense of responsibility for getting the work done, hate those who do get the work done, and believe that the company and their supervisor are remote and unconcerned about their welfare. Measures of employee attitudes provide a more sensitive index of integration.

INTEGRATION AND PRODUCTIVITY

The management and the psychologist want to improve productivity; they also want to improve integration. In deciding on the effectiveness of a course of action, therefore, it is important to have measures of both. How important it may be is shown by a study of 500 clerical workers in four divisions of a large corporation. They were all performing the same kind of billing operations (Likert, 1961).

The management of the corporation was anxious to increase the productivity of these units. It was impossible to increase the volume of work done, for it varied from time to time depending on factors beyond the control of the units. It was possible to decrease the number of workers who were performing the work. The question was: How can the number of workers be decreased without altering the volume of work done?

Two of the four divisions tried a "hierarchically controlled program." Part of the program involved intensive training for supervisors which stressed company policies, information about the company, and above all, the importance of supervisors carrying out the instructions given them by their superiors. A check on the level at which decisions were made before and after the training showed that after training, more decisions were made at a higher level. That is, the training had a significant impact on day-to-day supervisory behavior.

Another step in the program was to have all the jobs timed by the methods department and to have standard times computed. The study revealed that the billing units were overstaffed by about 30 percent except during the occasional peak-load periods. The general manager then ordered the managers of the billing units to cut their staff by 25 percent. No one was to be dismissed: workers were to be transferred and not replaced.

The program worked. A comparison was made between salary costs for the year before the program was installed and costs for the year after. They had declined 25 percent.

What happened to integration while productivity was being raised? The psychologists compared employee attitudes during the year before the program with attitudes during the year after. They found that attitudes had uniformly changed in an unfavorable direction: the employees felt less responsible for getting the work done, less favorable toward high producers, less close to the managers, and less confident that their superiors were pulling for them. In other words, while productivity was increasing, integration was drastically declining:

> If the company had had an accounting procedure which showed the investment in the human organization, it would have shown . . . the value of the human organization was less at the end of the experimental year than at the beginning. In other words, some of the increased productivity was achieved actually by liquidating part of the investment which the company had in the human organization. . . . the increase in productivity should have been charged with this cost (Likert, 1958).

The other two of the four divisions used a "participative program" to increase productivity. Its aim was to give employees more freedom of action in planning and doing their work. To achieve this supervisors were instructed to involve their subordinates in more activities, allow them to make more decisions, and supervise the details of their work less. Salary costs were measured before and after the program was put into effect. As in the first program, they declined, but not quite as much (20 percent). Unlike the hierarchically controlled divisions, however, integration in the participative divisions *increased*: employees felt more responsible, more favorably inclined toward high producers, closer to their supervisors, and more confident that their supervisors were pulling for them.

While productivity is going up, integration may be going down. In order to make sound decisions, therefore, a company must evaluate its actions in relation to measures of both.

MORALE

The morale of workers—their interest in and enthusiasm for doing their work—is vital to the success of a company. While nearly everyone involved agrees on the importance of morale, each has his own somewhat different definition of it. Guion (1958), for example, lists the following types of definitions and comments on them:

Morale as group cohesiveness: "Extremely meaningful as a basis for useful work . . . seems to ignore the individual."

Morale as job-related attitudes: "attitudes toward supervision, attitudes toward financial rewards, attitudes toward product, and the like . . . 'job satisfaction.' "

Morale as the absence of conflict: "seems rather negative . . . but it is certainly implied in much management action and conversation."

Morale as good personal adjustment: "we need a concept that is more job related than adjustment as such."

Morale as a feeling of happiness: "a person might be quite euphoric while at work in spite of his job, not because of it."

Morale as ego-involvement in one's job: "when is a man to be considered ego-involved in his job as opposed to being involved in the job as a symbol of some other involvement?"

Morale as the personal acceptance of the goals of the group: "considers morale an attribute of the individual, but it is an attribute which exists only with reference to a group of which he is a member . . . this hybrid definition is probably the one most widely accepted."

How can the confusion be reduced? One method is to define morale in a way that combines the most useful features of all definitions. Guion offers such a definition, which recognizes the complexity of the term, considers morale as an attribute of the individual in relation to his job, and can be applied to employees at any job level: "Morale is the extent to which an individual's needs are satisfied and the extent to which the individual perceives the satisfaction as stemming from his total job situation."

Another way of reducing the confusion, and the one used in this book, is to separate different components of morale, give them different names, and define them so that they overlap as little as possible. Thus *integration*, the ability of a company to maintain its structure and function, covers such aspects of morale as group cohesiveness, job-related attitudes, and the absence of conflict. In general, integration stresses conditions that surround the work to be done.

Morale, as here defined, concerns the work itself: *Morale is the worker's intrinsic interest in what he is doing as measured by his work effort, initiative, and satisfaction.* An individual or a group has high morale when there is a high level of involvement in the task to be done, great effort expended, and considerable happiness with the work itself. Low morale exists when the individual or group acts and feels apathetic, uninvolved, and indifferent about the work and its outcomes. Morale lies in the *interaction* between a worker and his work. That is, one employee may be interested and another uninterested in the same work, and some work may be more interesting to all workers than other work.

Why use two words (integration and morale) instead of one? The need for isolating attitudes toward work from attitudes toward conditions that surround the work is best shown by the confusion that occurs when the two are lumped together. Herzberg et al. (1957), for example, found 26 studies that related some measure of employee productivity (output, earnings, sales, supervisory ratings, etc.) to some measure of job attitudes (questionnaire scores, interview ratings, self-estimates of "mood," participation in activities, etc.). Table 2-3 gives the overall conflicting results. While 54 percent of the studies showed a positive relationship between productivity and attitudes, 35 percent showed no relationship and 11 percent showed an *inverse* relationship (the more favorable the attitude, the lower the productivity). Why the conflicting results? One explanation is that favorableness of any attitude is only loosely related to productivity. A more likely explanation is that some studies measured attitudes toward conditions that surround the job and some measured attitudes toward the work itself; and that these two kinds of attitudes have quite different effects. Attitudes toward the conditions that surround the work are only loosely related to immediate productivity. Morale, however, as the following studies indicate, has a more direct and positive relationship to productivity.

TABLE 2-3   The relationship between productivity and employee attitudes

Relationship between productivity and attitudes	Percent of 26 studies
The more favorable the attitude, the *higher* the productivity	54
No relationship	35
The more favorable the attitude, the *lower* the productivity	11
Total	100

SOURCE: Data from Herzberg et al. (1957), pp. 99–100.

MORALE AND PRODUCTIVITY

Morale is the degree of intrinsic interest a worker has in doing a job. The Strong Vocational Interest Blank is a widely used test designed to measure a person's degree of interest in many occupations. A high level of interest in an occupation, as measured by the test, is related to high productivity. Table 2-4, for example, shows the sales records of 160 life insurance agents, of whom 17 received C interest ratings in life insurance work, 22 B ratings, and 121 A ratings. The greater the interest in the work, the higher the sales. For instance, none of the C agents sold over $200,000, yet more than a third of the A agents did.

Interest in an occupation is also related to proficiency. Stone (1960), for example, tested the shorthand skill of 1,100 women in an advanced course by dictating typical business letters. Performance was rated on the basis of language skill, penmanship, and mastery of shorthand principles. Scores on an especially developed interest test sharply differentiated the high from the low performers.

TABLE 2-4   Life insurance sales in relation to interest in being an agent

Average annual sales	Percent of agents who sold indicated amount		
	C interest	B interest	A interest
200,000 and up	—	5	34
100,000–199,000	24	23	41
0–99,000	76	72	25
Total	100	100	100

SOURCE: Data from Strong (1943), p. 492.

MORALE AND FREEDOM

High morale is a product of what work a group is expected to do. It is also, and even more, a product of *how* the work is expected to be done. No element has more influence on morale than the amount of freedom the group is given to decide how to work. When a group is given the freedom it wants, both its morale and its productivity tend to rise. Yet many aspects of modern enterprise—the way the engineer designs the job, the way the executive supervises, the way company policies are formulated—tend to reduce the freedom of the worker and his work group.

No worker in modern industry has less freedom than the auto assembly worker on the "final line." He does not determine the position of his tools; the position is predetermined. He does not decide what to do next; the next thing is the same as the last thing. He does not decide when to go fast and when to go slow; the speed of the line and of his work is mechanically paced.

Jobs on the assembly line look much the same to the casual observer. From the standpoint of workers, however, there are small but important differences. For example, most of the jobs are mechanically paced, but some permit the worker to vary his pace. He may be able to "work up the line": work very fast on four or five units and then rest while the conveyor catches up to him. He may also be able to "bank-build": rapidly accumulate a pile of the products he is working on and then release them according to the demands of the line. Most of the jobs involve performing a single operation, but some permit the worker to rotate among several operations. Most do not require teamwork, but some do.

Small differences in freedom make big differences in morale. Walker and Guest (1952), for example, asked 180 assembly-line workers, "Would you say your job was very interesting, fairly interesting, not too interesting, or not at all interesting?" They related each worker's answer to the number of job operations he performed. As shown in Table 2-5, 70 percent of the

TABLE 2-5 Job interest and assembly-line operations performed

Operations performed	Percent answering very or fairly interesting	Percent answering not very or not at all interesting	Total percent
1	33	67	100
2–5	44	56	100
5 or more	70	30	100

SOURCE: Adapted from Walker and Guest (1952), p. 54.

workers performing five or more operations said their jobs were at least fairly interesting; only 33 percent of workers performing one operation made such a reply.

MORALE AND INTEGRATION

Morale and integration are not entirely independent goals; as morale goes up, integration tends to go up. Walker and Guest (1952), for example, related a measure of integration (absenteeism) to a measure of morale. The morale measure included six factors related to job interest and freedom: (1) degree of repetitiveness, (2) degree of mechanical pacing, (3) skill as measured by length of learning time, (4) frequency of breaks in job routine, (5) frequency of social interaction, and (6) size of interacting group. A man's job was given a zero score if he performed only one operation, if his learning time was less than one week, if he could rarely take a break, and if he had little actual interaction with other workers. On the other hand, his job received the maximum score of 12 points if he worked at several operations not on a moving conveyor, if there was a considerable learning time for the job, if there were frequent breaks in routine, and if the job involved frequent inter-action with others.

The authors of the study related absenteeism to the morale scores of 175 men as shown in Table 2-6. The results are clear: The higher the morale score, the lower the absenteeism. Thus, over three-fifths of those in the high-morale group were below the median in absenteeism; less than two-fifths of those in the low-morale group were below.

As morale goes up, integration goes up. The reverse, however, is not always true. Increasing the integration of a company does not necessarily increase morale; it may actually lower it. As integration increases, morale first rises and then declines. In a company with a chaotic organization, workers are likely to be apathetic about their work and to feel hemmed in

TABLE 2-6   Absenteeism and morale

	Percent with low morale score	Percent with high morale score
Low absenteeism (89 workers)	39	63
High absenteeism (86 workers)	61	37
Total	100	100

SOURCE: Adapted from Walker and Guest (1952).

and limited by the lack of orderly procedures. As things become better organized, workers feel freer and more interested in their work because they know what they are supposed to do and how they are supposed to do it. As organization becomes more rigid and detailed, however, morale again declines.

THE GOODNESS OF CRITERIA

Criteria are measures of goal performance. The company's goals are usually general and abstract and the psychologist works to translate these general, abstract statements into terms that can be measured. We have already looked at a variety of criteria: production of rubber-sealed terminals per man hour, number of loan applications processed, salary costs per unit of work, labor turnover, absenteeism, and employee attitudes. In developing these criteria it is not enough just to measure something. There are criteria for criteria (Weitz, 1961); they must meet certain standards if they are to be truly useful.

Some organizations measure things that are easy to measure or have "always been measured" and assume that these are criteria. However, unless what is being measured is related to company goals, the time spent in measurement is wasted (Wallace, 1965). Sometimes organizations avoid the difficult task of developing measures of integration and morale, what McGregor (1960) calls *The Human Side of Enterprise*. Likert (1967) suggests how costly it can be if one fails to keep track of the human organization:

> Assume that tomorrow morning every position in the firm is vacant, that all of the present jobs are there, all of the present plants, offices, equipment, patents, and all financial resources but no people, how long would it take and how much would it cost to hire personnel to fill all of the present jobs, to train them to their present level of competence, and to build them into the well-knit organization which now exists? (p. 103)

Executives and managers who were asked this question replied that if it could be done at all, which was doubtful, it would cost about twice the annual payroll of the company.

Measuring the easy may be a waste of time. Failing to measure the hard may lead to a false evaluation of the progress an organization is making. How can a psychologist know that he is measuring the right things and that his measures are good criteria? How does he go about developing better criteria?

WHAT SHOULD BE MEASURED?

Criteria may be classified as ultimate, intermediate and immediate. (Thorndike, 1949) The ultimate criterion is one which allows you to know that the goal statement has come true. In an industrial organization this would mean that productivity could not be improved, integration left no doubts about the organization's ability to maintain its structure and function, and morale was such that each employee considered his job the most important and satisfying thing he could do with his time. In the practical world, the ultimate is never reached. For a dead company one might be able to determine by a study of its history when the organization was best achieving its goals and which criteria came closest to being the ultimate ones. For live organizations criteria are immediate, dealing with what we can measure now, or intermediate, between what we can measure now and what we ultimately would like to measure: The ratio of man hours to light bulbs manufactured today, the percentage of people who started work last Monday who can do their job properly today, or the rate at which people quit during the past twelve months.

Psychologists are interested in discovering some absolutes and finding ultimate criteria. Usually, however, they must settle for immediate and intermediate criteria. The psychologist *working with members of the organization* should measure those immediate and intermediate activities which are the best approximations of the goals of the organization. Thus, what should be measured is a matter of judgment, not guesswork. The psychologist brings to the judgment task his knowledge of measurement and his ideas of what is likely to be relevant to the goals. By working with members of the organization he also gains their special experience and their ideas of what is likely to be relevant. If what is to be measured does not appear relevant to workers, psychologists or the management, then it is not a good criterion. The best criterion is the one managers, workers and the psychologist consider to be most relevant.

How can the psychologist know how good an apparently relevant criterion is? How does he know one is better than another? To answer these questions it is important to know the cost in time, money and effort to get the measures and the relationship of cost to benefits obtained from developing the criterion. However, the most important qualities for evaluating a criterion are its reliability and validity.

RELIABILITY

A criterion should be as reliable as possible. The techniques of estimating the reliability of criteria are difficult to master and even more difficult to apply (Dunnette, 1966; Guion, 1965); the general concept of reliability, how-ever, involves only two essential elements. Reliability concerns the *con-sistency* of the criterion. Does the measure give the same results from one time to another, from one place to another and from one measurer to another? Reliability is *relative*, not absolute. Thus, one criterion can be more reliable than another, and a criterion which is unreliable in one situation may be re-liable in another.

Measurement is a process. The process is that

> someone—
> does something—
> to something—
> with something—
> under a certain set of conditions.

For example,

> you—
> estimate the length—
> of a bean—
> with a ruler—
> under certain conditions of light, heat, moisture, etc.

If you use the same bean, ruler, and conditions to make two separate esti-mates of the length of the bean and they agree perfectly, then the measuring process is perfectly consistent. You have perfect reliability. However, if you are careless, or the bean shrinks a bit, or the ruler expands a bit, or the conditions change, then the two estimates will not agree and reliability is less than perfect. Of course, you would not make a decision about your measuring process based on only one bean; you would prefer to use ten, or a hundred, or a million beans.

If you used one hundred beans, the procedure for estimating reliability would be to measure all the beans once and then measure all the beans again. The two groups of measures would be compared with each other using the statistical method of correlation. The degree of consistency between the two groups of measurements, the estimate of reliability, would be expressed as a *coefficient of correlation*. The lowest possible coefficient of correlation is .00; the highest, 1.00. If the two groups of measures have a correlation of .00 there is no consistent relationship between them. If they have a cor-relation of 1.00, there is a perfect relationship. That is, the order of beans from longest to shortest will be exactly the same both times. A coefficient of -1.00 would also show a perfect relationship. However, this would mean that the order of beans from longest to shortest was exactly reversed from one time to the next.

Psychologists are not interested in beans, but in human beings. They are interested in such measurement problems as the morale of a foreman. The problems of such measurements are, of course, more difficult. People are by nature less consistent than beans. Mental and attitudinal qualities are less consistent than physical qualities. Furthermore, the instruments for estimating physical qualities are more highly developed than those for estimating such qualities as morale, integration, or even productivity. For these reasons, the psychologist neither expects nor finds perfect reliability. Criteria may have relatively good, not perfect, reliability and the psychologist needs to judge whether relatively good is good enough for any particular problem. In general, psychologists consider reliabilities above .90 excellent, between .80 and .90 good, and below .80 not so good. When they must choose between two measures that have unsatisfactory reliabilities, as often happens, they will settle for the measure of higher reliability. A half loaf is better than none.

Criteria must have some reliability or they are useless. If the measure of an employee's production yesterday has no relation to that of his production today, neither is likely to be related to anything else about the employee. If the merit ratings of the same workers by two supervisors have no relation to each other, neither supervisor's ratings are likely to be related to anything else about the employees. That is, if two measures of what is apparently the same factor have no relation to each other, they certainly will not be related to measures of other factors.

VALIDITY

It is necessary but not sufficient that a criterion be reliable. The criterion must also be *valid*, i.e., must actually measure what it is supposed to measure. Now criteria of low reliability cannot be valid, but criteria of high reliability may not be valid either. For example, differences in the neatness, completeness, and accuracy with which salesgirls in a department store fill out sales forms can be measured with a high degree of reliability. That particular measure, however, may not be valid for measuring sales performance, since this is determined largely by the salesgirls' skills in dealing with customers and not by their skills in filling out forms.

Many figures that are supposed to be measures of productivity are contaminated and thus invalid. For example, the number and amount of daily sales may be used as a measure of a salesman's productivity when actually his sales are largely determined by the department he is in or the territory he has. Again, the number of pages typed per hour may be used as a measure of a typist's productivity when actually the number of pages completed is greatly affected by the kind of material typed or the kind of machine employed.

Determining the validity of a criterion is an even more difficult, time-consuming, and expensive task than determining its reliability. To be valid the criterion must have high reliability, be relevant, and be free of contamination or bias.

MULTIPLE CRITERIA

Companies have three basic goals: productivity, integration, and morale. Even the most reliable and valid criterion generally measures progress toward only one of them. At best, therefore, a single criterion is an incomplete measure of a worker's or a company's performance. At worst, a single criterion, while valid in itself, may lead to wrong actions. In Likert's study of the four divisions of clerical workers doing billing operations, for example, we saw that if the investigators had used productivity measures alone, they would have been led to quite a different conclusion from the one they reached by using both a productivity and an integration criterion. One should have measures not only of productivity, or integration, or morale, but of all three. And ideally, one should not have just one measure of each, but several.

It is necessary, however, to differentiate sharply between what is and what ought to be. A company ought to have several reliable and valid measures each of productivity, integration, and morale. No company does, and only a few come close. The vast majority use quite inadequate criteria to measure goal performance. It is a continuing and difficult task of the industrial psychologist to help companies develop more, and more valid, criteria.

THE USES OF CRITERIA

Several parts of this book will discuss studies made by psychologists. In each of these, psychologists have used one or more criteria. Criteria are necessary in order to conduct any research concerning people working in organizations. They are also needed by a company to evaluate its own performance. Knowledge of criteria, and the criteria of criteria, is essential for the reader if he is to understand fully these studies, to evaluate their limitations and significance, and to make the best use of the results.

SUMMARY

Every company strives to increase its *productivity*, its output per ·nit of input; its *integration*, its ability to maintain its structure and function under stress; and its *morale*, the intrinsic interest of its workers in what they are doing. Achievement of one of these goals is only loosely and indirectly related to achievement of the others. It is best, therefore, to view them as independent goals.

A *criterion* is a measure of productivity, integration, or morale. Thus production of rubber-sealed terminals per man-hour is a criterion of productivity, number of grievances and amount of labor turnover are criteria of integration, and absenteeism and job interest scores are criteria of morale. Criteria are essential for evaluating the effects of *any* condition upon company goals. The determination of the influence of work music, rest periods, selection procedures, job orientation programs, work organization, or systems of organization requires criteria.

The goodness of criteria is determined by their reliability, validity, and comprehensiveness. The *reliability* of a criterion is its consistency, the extent to which the same measurements made at different times or in different ways agree with each other. The *validity* of a criterion is the extent to which a measure actually measures what it is supposed to measure. The use of *multiple criteria*—two or more measures of company goals—is necessary for comprehensiveness in measurement. In order to help a company, the industrial psychologist must have a deep concern with developing and using better criteria of productivity, integration, and morale.

2

HUMAN RELATIONS
IN ORGANIZATIONS

People working in organizations relate to supervisors, subordinates, peers, and friends, as well as to machines, noise, air, and other environmental factors. These elements combine into two kinds of systems—people-to-people systems and people-to-environment systems. But why do people relate to and work in the organization at all? After considering this basic question this section deals in turn with the questions: How do people relate to the physical environment? How do people relate to the groups of people with whom they work? How do people relate to their leaders? How do people communicate within the organization?

3

WHY PEOPLE WORK

To reach its goals, a company must have productive employees interested in their work. But why do people work? Why are some people productive and others not? Why do they work in certain organizations and not others? To answer these questions we must define what we mean by work. (Shimmin, 1966).

McGregor (1960) says that man works because work is as natural as play or rest. To be alive is to be active and doing, and work is a form of activity. A person works because he exists. If this kind of answer seems unsatisfying, try the following exercise. In a general way that does not depend entirely on your own set of values, make a distinction between work and play.

Psychologists answer the question of why people are active by saying they do things to reach certain goals. Man is motivated to action because he expects that his act will move him to a state of being which is more satisfying than his present state (Vroom, 1964). For example, you are reading this because you expect that when you finish you will know more than when you started and because you value knowledge more than you do ignorance. When alternative actions are open to him, a person behaves as if he were computing the relative instrumentality of the actions and the relative satisfaction (value) of the possible outcomes. Then, based on these calculations, he does what will lead to the highest anticipated satisfaction. An individual does not, of course, sit down with paper and pencil to figure out his next move. However, unconsciously a person probably does go through the process which Vroom describes.

While the particular goals of individuals may differ greatly, each person works to reach goals he thinks—rightly or wrongly—will satisfy his needs for food and safety, for belonging and status, for self-actualization.

Studies have shown that employees at all levels of an organization seek the same general goals and are in general agreement about the importance of various job characteristics. One study (Ronan, 1970) asked a sample of more than 1,000 managerial-supervisory employees, 3,500 salaried employees (e.g. engineers and accountants) and 6,000 hourly rated employees to rate various job characteristics for importance. All three groups rated the characteristics about the same way. The ratings by managerial-supervisory people correlated .87 with the ratings by salaried people and .68 with those of the hourly people. Ratings by salaried and hourly employees correlated .81. What all groups considered most important were characteristics such as satisfaction with the type of work and with doing good work, being with a company that plans for the future, job security and fair pay.

This chapter examines the conflict between the needs of the company and those of its workers, describes a theory of human needs, and suggests ways of applying the theory in company policies and practices to reduce conflict.

THE ORGANIZATION VERSUS THE MAN

In *The Organization Man*, W. H. Whyte (1956, p. 448) argues that the goals of the organization and the man in it are in conflict and that he must learn to fight:

> Not stupidly, or selfishly, for the defects of individual self-regard are no more to be venerated than the defects of cooperation. But fight he must, for the demands for his surrender are constant and powerful, the more he has come to like the life of organization the more difficult does he find it to resist these demands, or even to recognize them. It is wretched, dispiriting advice to hold before him the dream that ideally there need be no conflict between him and society. There always is;

there always must be. Ideology cannot wish it away; the peace of mind offered by organization remains a surrender, and no less so for being offered in benevolence. That is the problem.

Argyris (1962, 1964) and McGregor (1960, 1967) also believe people are in conflict with the organizations in which they work. They see people as trying, and able to be, mature when they work. Maturity they describe as man's need to be independent and autonomous, to develop his individual skills and abilities and to show that he is *self*-motivated and *self*-controlled. While Argyris and McGregor see people attempting to be mature, they see most jobs in most companies as highly specialized, overly controlled and requiring only parts of people instead of whole people.

Man and his social organizations are not inevitably in conflict. Quite the contrary. On the whole, social organizations satisfy his needs for food, shelter, protection, belonging, and status far better than he could possibly satisfy them alone. One could well say that man's most significant trait is his sociability and his greatest achievement is his ever-increasing efficiency in building social organizations that meet his needs.

A man is better off with some social organization than with none. But is he better off in a modern, complex organization than he was in a more primitive one? Banfield (1958) would answer yes. He describes the activities reported in a single issue of the weekly paper in St. George, Utah (population 4,562). Among other things, meetings of the PTA were being held in the local schools, the business and professional women's club was raising funds to build an additional dormitory at the local junior college by putting on a circus, the chamber of commerce was discussing the feasibility of building an all-weather road between two nearby towns, a local church had collected $1,393.11 in pennies for a children's hospital 350 miles away, and the county farm bureau was flying one of its members to Washington, 2,000 miles away.

Most of the people in the world are living and dying in social organizations no more complicated than the family. For example, Banfield contrasts St. George with Montegrano, a town of comparable size in southern Italy. Here there are no leaders, no followers, no public zeal, no interest in the welfare of the community, no respect for the law. The social behavior of the citizens seems guided by this principle: Maximize the immediate material advantage of the family; assume that all others will do likewise. The community has no newspaper or organized charities, and its churches engage in no welfare activities. No one in the town is animated by any desire to do good for all the population. The people are as ignorant, as sick, and as poor as those in any town of the Western world.

Even if we agreed that the advantages of the complex organization of our technological society outweighed the disadvantages, we might well see the favorable balance as small, for the weaknesses are serious. Allport (1945) has dramatized these weaknesses with a fictitious picture of a day in the life of a typical citizen:

> Citizen Sam . . . moves and has his being in the great activity wheel of New York City. Let us say that he spends his hours of unconsciousness somewhere in the badlands of the Bronx. He wakens to grab the morning's milk left at the door by an agent of a vast dairy and distributing system whose corporate maneuvers, so vital to his health, never consciously concern him. After paying hasty respects to his landlady, he dashes into the transportation system whose mechanical and civic mysteries he does not comprehend. At the factory he becomes a cog in a set of systems far beyond his ken. To him (as to everybody else) the company he works for is an abstraction; he plays an unwitting part in the "creation of surpluses" (whatever they are), and though he doesn't know it, his furious activity at his machine is regulated by the "law of supply and demand" and by "the availability of raw materials" and by "prevailing interest rates." Unknown to himself he is headed next week for the "surplus labor market." A union official collects his dues; just why he doesn't know. At noontime that corporate monstrosity, Horn and Hardart, swallows him up, much as he swallows one of its automatic pies. After more activity in the afternoon, he seeks out a standardized day-dream produced in Hollywood, to rest his tense but not efficient mind. At the end of his day, he sinks into a tavern, and unknowingly victimized by the advertising cycle, orders in rapid succession Four Roses, Three Feathers, Golden Wedding and Seagram's which "men who plan beyond tomorrow" like to drink.

What's to be done? On the one hand, our modern social organization has freed us from the hunger that plagues most of mankind and has empowered us to do many more things than men have ever been able to do in the past. We are freer than the masses of ancient Athenians, freer than our grandfathers on the frontier, and freer than our fathers who were raised in the small strait-laced town. On the other hand, some say that we are selling ourselves to the organization for a mess of pottage, swapping our personal integrity and happiness for material gains. We can't go back to simpler forms. On the contrary, we seem to be pushed toward ever more complex ones.

Social organizations, like space vehicles and television, are human inventions to satisfy human needs. But although we understand the principles behind space vehicles and television, we are still remarkably ignorant about how organizations really function and remarkably clumsy in our use of them to satisfy human needs. What are our needs as human beings, and how can a company be organized so that its own goals are better achieved while our needs are better satisfied? The problem is not to consider the organization versus the individual, but to link the organization *and* the individual.

A THEORY OF HUMAN NEEDS

A theory aims to unify the facts we have and to suggest new facts to look for. The theory of human motivation advanced by Maslow (1943, 1948, 1970) is admirably suited for understanding why men work, for it helps relate some apparently conflicting facts about men at work and suggests new ways of looking at old facts.

To begin with, the theory states that there are five general types of needs: physiological needs, safety needs, belonging needs, status needs, and self-actualization needs. The *physiological needs* are the food, water, oxygen, sex, elimination, and rest needs that are largely controlled by chemical and neural conditions within the body. Some of these needs are lacks which lead to intakes (hunger and sex) and some are distensions which lead to outputs (sex and excretion). The economic importance of these needs is suggested by advertising appeals such as:

"Taste that beats the others cold"
"The pause that refreshes"
"Take it off. Take it all off."

Many advertisements appeal to several types of needs. For example, "Go Pullman . . . comfortable, convenient, and safe" appeals to the need for safety as well as the need for rest.

The *safety needs* involve the avoidance of such physically harmful situations as excessive heat and cold, poisonous chemicals, accidents, pain, etc. Unlike the physiological needs, safety needs are not controlled by any special chemical or neural condition within the body. Frequent appeals to safety needs are made in advertisements:

"It happens within two seconds—Fast Pain Relief!"
"Feel the knot of pain fade away"
"Nothing you buy compares in importance with the things that protect your family's safety"

The last combines an appeal to both the belonging and the safety needs.

The *belonging needs* refer to the need for acceptance by other people and the need to have satisfying relationships with them. Man's inherited traits, his long dependency on his parents, and his life experiences make him aware that satisfaction of many of his needs comes through others: family, friends, work associates, and bosses. Consequently, the worker feels a strong need to be liked and accepted by his group and fears its rejection of him. The "everybody's doing it" advertisements appeal to the need for belonging:

> "In Philadelphia nearly everybody reads the Bulletin"
> "Everybody wants a DuPont sponge"

How to Win Friends and Influence People combines an appeal to both the belonging and the status needs.

Status is a position in a group that carries duties and privileges. All members of a group have status, but some have a higher status than others. It is generally recognized, for example, that mothers and fathers hold more important positions in a family than sons and daughters.

In work groups, too, some workers have positions that are recognized as being more important than the positions of other workers. The need to at least maintain and at best increase the importance of one's social position is often a powerful motive. The "keeping up with the Joneses" type of advertising appeals to the need for status:

> "When only the best will do . . ."
> "The smarter you are . . ."
> "Now, the nicest people use . . ."

Status appeals are also sometimes combined with appeals to the need for self-expression: "A man wears his Countess Mara tie for the personal pleasure it provides . . . not just for prestige. But, like the law of gravity, there's no escaping the latter."

The need for *self-actualization* is the need to become what one is capable of becoming. In a job, it is the need to do work that is of itself satisfying:

> "When I was a young engineer I designed a bridge which stands over one of the rivers around Pittsburgh. I got a tremendous feeling of satisfaction from seeing the bridge actually arise out of the plans I had drawn. I still feel wonderful every time I pass the bridge and point to it and say, 'I built that.' "
>
> A salesman tells about visiting a building in which materials on which he had "worked" were a part of the construction. It made him feel very good to see this because "I sweated out a lot of stuff working the thing out. It really gave me a new inspiration; I really had a feeling that I had a function, that I was an important part of the job."

An accounting supervisor reports that he felt wonderful during the period he was working on installing new IBM equipment. He felt especially good when it turned out after a period of time that the equipment was working, statements were going to come through on time, and a real difference had been made in the functioning of his section (Herzberg, Mausner, and Snyderman, 1959).

THE HIERARCHY OF NEEDS

Needs are arranged in a hierarchy from low to high. The "lowest" are physiological needs; next come safety needs and then the belonging and status needs. The "highest" is the need for self-actualization. The lower needs, those that adults share with animals and children, are the most urgent. We will sacrifice higher-need satisfactions to satisfy them: the starving man sacrifices safety to gain food; the well-fed but endangered man will sacrifice the satisfactions of belonging in order to make himself safe; the safe and well-fed man will sacrifice status to gain acceptance; and finally, the well-fed, safe, and accepted but status-anxious man will sacrifice self-actualization to gain status. Maslow (1948) summarizes his theory of the hierarchy of needs in this way:

> It is quite true that man lives by bread alone—when there is no bread. But what happens to man's desires when there is plenty of bread, and when his belly is chronically filled? At once other (and higher) needs emerge and these, rather than physiological hungers, dominate the organism. And when these in turn are satisfied new (and still higher) needs emerge and so on.

This theory suggests that work is most likely to satisfy the lower needs, least likely to satisfy the higher needs. L. W. Porter's results (1961) support the suggestion. He asked 75 middle managers in three large companies to say how much feeling of security, opportunity to develop close friendships, chance to satisfy their self-esteem, and possibilities of self-fulfillment they thought a person *should* get from being in their particular jobs. Porter then asked them how much they *did* get. If a manager said he got as much satisfaction in a particular area as he thought he should get, he was judged not deficient. If he said he got less satisfaction than he thought he should get, he was judged deficient for that particular need. The largest number of managers reported deficiencies in the satisfaction of their need for self-actualization (53 percent), and the smallest number reported deficiencies in the satisfaction of their physiological and safety needs (27 percent).

Porter reported further findings in a series of four research reports (1962, 1963a,b,c). In these studies Porter compared many different groups on how

TYPE OF NEED:

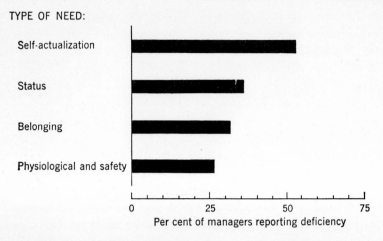

FIGURE 3-1 Deficiencies in the Satisfaction of Needs Among 75 Managers (Adapted from L. W. Porter, 1961).

important the lower and higher needs were to them and on how well they thought the needs were satisfied. His comparisons included groups working at different levels within organizations, groups working at the same level, i.e., staff versus line jobs, and groups working in large companies versus groups working in small companies. The volume of findings and the systematic way they were obtained have greatly improved our understanding of the relationships between work and the satisfaction of needs. In general, they support Maslow's theory.

DEFICIT VERSUS GROWTH NEEDS

Maslow's theory divides types of needs into *deficit* needs and *growth* needs. Only self-actualization is a growth need, an inner need to grow into what one is capable of becoming. The other needs are *deficit* needs, external needs stimulated by lack of food, lack of safety, lack of love, or the lack of status. The deficit needs must be met before the growth need emerges in the conscious life of the individual to organize his thoughts and behavior. Yet meeting his lower needs brings him not satisfaction, but the removal of dissatisfaction; not pleasure, but the absence of pain; and not happiness, but relief. That is, the lower needs are not satisfiers, but potential dissatisfiers; the need for self-actualization is not a dissatisfier, but a potential source of satisfaction and happiness.

If we apply this theory to the work situation, we see that certain relationships and conditions that are present on the job, such as poor working conditions, lack of job security, unfriendly associates, and bad bosses are closely related to the deficit needs. Their presence may produce intense dissatisfaction; their absence, however, produces not satisfaction but relief. Having a responsible, interesting, and demanding job is intimately related to the need for self-actualization. The presence of these elements leads to high job satisfaction; their absence, not to dissatisfaction, but to neutral and indifferent feelings about the job. There are dissatisfiers and satisfiers; the removal of the dissatisfiers does not make a worker happy; the absence of the satisfiers does not make him unhappy.

The dissatisfiers and the satisfiers are directly related to integration and morale. Good working conditions, job security, friendly associates, and helpful supervisors lead to high integration but not necessarily to high morale. Interesting and challenging work leads to high morale but not necessarily to high integration. The dissatisfiers, in other words, are related to integration; the satisfiers, to morale.

In one attempt to see if facts fit the theory, several hundred engineers and accountants were asked to tell a story about their actual job experiences and to "start with any kind of story you like—either a time when you felt exceptionally good or a time when you felt exceptionally bad about your job." If their first story was a "good" one, they were then asked to tell a "bad" one. If their first was "bad," they were asked to tell a "good" one (Herzberg, Mausner, and Snyderman, 1959).

After a story was recorded, it was broken into thought units ("I wasted time doing unnecessary work," "I felt eager to come to work," etc.) These thought units—more than 3,000 were eventually isolated—were typed on 3 by 5 cards. Some units concerned the feelings of the worker, some the causes of his feelings, and some the consequences of his feelings.

The reported causes of satisfaction and dissatisfaction were *not* the same. Figure 3-2 contrasts the frequency with which various job elements were related to satisfaction stories and dissatisfaction stories. Thus, 90 percent of the satisfied mentioned the work itself and only 7 percent mentioned company policies and supervision. On the other hand, only 27 percent of the dissatisfied stories mentioned the work itself and 62 percent mentioned company policies and supervision. Job dissatisfaction arose from poor interpersonal relationships, supervision, and company policies; job satisfaction, from a challenging job well done.

Active research about satisfiers and dissatisfiers continues. The theory itself needs to be made more explicit so that better ways of testing it can be devised. King (1970) found that three versions of the theory are not supported by the facts and that two other versions have not been adequately

JOB ELEMENTS:

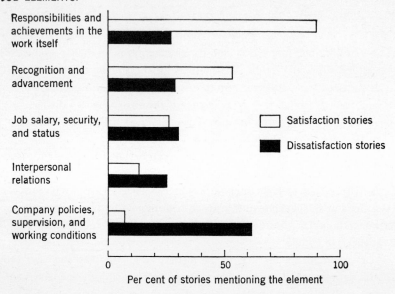

FIGURE 3-2 Elements Related to Satisfaction and Dissatisfaction in Work (Adapted from Herzberg, Mausner, and Snyderman, 1959).

tested. Obviously, much work remains to be done, both in theory and practice.

THE GROWTH NEED AND PRODUCTIVITY

As deficit needs are met, the growth need becomes more dominant: carpenters, who have little job security, report "steadiness and permanence of work" as the most important aspect of work; professional workers and executives, however, report "opportunities to make use of all one's knowledge and experience" as most important. Furthermore, Maslow's theory maintains, as the growth need becomes dominant, people are not only happier but also more creative and productive.

A study of 72 decision-making business conferences supports the relationship between growth needs and productivity (Fouriezos, Hutt, and Guetzkow, 1950). People dominated by deficit needs are *self-oriented* while people dominated by growth needs are *task-oriented*. Observers rated each meeting on a scale from self-oriented to task-oriented. A rating of zero indicated "no expression of self-oriented need" and a rating of 10 signified "all behavior of the self-oriented type."

The self-oriented need was measured by the number of expressions with dependency, status, dominance, aggression, or catharsis aspects. Remarks exemplifying each of these are as follows:

Dependency: "Mr. Chairman, would you clear this up for me?"
Status: "I was a member of a coordinating committee once and we did some wonderful work in this field."
Dominance: "This is the way it must be done."
Aggression: "I disagree. I think that all you guys are on the wrong track!"
Catharsis: "Once I was in a situation where I was forced to . . . ."

The ratings were very reliable: one observer's ratings agreed with those of others at the same meeting.

The study revealed that self-oriented behavior varied greatly from one meeting to another. Some meetings were dominated by self-oriented expressions, others by task-oriented expressions. The productivity of the meetings was related to these ratings. The participants who attended self-oriented meetings were less satisfied with the meetings, the chairman, the decisions of the meeting, and the way decisions were reached. The observers reported a high degree of conflict in such groups. Their meetings were longer but covered fewer items on the prepared agenda.

PRODUCTIVITY IN THE CLASSROOM

The dissatisfiers are related to the deficit needs; the satisfiers to the growth need. Does the removal of dissatisfiers or the creation of satisfiers lead to higher productivity? This is a hard question to answer by experiment. It requires measures of the sources of satisfaction and dissatisfaction among a large group of workers as well as measures of their individual productivity. Armour (1954) came close to meeting the requirements, but in a college class.

Armour's "workers" were 100 students with the same instructor in several different sections of a quarter course in psychology. He measured their "productivity" by the amount of knowledge they gained from the beginning to the end of the quarter. He gave the 90-item final examination on the first day of the course as well as on the last day. A student's productivity was, then, the difference between the two test scores. If, for example, he got 30 questions correct on the first day, and 70 correct on the last day, his gain score was 40 (70–30).

To measure sources of satisfaction and dissatisfaction, Armour developed and gave the students attitude scales designed to measure their enthusiasm for the general kind of work they were doing; their interest in the particular work of the course; their satisfaction with classroom working conditions; their liking for their immediate supervisor, the teacher; their liking for their coworkers, their fellow students; and their satisfaction with the incentive system. The following are typical items from the scales:

General Kind of Work (Being a student)
Being a student is just about the most enjoyable thing I have ever done.
The work of a student is eventually a great service to mankind.
I often wish I was not a college student.

Particular Work (Psychology)
Psychology is one of the most interesting subjects that I have taken.
The importance of psychology seems to me a bit overrated.
I wouldn't want to take any more courses in psychology.

Working Conditions (Class activities)
I am enthusiastic about the way the psychology classes are conducted.
I only occasionally feel satisfied with the meetings of this class.
I seldom feel satisfied with the meetings of this class.

Coworkers (Fellow students)
The students in the course are about the most pleasant I have ever met.
In general, I think the students in this class are a pretty good lot.
I don't think I would care to have these students as classmates again.

Supervisor (Instructor)
I find this instructor to be highly stimulating as a teacher.
This teacher is sometimes difficult to pay attention to.
The teacher of this course is below par as far as I'm concerned.

Incentive System (Grading method)
The grading in this course seems quite good, and I am pleased with the
    mark I'm receiving.
Although the grading system doesn't measure knowledge of the work
    very well, I still may receive a good grade.
I feel the grading in this course is very unfair, and certainly does not
    show what I know about the work.

There were eight or more statements in each subscale and the students answered each on a scale from 1 (strong disagreement) to 5 (strong agreement). In about half the statements, agreement indicated satisfaction; in the other half, dissatisfaction.

The first two scales (general kind of work and particular work) are measures of potential satisfiers. The last four scales (working conditions,

TABLE 3-1   The relation between student attitudes and productivity

Attitude scales	Correlation with gains in the course
General kind of work (being a student)	.41
Particular work (psychology)	.30
Working conditions (class activities)	.11
Coworkers (fellow students)	.01
Supervisor (instructor)	-.01
Incentive system (grading)	-.03

SOURCE: Data from Armour (1954).

coworkers, supervisor, and incentive system) are measures of potential dissatisfiers. Table 3-1 shows the correlation between scores on each of these scales and gains in the course. The results fit Maslow's theory and the industrial findings of Herzberg et al. (1959). Attitudes toward the work itself were related to productivity (.41, .30). Attitudes toward things surrounding the work (working conditions, supervisor, incentive system, etc.) were not.

The potential dissatisfiers might determine whether a student would be absent, drop the course, complain about the course, or fail to take another course in the subject. They do not seem to determine how much he learns in a course.

THE THEORY AND THE COMPANY

The theory of a hierarchy of human needs suggests new and better ways of managing workers. Managers may resist such ways because, they say, they are "practical" men. Yet it is impossible to reach any managerial decision without *some* theory about human needs. McGregor (1960) gives the following example:

> A manager . . . states that he delegates to his subordinates. When asked, he expresses assumptions such as, "People need to learn to take responsibility," or "Those closer to the situation can make the best decisions." However, he has arranged to obtain a constant flow of detailed information about the behavior of his subordinates, and he uses this information to police their behavior and to "second-guess" their decisions. He says, "I am held responsible, so I need to know what is going on." He sees no inconsistency in his behavior, nor does he recognize some other assumptions which are implicit: "People can't be trusted," or "They can't really make as good decisions as I can" (p. 7).

Every manager's acts rest on a theory. His statement "Let's be practical" actually means "Let's accept my theory without question." The psychologist cannot accept it, however, because he has put his own theory into words, found that its parts are consistent with each other and with the known facts, and believes, consequently, that it is a more effective guide for increasing productivity, integration, and morale. What are the differences between the typical manager's theory and that of the psychologist? Table 3-2 presents a comparison of the theories and their implications.

"Controllable" is the key word in the table. The psychologist sees as well as the traditional manager that the workers dislike their work and must be forced to do a fair day's work, that they avoid responsibility and show little ingenuity in solving their work problems. The psychologist, however, sees these realities as largely controlled by the theory of the manager and the

TABLE 3-2   Contrasts in the theories of the manager and the psychologist

	A traditional manager's theory	A psychologist's theory
Motivation	The average worker has an inherent dislike of work and will avoid it if he can.	The average worker does *not* have an inherent dislike of work. Work is as natural as play or rest. Depending upon *controllable conditions*, work can be a source of satisfaction and will be sought or a source of punishment and will be avoided.
Incentives	The average worker must be forcefully directed and threatened with punishment to get him to do a fair day's work.	The average worker likes to and will exercise self-direction and self-control in the service of goals to which he is committed under *controlled conditions*.
Leadership	The average worker likes to be directed, wants to avoid responsibility, and seeks security above all.	The average worker likes responsibility and will seek and accept it under *controlled conditions*.
Problem solving	Few workers have either the imagination or the ingenuity to solve organizational problems.	Many workers have the capacity to solve organizational problems. Under *controllable conditions* they will use this capacity.

SOURCE: Adapted from McGregor (1960).

policies he uses in putting his theory into action. Change the manager's theory and his policies, and these realities change.

THE PRINCIPLE OF COMMON GOALS

How can the greater potentialities of the psychologist's theory be realized? *The more goals in common a company and its workers can develop, and the better their different goals can be fitted together, the more fully realized will be the potentialities of the organization and its members.* The first step in applying this principle is to consider the goals of the worker to be as important as those of the company. Some men who run companies would rather break a leg than take this step. For example:

> A district manager in a large company is told that he is being pro-moted to a much more important policy level position at headquarters. The headquarters group carefully considered many possible candidates and had little doubt that he was not only the man for the promotion but also an obvious eventual choice for an even higher position. The group takes genuine satisfaction that such an outstanding candidate is available.
>
> The manager is appalled. His goal is to be the "best damned district manager in the company." He doesn't want a policy level job, he dis-likes the social obligations of the headquarters city, he enjoys his associ-ations with operating people in the field, he and his wife enjoy the life they have created in a small city. He expresses his feelings, but his ob-jections are brushed aside. He feels forced to take the job. Two years later he is in an even higher position. Privately, however, he expresses considerable unhappiness and dissatisfaction. He would "give anything" to be back in the situation he left two years ago (McGregor, 1960, p. 50).

The idea that the company is more important than the employee is so deeply seated in management thinking that it generally goes unquestioned or even unthought of. It is rare indeed for management to give an individual the opportunity to be an equal partner in such a decision, even though it may affect his most important personal goals. The goals of the company and the worker will never be either entirely identical or entirely harmonious. None-theless, nothing is more important to the success of a company than reducing the conflicts between worker and company goals and developing more and stronger common ones.

THE PRINCIPLE OF SUPPORTIVE RELATIONSHIPS

The most successful company is the one that most successfully builds supportive relationships. Likert (1961) defines the principle as follows:

> The leadership and other processes of the organization must be such as to ensure a maximum probability that in all interactions . . . each member will . . . view the experience as supportive and as one which builds and maintains his sense of personal worth and importance.

A person has the support of others when he feels he is understood, accepted, and liked; that his work is generally approved and respected; and that others are trying to help him to do a good job and satisfy his needs. A supportive relationship exists when each person supports the other. A supportive relationship does not necessarily exist when the boss supports the worker; it does exist when boss and worker support each other.

The absence of a supportive relationship and its pervasive consequences is suggested by the following example:

> I really think I was almost ready to have one of them nervous breakdowns or whatever you call them. I was dreading going down there all the time, and then when I'd get to work I'd be worrying about what Sam (the foreman) was going to do next, and it really was doing something to me. It works this way: I go to the foreman and I ask something about what I'm supposed to be doing and he gets nasty and sarcastic to me, and he don't give me any help, or he tells me to figure it out for myself, or that I'm the operator and what do I want him to do about it.
>
> And then one of the girls comes up to me and asks me a question and I get nasty to her, just because this guy's been sarcastic to me. Like one of the girls will come up and ask me to help her, or she'll ask me a question about how to do something, and I'll tell her to do it herself, I haven't got time, or to use her head and maybe she wouldn't have to ask so many questions. And it isn't because I don't want to help her, because usually I would. It's just that it makes me feel better to be yelling at her after somebody's been yelling at me all the time. Now, if I didn't feel that way I'd tell her, sure I'd help her and if I didn't have time right that minute I'd tell her to wait for half an hour or something and then I'd be down to help her. I like to be helpful to people when I can, but when you got somebody over you that's making things miserable for you, why you just seem to naturally take it out on the ones beneath you. So I'd act this way to the girls, and then when I'd come home I'd be a crab to my wife and kids. It worked that way with everybody down at the plant in the department—pretty soon everybody

was yelling at everybody else. You know what they say—one rotten apple is enough to ruin a whole barrel (W. F. Whyte and Gardner, 1945).

The development of a supportive relationship takes more than a hearty "first name" informality and more than a "personal interest" in the family and problems of the worker. The answers to questions like the following determine the degree of support in a supervisor-employee relationship: Does the supervisor accept or reject the employee as a person? Does he generally approve or disapprove of him? Does he like or dislike him? Do the supervisor and employee have a mutual sympathy and understanding, or is the relationship distant and formal? Is the supervisor critical of the employee's work or critical of the employee?

In composite, the supportive supervisor accepts, likes, and understands his subordinates, generally approves of their activities, and is interested in satisfying their needs. The nonsupportive supervisor rejects, dislikes, and disapproves of his subordinates, does not understand them, and is not interested in finding out about them. The nonsupportive supervisor generates anxieties and opposition regardless of his competence or the merits of his proposals.

THE PRINCIPLE OF RESPONSIBILITY

A worker is happiest and his organization is most productive when the responsibilities of his job encourage him to use all his knowledge, skill, and ingenuity to fulfill them. To achieve this state, *the processes of the company must be such as to ensure a maximum probability that each member will seek and accept responsibility for his own work and for the work of his organization.*

The presence of common goals and supportive relationships encourage, but do not ensure, that the principle of responsibility will be applied. The presence of supportive relationships and the absence of responsibility can be an explosive combination. For example, in a Pittsburgh cork plant working conditions were excellent, pay was high, and the supervisors were friendly. Yet resentment against the management was high, and the more than one thousand workers were forcefully behind a drive to unionize the plant. Typical of worker attitudes was the girl who said, "It's about time something like this happened. We have got to stand on our feet. They do everything for you but provide you with a husband, and I even know girls they got husbands for. And them what ain't got time to get pregnant, they get foster kids for" (Golden and Ruttenberg, 1942).

When responsibilities are great, men tend to respond to the challenge. Grinker and Spiegel (1945) made these comments after an intensive study of bomber crews during World War II:

> It is an interesting fact that, although the members of combat crews are thrown together only by chance, they rapidly become united to each other by the strongest bonds while in combat. . . . The men and their plane become identified with each other as "my pilot," "my bombardier," "my gunner" and so on. The emotional attitudes the fliers take toward each other have less to do with the accident of their individual personalities than with the circumstances of their association (p. 22).

Developing effectively functioning work groups like the bomber crews is essential if a company is to make full use of the capacities of its workers. In such groups, a worker seeks to get the support and recognition of other members, learns to accept the goals of the group as his goals, and strives with all his skill to make the decisions of the group effective.

Participation of the worker in decisions that affect him is also vital if he is to accept full responsibility for them. The more he has to say about the work he does, the more likely he is to become personally involved in it. The worker's participation demands are growing and are likely to continue to grow, for these demands are related to the level of his education. In 1940, less than 40 percent of the work force had a high school diploma; in 1950, 50 percent; in 1960, more than 60 percent; and very likely the percentage will rise to 75 to 80 percent by 1980. At the same time, according to one estimate, the number of bachelor's and first professional degrees awarded in 1980 is expected to be nearly twice the number of such degrees awarded in 1965 (Tickton, 1968), an increase that far exceeds the expected rate of growth of the population.

It is hard for a leader to apply the principles of common goals, supportive relationships, and responsibiltiy in handling his everyday problems; it is impossible if he holds the traditional manager's views about worker motivation. If he believes the average worker really dislikes work, has little ingenuity, has a distaste for responsibility, and needs to be forcefully directed, he cannot apply the principles.

THE SCANLON PLAN

It may be decades before we have enough skill to apply the principles of common goals, supportive relationships, and responsibility to some kinds of industrial situations. For example, a large corporation with a mass production operation and with a hostile union can do little, although even in such organizations, the principles have been successfully applied to the management of executives and professional people. Some companies, however, have made massive and effective applications of the principles. Notable among these are the companies using the Scanlon plan.

Joesph Scanlon, a cost accountant and labor leader, first proposed his plan (which will be described below) in 1938 for a steel company on the verge of failure. He was president of its local union at that time. In 1957, 21 plants using his plan met to discuss their common experiences. The plants varied widely in size, union affiliation, and economic status when the plan was adopted. Five of the plants had less than 100 employees, thirteen had between 100 and 1,000, and three had more than 1,000. Eighteen of the companies had unions; one was affiliated with the United Mine Workers, three were independent, and fourteen were affiliated with the AFL-CIO. Four were losing money when the plan was installed, twelve were about average for their industry, and three were more profitable than the average company in their industry.

In 1964 a group of about ten Midwestern companies using the Scanlon plan held their first annual conference. By 1969 the informal group of ten had added several members and become the Midwest Scanlon Associates. Their 1969 annual conference attracted representatives from more than fifty organizations which were either using or were considering using the Scanlon plan. They included banks and heavy industries, one-plant operations and international operations, unionized and non-unionized companies, family-owned and operated companies and publicly owned corporations—a broad and representative cross section of work organizations. Today the Midwest Scanlon Associates is a non-profit corporation which fosters improved management practice (Gooding, 1970), encourages research on the development of better organizations (Morrison, 1970; Ruh, 1970), and assists non-member companies who are considering using a Scanlon plan in their own operations.

COMMON GOALS

The core of Scanlon's idea was the development of stronger common goals between the company and the workers. Although his plan has many variations, it is typically embodied in a "memorandum of understanding" between a company and its union.

> This memorandum of understanding establishes a plant-wide incentive plan designed to enable all employees and officers of the _____

Company, up to and including the President, to benefit from their increased cooperation and efforts as reflected in increased productivity.

In order to assure full participation in the benefits of the increased productivity which should result from the employee-management cooperation plan, a plant-wide monthly productivity bonus shall be applied, effective _____ 19__, to remain in full force and effect for a trial period of one year, after which time its continuance will be subject to the approval of both the management and the union (Lesieur, 1958).

The bonus is based on the average payroll cost for making each dollar's worth of production in the three to five years before the plan was installed. This cost establishes a *productivity norm* (for example, 50 cents). If you were an employee, the system might be explained to you in this way:

1	Assume that this month the *sales value of production* comes to	$100,000
2	If employee work performance had been no better this month than the average for the base period, the payrool would have come to	50,000
	This is the *allowed payroll* (.50 X 100,000)	
3	Assume, however, that the actual payroll for this month figured out to be	40,000
4	This would mean an improvement over the norm amounting to	10,000
	This is the *bonus pool* (50,000 – 40,000)	
5	Set aside 20 percent of this as a reserve	2,000
6	This leaves for *immediate distribution* the sum of	8,000
*7	Deduct the company's share (25 percent of 8,000)	2,000
8	This leaves the employee's share (75 percent of 8,000)	6,000
9	The employees share amounts to	15%
	This is the *bonus percentage paid* (6,000 – 40,000	
10	Your own pay record for this month would look like this:	

Name	Total hours worked	Hourly rate	Total pay	Bonus percent	Bonus	Total
John Doe	160	$3.00	$480	15	72	$552

*Most companies in the Midwest Scanlon Association do not deduct a share for the company. They have shown they can pay the total amount as bonus and still improve profits through improved quality, reduced turnover, and improved delivery to customers.

This example does not answer the hard questions: How was the 50-cent productivity norm decided upon? Why was 20 percent put into a reserve? How was it decided to split the bonus on a 25-75 basis? The cooperative process by which these answers were reached is indicated in the following sections.

What effect does the plan have on productivity? Puckett (Lesieur, 1958) studied changes over a 2-year period in 10 plants that had the most reliable measures of productivity. The production processes in the plants varied from job-shop situations to mass production, from highly skilled toolmaking to low-skilled manual operations, and from operations employing antiquated equipment to those with entirely new equipment. The average increase in productivity was 23 percent, with a low of 10 and a high of 39 percent. Bonuses to the workers thus ranged from 8 to 29 percent. In none of the plants had employment declined, and in most it had increased. Plants also reported lower capital requirements because of more efficient use of equipment and the reduction of inventories. They also reported better quality in their products and more promptness in meeting delivery schedules. Puckett concluded, ". . . our human resources contain a potential that is apparently not fully utilized in even relatively efficient and profitable manufacturing companies. To tap this reservoir of human potential is the great challenge facing labor-management relations today."

SUPPORTIVE RELATIONSHIPS

To those who work under the plan, the increase in supportive relationships seems to be more apparent than the increase in productivity. Since supervisors and employees see themselves as working toward the same goals, friction between them is reduced. In fact, all members of the enterprise are likely to see themselves as benefiting from team effort, so interpersonal frictions are reduced. The resulting improved performance of the company increases the job security of the worker as well as increasing his pay. These increases are in addition to what he would get without the plan, for it is a basic principle of the plan that bonuses have no influence on normal wage and salary levels and normal increases. One worker, describing the changed atmosphere under the plan, said, "Formerly everyone was on his own. Now we all work for each other."

RESPONSIBILITY

The Scanlon plan increases the worker's responsibilities, because decisions are made with employee participation. Departmental committees composed of management and union representatives typically meet at least once each month to discuss ways of increasing productivity. At a higher level, a labor-management screening committee deals with suggestions that have not been disposed of at the production committee level.

Both the mechanics and the spirit of the plan free the employee to work to his capacity at his own job. They also encourage him to accept responsibilities far beyond his own, as an incident at the Lapointe Machine Tool Company in Hudson, Massachusetts illustrates. The sudden increases in production when the plan was installed began wiping out what the management had thought was a comfortable backlog of orders. By strenuous efforts, management was able to gain additional orders by June. Before the orders could be translated into work, however, weeks of designing were necessary. The usual practice of the plant was to shut down for vacations for two weeks in July. If the engineers went on vacation, no designing would be done. Davenport (1950) reports:

> Would anybody dare to ask the engineers to give up their vacations?— especially in view of the fact that, as is usual in machine shops, there was continuous bickering between the engineers and the machine operators, who were inclined to criticize the drawings as unrealistic? A delegation from the union approached Vice President Dowd, who said that he would put it up to the men themselves. When he went to the men, however, he found that agreement had already been reached at the workers' level—the engineers had sacrificed their vacations. They worked hard during July in an otherwise empty plant, and by August drawings were pouring out of the drafting room.

QUESTIONS

The limits of the Scanlon plan's application are not now certain. The plan has been typically applied in companies of several hundred employees and never in a company of over ten thousand. Would it be effective in larger organizations? Companies are becoming increasingly automated. Will the plan work in such companies where there seems little room for improvement originating anywhere except in engineering or research? Does it take special types of personalities to overcome anxieties about the plan and "sell" the philosophy successfully? Can the plan work in service organizations as well as in production organizations? There are no sure answers to these questions.

Even the present achievements of companies under the plan are not entirely certain. It is not known, for example, how many companies have thought of using the plan but did not. It is not known exactly how many have tried the plan and abandoned it. Of those using the plan, only a few have measured with any exactness the changes resulting from its installation. None have compared achievements under the plan with achievements under alternative plans.

Still, the known achievements support the newer theory of human needs and the principles derived from it: common goals, supportive relationships, and responsibility. While not all job situations permit the global applications of the principles seen in Scanlon companies, all situations provide some opportunity for some application. The theory provides, not a utopian blueprint, but a guide to the best places to look for a solution to a concrete problem at a given moment. Later chapters will turn to a consideration of everyday personnel, organizational, and management development problems in the light of the theory.

SUMMARY

While a company pays its employees to meet its needs, employees work only to meet *their* needs. Conflicts between company and employees are not inevitable; they are the result of efforts to apply theories of motivation that are inconsistent with our present knowledge of human behavior. Maslow's theory fits the facts and suggests constructive ways of resolving conflicts. It assumes there are five general types of needs: physiological, safety, belonging, status, and self-actualization needs. The needs are arranged in a hierarchy with the physiological needs being the "lowest" and the self-actualization need the "highest." The lower needs are *deficit* needs; the self-actualization need is a *growth* need. The lower needs are more urgent. Their satisfaction does increase company integration, but it does little to improve either productivity or morale. The satisfaction of the growth need, on the other hand brings personal satisfaction as well as increases in morale and productivity.

The principles of common goals, supportive relationships, and responsibility are derived from Maslow's theory and serve as general guides to the constructive solution of human problems in work situations. The Scanlon plan of management is a dramatic and successful example of the application of these principles. A study of 10 companies using the plan concludes, "Our human resources contain a potential that is apparently not fully utilized in even relatively efficient and profitable manufacturing companies. To tap this reservoir of human potential is the great challenge facing labor-management relations today."

4

THE ENVIRONMENT
OF WORK

Man has always worked to meet his needs. He has tried to make work easier and more effective by improving his relationship with the environment, and by inventing and continually perfecting tools to ease his labor. He has progressed from building pyramids with only human muscle power to constructing immensely complex machinery which can land him on the moon. In achieving this technological progress he has endured the hazards of the natural environment such as extremes of heat and cold, as well as such man-made hazards as noise pollution and foul air.

Environmental improvements have come about with the development of central heating, air conditioning, indirect lighting and sound-absorbing walls. Better tools for making use of man's energy have been engineered. For example, the goose quill pen evolved into the electric, tape-directed typewriter. Man has found ways of controlling the release of muscular energy to fit his ability to regenerate it: the lever, the inclined plane, and the pulley let him trade his time for the chance to use his energy at a lower rate. For human muscles he has substituted animal labor, water power, and finally power machinery, which represented a great break with the past and set the stage for the industrial revolution. Over the past few decades, man has developed substitutes for his senses: mechanical seeing, hearing, touching, and even smelling devices that control his mechanical muscles. Now, most revolutionary of all, he is developing substitutes for his brains: computers that receive the mechanical sensations and control the mechanical muscles.

The engineer has played an increasingly important part in making man's work easier and better. He has used his knowledge of the mechanical, chemical, and electrical properties of matter to create things that satisfy our needs: safety pins and automobiles, mousetraps and missiles. He creates machines to produce the things: hammers and punch presses, pulleys and computers. Unfortunately, he sometimes creates problems for consumers and workers: products they cannot use and machines they cannot run. The role of the psychologist in making work easier and better is to gather basic data about how human beings perform and to apply this knowledge to problems which arise in man-machine systems. (Howell and Goldstein, 1970). The endeavor to solve these problems by matching human beings and machines so that the combination is comfortable, safe, and efficient constitutes the field of human engineering.

Human engineering has many synonyms—engineering psychology, biomechanics, ergonomics, applied experimental psychology, and human-factors engineering. Like the personnel worker, the human engineer aims to increase the productivity, integration, and morale of workers. Unlike the personnel worker, the human engineer does not stress fitting the man to the job; he stresses fitting the job to the man. He aims to reorganize the job, redesign machines, and modify the environment so that work is easier and more effective. The fields of human relations and human engineering are both concerned with improving the work environment. Human relations, however, focuses upon the psychological environment; human engineering upon the physical environment.

The human engineer of a kind existed long before psychologists became interested in the field. During World War II, however, his contribution became critical. Military equipment was being designed and used that required too many hands, too many feet, or too many heads; that required operators to see invisible targets or to hear speech in the presence of deafening noise; and that required complex life-and-death decisions to be made in split seconds. "Human errors" mounted: bombs missed their mark, planes crashed, whales were depth-charged, and friendly ships were sunk. Psychologists joined with anatomists, physiologists, and engineers to form a new scientific discipline to help solve these problems.

Human engineers now influence the design of all major types of military equipment and many other things as well: control towers, aircraft instruments, telephone sets, artificial limbs, post office sorting equipment, theodolites, equipment for the earth satellite program, control panels for atomic reactors, automobiles, and numerous industrial machines. Before 1950 there was only one company with an organized program for human engineering activities. By 1957 there were 35 to 40 such companies, and by 1967 there were about 260. (Grether, 1968). Security provisions, proprietary rights, and the complexity of problems involved have combined to keep the public largely unaware of the growing impact of the human engineer on modern technology.

THE MAN-MACHINE SYSTEM

Machine and man interact as one system to accomplish what neither can do alone. If the system is to do the specified job, certain functions must be accomplished. Things need to be lifted, decisions must be made, and energy has to be controlled. How are these functions to be divided between man and machine?

Fitts' (1951) way of dividing functions between man and machine is to list all functions needed in the system and then *compare* man and machine to see which can perform each better. Whichever can perform the function better takes that function in the system. For example, in most systems the machine is better able to perform in the areas of speed and power while man is more capable of performing those functions requiring unprogrammed judgments and improvisations.

Jordan (1963) challenges Fitts' idea of comparing and then assigning man and machine to separate areas. Jordan says man and machine are *complementary* and that this fact should be the basis for allocating functions in the system. His main argument is that it is, at least theoretically, possible to design and create for any single function a machine which is better than a man, while it is impossible to design a machine which can do all of the things a man can do. Machines are consistent but not flexible; men are flexible but not consistent. Thus, while a machine will very likely be better at a particular function in a predictable and controlled environment, man is frequently needed to perform the same function when predictability and control are absent. Another way in which machine and man complement each other is that the machine degrades abruptly, it either does the job or it does not, while man degrades gracefully and can continue to do parts of the job or even all of the job if there is sufficient time. Finally, integration and morale as well as productivity must be considered in putting together man-machine systems. (Jordan, 1963, p. 169)

"When a man is forced to function like a machine he realizes that he is being used inefficiently and he experiences it as being used stupidly. Man cannot tolerate such stupidity. Overtly or covertly men resist and rebel against it. Nothing could be more inefficient and self-defeating in the long run than the construction of man-machine systems which cause human components in the system to rebel against the system."

Chapanis (1965) believes that instead of trying to develop a general solution to the problem of allocation, each situation should be treated individually. He argues that in each situation the answer depends on whether the best solution or an adequate solution is desired, on how long the system is expected to last, and the actual characteristics of the machines available.

A MODEL OF THE MAN-MACHINE SYSTEM

In whatever manner functions are distributed, man and machine become interacting parts of a system. In most cases the human engineer sees man as an information-gathering and -processing link between the "displays" and "controls" of the machine. The psychologist aids the engineer by providing information about the man component of the system, using his knowledge of human variability to evaluate systems and participating with the engineer in the actual design of new systems. At the simplest level, he works with details of a single display or control; at a more complex level, with a panel of displays and controls; and at the most complex level, with the man-machine system as a whole.

The major parts of a man-machine system are illustrated in Figure 4-1: input, mechanisms, displays, operator, controls, output, and the work environment. Driving a car is an illustration. The system requires inputs (water, oil, and gas) into the mechanisms (battery, motor, tank). The mechanisms operate displays (speed, gas, oil, and temperature gauges). The operator uses the information he gets from the displays in operating the controls (accelerator, clutch, brake, light switch). The controls determine output of the mechanisms (lights, 60 miles per hour, etc.). The heater and air conditioner determine the temperature of the work environment.

Telephones illustrate a simple two-operator system. The dialing is the input, the mechanism is the phone, the ringing is a display, and lifting the receiver is a control. A strategic missile system is a complex system made up

THE WORK ENVIRONMENT

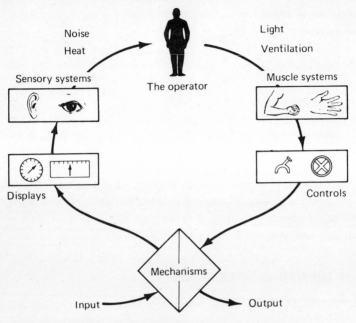

FIGURE 4-1 The Man-Machine System.

of many subsystems, each with many inputs, mechanisms, panels of displays, operators, and panels of controls. It has a single final desired output: to hit a small target thousands of miles away.

MATCHING INPUTS TO OUTPUTS

Developing an effective man-machine system is, of course, a highly technical and complicated task. One basic principle that guides the human engineer in his task is to make the best match of inputs to outputs.

Each part of the system, as well as the system as a whole, has an input and an output. Gasoline, for example, is fed to the engine; the output of the engine determines the input to the displays, the output of the displays determines the input to the operator's sensory system. Sometimes the adjacent parts are both mechanical, as in the case of the output of the engine determining the input to the displays; sometimes one is mechanical and the other is human, as in the case of the display output affecting the operator input or the operator input affecting the control output; sometimes both are human, as in the case of the hand signal of one operator determining the output of a second operator.

The car speedometer in relation to the driver illustrates a matching problem. What shape dial can the driver most accurately read: horizontal? circular? vertical? Graham (1956) drew a series of scales in white ink on black paper, each with a pointer opposite one of the numbers from 1 to 10. The scales were drawn so that the intervals between the horizontal, circular, and vertical scales were the same. All the drawings were then photographed and shown on a screen to 60 engineering students, each scale being exposed for a half second. After each exposure the students were asked to check what they thought the reading was. The percents of correct readings for the circular and horizontal dials were much higher than for the vertical ones. Why? Our eyes move more quickly and easily from side to side than up and down. Consequently, circular and horizontal dials are a much better match for the human eye than vertical ones.

ADJUSTING TIME CONSTANTS

Generally, other things being equal, the faster a system operates, the better. The parts of a system, however, are seldom equally fast. Consequently, one part of a system may be operating too fast for the next part: the gas may flood the carburetor, the speed of the motor may jam the cogs of the speedometer, or the car may be going too fast for the driver to put on the brakes in time to stop. The designer of the system must be alert to the time constants of the various parts of the system and adjust the speed of the various parts so the system as a whole works effectively.

In many systems, the speeds of the operator's responses are critical. The psychologist has been helpful in clarifying the nature and causes of these speeds. Fleishman (1954) found, for example, that speed of simple reaction time (pressing a button when a light shows), speed of wrist-finger movements (tapping a key), and speed of large arm movements (turning a crank) are relatively independent. That is, the operator who has a fast simple reaction time may well have only moderate wrist-finger speed and slow arm movements. Furthermore, the fact that he is fast does not mean he is accurate. Instead, accuracy seems dependent upon other abilities that vary with the size of the muscle groups involved. For example, the accuracy of the skilled watchmaker, who makes primary use of his fingertips, is largely determined by his finger dexterity. The accuracy of the skilled ballplayer, who uses the larger muscles of his back, arms, legs, and wrists, is largely determined by the factor of psychomotor coordination.

The faster we move, the less accurately we move. Similarly, the greater the accuracy of response the system demands, the slower our responses should be, and in fact, the slower we voluntarily choose to go. Fitts (1954) gave subjects tasks that required wrist-finger speed and dexterity. Some were easy, some hard. They were asked to adjust their speed so as to maintain the same level of accuracy. The typical subject maintained the same overall level of effectiveness by slowing down on the hard tasks, speeding up on the easy ones.

The human engineer sometimes slows the required speed of input or output to fit the operator. Sometimes he changes the task so that the operator can go faster. Suppose a system requires an operator to crank a horizontal wheel which has a radius of 10 inches. An individual can turn such a wheel at about 150 revolutions per minute (Reed, 1949). The engineer might then adjust the system so this speed meets the demands of the system. Or he might decrease the radius of the wheel so the operator can turn it faster. When the radius of the wheel is reduced to 1 inch, the operator can make almost twice as many revolutions per minute.

PREVENTING OVERLOADS

Although a system may have individual inputs properly matched to individual outputs and adequately adjusted for the individual time constants, it may still be overloaded. That is, too many different inputs may be coming in and too many outputs may be required. Improved *coding* is one way of preventing overloading. The code for an object or situation is the cue required to recognize its presence. The fewer, simpler, and clearer the cues are, the better.

Better coding improved a system for guiding aircraft into a landing field. Normally, different aircraft appeared on the radar screen before the controller as small blobs of light, and he could determine which blob stood for which airplane only by remembering their relative positions, headings, and speeds as shown on the display panel. Meanwhile, he had to tell the different pilots what direction they should go in, where to turn and how fast, and how high they should be traveling. A clock code was introduced which clearly identified each airplane as it entered the traffic patterns. Checks showed considerable improvement as a result of using the clock code (Schipper et al., 1957).

EQUIPMENT DISPLAYS

The senses of the caveman gave him information essential for his well-being and survival: he saw food and ate; he heard dangerous animals and ran; he felt cold and he warmed himself. Modern man has devised many ways of improving the amount and accuracy of information received through his senses as well as his ease in getting it: books, radios, and television are the most obvious and widespread. The modern worker, too, has aids: gages to read, warning signals to listen to, and even vibrations to feel. Improving the design of such information displays is a vital task of the human engineer.

"Have you ever made or seen anyone else make an error in reading or interpreting an aircraft instrument, detecting a signal, or understanding instruction?" The answers experienced Air Force pilots made to the question indicated many dangerous errors resulting from poor displays (Fitts and Jones, 1947). A typical pilot reported:

> It was an extremely dark night. My copilot was at the controls. I gave him instructions to take the ship, a B-25, into the traffic pattern and land. He began letting down from an altitude of 4,000 feet. At 1,000 feet above ground, I expected him to level off. Instead, he kept right on letting down until I finally had to take over. His trouble was that he had misread the altimeter by 1,000 feet. This incident might seem extremely stupid, but it was not the first time that I had seen it happen. Pilots are pushing up plenty of daisies today because they read their altimeter wrong while letting down on dark nights.

The principles for improving displays are the same as those for improving the man-machine system as a whole: match inputs to outputs, adjust time constants, and prevent overloads. However, the goals of man-machine systems have become more exact and complex; the amount of information and consequently the number of displays needed by the operator have expanded. Overloading, therefore, has become the key problem, and its prevention has become the major objective of the human engineer in designing displays. Eliminating unnecessary displays, making greater use of nonvisual channels, using check displays where possible, using the most effective indicator design, and patterning the indicator display are among the methods he employs in solving the overload problem. These methods are examined below.

Overloads can be reduced by cutting out *unnecessary displays.* To decide what is necessary and what is not, however, is often not easy, for the decision requires a realistic understanding of the goals of the entire system. An operator may have all the information displays required to move cars through a traffic control system in the quickest possible way. Moving them in the safest way possible, though, is also a goal, whose achievement may require additional information and displays. A more common problem is that the engineer who designs a machine makes good use of a particular display when *he* is running the machine, but the typical operator of the machine does not. Thus, an engineer driving a car might use a gage recording the revolutions per minute of the engine, but the typical driver would not. Consequently, knowledge of the behavior of the typical operator in the system is often required before the worth of a particular display can be assessed.

Overloads can be reduced by substituting *nonvisual displays* for visual ones. Machines exist which are much more sensitive to light, sound, touch, or smells than men are. Still, one potent reason for maintaining the man in the man-machine system is that, in balance, his sensory capacities are much greater than those of any machine: he is sensitive to a much greater variety of physical stimuli, he is exceedingly sensitive to many of these varieties, and he is much more capable of simultaneously sensing both very weak and very strong stimuli. Because his eyes are outstanding in these respects, panels often consist of nothing but visual displays and, consequently, run the danger of overloading the eyes. The danger can be reduced by using nonvisual channels wherever possible. Auditory channels—bells, buzzers, and clicks—are the most common alternative. Vibrations, too, have been used as an alternative. The lifetime habits of operators interfere with the acceptance of nonvisual alternatives. Still human engineers are seeking and finding useful ones.

Overloads can be reduced by substituting *check displays* for quantitative and qualitative ones. *Quantitative* displays—speedometers, altimeters, and pressure gages—give relatively precise information. The *qualitative* ones give information that tells the operator whether a machine is working all right and, if it is not, the general direction in which it is off. Most automobiles now have qualitative temperature indicators: they do not give the precise temperature, but they do show whether it is in the normal range and, if it is not, whether it is too cold or too hot. Check-reading indicators just tell the operator whether something is on or off, working or not working. Car turn signals now have a double-check indicator to show when the signal is operating (blinking light and clicking sound). An increasing number of oil and battery gages have red lights that go on when the oil pressure and battery charging devices are not working adequately.

The substitution of qualitative displays for quantitative ones simplifies the display panel; the substitution of check displays for qualitative and quantitative ones simplifies the panel even more. If a check display can be substituted for a qualitative or a quantitative one, the dangers of overloading the panel are reduced.

Now, assume that all indicators that could be eliminated have been, that all visual displays that could be made nonvisual have been, and all quantitative displays that could be changed to check ones have been. What, then, is the best design for the remaining visual and quantitative displays? Some form of dial might seem to be the obvious answer. Often, however, it is not. In fact, the substitution of *counter displays* for dial displays is a principle of wide applicability. The typical car speedometer is a dial display; the typical car odometer that shows accumulated mileage is a counter.

The superior speed and accuracy of counters is shown by the records of male students who checked thousands of readings on dials and counters (Weldon and Peterson, 1957). The average student took much less time and made fewer errors by far in checking counter readings. The same students were also asked to set given readings into the dials and counters. Again, they took less time and made fewer errors in setting the counters. Watches and clocks, as a consequence, are shifting from dials to counters.

Should an airplane's altitude indicator be a counter rather than a dial? A reading test showed that a counter indicator could be read more quickly and accurately than any of eight different dial designs (Grether, 1947). Reading an altimeter in a test booklet, however, is not the same as reading it in a cockpit. For one thing, the altimeter in the cockpit sometimes changes so quickly that it is difficult to read the changing numbers on a counter. Actually, the practical solution was a combination dial and counter with the counter set in the middle of the dial. The counter measures in units of 1,000 feet; the dial, in units of 100 feet. For example, the counter reads 8 for 8,000 feet and the arrow on the dial points to 2 for 200 feet. The pilot, combining these, knows that he is at 8,200 feet.

Even when operating conditions require a dial rather than a counter, the dial that is most *like* a counter often turns out to be best. For example, the speed and accuracy with which the dial shapes shown in Figure 4-2 could be read were determined by having 60 subjects make quick readings on the different dials. All the dials have the same size numbers and pointers and the same distance between the numbers. In Figure 4-2 the dials are arranged from top to bottom in order of the accuracy of readings. Again, the circular and horizontal dials were more accurate than the vertical ones. However, the open-window dial, which is most like a counter, was most accurate of all (Sleight, 1948).

If it has been determined that a circular dial would be most effective in a given situation, what specific design is best? Should the dial be small or large? How far apart should the marks or numbers on it be? In what direction should the numbers increase? The answers vary somewhat with the situation. A dial with a diameter of about 3 inches, for instance, gives the best results when it is to be read from a distance of 30 inches or less. The numbers on it should be about a half inch apart and should progress in the same direction as those of a clock (Chapanis et al., 1949).

Finally, the way dials in a panel are related to each other has an important bearing on the ease with which they can be read. In general, the simpler and more definite the pattern, the better. Suppose the operator has to read six clocks located together in a panel. If twelve o'clock were at the top of some dials and at the bottom of others, he would take more time to read them and make more mistakes than if twelve o'clock were always at the top. This principle of simplifying the pattern is being widely applied in panel designs. Most of the time, the twelve o'clock position is used to indicate a "normal" reading and variations from it to register an "out of line" reading. This pattern not only makes it easier for the operator to read all dials but also calls his attention to the dials it is most important for him to check (Woodson, 1954).

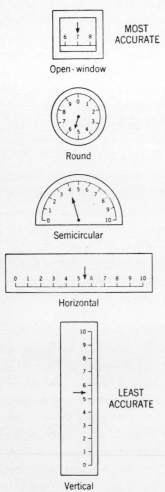

FIGURE 4-2 Dial Shapes in the Order in Which They Can Be Most Accurately Read. (Adapted from Sleight, 1948.)

EQUIPMENT CONTROLS

Since the displays of a machine give the operator the information he needs to control it, the better they are, the better his control. Likewise, the quality of the controls on the machine influences the effectiveness of his control. The ways of improving controls are similar to the ways of improving displays: Eliminate unnecessary controls, substitute on-off or position controls for continuous ones, substitute nonmanual for manual controls, make controls natural, make them distinguishable, and—even more critical than in displays—place the controls in a safe and effective pattern.

Controls can often be eliminated by redesign. Automatic transmissions, for example, eliminated the need for clutch controls in cars. Changes in radio receivers achieved an even more dramatic reduction in the number of controls. A 1923 Zenith table radio had six control knobs and required fifteen steps to turn it on and tune in a station. The recent models have two control knobs and three required steps.

Like displays, controls can be divided into three types: *on-off* controls (house light switches, car direction signals), *position* controls (station selector on a TV set, gearshift on a car), and *continuous* controls (brakes and steering wheel of a car). The on-off control is simpler than either the position or the continuous control, and the position control is simpler than the continuous one. If an on-off or position control is sufficient for the job, it should be substituted for the continuous one. Early electric stoves, for example, had continuous heat controls for each burner. Later ones had position controls. These give as much heat variation as the typical cook actually uses.

Since our hands are more accurate and adaptable than our legs or feet, controls are normally designed for manual use. As the number of controls increases, however, the hands become overloaded, and it becomes critical to relieve them. The first step in this direction is to substitute stick controls (operated by one hand) for wheel controls (operated by two hands) wherever possible. The step is often an easy one, for a stick control can be just as accurate as a wheel (Grether, 1947). Foot and knee controls are less accurate than hand ones. The slight loss of accuracy is more than compensated for by the reduction in manual overload. The substitution may also increase the safety of operation, for as the number of manual controls is increased, the dangers of accidentally hitting them mount.

The more natural the controls, the more easily and safely they can be used. If we want a car to go right, turning the steering wheel to the right should make the car go in that direction; if we want to produce a downward movement, pushing down on the control should produce such a movement. Though this is a commonsense principle, it is sometimes forgotten and sometimes hard to apply correctly in a concrete situation.

Nearly everyone assumes, for example, that turning rotary controls in a clockwise direction to increase and in a counterclockwise direction to decrease is the most natural way to operate. Is the assumption correct? To answer the question, Bradley (1959) had 300 men and women turn the knob on a box. A light was placed above the knob, and the subjects were instructed, "On this box is a light which is controlled by the knob below it. I would like for you to take hold of the knob and. . . ." At this point, different subjects were told to "increase the light," "make the light brighter," "increase the brightness of the light," or "decrease the dimness of the light." Other subjects were given the opposite instructions: "Decrease the light," "Make the light dimmer," "Decrease the brightness of the light," or "Increase the dimness of the light." The common assumption was verified: Three out of four subjects turned the knob clockwise to increase and counterclockwise to decrease the brightness of the light. The assumption was as true for women as for men and almost as true for left-handed as for right-handed men.

Telephone dials operate in the most natural direction—clockwise. What about the numbers: Is it easier for a person to use the traditional letter-numeral dial (UNiversity 4-5271) or all-numeral dials (864-5271)? Bell Laboratory scientists conducted a series of studies to find the answer. To discover the speed and accuracy with which persons could look up and dial numbers under the two systems, nine subjects went once a day for 10 days to a special test room where they looked up the numbers of persons in the regular Manhattan telephone directory and placed calls to them. The next 12 days they repeated the study with a modified directory that had numbers in the all-numeral form. The result was that while using the all-numeral form, subjects were 10 percent faster and slightly more accurate.

In the next experiment, short-term and long-term memory for numbers under the two systems was determined. This study indicated that memory is the same for a short term but slightly poorer for a long term under the all-numeral system. Long-term memory, however, is not very important, for the average telephone user "permanently" memorizes only four or five numbers.

In the final experiment, the all-numeral system was tried by 73 users in their homes for 10 weeks. At the end of this study, 43 percent preferred the all-numeral system, 24 percent had no preference, and 33 percent preferred the letter-numeral system. The Bell scientists concluded that with AND (all-numeral dialing), "dialing speed should increase and the error rate should be about the same or slightly lower. There should be little strong feeling against AND and there is a good chance that it would be widely accepted" (Karlin, 1961).

The more controls a mechanism has, the more chance there is the operator will confuse them. Bathers turn on the hot water when they mean to turn on the cold, drivers push the clutch when they mean to push the brake, etc. One way of reducing the confusion is to distinguish a particular control from every other by giving it a special size, color, or shape. Green and Anderson (1955) investigated a series of 16 possible shapes for the knobs of controls: round, rectangular, bullet, cross, half-moon, dumbbell, etc. The frequency of confusions between them was experimentally determined, and a handful of shapes that were least often confused with each other was picked. Small handles were as easily identified as large handles, and operators made few errors in transferring from one size to another. The conclusion: "These experiments strongly suggest that tactual coding of switch handles can aid an operator materially in many applications."

The confusion between controls can be reduced by proper positioning; controls that are far apart are less likely to be confused than those that are close together. The principle is limited in application, however, for the feasible places for controls are few. The operator must be able to reach each one, he must be able to move it without undue bodily distortion, and he must be able to maintain contact with some controls while moving others. Placement is also severely limited by habits, as is exemplified by the difficulties drivers have when the reverse gear of a car is placed in an unusual position. So many airplane accidents have been traced to variation in the position of controls from one type of plane to another that strenuous efforts are now being made to standardize their placement. The problems involved in introducing better typewriter keyboards are another example of the conflict between old position habits and new but basically more efficient ones.

THE WORK ENVIRONMENT

The physical environment in which a man works is a critical element in determining his efficiency in the man-machine system. It may be too dark for him to see the displays, too noisy for him to hear signals, or too cold for him to work the controls. The task of the human engineer, therefore, includes defining and creating the best possible environment for the operator of the machine.

As we enter the space age, this task is becoming extremely complicated, for space vehicles can function well in environments that man cannot. Also, they *create* environments that man cannot tolerate. They can, for example, accelerate with speeds well beyond 5 *g*. A pilot, however, finds it hard to lift his feet at a centrifugal acceleration of 2 *g*. Between 3 and 4 *g*, it becomes hard for him to move either his hands or his feet. Above 5 *g*, his field of vision blacks out, and his ability to control the machine is practically zero.

LIGHTING

In the dark we can see nothing. A very little light increases our vision enormously. More and more light continues to improve our vision, but with rapidly diminishing returns. Still, almost any increase in light short of blinding intensities improves our vision somewhat. Consequently, there is no "best amount" of light. The problem, rather, is to get as much light as we need to do what we are going to do as quickly, accurately, and comfortably as possible.

The light we need is often less than we might think. In one phase of the first of the classic Hawthorne studies (Roethlisberger and Dickson, 1939), the illumination for a control group of girls winding the coils for small relays was maintained at 10 foot-candles—the light that a 40-watt bulb produces on a surface 2 feet away. The illumination of the experimental group started at 10 foot-candles and was gradually decreased to 3 foot-candles. The productivity of the girls under 3 foot-candles was as high as under 10 foot-candles. In the final phase of the study, two girls volunteered to work under lighting that was equivalent to bright moonlight. They were just as efficient and reported no eyestrain.

Tinker (1939) summarized a large number of experiments done in actual work situations and reported the foot-candles beyond which there was neither a measurable increase in efficiency nor a decline in visual fatigue. The following is a sample of the work situations with the recommended illumination:

Work situation	Recommended foot-candles
Ordinary reading	3
Clerical work	6
Sorting mail	10
Drafting	12
Playing tennis	24
Sewing	30
Surgical operations	700

Tinker concluded, "The vast majority of industrial operations can be carried out at maximum efficiency with an illumination intensity in the neighborhood of 10 foot-candles." Many factories are far below this level. A survey of six industrial operations revealed an average illumination of 2.4 foot-candles. Raising this level to 11 foot-candles resulted in an increase in production of more than 15 percent.

Well designed machines and good arrangement of the work situation can do much to lower the amount of illumination required. Thus, the greater the *contrast* (the difference in brightness between the object being worked on and its immediate background), the less the illumination required. Suppose, for example, we are looking at dark numbers on the white background of a dial. Our visual acuity will be better when the letters are coal black than they are light gray, because black makes a greater contrast with white than gray does. Also, the closer the illumination of the *surround* (the general work area) approximates the illumination of the work object, the easier it is to see the object. That is, we can read a dial with 5 foot-candles of illumination best when the room in which we are reading the dial also has 5 foot-candles of illumination.

NOISE

A *decibel*, like a degree of temperature in the measurement of heat, is the standard unit for the measurement of noise. The zero on a decibel scale is at the threshold of hearing, the lowest sound pressure that can be heard. On this scale, 20 decibels is a whisper, 40 the noise in a quiet office, 60 normal conversation, 80 a bus, 100 a subway train, 120 loud thunder, and 140 the level at which a sound becomes physically painful. Small portable meters measure sound-pressure levels with considerable accuracy.

No authorities claim that noises below 90 decibels do any physical harm. In fact, sensory deprivation—the complete absence of sounds and other physical stimuli—may be extremely disturbing. As high-pitched sound rises beyond 90, however, the claims mount. Beyond 110 decibels, there is little doubt that prolonged exposure to noises, particularly high-pitched ones, produces temporary or permanent deafness as well as symptoms of nervousness and emotional instability.

Noise interferes with communication: the louder the noise, the harder it is for us to speak so we can be heard. We can be heard and understood even when our speech is no louder than the noise. We can even be heard when our speech level is *lower* than the noise level, as attenders of cocktail parties can testify. The accuracy and completeness of communication, however, declines as the noise level rises. Designers of systems that produce noise, therefore, must provide for enough amplification of voice communication delivered by means of headphone or speaker to ensure that speech will be readily understood.

The psychological effects of noises have long puzzled psychologists. On the one hand, noise has been attacked as a kind of devil by both industrial and community groups who energetically develop and enforce noise-abatement programs in the confident belief that quiet is good for people and for production. On the other hand, Ryan, in summarizing the available evidence in

1947, could only conclude, ". . . intense noises are likely to reduce output when they first begin, and, for that matter, when they first cease." More recent studies suggest a solution to the puzzle: Noise is a source of psychological stress. Under noise, as under other kinds of stress, we may for a time work as hard or even harder than we usually do. In the long run, however, we become more fatigued, make more errors, and produce less.

Noise has little immediate effect on the performance of even complex tasks. College sophomores, for example, were paid a dollar an hour plus prizes for good performance to learn short words, statements such as "The elevation of Jones Field is 2,000 feet," and a series of dial settings such as "Set the black dial at 39," The students first learned a task, one group under quiet conditions and one group under noisy conditions (110 decibels, equivalent to that produced by a jet airplane engine). They then saw a half-hour movie, after which both groups were asked to recall what they had learned. The conclusion was that "Noise . . . does not significantly affect the recall of verbal material." Some students complained initially that they were irritated, distracted, or disturbed by the noise, but all quickly adapted to it (Miller, 1957).

Noise, however, does have long-term effects. If the task is repetitive and unchallenging, performance declines more rapidly under noisy than under quiet conditions. Undergraduates were paid to watch a clock for 2 hours and to press a switch whenever the clock hand made one of its haphazard double steps, which it did about once every minute. Some worked under conditions of "quiet" (80 decibels) and some under conditions of "noise" (110 decibels). The percent of correct responses for the two groups was determined for each half-hour period. The group working in quiet made about the same percent of correct responses in each of the four periods. The group working in noise did as well in the earlier periods but dropped significantly in accuracy during the last half hour (Jerison, 1959).

The most convincing study of the effect of noise would be one conducted not in the laboratory, but in a natural setting over a long period of time with precise experimental controls. Unfortunately, there have been few of these. Berrien (1946) in his summary of studies concluded that "only one field study in this country has been completed with sufficient control and covering a sufficient time to place confidence in the results." It showed an increase in productivity as noise was reduced among office workers.

A more recent careful field study verifies the declines in communication and quality of production with noise (Broadbent and Little, 1960). A room with rows of machines which perforate the holes in the edges of movie film was treated by placing absorbent material on the walls and ceilings and between the machines. Before treatment, the sound pressure in the middle of the room was 99 decibels; after treatment, 89 decibels. To determine the influence of the treatment on communication, experienced operators stood along the wall, listened to tape recordings of single-syllable words, and tried to write the words down as they heard them. Some operators listened before and some after the soundproofing. The sound level of the recording remained the same. Before the soundproofing, operators correctly identified 54 percent of the words; after soundproofing, 69 percent.

Quality of production was measured by counting the number of broken rolls of film that were due to operator errors before and after soundproofing. The number of broken rolls in the 6-week period after treatment was significantly smaller than before. The benefits did not "wear off"; just the reverse happened. In succeeding 6-week periods, the difference between treated and untreated areas *increased*. "Noise," the investigators concluded, "does produce human error in a real-life situation, even among people who are used to it."

Expected and unexpected noise can also create problems. Generally, unpredictable noise interferes with work more than predictable noise. In one experiment (Finkelman and Glass, 1970) volunteers simulated steering a car in a device which used a sports car steering wheel and an oscilloscope. While driving, each person was presented various numbers. As each number was presented the subject tried to recall the previous number. One group of subjects was exposed to predictable noise at 80 decibels and the second group was exposed to unpredictable noise at the same level. Results showed the two groups did not differ significantly in driving performance, but the group subjected to unpredictable noises made twice as many errors in recalling numbers.

In spite of some doubts about the precise effects of particular noises on particular individuals, it is clear that intense noises do some physical damage. In addition, loud ones result in symptoms of stress, in some interference with production, and in some dissatisfaction among practically all workers. Finally, unpredictable noise interferes with performance and is especially troublesome to workers who are trying to do two things at once.

Planning can often reduce noise at little cost. Low, soundproofed ceilings with walls slanted outward give maximum sound absorption. Man-machine system designs can eliminate noise at the source. Cushioning, rubber and felt mountings for equipment, and even floor suspension have decreased the noise problem in many enterprises. Quiet operations such as welding can be substituted for noisy ones such as riveting. The proper maintenance of equipment to keep it free from rattles and squeaks is an obvious help. Even after equipment has been installed in a plant, proper acoustical treatment can reduce sound-pressure levels by as much as 10 decibels.

Earplugs are an effective last resort. The "Ear Warden" earplug developed by the Psycho-Acoustic Laboratory at Harvard University is clean, durable, cheap, and comfortable. Workers, however, resist any interference with their normal hearing. Under circumstances such as work in areas affected by sounds of explosions, a company should insist on earplugs being worn as firmly as it insists on safety goggles where there is danger to the eyes.

VENTILATION

Heat produced by physical activity must be dissipated in order for a man to continue to work. The chief mechanism for dissipating heat is the evaporation of perspiration from the skin. Ventilation determines the effectiveness of this mechanism. Consequently, changes in ventilation produce changes in productivity, in the accident rate, and in morale. The best ventilation in a particular situation is determined by the interaction of temperature, humidity, and air motion; by the amount of physical effort required; and by the attitudes of the worker.

In general, at temperatures in the immediate neighborhood of 70°F most workers feel most comfortable, have the fewest accidents, and are most productive. This optimum range can be greatly modified by abnormal variations in humidity and air motion. Thus, 90°F at 10 percent humidity feels as comfortable as 80°F at 60 percent humidity or as 75°F at 100 percent humidity. Also, low temperatures with no air motion may be less comfortable than considerably higher temperatures with a great deal of air motion. Consequently, ventilation engineers use as *effective temperature scale* that combines the subjective effects of temperature, humidity, and air motion.

The optimum effective temperature varies with the work being done. Below 50°F, however, performance of any kind of work suffers. Temperatures in the 60s are best for heavy physical work, performance of which deteriorates at an increasingly rapid rate as the temperature rises beyond 70°F. On the other hand, while workers on light physical jobs or mental tasks prefer temperatures around 70°F, their performance shows little or no deterioration up to 85°F.

Wireless telegraph operators during World War II, for example, heard and recorded Morse messages for 3 hours in rooms of different temperatures: 79°, 85°, 88°, 92°, and 97°. The average number of mistakes made per man per hour was determined for each temperature. The number was about the same through 88°, rose slightly during the 92° period, and jumped high during the 97° period. For the lower temperatures, there was no evidence of fatigue over the 3 hours. That is, errors increased for all temperatures from the first to the third hour, but the number of third-hour errors was the same (20) for the 79° and 85° periods. Above these temperatures, however, the affects of fatigue became increasingly apparent (Mackworth, 1946).

Fortunately, most workers on the same job are comfortable at about the same temperature. Ryan (1947) summarized nine studies of worker reports on the temperature at which they felt most comfortable. The effective temperatures ranged from 66° to 77°, the locations ranged from Toronto to Texas, and the seasons varied, but all the workers were engaged in light physical or office work. Those who reported being comfortable at the optimum temperature ranged from 75 to 98 percent of the groups. That is, about 9 out of 10 workers were comfortable at the temperatures which were finally selected.

Not all ventilation problems can be solved by simply providing the optimum ventilation. During World War II a new aircraft plant in Texas was constructed without windows or skylights but with modern air conditioning equipment for controlling temperature, humidity, and air circulation. The air vents were high, for the ceilings were over 50 feet from the floor. From the beginning, the employees complained that it was "too hot," "too humid," "too close," etc. The equipment was checked and found to be in excellent condition and providing an optimum effective temperature. The complaints persisted. It was finally suggested that the rural workers might feel cooped up in a windowless plant where they could feel no breeze blowing. Tissue streamers were tied to the high vents so that workers could see that the air was moving, and employee complaints quickly dropped (Davis, 1957).

Ventilation studies have clear implications for the human engineer: The man-machine system that is operated in an environment that is too hot, too cold, or too stuffy will be less than maximally efficient. Effective ventilation systems, therefore, are generally a sound investment.

AUTOMATION

The man in the man-machine system is often the greatest threat to the efficiency of the system: he cannot read the displays accurately enough, he cannot make decisions well enough, he cannot operate the controls fast enough, or he cannot stand the noise and heat that the machine can. The most radical solution to the problem is to eliminate the man. A Ford executive coined the word *automation* in 1946, and it has since been used by one person or another to mean any kind of technological improvement.

With increasing frequency, however, automation is used in a more limited and exact sense to mean (1) the substitution of mechanical senses (electric eyes) for human senses to receive display information, (2) the substitution of mechanical decision-making devices (computers) for human decisions, (3) the substitution of mechanical muscles (thermostats) for human muscles to operate controls, or (4) in the purest form, the simultaneous substitution of all these mechanical devices for their corresponding human functions so that the man in the system is eliminated.

Generally, engineers have achieved complete automation of a job by the substitution of more and more mechanical devices over a period of time. The "cup" line of the Bucyrus plant of the Timken Roller Bearing Company illustrates automation in a relatively pure form.

> A steel tube advances against a stop. Three sets of tools work to shape the end, inside, and outside of the outer ring for a tapered roller bearing. At the same time, a fourth tool is cutting the ring from the end of the tube.
>
> A steel finger advances and catches the ring as it drops and deposits it on a conveyor. The cup, as it is called, rides through a washing machine, up an elevator, is turned over—if it needs to be—so that size and model can be stamped on one edge, goes through three furnaces and washing machines to increase the carbon content, harden, and temper it. The cup is ground all over in a series of four machines and then honed to a fine polish on the inside. It is measured by a series of gauges that use air pressure to check the size and taper of the bore.
>
> Finally, the cup is washed, dried, dipped in oil, and wrapped in paper. The size has been so accurately controlled that cups need not be matched to the rest of the bearing. They will fit perfectly with the rollers and inner ring when eventually mated with them during the assembly of an automobile (Ashburn, 1962).

A bearing cup can go through the entire production sequence without being worked on by a human being. The line is one of 11 in the plant that employs only 700 workers, yet manufactures 30 million tapered roller bearings a year. The investment per worker is more than twice that of comparable unautomated plants. After the plant was opened, however, the selling price of the bearings dropped by 15 percent.

One objective measure of the degree of automation is the amount of automatic equipment being used, by this measure, the automobile industry, the first user of automation, is still its largest user. In 1958, an *American Machinist* survey revealed that of the 16,000 automatic assembly machines in the United States, over half were in the automobile industry. A 1960 survey (Diebold, 1962) showed that manufacturing had made the highest percentage of possible applications of computers and that there were over 5,000 general-purpose computers in use in the United States. The same survey showed there were over 7,000 such computers *on order*. In other words, more were on order than had been built in the 16 years since the first commercial computer was marketed. The actual expansion is even greater than this statement would suggest, for the newer computers are larger, faster, and more flexible than the older ones.

About one in four manufacturing plants has made some applications of automation. The number has been growing, and growth has been accelerated by the invention of the numerical control of machines. In the past, automation was mostly limited to large plants because of the high cost and high degree of specialization of equipment. The numerically controlled machine is the antithesis of machines that make a million identical parts in an identical way. With numerical control, one can change the part produced by changing the magnetic tape or punch card that controls the machine. This adapts automation to the needs of the small plant making small quantities of many different things.

While manufacturers have made the greatest use of automated equipment in the past, the range of present and contemplated applications is nearly limitless. The Telephone Company has estimated that it would require all the employable women in the United States to carry on its present activities if there were no automation. The president of the Michigan National Bank stated that "in two years there will be no such thing as a bank clerk" in his organization as a result of the installation of automated equipment for processing deposits and checks. A gas and electric company is experimenting with devices for reading meters through calls to customers where the phone would not ring. Traffic control of air and ground vehicles is being taken over by automated systems. Automated long-range weather forecasting is also becoming a reality. Automated teaching machines, language-translation machines, and medical-diagnosis machines are passing from experimental to commercial models.

HUMAN PROBLEMS IN AUTOMATION

The onrush of automation is reducing the number of humans involved in production and service systems. At the same time, it is producing new kinds of human problems. Men resist changes in the nature of their work, they dislike some aspects of their automated jobs, they find new demands being made of them, and above all, they are fearful of being "disemployed."

Automation has created little organized resistance. Business, government, and union leaders are, in principle, in favor of it. For example, the AFL-CIO Collective Bargaining Report states:

> Unions in the United States are not opposed to and do not stand in the ways of technological improvement. They well recognize that technological advance and the resulting increasing productivity are needed to enable improvement in standards of living.
>
> They typically cooperate with and indeed frequently encourage and stimulate management efforts to improve technology. This is well reflected in the fact that, although billions of dollars worth of new equipment is installed each year, there are barely a handful of claims or complaints of union opposition.
>
> At the same time, unions want to see to it that workers get wage increases to provide them with a fair share of the benefits of increased productivity (April, 1958).

The report, however, adds that unions are "greatly concerned about the manner in which technological change is introduced." They want *advance notice and consultation* before changes are made. They want *negotiation on questions raised* by the innovations so that workers derive some benefit from them. They also want *protection for workers* whose work is taken over by a machine. In most cases, managements have been quite ready to meet these conditions.

Most workers welcome some mechanization. For example, a survey of attitudes toward automation among the employees of the central office of an insurance company revealed that the majority of them would like to have some parts of their work mechanized (Trumbo, 1961). Although some resisted the idea of basic changes in their jobs, others expressed readiness for this. Those ready to change had qualities related to the ability to deal effectively with change: They were more intelligent, better educated, and more emotionally stable than average. Leadership also influenced the readiness to change: workers with more democratic leaders were more ready to change than workers with less democratic leaders (Nangle, 1961). Organizational policy also influences the readiness to change. Workers from organizations that had a record of protecting the positions of workers were more ready to change than workers in organizations without such a record (Mann and Williams, 1959).

The worker who goes from an unautomated to an automated job meets new problems. For example, automobile workers transferred to an automated engine plant were disturbed by the additional attention required by the job, the greater noise on the job, and the greater distance between workplaces.

The greater distance meant that workers were less able to talk to each other while working and that they tended to confine what talks they had to work-related matters. On the whole, they reported they were making fewer friends on the job and in general felt more socially isolated. Many of the workers felt a greater pressure to avoid machine breakdowns and were more tense and fatigued.

A most serious problem for many workers on automated jobs is the need to adjust to night work. Automation requires a greater capital investment per employee. In order to spread the investment over more units of production, companies tend to operate on two and even three shifts per day. Around-the-clock operation means more night work for more workers. There is little doubt that night work is unpopular and detrimental to health and efficiency. Findings at an automated power plant (Mann and Hoffman, 1960) are typical: 40 percent said they disliked shift work, 47 percent said they did not mind it, and only 14 percent said they liked it; 84 percent reported sleeping difficulties as the biggest problem resulting from shift changes, 45 percent reported eating difficulties, and 11 percent reported family and social problems.

Overall, workers seem to like their automated jobs more than their old ones. Three-fourths of the workers in the automated engine plant said they preferred their new job to their old one. Also, the strongest preferences were expressed by those with the most highly automated jobs (Faunce, 1958). A comparable study among workers transferred from an old power plant to a more automated one showed that 94 percent were more satisfied with their new jobs (Mann and Hoffman, 1960). They liked the increased freedom to move around in the plant, their cleaner surroundings, their greater responsibilities, and their opportunities to learn while on the job.

The worker who moves to an automated job is likely to get more attention from his supervisor, since the supervisor has more time for him. For example, a manager of an automated operation who had also been the manager in unautomated days reflected upon the changes in his own job. Much of his hectic day-to-day planning had been taken over by the computer, so that he could now pay more attention to parts of his job he had slighted before. Most of these concerned interpersonal relations with customers and employees. He now finds that he spends more time building a good staff and getting to know customers' needs than was possible in previous years. He also reports that he thinks these activities are more what he, as a manager, should be doing (Whisler and Shultz, 1962).

The major problem caused by automation does not involve workers moving from unautomated to automated work; it involves workers moving from unautomated work to the ranks of the unemployed. Fortunately, unemployment directly caused by automation is infrequent, for companies typically have not discharged old workers but have retrained and transferred them to new jobs. The installation of a computer in a Michigan bank, for example, reduced the required number of employees from 175 to 75. The bank president said that persons involved in the net reduction of 100 jobs were staying on the payroll in other tasks or were being retrained, but that they *would not be replaced when they left.*

Disemployment is the decline in total jobs caused by increased output per worker. Automation, as a common and dramatic fact of modern industrial life, has been identified frequently with increasing disemployment. Predictions have been made that the day will come when machines will do all the tasks that need doing and man will work no more. Some view the day with delight and others with dismay.

For most of the industrial history of the United States technological change has been a fact and the rate of change is increasing. However, with very few exceptions, such as the depression years of the 1930's, about 95 percent of the work force has remained employed. Evidently, as technology has destroyed jobs in some areas of the economy, it has created jobs in others. Also, since total population has been increasing, it is a fact that more jobs have been created than have been destroyed. Since 1947 the annual growth of output per man hour (productivity) has been between 3.0 and 3.5 percent. This is a substantial, but not a dramatic, increase.

A National Commission on Technology, Automation and Economic Progress reported to the President of the United States in 1966. (Bowen and Mangum, 1966). The commission indicated that automation does not play a major role in the increase of unemployment or disemployment. Their report showed that the number of jobs is not decreasing, while its projections indicated that 18,300,000 or more new jobs have been and will be created in the period 1964-1975. The number of farm workers will decline which continues the trend of the past 100 years. All other categories of white-collar, blue-collar, and service workers show increases. Blue-collar increases are not projected to be as great as white-collar increases, but they still account for approximately 4,500,000 new jobs.

Disemployment does not appear to be a serious national problem. Displacement is. The man who has just lost his job because of a technological improvement may not know where automation has created the new job or may get hungry waiting for a new job to be created where he is. What the discussion of automation has done is focus attention on unemployment figures. As the Commission on Technology pointed out in its report, technological change probably does not have any major responsibility for the general level of unemployment, but it does play a role in the unemployment of particular persons in particular jobs, in particular industries at particular locations. What unemployment figures show is that the unemployed include an unusually high percentage of the young, the undereducated, and the black. What these figures mean is not that technological change is too fast but that social change is too slow.

While the rate of technological growth is relatively slow and appears well within control, it does have a considerable effect over an extended time period. Today's average worker is better housed, better fed, and in all ways enjoys a higher economic standard of living than the average worker of 100 years ago. Moreover, he works far fewer hours to accomplish this standard. The average worker of 1890 worked about 60-62 hours per week. In the 1970's the average is 40-42 hours per week. This means that each worker today compared with the worker of 1890 has about 1,000 more hours a year when he is free from "earning a living." What shall we do with this free time? What shall we do when the work week goes to 30 hours and we gain 500 more hours of free time per year? What can be done with 1,500 hours per person times the eighty million people in the work force? The answers will increasingly determine the quality of our society.

SUMMARY

The human engineer deals with man-machine systems in which the worker is viewed as an information-gathering and -processing link between the "displays" and the "controls" of the machine. The human engineer's major aims are to match inputs into the machine with desired outputs, to adjust the time constants within the system, and prevent overloads within it. In the development of displays, for example, he seeks to give the operator, through multiple channels and in the easiest form, only the information he really needs. In the development of controls he strives to give the operator the varying types of controls that will permit him to perform the really necessary operations in the easiest way. Since the work environment is also part of the system, the human engineer is also concerned with problems of lighting, noise, and ventilation.

Over the years, as he works with a system, the human engineer is continually substituting mechanical senses for human senses, machine decisions for brain decisions, and mechanically operated controls for muscle controls. This trend is called automation, which in its final form eliminates the man from the man-machine system. Executives and workers, unions and management, citizens and government, all generally favor automation. Few of these groups, however, have fully recognized the human problems which automation is creating, and none have proposed any satisfactory solutions.

5

GROUPS IN THE ORGANIZATION

A worker is a part of a man-machine system; he works with machines in a physical setting. Even more important to the psychologist, the worker is a part of a man-people system; he works with other people in a social setting. As we shall try to show, it is only as a member of an integrated group with high morale that the worker can make his maximum contribution to an enterprise. What constitutes a group, how effective groups can be developed, and how different groups can be linked together are the questions to be dealt with in the present chapter.

THE MAN-PEOPLE SYSTEM

Until recently the importance of the man-people system in organizations has been largely ignored. Formal organization with its rational blueprint of how things should be done has treated people much like interchangeable parts. Consequently, the relationship of the person to his task in the organization has been stressed; the relationships of the person to his fellow workers has not been. The tradition of individuality in our culture has contributed to our slowness in recognizing the importance of the psychological and social environment of the work place.

Both common sense (it was uncommon sense thirty years ago) and research reenforce the knowledge that people-to-people relationships in organizations are of primary importance to the individual as well as to the productivity of the organization. For most people, the organization *is* the people they work with.

What the organization means to a person is determined in large measure by his co-workers. If they are industrious, friendly, supportive and see their jobs as important, then that is the way the company is. Of course, the company has policies and procedures which influence the individual as he goes about his job day by day. However, each individual tries to make sense of the policies and fit them to his particular situation by talking to and watching other people in the organization. Vice-presidents check reality with other vice-presidents and with their secretaries; lathe operators check reality with other lathe operators and with their bosses.

The Hawthorne studies (Roethlisberger and Dickson, 1939) which we mentioned before and will again, show the importance of the work group. Coch and French (1948) found that workers who belonged to groups with a strong "we feeling" were less likely to quit than workers who were not in such groups. Rose (1951) found that soldiers who went AWOL were more socially isolated, had fewer acquaintances or friends than soldiers who did not go AWOL. Walker and Guest (1952) found when they studied mass-production jobs that lack of social interaction had a negative effect on workers' attitudes toward their jobs and was correlated with high rates of tardiness and absenteeism. These early findings have been confirmed consistently in a variety of organizations during the past twenty years.

Any particular person's man-people system in the organization is more than his immediate work group. He may be part of a car pool, a relative may work in a different part of the company, or the switchboard operator may be a friend. Each person has a unique man-people system. However, for most individuals the work group is the center of his system.

THE WORK GROUP

A group is different from a collection of individuals. Six people on an elevator are not a group. Schein tries to make this difference clear when he defines the group is psychological terms:

A psychological group is any number of people who (1) interact with one another, (2) are psychologically aware of one another, and (3) perceive themselves to be a group. (Schein, 1965, p. 67)

A work group is a special kind of psychological group. It requires that each of its members be assigned specific tasks which fit together in such a way that the group can do a job which is helpful to other work groups. Unlike many psychological groups, the work group endures: old members can leave and new ones can enter, but the group as a producing social system can still be identified as the same.

To get a clearer idea of the similarities and differences among work groups, we will look again at the two best-known work groups of all time: the six girls in the relay assembly room and the fourteen men in the bank wiring room of the Western Electric Company during the Hawthorne studies (Roethlisberger and Dickson, 1939).

The relay assembly room group was smaller than some groups, larger than others. Size of a group is clearly a dimension of great importance since it affects interaction and people's ability to be aware of each other (Thomas and Fink, 1963). In addition to size, groups can be helpfully compared on the 13 other dimensions shown in Figure 5-1 (Hemphill and Westie, 1950). The authors have grouped the dimensions most relevant to the integration goal together and those most relevant to the morale goal together. *Homogeneity*

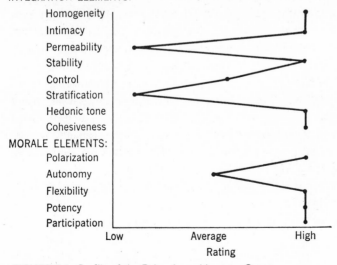

INTEGRATION ELEMENTS:
Homogeneity
Intimacy
Permeability
Stability
Control
Stratification
Hedonic tone
Cohesiveness
MORALE ELEMENTS:
Polarization
Autonomy
Flexibility
Potency
Participation

Low   Average   High
Rating

FIGURE 5-1 Profile of the Relay Assembly-room Group.

is the degree to which members of a group are similar in social characteristics. Thus, the fact that the members of the assembly-room group were all of the same sex and of similar age, race, socioeconomic status, interests, attitudes, and habits indicates that they were a highly homogeneous group. *Intimacy* is the degree to which members of a group know each other. Since most of the girls were friends to begin with, spent several years together, and talked a great deal with each other, they became a most intimate group. *Permeability* is the degree to which people can enter the group. The experimenter made the group impermeable. *Stability* is the degree to which the group persists unchanged over time. The assembly-room group was less stable than a family but more stable than most work groups. *Control* is the degree to which the group regulates the behavior of its members while they are in the group. While the girls exercised some control over each other, it was probably no more than in the average group. *Stratification* is the degree to which the group is arranged into status hierarchies. Stratification was practically absent among the girls. *Hedonic tone* is the extent to which group membership is accompanied by a general feeling of pleasantness and agreeability. The girls reported that they enjoyed working with each other much more than with their former groups. *Cohesiveness* is the degree to which members of a group function as a unit. The girls worked closely together with little evidence of dissension and conflict.

Polarization is the degree to which a group is oriented toward and works toward a goal that is clear to the members and shared by them. The assembly-room group was not only aware of the production goal but worked effectively toward it: productivity increased from less than 2,400 units to more than 3,000. *Autonomy* is the degree to which a group determines its own activities. While the assembly group was not closely supervised, the production goals and work methods were largely beyond the control of the group. *Flexibility* is the degree to which the group's activities are marked by informal rather than formal procedures. The activities of the assembly group were highly informal. *Potency* is the degree to which the individual's needs are satisfied by membership in the group itself. The assembly group was highly potent, for it not only satisfied the economic needs of its members but also satisfied their needs for belonging and status much better than their former work groups. *Participation* is the degree to which members of a group apply themselves to their assigned duties and accept unassigned duties. It relates also to the total amount of time spent in group activities. From this point of view, the assembly group was highly participative, for members worked more than 40 hours per week together, fully accepted both assigned and unassigned responsibilities, and spent time with each other off the job.

The bank-wiring group, which was also assigned to a separate room, was more than twice as large as the relay assembly-room group. Its task was wiring "banks," a repetitive manual job that involved wiring, soldering, and inspecting the connections in panels to be installed in the central offices of the telephone company. The observer of this group assumed the role of a disinterested but not aloof spectator. He did not demonstrate any authority, he did not take part in arguments, and he did not betray employee confidences. Although the men had agreed to cooperate in the study, they were initially suspicious. It was almost a month before they started to relax and behave as they did in their regular department. The observer remained with the group for more than 6 months, noting the formal organization of supervisor and employees, the informal groupings of the men, and interrelationships between these two types of organization.

In most of the group dimensions, the bank-wiring-room group rated about the same as the relay assembly-room group. It was similarly high in homogeneity, intimacy, stability, hedonic tone, cohesiveness, polarization, flexibility, and participation. It was similarly low in permeability. The bank-wiring group, however, was more stratified. It was divided into two cliques: Clique I considered itself superior to clique II, felt that its conversation was on a higher plane, and was less boisterous. A member joined his other clique members in eating, in trading jobs, in playing games, and in socializing after hours.

The bank-wiring group also exercised more *control* over its members. It used ridicule, sarcasm, and "binging" (a sharp blow with the fist on the upper arm) to discipline "rate busters" (workers producing more than the group judged proper), "chiselers" (workers producing less than the group judged proper), and "squealers" (workers who told the supervisor anything that would harm a member of the group). These methods were particularly effective because the membership had high *potency*: members wanted to be accepted by the group and feared ostracism from it.

Extending Schein's definition, we would say that *A work group is a social system composed of two or more members playing different roles who are psychologically aware of each other, who perceive themselves to be a group and who interact with one another in such a way that members can enter and leave and yet the system can be identified as the same.* The members of the bank-wiring room were a work group. They were a social system which included a number of people (14); they knew each other; they perceived themselves to be a group; they played different roles (electrician, solderer, inspector); they talked, worked, played, and ate together; the system was arranged so that workers could quit and others be hired and still the bank-wiring group went on.

EFFECTIVE AND INEFFECTIVE GROUPS

From the point of view of management, the bank-wiring group was ineffective. It regularly violated job rules, distorted official records, communicated as little as possible with the supervisors, and produced far less than it was capable of producing. On the other hand, the relay assembly-room group was effective. It followed company rules, kept accurate records, communicated in detail with the management, and made steady and significant increases in its production. The reasons for the differences were not entirely clear, although differences in the size of the two groups, the sex of their members, their formal and informal organizations, and the management attitudes all had some influence.

The effectiveness of a group is measured by its success in achieving its goals. A group, however, may and generally does have many goals, some consciously specified and some not. The bank-wiring group, for example, consciously tried to limit its production to two banks per day. It was very effective in achieving this end. The members also tried to increase the stability and cohesiveness of the group as well as its potency for satisfying the belonging, status, and self-actualization needs of its members.

Some conflicts between goals are nearly inevitable in groups. Thus, goals of the group may conflict with goals of individuals so that it is necessary for the group to sacrifice its goal achievement for the individual, or vice versa. Also, some goals of the group may conflict with other goals of the group, so that achievement in one direction must be sacrificed for achievement in another. Finally, the goals set for itself by the group may conflict with the goals set for the group by someone else, as was the case with the bank-wiring group. The effectiveness of a group, then, cannot be completely determined by measuring only the satisfaction of its members, or the achievement of group goals, or the contribution of the group to the larger organization. Its overall effectiveness must be assessed by considering its achievements in all these directions. In general, the fewer the conflicts between the members, the group, and the organization, the more effective the group is likely to be.

Group effectiveness is determined not only by its goals but also by the way it goes about achieving them. McGregor (1960) contrasts the characteristics of effective with ineffective group meetings in the following manner:

Effective group	Ineffective group
1. The *atmosphere* tends to be informal, comfortable, and relaxed.	1. The atmosphere reflects boredom, indifference, and tension.

Effective group	*Ineffective group*
2. Everyone *participates* in the discussion and the discussion remains pertinent to the task of the group.	2. A few people dominate the discussion and often make contributions that are way off the point.
3. The task of the group is well *understood and accepted* by the members.	3. Different members have different, private, and personal objectives that are in conflict with each other and the group's task.
4. The members *listen* to each other! Every idea is given a hearing.	4. Ideas are ignored and overridden and members make speeches intended to impress someone rather than to solve the problem at hand.
5. There is *disagreement* but no "tyranny of the minority." Individuals who disagree do not try to dominate the group or express hostility.	5. Disagreements are either suppressed by a leader who fears conflict, or cause open warfare, or are "resolved" by a vote in which a small majority wins the day.
6. Most decisions are reached by a *consensus* in which it is clear that everybody is in agreement or at least willing to go along.	6. Decisions are often made prematurely before the real issues are examined or resolved.
7. *Criticism* is frequent, frank, and oriented toward removing obstacles.	7. Criticism is present, but is embarrassing and tension-producing. It involves personal hostility and the members are unable to cope with this.
8. Members are *free in expressing their feelings.* Little pussy-footing, few "hidden agendas."	8. Personal feelings are hidden rather than being out in the open.
9. When action is taken, *clear assignments* are made and accepted.	9. Action decisions are often unclear so that no one really knows who is going to do what.
10. There is little evidence of a struggle for *power.* The issue is not who controls but how to get the job done.	10. The formal chairman may be weak or strong but he always sits "at the head of the table."

The more effective a company's work groups, the more fully it can make use of its human resources. It can develop more effective work groups by taking action that encourages the development of group goals, the growth of supportive relationships within the group, and the enlargement of the responsibilities of the group.

THE DEVELOPMENT OF GROUP GOALS

The rigid assignment of sharply defined tasks to each individual in a group discourages the development of group goals. For example, group goals do not develop in a conventional college class where each student has his own learning tasks to do and his own grade to get. Even when he is given group tasks and group rewards, the typical student finds it hard to shift from his accustomed pattern (D. M. Johnson and H. C. Smith, 1953). In most work groups, however, group goals may develop in the face of management efforts to set individual tasks and to give individual rewards. A department store, for example, installed an individual incentive system that created high production but also considerable hostility among the competing salesmen. The salesmen gradually worked out a procedure for pooling their efforts so that commissions were identical (Babchuk and Goode, 1951). The casual assignment of a common task to a group of individuals normally results in the development of group goals. Thus, the girls in the relay assembly room and the men in the bank-wiring room developed into cohesive groups with common goals as a result of being assigned similar work to do.

Stopping assignments at the group level is an effective way of deliberately encouraging the development of group goals. Modern technology often demands that many intimately interrelated tasks be done in a precise fashion at an exact time. It does *not* demand, however, that each particular task be assigned to a particular individual. A series of interrelated tasks can be assigned to the group. The group can then determine how they are to be done. Concretely, the assembly of an automobile requires that many specific tasks be completed on time and in the right way; it does not demand that each task be assigned to one man, although it usually is. In the final polishing of the car, for example, man A moves the car onto the main line, man B polishes the trunk, man C polishes the doors on the side, man D polishes the fenders, and finally, man E polishes the quarter panels (Walker and Guest, 1962). It would be possible, however, to assign the polishing tasks to the five men and let them decide how they would accomplish the necessary work. The value of such group assignments is suggested by the remarks of assembly workers who were accidentally given team assignments:

> I'm in a team of six. One man works inside the car body right with me. We're good friends. So are the others in my group. We talk and kid all day long. Makes the job sort of fun. I'd much prefer working with others than alone.
>
> I work with another fellow. He pulls the fender back, and I tighten it with bolts. If we do it wrong, it costs a lot of money. We have a lot of fun and talk all the time.
>
> I have one partner in a group of five fellows. We all help one another and change jobs for variety. No throat cutting. It's nice to work in that kind of atmosphere.

Interactive discussions in which workers and management representatives talk over the goals to be set for the group can help gain the group's acceptance of performance goals. The minimum requirement of the method is that workers ask questions and managers give honest answers. In particular, the workers must feel free to raise impolite questions concerning possible conflicts between their interests and those of the management.

Interactive discussions worked in a well-known men's apparel manufacturing company (French et al., 1958). The management had decided that extensive changes in its production methods were essential. Changes involved were rearranging the sequence of operations throughout the plant, speeding up the movement of materials, reducing material handling, and introducing mechanical aids for folding, trimming, and holding materials. These innovations required radical changes in tasks performed by many of the one thousand company employees.

In the past, employee resistance and conflict had largely washed out hope for benefits from changes in work methods. This time, the management, while retaining the right to make the changes it deemed necessary, laid down a policy of openness and fairness with the employees and stuck to it. It first introduced the program into its two smaller plants and then into its third and largest plant. The program was introduced in a series of about 80 meetings. The number of workers attending the meetings varied from one to eight. The local plant management met with each group of operators performing the same operation. When there were a few workers on a particular operation, they were accompanied to the meeting by a shop steward of the company's strong and progressive union.

The results of the method were determined by comparing productivity records for the 6 weeks before the changes were made with the same 6-week period a year after the change. Both production and productivity had increased. For the same periods, absenteeism and labor turnover had decreased. The success of the method was due to the fact that workers were convinced to begin with that management felt they were an important part of the company and were important for the new plan's success. They were convinced because the company had firmly held to three policies: (1) Let workers know about proposed changes as soon as possible, (2) pay the cost of retraining if this is necessary, (3) never change earning opportunities already set for a job because they turn out to have been too generous.

Letting a group decide on its own production goals is the most certain way of getting the group to accept them. In addition, performance standards the group sets for itself may be higher than those management sets. A psychologist, for example, met with three different groups of workers on the same job, each of whose normal production was 70 units per man-hour. In two of the groups, he discussed the desirability of setting higher goals, but the groups did not decide on specific goals for the following week. Their productivity did not change over the next 3 weeks. In the third group, the desirability of setting higher goals was not only discussed, but a decision to reach 90 units per man-hour the following week was made by the group. Productivity the following week was 86 units; the next week, 92 units; and the third week, 87 units (Bavelas, 1946).

Letting a group decide its own production goals is worker-management cooperation at its highest level. It seldom reaches this level. Managers are least willing to allow workers to make decisions in areas directly concerned with production: the setting of output standards, the planning of production, the utilization of machinery, or the innovation of technological changes. They are more willing to allow them to make decisions that directly concern the worker: on lateness, absenteeism, employee health, discipline, etc. They are most willing to allow them to make decisions in areas where workers and management have an obvious common goal, i.e., accident prevention (Dale, 1949).

Whether managers are willing or not, however, groups *do* make informal but effective decisions about production goals. The following are examples:

> In one company, a long assembly line with 1,100 employees assembled exactly 1,500 units on the day shift. The company scheduled higher production and sought to achieve it, but volume stayed at 1,500 units. The hourly production often varied, and by midafternoon, the number of units might be appreciably more or less than that required for a 1,500 day, but by the end of the shift there were always 1,500 units, no more and no less.

In a company with much of its work on either individual or group piece rates, virtually no employee produces above 150 percent of standard. An appreciable number of workers are at the level of 145 to 149 percent of standard, but the decision has been made—and not by management—that it is undesirable to reach or exceed 150 percent of standard (Likert, 1961, p. 211).

The setting of goals is important. It is equally important, however, that workers be motivated to achieve them.

Giving a group information about its performance is one of the most effective ways of increasing its goal achievement. The earlier it can get this information, the better. For example, a company manufactured a heavy boardlike material for the siding of houses. The quality of the material was tested as it came off a long machine. Thus, if something was wrong with the mixture at the beginning of the machine, over 6,000 square feet of the material had to be scrapped. Now the company tests the material in the very early stages, so that workers can make corrections in the mixture if necessary. As a result of this shortened feedback cycle, only a few hundred square feet at most ever have to be scrapped. Without this early information, the group could not have improved its scrap record.

The more complete the information given the group, the better. The district managers of a large company, for example, had come to the home office of the company for a semiannual reporting and planning meeting. Many of them complained about one of their important products and suggested needed improvements. Actually, the research department was secretly working on an improved product, but it would take another year before the product was on the market. It was important that news of the development be kept from competitors. Should the managers be told? They were, and were asked to keep the information confidential. The secret was not betrayed; the managers had information that would help them plan their activities more intelligently, and their integration and morale were significantly increased.

Development of performance measures to give the group is one of the hardest, most important, and largely unrecognized tasks of a company. Eddy (1963), examining the performance measures available in a series of companies, concludes:

The paucity of objective productivity data available at the departmental level and the disagreement among interviewees as to the nature of the relevant criteria or their application to the situation suggest a lack of recognition on the part of management of the need for clearly specified criterion data . . . setting clear and attainable goals should lead to more effective performance and to ultimate job satisfaction when goals are reached.

That is, companies often do not have useful information to give the group. In such common situations, the group itself may be in the best position to urge the development of measures that would most usefully and realistically evaluate its goal achievement.

THE DEVELOPMENT OF SUPPORTIVE RELATIONSHIPS WITHIN THE GROUP

To do his best, a man must feel his work experiences are supportive—that they maintain or add to his sense of personal worth and importance. Compared to the lone worker competing against other workers, the worker in a group is much more likely to feel accepted, liked, and respected. But while the likelihood of supportive experiences is increased in a group, it is not made inevitable. Interpersonal frictions, antagonistic cliques, and wide variations in ability may weaken or destroy group support of its members. The methods used by a company in handling its work groups can never guarantee that every worker will feel supported; they can, however, increase or decrease the chances of such feelings developing.

Fitting the members of a group together is more likely to result in the development of supportive relationships than throwing them together by chance. They can be fitted together on the basis of age, sex, nationality, and local factors which are known to be sources of conflict. Employees of similar seniority generally fit together more readily than those with wide differences in seniority. The placement of men and women in the same work group must be handled with care. The employment of Negroes and whites on the same job must be planned with understanding if it is to be successful.

Sociometry can be a valuable aid in fitting teams together. In its simplest form, it consists of asking (privately) each member of a potential work group to list in order the names of the people he would like to work with. The simplest use of the answers consists in fitting pairs of workers together. This method was used to group 74 carpenters and bricklayers who were working on a large construction project in the Chicago area (Van Zelst, 1952). They were all experienced men on a fixed-wage scale. They were constructing homes in identical rows of eight each, half on one side of the road, half on the other. Before the introduction of the sociometric procedures, careful records of labor turnover and material costs were compiled.

The sociometric procedure was started by assembling the men and giving them the following instructions:

> You are now working with a partner who was not chosen by you, nor were you chosen by him. You are now given an opportunity to choose the persons with whom you would most like to work. You can choose any of the individuals in your own group. Write down your first choice, then your second and third choices in order.

On the basis of these choices, the men were first arranged in pairs and then in groups of four. Since the work was of the type that seldom required more than four men to work as a team, the procedure did not go beyond this point. The greater satisfaction of the workers under the new arrangement was suggested by the comments of a typical worker:

> Seems as though everything flows a lot smoother. It makes you feel more comfortable working—and I don't waste any time bickering about who's going to do what and how. We just seem to go ahead and do it. The work's a lot more interesting too when you've got your buddy working with you. You certainly like it a lot better anyway.

Highly significant reductions in costs and turnover were found: "The end result in this study has been a happier, more productive worker, who has given management a 5% saving in total production cost."

The method is applicable to the development of large groups. In such cases, however, it is necessary to relate the choices on a *sociogram*. The *sociogram* in Figure 5-2, for example, shows in view a a highly integrated group with strong leadership. A dotted line with a single arrow indicates a one-way choice; a solid line with a double arrow indicates a "mutual pair." Note that individual 3 is chosen by everyone else in the group and that no one is an "isolate"—that is, everyone is chosen by at least someone. In b, there are many mutual choices, but no one in the group is the favorite. In c, there are few choices, and individual 1 is completely isolated—he chose no one and no one chose him.

The sociograms of two naval air squadrons during World War II were compared to determine why one was effective and the other ineffective and and to discover how the ineffective squadron might be made more effective. Each squadron was made up of a commanding officer, an executive officer, and 17 flying personnel. Each man was privately asked to name those whom he would like to have fly beside him and those whom he would *not* like to

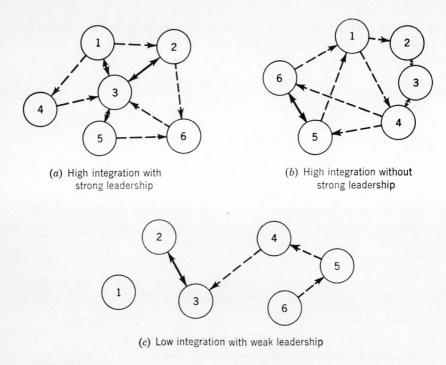

(a) High integration with strong leadership

(b) High integration without strong leadership

(c) Low integration with weak leadership

FIGURE 5-2 Sociograms Showing Groups with Low and High Integration and Strong and Weak Leaders.

have fly beside him. A comparison of the two sociograms showed the following (Jenkins, 1948):

1. The effective squadron had no cliques; the ineffective squadron had two tight cliques, the members of which chose no one outside their own group.
2. In the effective squadron, half of the men chose their commanding and executive officers; no one said he would not like to fly beside either. In the ineffective squadron, no one chose either the commanding or the executive officer; no one rejected the executive officer.
3. In the effective squadron, there were no choices of men outside the squadron. In the ineffective squadron, there were four choices of men outside the squadron.

In sum, in the effective squadron the men respected their leaders, they had a closely knit organization, and they preferred the members of their own group to outsiders. In the ineffective squadron, the leaders were disliked, the organization was split, and some wanted to get out of it. The comparison strongly showed the need for a change in leadership of the ineffective squadron as well as for certain transfers into and out of it.

Encouraging interaction among the members of the group helps develop supportive relationships. Such interaction is made easier by the presence of common goals as well as by the existence of compatible members in the group. It is made harder by excessively noisy work environments and by policies that try to reduce conversation between workers. Aside from these positive and negative factors, many opportunities exist in an organization for promoting interaction. The introduction of a new worker to his job provides a natural time to acquaint him with his coworkers, the time and place for rest and lunch periods can be arranged to help workers to get to know each other, company social and recreational activities can be planned, etc.

Stabilizing work groups also helps. The members of a group require time to get to know each other and to develop the close ties upon which support is built. For, like family ties, work ties develop slowly. How much time is suggested by a study of aircraft workers in southern California during World War II (Mayo and Lombard, 1944). Three types of groups were discovered: The *organized* group grew out of the efforts of a skillful supervisor to create a cohesive and cooperative team; the *natural* group was one limited to not more than seven workers on closely related jobs; and the *family* group was one of larger size that was based on a core of relatively long-service workers whose behavior set an example for new workers. The formation of an effective family group took about 6 months. This period of time seemed necessary in order for the example of the older group to be communicated to the newer workers. The departments with the best-developed groups had both good attendance and good output records.

When the stability of groups was about the same, differences in the type of leadership made big differences in the cohesiveness and productivity of the groups. For example, the high cohesiveness and productivity in one department seemed largely due to the efforts of one "leadman." He was a college graduate who did not rank as a supervisor. This man tried to help the individual worker in such ways as listening to him, introducing him to his companions, getting him congenial work associates, and helping him to handle his personal problems. He helped the workers with their technical problems and acted as contact man in the group's relationships with inspectors, time-study men, and the department foreman. Among other things, he arranged trips for the worker to other parts of the plant so that he could see, in place on finished assemblies, the parts he produced.

The necessary technological changes and improvements characteristic of modern industry are a constant and serious threat to group stability. Managers are in a dilemma. They must introduce changes to survive but the changes may weaken or destroy the fabric of social relations. In handling the problem, managers should give serious attention to these questions:

1. Will the technological improvements, considering the probable detrimental effects upon employee integration and morale, actually result in increased productivity?

2. If so, how can the introduction of the improvements be timed in order to least disturb the stability of work groups?

3. What is the best way of introducing a particular change so as to least disturb group stability?

THE DEVELOPMENT OF GROUP RESPONSIBILITY

Group responsibility involves (1) tasks the group is assigned to do and (2) the dependability of the group in getting them done. To do its best, a company needs groups who can be given many tasks and can be confidently depended upon to do them. How can the development of these two aspects of responsibility be encouraged?

For a group to be depended upon, the workers in it must be dependable. The more supported a worker feels—the more he feels liked, accepted, and respected—the more dependable he is likely to be. This principle is verified by studies outside the industrial setting as well as in it. For example, 192 students in the tenth grade of a medium-sized city in upstate New York were rated on responsibility ("Can be counted on to fulfill obligations . . . . Cannot be counted on to fulfill obligations"). On the six-point rating scale, a rating of 1 was given to the least responsible students and a rating of 6 was given to the most responsible. Each student filled out a long questionnaire designed to measure 20 different dimensions of parent-child relations. Responsibility ratings were then related to questionnaire ratings. The result was that "The adolescent receiving lowest ratings in responsibility describes his parents as most likely to complain about and ridicule him, compare him unfavorably with other children, spend little time with him, and avoid his company." The study concluded "In American middle-class culture, the major obstacle to the development of responsibility and leadership in boys stems from inadequate levels of parental support" (Bronfenbrenner, 1961).

Personal responsibility develops as supportive relationships develop. Of course, all workers who feel supported are not necessarily responsible people.

Any group of workers, though, is more responsible when the members feel supported, when they feel that what they are doing is important. They have this sense of importance when they feel the goals of their organization are significant and they have an indispensable part to play in achieving the goals. When they feel their jobs are trivial and unimportant ones, they feel unsupported and irresponsible.

When jobs are felt to be unimportant by those assigned to do them, they should, if at all possible, be made more important. Ideally, the actual responsibilities of a group should match its capacity to fulfill them. Sometimes the responsibilities of a group exceed its capacity but most problems in this area arise in situations where the capacities of a group far exceed its responsibilities. How can the responsibilities of groups be effectively expanded?

The management that stops assignments at the group level, encourages interactive discussions, and lets the group make some of its own decisions is developing common goals by increasing the responsibilities of the group. No matter what type of structure the company has, these methods all can be used with only minor changes in organization. In addition, there are several major changes a company can make that will profoundly and permanently increase responsibilities of the group.

Decentralizing the organization tends to increase the responsibilities of groups within it. As companies grow, they often locate their plants in different places. They may do this for a variety of reasons: to be near the sources of raw materials, to be near sources of power, to be near available labor supplies, to be near marketing areas, or to achieve tax advantages. Whatever the reason, the decentralization usually increases the responsibilities of smaller units. It does not inevitably have this effect, however. A central authority can still specify in detail how and when things should be done. For example, local plants often have no authority to make agreements with local employee organizations. When a distant central management holds power tightly in its own hands, the local plant may actually have less responsibility than it would if it were under the same roof with management.

More and more companies are decentralizing for psychological as well as economic reasons. Plants are being made small even when there is no obvious financial reason for it. More important, an effort is being made to decentralize responsibility at the same time. The American Brake Shoe Company, for example, shifted from a centralized to a decentralized organization (Given, 1949). Before decentralization, the central management once each year set arbitrary budgets for each of its 10 divisions. After decentralization, each division made up its own budget, which it could generally expect the central management to approve. Responsibility in other matters was similarly decentralized.

Moving from more to less specialized organizational structures increases group responsibilities, for it increases the size and variety of tasks the group has to perform. The difference between moving toward a specialized organization and moving toward a nonspecialized one has been described in the following way:

> Let us suppose an organization performs three essential functions, A, B, and C. Let us suppose further that the volume of output requires three units of each function. Under these circumstances, the organization could be set up in either of two ways:
>
> 1. It could be set up in large divisions, each function (A, B, and C) being represented in each division and each division, therefore, being a relatively independent administrative entity. [See Unspecialized Organization at the top of Figure 5-3.]

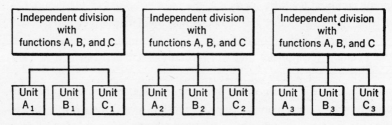

UNSPECIALIZED ORGANIZATION

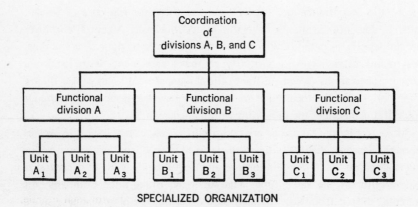

SPECIALIZED ORGANIZATION

FIGURE 5-3 Specialized and Unspecialized Ways of Organizing the Same Functions. In the specialized way none of the three divisions is independent; in the unspecialized way all three are relatively independent.

2. On the other hand, the organization could be set up in three functional divisions, one division having all three A units, another all three B units, and third all three C units. In this case, none of the three divisions has any independence; each can operate only in closest coordination with the other two. [See Specialized Organization at the bottom of Figure 5-3.] (Worthy, 1950b)

In this illustration, the unspecialized way provides for three small and independent units; the specialized way provides for only one unit. In general, the nonspecialized organization makes it easier to decentralize authority and increase the responsibilities of individuals and groups within the organization.

Flattening the organizational structure is a radical way of increasing the responsibilities of groups. It not only facilitates but actually forces decentralization of responsibilities. The *pyramid* organization, shown at the top of Figure 5-4, embodies traditional ideas about good organization. It is based on the hallowed principle that a tight "span of control" is desirable. That is, each executive should have only a small number of subordinates so that he can keep close control over their activities. The essential difference between the pyramid organization and the flat organization is shown in the illustration. The executive in the flat organization has many more subordinates than the executive in the pyramid. Consequently, it is impossible for him to maintain tight control over his subordinates.

Moving from a pyramid to a flat organization inevitably enlarges the responsibilities of workers and subordinate work groups. Sears, Roebuck and Company is an outstanding example of an organization that made this move successfully.

THE GROUP SYSTEM

The actions thus far discussed for creating more effective work teams—stopping assignments at the group level and letting groups make their own decisions, fitting compatible teams together and stabilizing them, and decentralizing and flattening the organizational structure—are all aspects of a *group system* of organization. They grow from a group theory of effective organization, and are applied in companies with a group "climate."

Under a group system of organization the leader's primary task is the development of a productive and well-integrated group with high morale. His real authority arises from group customs and codes. Written rules are a source of authority only when they reflect ideas accepted by the group. The more the leaders in an organization feel this way and the more in-

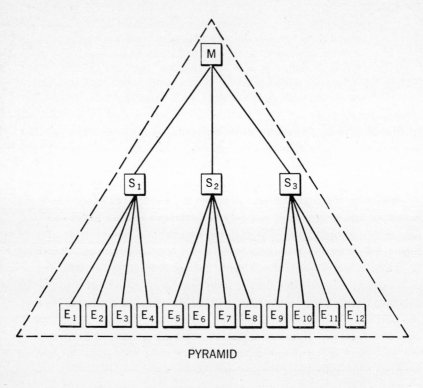

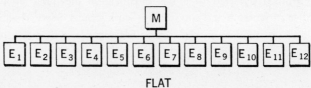

FIGURE 5-4 Pyramid and Flat Organization Structures. In the pyramid, each leader has a few subordinates; in the flat, each leader has many.

tense their feelings, the stronger the group-system climate and the more likely the organization is to take actions promoting the system's development.

An episode in the life of a group-system organization shows how it works. The president of a subsidiary of a large corporation was younger (forty-two) than most of his staff and much younger than two of his vice-presidents (who were sixty-one and sixty-two). The subsidiary had done quite well under its previous president, but the young president was eager to have it do still better. In his first two years as president, his company showed substantial improvement. He found, however, that the two older vice-presidents were not effectively handling their responsibilities. Better results were needed from them if the company was to achieve the record performance which the president and the other vice-presidents sought.

The president met the situation by using his regular staff meetings to analyze the company's present position, evaluate its potential, to decide on goals and the action required to reach them. The president had no need to put pressure on his coasting vice-presidents; the other vice-presidents did it for him. One vice-president in particular, slightly younger but with more years of experience than the two who were dragging their feet, gently but effectively pushed them to commit themselves to higher performance goals. In the regular staff meetings, progress toward objectives was watched and new short-term goals were set as needed. Using this group process, steady progress was made. The two oldest vice-presidents became as much involved and worked as enthusiastically as the rest of the staff (Likert, 1961).

THE MAN-TO-MAN AND BUREAUCRATIC SYSTEMS

The group system embodies the best parts of the *man-to-man* and the *bureaucratic* systems. On the formal organizational chart, all three systems look the same. In practice, however, they work quite differently and have quite different effects.

The man-to-man system stresses the individual and his responsibilities rather than the group and its responsibilities. It stresses decisions by individuals rather than by the group: "I've been made supervisor here because I'm better trained and have had more experience than anyone else. It is my responsibility to make the decisions." It stresses the need for an intimate knowledge of individuals rather than an intimate knowledge of groups. It rewards individuals rather than groups.

The man-to-man system demands ambitious men who will strive to advance themselves. How does a man advance in a man-to-man organization? By being assigned ever larger responsibilities and by achieving the goals set for him. The system encourages him to become an empire builder—to increase the number of workers under him and enlarge the area of his responsibilities by encroaching on the responsibilities of others. Since he must achieve the goals set for him, he maneuvers to have easy goals set.

A day-to-day operation of the man-to-man system is illustrated by the production manager who went to the president to recommend a model change. The president called in the sales manager, asked for his opinion, made the decision to produce the new model, and gave orders to implement the change. Unknown to the president, however, the production manager had picked a model that would be easy for him to make and had withheld information about a better model that would be more difficult. The sales manager had found out something about this on his own but went along with the decision. He thought he could get the president to set a price on the model later that would make it easy for him to sell it, although it would be hard for the company to make a profit. When the heads of other departments heard about the decision, they were unenthusiastic and began to plan how they could at least protect and at best promote the well-being of their own organization. The system, in other words, encourages the setting of low and unrealistic goals, distorts communication, and promotes suspicion and hostility between members of the organization.

The bureaucratic system shifts the stress from the norms of the small group to the rules and regulations of the "bureau." Bureaucratic leaders are preoccupied with maintaining and, if possible, expanding the bureau regardless of the desirability of the expansion. Bureaucratic leaders in a company demand loyalty from their subordinates. In turn, so long as the employee shows his loyalty by conformity to the rules and regulations of the company, he can feel secure even if he is not interested in what he is doing or is not productive on his job.

LABORATORY STUDIES

Laboratory studies disclose that members of a group system have higher morale than those of the other systems. Experiments contrasting the group and man-to-man systems are especially numerous. A typical example is a study in which four people are each given information necessary for solving an arithmetic problem. No one person has all the information necessary, but by exchanging information the group is able to solve the problem. Some groups are organized in a man-to-man pattern, where one of the four is the leader and the other three can only communicate with and receive communication from him. Other groups are organized so that all members can communicate with each other. The study found that under the man-to-man system the leader was happy, but the other members got bored and felt left out. Under the group system, on the other hand, the average member was much more interested in what he was doing (Glanzer and Glaser, 1961).

Although laboratory groups organized on the man-to-man principle have lower morale, they show higher productivity on *simple* problems. For example, in the above type of situation they tend to be first to solve the problem.

With more complex problems, however, they do not do as well, for they do not correct errors as quickly and may not be as quick to discover errors. In some studies the members were given information necessary to solving the problem and additional information which did not relate to the problem. It was shown that members under the group system discovered the extraneous information sooner and solved these harder problems more quickly and accurately than members under the man-to-man system.

The best system of organization depends, then, on the problem to be solved. The group that has a simple but urgent problem is likely to be more successful with the man-to-man system; the group with a difficult problem is likely to do better with the group system.

What are the implications for industrial organization? Since the production problems of some groups are simple ones and those of others are hard, it might seem that *varying* patterns of organization in a company would be best. However, permanent work groups have not only the goal of increasing productivity but also the goals of increasing integration and morale. While some groups may have a simple problem to solve to increase productivity, no group ever has a simple problem to solve in raising its integration and morale while raising its productivity. Thus, overall, the group pattern would seem to have the best chances of success in practically any work group.

How successful any particular group is depends in part upon its success in developing high performance goals, group support for its members, and group responsibility. In part, it depends upon the effectiveness of the *linking-pin* function.

THE LINKING-PIN FUNCTION

The group system gives the worker more responsibilities and more opportunities to exercise initiative than the bureaucratic system does. Compared to the man-to-man system, the group system ties the worker's goals more closely to company goals. To be fully effective, however, the various groups must be harmoniously linked together. The critical linking-pin function in a group system of organization is illustrated in Figure 5-5: The triangles represent the hierarchy of groups in the organization, the small circles the men with a linking-pin function, and the arrows the directions in which these men work.

The supervisor leads his group in the development of common goals, supportive relationships, and responsibility. In turn, he is a member of the group led by the division head, who also, in turn, is a member of the group

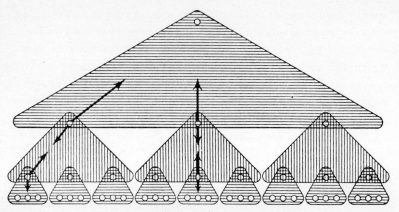

(The arrows indicate the linking pin function)

FIGURE 5-5 The Linking Pin in the Group System of Organization. The triangles show the groups in the organization; the arrows, the linking pin function. (From Likert, 1961, p. 113.)

led by the president. The diagram, of course, is not comparable to an organization chart. It is only intended to focus attention upon the linking pin and to suggest the great influence that its good or bad functioning may have upon an organization. It even oversimplifies the linking-pin function, for a company takes a serious risk when it depends upon a single chain of links to tie the organization together. Multiple and overlapping links make the organization safer and stronger. Thus, in addition to the regular links shown in the figure, a company may have staff groups, temporary and permanent committees, and informal groups at the same and varying levels.

The superior who is fulfilling his linking-pin function holds frequent meetings with his immediate subordinates. He also holds occasional meetings over two levels to see if there is any breakdown in the linking process. He may, for example, observe in such meetings that the men are reluctant to talk, that they never question any policy, and that they give evidence of being fearful. These signs suggest to him that his subordinate is failing in the linking function and needs help in learning how to build his own subordinates into a work group with high loyalty and trust in their supervisor.

The capacity to exert sufficient influence upward is essential if the leader of a work group is to function effectively. The establishment of linking pins establishes the roads over which the supervisor must travel to exert his influence. Whether the roads are good or bad ones depends in large measure upon the effectiveness of communication in the organization. Therefore, this topic will be examined in Chapter 7.

SUMMARY

The group system of organization is a compromise between the man-to-man and the bureaucratic systems. The group system stresses cooperation more than the man-to-man system and individual responsibility more than the bureaucratic system. The man-to-man system rewards the personally ambitious, the bureaucratic system rewards the conformist, and the group system rewards the interpersonally competent. *Linking pins*, effective ways of tying subgroups together, are essential for the success of the group system. Regardless of the system, an organization's success depends upon the development of (1) common goals with its employees, (2) a supportive environment, and (3) worker responsibility. The group system provides the setting most likely to encourage all three.

The development of common goals is helped by stopping work assignments at the group level, encouraging interactive discussions between workers and managers, giving a group complete information about its performance, and letting a group decide on its own goals wherever possible. The development of supportive relationships is fostered by fitting workers together into teams and by stabilizing the membership of the group. The development of personal responsibility is encouraged by decentralizing the organization and making it flatter and less specialized.

6

LEADERSHIP AND
SUPERVISION

The preceding chapter points out that the work group is the basic unit from which organizations are constructed, and that it provides a social system where individuals can satisfy their psychological and social needs while the job proceeds. Since the key figure in every work group is the leader or supervisor, his job is crucial to the success of the total organization. Thus, every company wants to select and develop good leaders.

After looking at the availability of business managers in this country, Nadler (1968) concludes there is a nationwide shortage of leaders. The number of people in the group from which business leaders have traditionally come, white men between the ages 35 and 45, is not sufficient to meet the need. He urges that younger people, women, and members of minority groups be recruited and trained to fill present and future vacancies.

Selecting and developing leaders requires a knowledge of leadership qualities, knowledge that has been discouragingly slow in coming. The "great man" theory, for example, was long thought to provide an adequate explanation of effective leadership. Now psychologists and an increasing number of business leaders have changed their thinking on this question. This chapter examines the great man theory first and then turns to more recent and more fruitful approaches.

THE WEAKNESS OF THE GREAT MAN THEORY

The great man theory is the oldest, simplest and until recently the most widely held notion of effective leadership. The past achievements of an organization, the theory implies, have been due to the great executives in it. Its present and future achievements will depend upon the greatness of the executives now in the organization. To improve its leadership, then, a firm must find what traits make leaders great and then find men who have the traits. It is easier to say than to do these things.

Great leaders do *not* have universal traits in common. One might imagine, for example, that all great leaders would at least be emotionally stable. Stogdill (1948), however, found 19 experiments where measures of emotional control had been related to leadership success. Overall, 11 showed that the leaders had more control than average, 3 showed no relationship between control and leadership, and 5 showed that the leaders had *less* control than average. Thus, while the typical leader is more controlled, some successful leaders are particularly lacking in emotional control. In general, equally good leaders may, and often do, have widely varying personalities. Why?

Different societies demand different leadership traits. Among the Manus in Oceania, efficiency and aggressiveness in leaders are rewarded; among the Dakota Indians, who value generosity and conformity, a Manus-type leader would be rejected. Among the Kwakiutl Indians in the Pacific Northwest, the ideal chief is the one who wins out in financial competition with other chiefs; among the Iroquois, who prize cooperation and generosity, a Kwakiutl-type leader would fail.

Different organizations in the same society demand different traits. L. W. Porter (1962), for example, related the masculinity scores of executives in companies with less than 50 employees to various measures of these executives' success. He found that the more masculine their interests, the more successful they were. He made the same comparison for executives in medium-sized companies and found less relationship. Finally, he compared executives in companies with more than 15,000 employees. Here, the more masculine the executive's interests, the *less* successful he was likely to be! Possibly, large companies need leaders who are more interested in reading books (a feminine interest) than in hunting and fishing (masculine interests). In any case, a trait that is a weakness in a small organization seems to be a strength in a large one.

Different parts of the same organization may demand different traits. In any part of an organization in our democratic society, one might think, democratic leaders would be more successful than authoritarian ones. The data do not support this idea. Vroom and Mann (1960), for example, used the F-scale to measure the authoritarianism of 52 supervisors in a single plant of a large delivery company. The F-scale (for fascist) is composed of 40 statements like "There are two kinds of people: the strong and the weak." As a whole, the scale measures the readiness of the respondent to condemn and punish anyone who violates conventional standards, to stress the importance of dominance and power, to assert his personal toughness, and to believe that the world is wild and dangerous.

Of the 52 supervisors, 28 were in charge of groups of drivers; the other 24 were in charge of groups of positioners. There were 30 to 50 drivers under each supervisor. Each driver checked in with his supervisor in the morning between 8:30 and 9, got his truck loaded, delivered his packages, and then reported back in the afternoon when he had finished. The positioners remained at the plant all day and worked in small groups, taking packages from conveyor belts, getting them ready to load into trucks, and actually loading them.

The satisfaction of the drivers and the positioners with their work group, with their overall work situation, with their supervisor, with their pay system, and with higher management was measured by means of attitude scales. The average score of each of 28 groups of drivers and 24 groups of positioners was then determined. Finally, these satisfaction scores were related to the authoritarianism scores of the respective supervisors. Table 6-1 shows the correlations.

The most surprising result was the difference between the drivers and positioners. Among the drivers, the more authoritarian their supervisor, the better they liked him and other aspects of their jobs as well. Among the positioners, the case was the opposite. Why? The two groups were not in the same situation: the drivers saw their supervisors for only a short time each day; the positioners saw their supervisors and their fellow positioners for most of the day. The variations in job *situations* seem to account for the radical differences in the effectiveness of authoritarian leaders.

Faced with facts like these, social scientists have decided that leadership is best defined, not as the property of a person with rare traits, but as a *relationship* between a person and a situation. *Specifically, leadership is the*

TABLE 6-1 Authoritarian leadership and worker satisfaction

Satisfaction with:	Correlation with F-scale	
	Drivers	Positioners
Work group	.47	.01
Overall work situation	.42	−.37
Supervisor	.41	−.41
Payment	.29	−.19
Higher management	.22	−.23

SOURCE: Adapted from Vroom and Mann (1960).

attempt to use interpersonal influence to gain a goal. Thus defined, leadership is the use of words rather than force to influence others. Pushing a man through a door is not leadership; persuading him to go through, even by threats, is. Thus defined, leadership is not a role but a process. The subordinate who tries to influence his superior, the member of a committee who tries to influence the chairman, and the housewife who persuades the salesman to leave are exercising leadership. And thus defined, leadership is applicable to all interpersonal relationships; it is not limited to relationships where one person has the title of "president," "general," "foreman," etc. A leader is anyone who attempts to exercise influence on another for a purpose.

Leadership may be effective or ineffective. A clear act of leadership may be clearly a failure. The leader may tell the follower, but the follower may not hear, or the follower may hear but may refuse to be influenced. Successful leadership is the *effective* use of interpersonal influence to gain a goal. In turn, the successful leader is one who succeeds in his attempt to exercise influence.

What makes a leader a success? From the broadest point of view, he is made a success by the *organization* of which he is a part, and by the *followers* whom he is attempting to influence. Finally, he is made a success by the *methods* he uses to influence others. It does not follow that any person can be a successful leader; it does follow that widely different kinds of people can be equally successful leaders. We shall now look more closely at each of these determinants of successful leadership.

THE INFLUENCE OF THE ORGANIZATION

Organization can make the difference between effective and ineffective leadership of the groups within it. A group must have sufficient authority to do its jobs well, and the leader of the group must have authority to fulfill his leadership functions.

The leader without adequate influence, regardless of his competence or the liking and the respect that his followers have for him as a person, is judged unsatisfactory by his subordinates. Pelz (1952), for example, measured the favorableness of the attitudes of nonsupervisory employees toward several hundred of their supervisors. He also had the supervisors rate themselves on more than fifty qualities assumed to be related to employee satisfaction. Their ratings on these qualities were checked against the attitudes of their subordinates. There was little or no relationship between ratings and subordinates' attitudes. In fact, some of the relationships were the reverse of what was expected. Thus, supervisors who reported "giving honest and sincere recognition for a job well done" more often had employees who rated them unfavorably. The more influence a supervisor had on his superiors, however, the more likely his employees were to hold a favorable attitude toward him.

In comparison with the man-to-man and the bureaucratic systems, the group system of organization (Chapter 5) gives greater influence to groups and to their leaders. Decentralizing the organization, moving from more to less specialized types of organization, and flattening the organizational structure are all ways of effectively increasing groups' influence. For better or worse, however, the organizational structure sets the limits on how effectively the leadership functions of its units can be fulfilled.

THE INFLUENCE OF FOLLOWERS

Followers have a profound influence on their leaders, so much so that one social scientist has suggested:

> There is some justification for regarding the follower as the most crucial factor in any leadership event and for arguing that research directed at the follower will eventually yield a handsome payoff. Not only is it the follower who accepts or rejects leadership, but it is the follower who *perceives* both the leader and the situation and who reacts in terms of what he perceives. And what he perceives may be, to an important degree, a function of his own motivations, frames of reference, and "readiness" (Sanford, 1950, p. 4).

"Followers" may be leaders, lead their leaders, select their leaders, or reject their leaders because they do not meet expectations. Bowers and Seashore (1967) believe it is a necessary function of the work group to provide leadership to its own members and also to supplement the leadership that the formal hierarchy of the organization may provide.

The skilled and intelligent worker who is a *constructive* follower may exercise considerable influence. He carries out orders but shows discretion and judgement in doing so, offers alternatives for himself and other workers when he thinks this is justified, and gives advice when he thinks it necessary. The *subversive* follower has the same amount of influence but uses it for his own ends or for the benefit of another group to which he is more loyal. The *routine* follower, the faithful subordinate who dependably carries out orders and does not try to influence his superior or his fellow workers, is less common than many think.

Followers may lead their leaders. For example, we may observe a supervisor directing one of his subordinates to go on vacation from July 1 to July 20 and assume that the supervisor is influencing his subordinate. We may miss the fact, however, that the subordinate is a hard-to-replace technician. We may also miss the fact that he has previously informed his supervisor that he might change his job because of difficulties in scheduling his vacation early in July at the same time as his brother-in-law's. Who is leading whom?

Followers reject leaders who fail to meet expectations. Army rifle squads, for example, were asked how they thought an ideal squad leader should act. They were also asked how they thought their own leader acted. The differences between the ideal and the real for each man were calculated and became his *discrepancy score*. The scores for men in a squad were averaged to find the squad's discrepancy score for a particular leader. When the discrepancy scores of different leaders were related to the effectiveness of their squads, it was found that the lower the discrepancy, the higher the effectiveness. That is, the more the leader acted the way the average member of his squad thought a good leader should act, the more effective the unit was. This held true even though different squads and different men in the same squad varied greatly in their ideals. The investigators concluded that the successful leader is able to meet the varying expectations of the men under him. He varies his leadership behavior to fit the expectations of each of his followers (Havron and McGrath, 1961).

Followers will not follow if they find their problems too difficult. If they feel the tasks facing them are overwhelming and the obstacles in their path are insurmountable, they cannot be led. They will either leave the group or lapse into apathy.

Followers will not follow if they find their problems too simple. If they feel that they face few problems, if they feel that they can solve those few with ease, and if they are highly satisfied with things as they are, they cannot be led. This is most often the situation with skilled and experienced groups, for problems that seem hard to the unskilled and inexperienced may seem easy to them (Bass, 1960). As groups continue to meet, leadership acts decrease; as combat crews progress in their training, the trainees participate more and the instructors criticize less; and as intelligence increases, the influence of propaganda decreases.

The closer a group is to its maximum productivity, integration, and morale, the less leadership is possible or necessary; the further a group is from the maximums, the more leadership is possible and desirable. In general, the maximum effective leadership can occur when the problems faced by a group are not so difficult that the members withdraw from them or so easy that little change in behavior is necessary to solve them. Thus, among 45 air crews of 10 members each who discussed work problems, the number of efforts to exercise interpersonal influence correlated with ratings of problem difficulty. That is, as the problems progressed from easy to hard, the number of interactions in the group increased (Ziller, 1955). Again, as problems were made systematically more difficult for 51 ROTC groups of 5 members each, the number of successful leadership attempts increased (Bass and Flint, 1958). When the problems faced by business and government conference participants are made more difficult by the failure of chairmen to lead, more acts of leadership are attempted by the other participants (Crockett, 1955).

THE MOTIVATION TO LEAD

The amount and the effectiveness of a leader's efforts are limited by the situation in which he finds himself, by the organization of the men below and above him, and by the nature of his followers and their attitudes. Still, we have leaders. Furthermore, different leaders in the same situation, with the same organization, and with the same kind of followers vary in their effectiveness. What makes the difference?

The *desire* to lead is one requirement for effective leadership. A leader must try to lead in order to have any chance of being effective. Of course, the attempt may fail, but without it no success is possible. Differences in the desire to lead are a central and stable trait of human beings. In his interactions with others, everyone seeks a satisfactory answer to the question: Who is the leader? Some find the answer in trying to be a leader—telling others how to do their jobs, supervising and directing the actions of others, persuading and influencing others to do what they want, settling arguments and disputes between others, making group decisions, and arguing for their own point of view. Some find the answer in being a follower—accepting the leadership of others, letting others make decisions, following instructions and doing what is expected, and getting suggestions from others. That is, some people consistently try to lead while others prefer to follow.

Children, at a very early age, differ in their motivation to lead, and the differences are sometimes painfully easy to identify. The following is a report on a nursery school child:

> The most outstanding characteristic of Agnes on entrance—and indeed as long as we knew her—was her egotism and her desire to dominate and boss others, and secure her own advantage by any method available. She had no notion of occupying any position but that of center of the stage. The first personality study made of her makes this comment, "At first she wanted literally to run the school." Whenever anything was to be done, Agnes was the first to volunteer. Her constant expressions were ... "I want to—I am going to." Her voice was loud and rasping, and was constantly sounding out above the others. Indeed so insistent and ubiquitous was she that it was difficult to conduct the school with her in it. She had no conception of her own limitations . . . (Wooley, 1925).

Some studies suggest that the desire to lead is heavily influenced by our genes. Cattell, Blewett, and Beloff (1955) compared the relative influence of heredity and environment among 104 pairs of identical twins, 182 siblings reared together, and 540 children in the general population. They concluded that genes and environment are about equally important in determining differences in dominance.

Severe discipline received during childhood helps create a persisting desire to lead. For example, 60 Harvard students were divided in 12 groups with 5 students in each group. Each group met for 14 one-hour meetings over a period of 6 weeks and discussed the same topics, performed the same tasks, and solved the same problems. Observers attended each meeting and completed extensive ratings. The instruction for one of the ratings was stated like this (Schutz, 1958):

> In many groups there is someone who, regardless of how good his ideas are, seems to have a tremendous influence on the final group decision . . . . In your opinion was there any member (or possibly two members) of the present group who tried to behave in this way?

The 60 students also rated the severity of the discipline they had received as children. At the end of the sessions, these ratings were related to ratings. of leadership. The results showed that the more severe the parental discipline, the more likely a student was to be rated high on interpersonal influence.

High social status also helps create the desire to lead. In our society, men are thought to be more important by both men *and* women (McKee and Sherriffs, 1957). When the same dominance scale was given to both men and women, over 90 percent of the men exceeded the average score for the women. Women have less desire to lead than men. Compared to other women, however, women with high social status are more strongly motivated to lead than those with low status. The higher her husband's occupational level, the greater the family income, and the better educated she is, the higher a woman's dominance score is likely to be (Trier, 1959).

The desire to lead is not enough, for men may want to lead only to satisfy their own ends. Self-oriented leaders are likely to be rejected by their followers. Even when they are not, they lead their followers to failure. Effective leaders are oriented toward the goals of their group and toward the tasks that must be done to achieve them.

DIMENSIONS OF LEADERSHIP

During the 1950's researchers at Ohio State University and another group of researchers at the University of Michigan adopted *a behavioral* approach to the study of leadership. They stopped asking the questions suggested by the great man theory of leadership: What is a leader? What are the traits of leaders? Instead they asked: What do leaders *do*? The results of their studies have completely changed our ideas about leaders.

At Ohio State, for example, Fleishman (1953) started with 1,000 specific behaviors supervisors display. These were then classified and sorted into 10 categories that seemed to cover the range of supervisory activities: initiation, representation, fraternization, organization, domination, recognition, production emphasis, integration, communication down, and communication up. In order to determine the frequency of each of these kinds of behavior, items for questionnaires for each category were developed. The following applies to *initiation*:

>He tries out new ideas in the group
>   always____ often____ occasionally____ seldom____ never____

In general, subordinates rate supervisors as showing good leadership when they are high in any of the categories. The major finding of the study, however, was that there were two independent dimensions that accounted for most of the differences in supervisory behavior: *consideration* and *initiation of structure*.

At the University of Michigan, Katz, Maccoby, and Morse (1950) studied leadership in the home office of an insurance company using work groups of clerical workers and their supervisors. Twenty-four work groups were matched into twelve pairs of groups, so that each pair did the same type of work and contained the same number and type of people. Within each pair, however, there was one high productivity group, and one low productivity group. Supervisors of the groups were compared on several variables to see if they differed in any significant ways. The supervisors in the 12 *high* and the 12 *low* groups did not differ in their age, sex, or marital status. They did differ in attitudes. Those in the high-producing groups were *employee-centered* while those in the low-producing groups were *production-centered*.

These studies gave a new picture of leadership. Effective leadership could not be explained by one dimension, as previously thought, but rather two dimensions were required to explain the results. (See Figure 6-1.) We shall examine these two dimensions in more detail.

CONSIDERATION

Some supervisors are considerate of their subordinates; some are not. The subordinates of considerate supervisors strongly agree with statements like the following about their superiors:

> He sees that a person is rewarded for a job well done.
> He makes those in the group feel at ease when talking with him.
> He backs up his men in their actions.

The workmen under an inconsiderate leader strongly agree with statements like the following:

> He refuses to give in when people disagree with him.
> He changes the duties of people without first talking it over with them.
> He doesn't give credit when it is due.

That is, the considerate supervisor is friendly, trusting, and helpful. The inconsiderate supervisor is hostile, distrustful, and cold.

Workers like consideration, but does it pay off? University of Michigan

The Great Man Theory

Leadership ability depends on a leadership trait or the specific combination of a few traits. In the extreme view people either have leadership or they do not. The more moderate view would be that there is a continuum of leadership ability.

Low leadership ／————————————————／ High leadership
     ability   ability

Behavioral Theory

Leadership depends on the attitudes a person has about his job and how these attitudes fit the expectations of the group of followers. The two most important areas of attitudes are attitudes toward the people in the work group and attitudes toward the tasks the work group is supposed to accomplish.

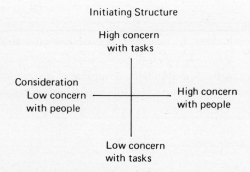

FIGURE 6-1 Theories of Leadership.

psychologists found a convincing answer to the question (Kahn and Katz, 1953). They systematically studied hundreds of supervisors in a variety of business organizations: supervisors of female clerical workers in an insurance company, supervisors of laborers on railroad section gangs, and supervisors of production workers in a tractor plant. They used a variety of objective criteria for measuring the productivity of each unit supervised by each supervisor: the average woman-hour cost of writing policies in the insurance units, the average rating by superintendents of the section gangs, and productivity on the tractor assembly line. These criteria showed marked differences in the effectiveness of the supervisors in the three companies. Finally, in each company, a group of high-producing and a group of low-producing supervisors were identified.

An intense effort was made to account for these differences in effectiveness. The supervisors, the people under them, and the people over them filled out questionnaires regarding their attitudes and beliefs. Intensive interviews with these groups were recorded and then analyzed. Finally, the attitudes and behavior of high-producing units were compared with the attitudes and behavior of low-producing units.

In all these studies as in the original study of the insurance company, the findings showed that high-producing supervisors were more considerate than low-producing supervisors. To begin with, they were more *interested* in their men. In the tractor factory, for example, workers were asked, "How much interest does your foreman take in you off the job?" Of the men in groups whose productivity was 100 percent of standard, 24 percent answered "a great deal" or "quite a lot." Of the men in groups whose productivity was 70 percent or lower, only 14 percent gave this answer. Workers in high-producing units in the insurance company and on the railroad also more often said their supervisors took a personal interest in them and their off-the-job problems. The high-producing supervisors themselves more often said that their subordinates wanted them to take a personal interest. The low-producing supervisor had such poor relationships with his subordinates that they did not want him to know about their personal problems.

High-producing supervisors were more interested in worker problems than work problems; low-producing supervisors were more interested in work problems than worker problems. That is, the high-producing supervisors were *employee-oriented* while the low-producing supervisors were *work-oriented*. In the insurance company, a typical low-producing and work-oriented supervisor said:

> I apportion the **work** to the people in my section and generally supervise the **work**. If a clerk is out, I have to make arrangements to have her **work** handled. The **work** must go on, even though there are absences. This involves getting the **work** redistributed to those who are there. That is all you are supposed to do. But I am from the old school and believe the head should **work** too (Kahn and Katz, 1953).

In the same company, a high-producing and employee-oriented supervisor said:

> My job is dealing with human beings, rather than with the work. . . . The chances are that people will do a better job if you're really taking an interest in them. Knowing the names is important and helps a lot, but it's not enough. You really have to know each individual well, know what his problems are. Most of the time I discuss matters with employees at their desks, rather than in the office. Sometimes I sit on a wastebasket or lean on the files. It's all very informal (Kahn and Katz, 1953).

High-producing supervisors were more interested in their workers than in their bosses; the low-producing supervisors were more interested in their bosses than their workers. In other words, the high-producing supervisors were *employee-identified* while the low-producing supervisors were *management-identified*. Thus, the high-producing supervisors, though they were generally more satisfied with their jobs than low-producing supervisors, were more critical of their bosses. The high-producing supervisors more often said that their bosses were not very good at handling people and that they were doing less than a good job. The high-producing supervisors were more likely to take the side of their subordinates in policies that affected them. At the time of the insurance company study, for example, both the dining-room setup and the company placement policy were being criticized by the workers. The high-producing supervisors were more aware of employee feelings about these matters and were also more critical of the company's position.

The greater interest of the high-producing supervisor in his workers more often showed itself in concrete and helpful ways. In the tractor company, for example, workers were asked, "If you talk over a problem with your foreman, does it do any good?" Of 327 men in groups whose productivity was 100 percent or more of the standard, the majority answered, "usually or always does some good." Of 275 men in groups whose productivity was 70 percent or less, only a minority gave this answer. The high-producing supervisors were more likely to be of practical help to their men in getting ahead. Men on the railroad section gangs, for example, were asked, "In what way does the foreman train men for better jobs?" Of 156 men in high-producing groups, 29 percent said their supervisors taught them new techniques and duties. Of 142 men in low-producing groups, only 17 percent made this answer.

One beneficial outcome of the high-producing supervisor's greater interest in his men was their greater sense of belonging and greater pride in their work group. Men in the tractor plant, for example, were asked, "Do you feel you are really a part of your work group?" The percent of various work groups answering "really a part" is shown in Table 6-2. The general trend is clear: The greater the sense of belonging, the higher the productivity. The same workers were asked, "When it comes to putting out work, how does your work compare to others?" The same trend was found: The greater the pride in the work group, the higher the actual productivity. In the insurance company the results were similar: Three times as many workers under high-producing supervisors as under low-producing supervisors were classifiable as having "high pride" in their work group. The men in the railroad section gangs had no way of knowing how other section gangs were doing. Still,

TABLE 6-2 Relation of group belongingness to productivity
in a tractor factory

Employees' percent of productivity	Number of employees	Percent answering "Really a part" of work group
100–119	327	58
90–99	762	56
80–89	452	51
70–79	269	52
40–69	275	46

SOURCE: Adapted from Kahn and Katz (1953).

more of the men under high-producing supervisors said that they felt the performance of their group was better than most.

PSYCHOLOGICAL DISTANCE

While the good leader is considerate of his followers, he is not intimate with them. The idea that there must be some psychological distance between leaders and followers is reflected in the customs of practically all formal organizations. Most military organizations have different mess halls, sleeping quarters, and washrooms for officers and enlisted men. Hospitals frequently provide one set of dining and lounge facilities for the medical staff and one for nurses and administrative employees. And many corporations operate separate dining rooms for executives and employees.

The common reason given for these differences is that the familiarity of a follower with his leader breeds contempt. Evidence shows, however, that a more valid reason for the difference is that the leader who is close to his men has his decisions affected by his feelings for them in ways that harm the effectiveness of the group. The military officer finds it hard to send his friends on dangerous missions, and the executive who is a close friend of a subordinate finds it difficult to fire him.

Differences in the psychological distance of leaders from their followers has been measured by first asking leaders to describe themselves—to answer statements such as "I like good food," to check from pairs of adjectives such as "intelligent-unintelligent" and "calm-excited" the one that is more descriptive of themselves, etc. (Fiedler, 1961). The leader is then asked to use the same statements and adjectives in describing the man he thinks is his best worker and the man he thinks is his poorest worker. Next, the number of statements on which the leader assumed that these two workers were like himself is counted. Finally, the *difference* between the assumed similarity for the best and worst worker is measured. This difference score is the measure of psychological distance. Low scores suggest dependence on others, great concern for the attitudes of others, and unwillingness to reject a person with whom one cannot accomplish a task. High scores suggest independence of others, lack of concern for the feelings of others, and readiness to reject others when they are considered poor coworkers.

The relationship between a leader's psychological distance and his effectiveness seems to depend upon his power to discharge poor workers. In studies of basketball teams, surveying parties, open-hearth crews, and sales groups—organizations in which it is fairly easy to dismiss the incompetent—the most productive leaders are found to be the most distant ones (Fiedler, 1961). In civil service organizations, where it is more difficult to dismiss workers, the moderately distant leader seems to be most effective. Thus, among 41 supervisors in the San Antonio Post Office, the most productive were those with average distance scores (Carp, Vitola, and McLanathan, 1963). The reason is not hard to find: followers resent being rejected by their leaders. Their resentment does little harm if they are removed from the organization; it does a great deal of harm if they are not. If this reasoning is correct, one would expect the best corporal of drafted men to be the one who feels closest to them, for here one would find workers eager to be dismissed in an organization reluctant to dismiss them.

INITIATION OF STRUCTURE

Some leaders initiate structure and some do not. Those who do are described by their subordinates in statements like the following:

> He offers new approaches to problems.
> He asks for sacrifices for the good of the entire department.
> He assigns people to particular tasks.
> He criticizes poor work.
> He encourages slow-working people to greater effort.

The initiation of structure is independent of consideration. A supervisor who initiates a great deal of structure may be very considerate or very inconsiderate.

The more time a leader spends in initiating structure, the more successful he is likely to be. For example, insurance company, tractor factory, and railroad section-gang supervisors were asked, "How much of your time do you spend in supervising the men, planning the work, making out reports, and dealing with people outside your section?" The answer of high-producing and low-producing supervisors, divided into those who said they spent more than half their time in supervising activities and those who spent less than half, are shown in Table 6-3. In all three companies, the high-producing supervisors spent more time in supervising. Thus successful leaders play a *differentiated* rather than an undifferentiated role. That is, they do not play the role of a worker and do the same things he does. Rather, they take on tasks their subordinates cannot do as well: organizing the work, planning on-the-job training, trying to obtain promotions for subordinates, informing subordinates about policies, etc. Every leader, of course, spends *some* of his time in undifferentiated activity, and leaders in some situations spend more time in undifferentiated activity than leaders in other situations. In the same situation, however, good leaders spend more time than poor leaders in differentiated activities.

Workers see and appreciate the results of supervisory planning. The men in the railroad section gangs, for example, were asked, "How good is the foreman at figuring work out ahead of time?" Ten percent of the men under low-producing supervisors answered "not very good" for their supervisor; only 2 percent of men under high-producing supervisors gave this answer. Twenty-seven percent of the men under low-producing supervisors answered "very good"; 38 percent of men under high-producing supervisors gave this answer.

The need for a leader to initiate structure becomes more pressing as his responsibilities increase. Consequently, weaknesses of executives in this area are more apparent than similar weaknesses in first-line supervisors.

Any structure is better than none. If workers do not know what they are supposed to do or what to expect if they do or do not do certain things, they become inactive, uncertain, and frustrated. Indecisiveness is a serious

TABLE 6-3 Which supervisors spent more than half their time in supervising activities?

| | Percent of supervisors | | |
Company	High-producing	Low-producing	Difference
Insurance company	75	33	42
Tractor company	69	47	22
Railroad company	55	25	30

SOURCE: Adapted from Kahn and Katz (1953).

weakness. Still, the structure a leader introduces may be good or poor and may lead to success or failure.

The ability to initiate good structure is heavily dependent upon knowledge and experience and the ability to use them. The more technical the work, the greater the knowledge required: the successful hotel manager would have a hard time running an automobile factory. Even in apparently untechnical types of work, the leader's job knowledge is critical. For example, extensive studies of leadership in Army squads concluded, "The predictors which consistently showed the highest relationships with unit effectiveness were measures of leader job knowledge and measures of leader intelligence" (Havron and McGrath, 1961).

CONSIDERATION AND STRUCTURING

It has long been thought, and many still think, that a leader has to choose between being considerate and initiating structure. The facts, however, do not support this notion. For example, supervisors were rated by their subordinates from low to high on consideration; they were also rated from low to high on structuring. The two ratings were independent (Fleishman et al., 1955). That is, a supervisor who was rated high in consideration was as likely to be rated high as low in structuring; a supervisor who was rated high in structuring was as likely to be rated high as low in consideration. In general, as Figure 6-2 indicates, consideration and initiation of structure are most realistically viewed as independent dimensions. Supervisor A, a leader of the authoritarian type, is high in structuring and low in consideration. Supervisor D, however, is high in structuring and high in consideration— an equally likely combination. Supervisor B is low in structuring and low in consideration; supervisor C is also low in structuring but is high in consideration, a combination that is just as likely.

One reason for the independence of the two dimensions is that some structuring is unrelated to consideration. That is, a leader may attempt to structure the work or the workers. In doing this he uses his technical knowledge and know-how to order the work of his group on a long-range basis. The fame of Henry Ford, for example, rests upon his introduction of the assembly-line principle into the mass production of automobiles. Effective structuring of work can result in great increases in productivity. How great depends upon the technical skill of the leader. It also depends upon the work situation and the freedom he has to introduce such changes.

A leader's opportunity to introduce technical structuring, incidentally, varies a great deal with his situation. When he is at a high level in a firm

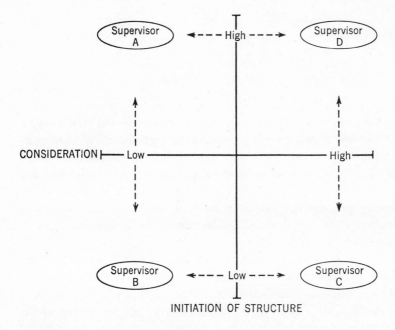

FIGURE 6-2 Consideration and Initiation as Coordinate but Independent Dimensions. (Adapted from Gagné and Fleishman, 1959, p. 325.)

engaged in a new and complex job, he may have vast opportunities for technical structuring. When he is at a low level in a firm engaged in routine production, which is typically organized and centrally controlled, his opportunities for introducing technical structuring may be very small. Supervisors on an assembly line, for example, see their main opportunities not in technical but in human-relations structuring:

> Ninety percent of my job is knowing how to break in and handle the men. . . . It's very easy for the men to rebel, and then things go to hell before you know it, and the foreman is left holding the bag.
> The two biggest problems we have here are absenteeism and relief. For example, we have a certain amount of work, and to do it we get a certain amount of manpower. Now, if I have two or more men out, that takes up my utility men, and then I have trouble getting relief for the men. This results in quality trouble.
> Let me show you how I have pulled a lot of operations off the line. Over here I have worked it so that a man can make up these mouldings and get a large stock of them built up quite far ahead of time. Then, if I have an absentee on the line, I can throw this man onto the line. I've done this throughout my group, and it allows me to ride a

long time. This kind of thing could be done much more in this department than it is. Some foremen have the theory that you must try and
put every operation on the line. The secret is to train men to do a lot
of different jobs. Some men like to do different jobs, and others don't.
You have to play that one by ear (Walker, Guest, and Turner, 1956,
p. 58).

Another reason for the independence of structuring and consideration,
even in the area of human relationships, is that such structuring may be inconsiderate. For example, a supervisor may structure his relationship with his
subordinates by telling them he is the boss, he will make all decisions, and
that he will see his decisions are followed by giving them detailed work
assignments and checking up on them frequently. Such a supervisor is
clearly structuring the situation. Equally clearly, he is showing a lack of
consideration.

The "Managerial Grid" of Blake and Mouton (1964) shows the independence of consideration and initiating structure. Blake uses the terms
concern for people and *concern for production* with a nine point scale on
each dimension. He shows that any combination of *concern for people* and
concern for production is possible and describes how leaders with different
combinations on these two dimensions behave. (See Figure 6-3). The best
manager is the 9,9 manager who shows high concern for people *and* production. Blake states that it is possible to train managers to be 9,9's through
management and organizational development.

The fact that consideration and structuring are independent means we
cannot predict one from the other. The considerate supervisor may or may
not initiate structure; the structuring supervisor may or may not be considerate. Ideally, of course, he should be both, and actually, supervisors often are.
The combination may occur by chance: the supervisor who happens to be
considerate may also happen to be good at initiating technical structure.
It may also be that he follows principles which lead to both consideration
and effective structuring.

DELEGATION OF AUTHORITY

Delegation of authority is one of the best ways for a leader to both structure and show consideration. If he sets goals for his men and then tells them
they can do the job the way they want to so long as they achieve the goals,
he is structuring the situation. At the same time, he is showing them he has
confidence in them and trusts them. Two, high-producing supervisors in the
insurance company study explained their approach in this way:

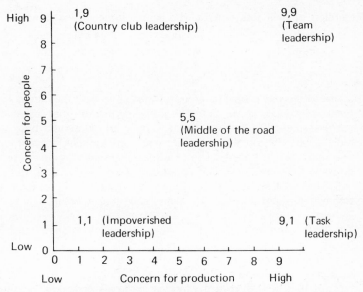

9,9 *Team.* Work is accomplished by committed people. All have a "common stake" in the organization and this leads to relationships of trust and respect.

1,9 *Country Club.* Thoughtful attention is given to the needs of people for satisfying relationships. This leads to a comfortable, friendly organization and work tempo.

9,1 *Task.* Efficiency in operations results from arranging conditions of work in such a way that human elements interfere to a minimum degree.

1,1 *Impoverished.* Minimum effort is exerted to get required work done and sustain organization membership.

5,5 *Middle Road.* Adequate organization performance is possible by balancing the necessity to get work done with the desire to maintain the morale of people at a satisfactory level.

FIGURE 6-3 Managerial Grid. (Adapted from Blake, Mouton, Barnes, and Greiner, 1964, p. 136.)

I never make any decisions myself. Oh, I guess I've made about two since I've been here. If people know their jobs, I believe in letting them make decisions. I believe in delegating decision-making. Of course, if there is anything that affects the whole division, then the two assistant managers, the three policy heads, and sometimes the assistant policy heads come in here and we discuss it. But I don't believe in saying, "this is the way it's going to be." After all, once supervision and management are in agreement, there won't be any trouble selling the staff the idea. . . .

I believe in letting them take time out from the monotony—it makes them feel that they are something special, not just the run of the mill. As a matter of fact, I tell them, "If you feel that the job is getting you down, get away from it for a few minutes" (Likert and Katz, 1948).

Regardless of their jobs, leaders who believe in delegating authority have the same general point of view. Two supervisors on an automobile assembly line, for example, are in agreement with the supervisors in the insurance company:

> I have often put it up to a group of men as to how they are going to break their work down. You take the seven men on that subassembly job over there. I got them together and said: "Now you boys know more about the job than I do. Do you want to break it down in any you think best?" I went on to explain to them that I wanted it broken down so that any of the men could do any of the different jobs . . . . Now there are some people who wouldn't go for that. . . . But if the foreman can put some trust in his men, they'll break it down fair enough.
>
> Once a foreman starts to poke into everything, he is lost. The utility man loses self-confidence and doesn't feel that he can make a move for fear that the foreman will step in and say something else. I can see that in certain kinds of industries under very stable conditions perhaps it is best to have the foreman keep his fingers on everything. But on an assembly line you must design your whole personnel setup for emergency conditions, because everything is in a constant state of emergency. As I like to tell my friends, an assembly line is just one damn emergency after another (Walker et al., pp. 29-30).

Supervisors who delegate authority have more productive units than those who do not (Kahn and Katz, 1953). In the life insurance company, for example, only 2 out of 12 high-producing supervisors said that they closely supervised their subordinates; 8 out of 12 low-producing supervisors said they did. Of the men under high-producing supervisors in the tractor company, 46 percent said they set their own work pace; of the men under low-producing supervisors, 37 percent. The significance of the difference between 46 and 37 percent is greater than it might seem, for most of the work of the men was set by the speed of their machines, an element beyond the control of the supervisors.

Supervisors who delegate authority have more satisfied workers. But how much authority should they delegate? The results of the following study suggest that the amount is higher than most think. Nearly 500 supervisors attending a supervisory conference were divided into groups of six and asked to solve the "new truck" and the "change of work procedure" problems (Solem, 1958).

The truck problem concerns the allocation of a new truck among the five members of a crew of repairmen, all of whom want the truck. The work-procedure problem involves a crew of three men on a routine assembly operation who rotate positions periodically in order to prevent boredom. Supposedly, a methods study has revealed that if each man remained on the position for which he was best suited, there would be a considerable saving in time per unit. The men, however, fear boredom and mistrust the management motives underlying the suggested alteration in job procedure. In solving these standard problems, one man in each group of six at the conference was asked to play the part of the supervisor, and the other men in the group were asked to take the roles of the different workers involved.

In 19 of the groups the man playing the part of the supervisor was asked to use a "limited-delegation" method. That is, he was asked first to decide what he thought was the best solution to the problem and then to discuss it with the group. The other 27 men playing the part of the supervisor were asked to use a "full-delegation" method—to present the problem to the group, discuss it, and accept whatever solution was developed. After 25 minutes, discussion was stopped and the supervisors of all groups were asked for their solutions. The supervisors and the men were also asked whether they were satisfied or dissatisfied with the solutions reached.

The kinds of solutions and the satisfaction with the solutions in the limited-delegation and the full-delegation groups were radically different. When solving the truck problem, for example, only one limited-delegation group in ten agreed to give the truck to the worker with seniority. In half the full-delegation groups the senior worker was given the truck. The limited-delegation groups had more than twice as many men who reported themselves dissatisfied with the solution reached. Furthermore, more of the *leaders* in the limited delegation group were dissatisfied. In explaining his results, Solem comments:

> . . . the differences in results appear to arise from the fact that the limited delegation procedure causes the superior to take an initial position as to what is the proper solution so that, in reality, he is presenting a solution to the group, not a problem. To the degree that the solution is at variance with the needs and ideas of the subordinates, it becomes a focal point for the expression of dissatisfaction and criticism. . . . an important contribution of the full delegation attitude of the superior is that it influences subordinates toward constructive solution of a problem on its own merits. In so doing, it helps to avoid any tendencies toward merely giving lip service to a superior's solution, of arguing with him, or of doing as directed with reduced motivation (1958).

THE FUTURE OF LEADERSHIP RESEARCH

Current research is beginning to replace the "great man" idea about leadership with more adequate interpersonal theories. It has established a clearer description of the leadership *process*. (Hollander and Julian, 1969). This process is one in which leader and followers influence each other and in which both attitudes and expectations play an important part. The behavioral approach to leadership has changed the thinking of social scientists and leaders on this question but it has not provided final answers.

Korman (1966), in reviewing twenty years of research exploring the concepts of consideration and initiating structure, concluded that much remains to be done before we can use these variables to *predict* how work groups will perform. Hersey and Blanchard (1969) think that it may be time to add a third dimension to leadership—effectiveness.

> By adding an effectiveness dimension to the task and relationships dimensions of earlier leadership models, we are attempting to integrate the concepts of leader style with situational demands of a specific environment. When the style of a leader is appropriate to a given situation, it is termed *effective*; when his style is inappropriate to a given situation, it is termed *ineffective*. (p. 76)

Bowers and Seashore (1966) have proposed four dimensions of leadership behavior. They believe leaders display two kinds of "consideration" behavior and two kinds of "initiating structure" behavior. Consideration is composed of behavior that *supports* (enhances someone else's feelings of personal worth and importance) and behavior that *facilitates interaction* (encourages members of the group to develop close, mutually satisfying relationships). Initiating structure is composed of behavior that *emphasizes goals* (stimulates an enthusiasm for meeting the group's goals or achieving excellent performance) and behavior that facilitates work (helps achieve goals by activities such as scheduling, planning, coordinating and providing resources).

Wofford (1967, 1970) has proposed six dimensions of leadership behavior. He believes the leader's behavior relates to keeping the work environment neat and safe; to being orderly and systematic; to being supportive and accepting support. to setting goals and innovating; to seeking status, power, and recognition; and to promoting team action and group achievement.

Future research, it seems likely, will produce models of leadership with more and better defined dimensions. These models will do a more thorough job of representing the complexity of leadership behavior. Consequently, they will permit not only a better description of leadership but also better predictions about the consequences of different kinds of leadership.

SUMMARY

The ideal leader is one who most effectively fulfills the leadership function. The function is always necessary; the leader is not. If the members of the group understand the nature and importance of the leadership function for them, the formal leader may be stupid and ignorant or even nonexistent, and still the group can effectively achieve its ends. The ideal leader's personality varies from situation to situation. An authoritarian and masculine leader may be a success in one situation and a failure in another; a democratic and feminine leader may be a success in one situation and a failure in another. The ideal leader is best defined not in terms of his own personality traits but in terms of his *relationship* to the group.

The ideal leader understands his relationship to the group is different from the relationship of the other members to it and that the success of his group depends upon his assuming the leadership role and playing it well. He is ready and eager, but not too eager, to play the role. He is accepted, liked, and respected as a leader by his superiors and by his subordinates. He has the general intelligence and special knowledge and skills required to initiate improvements in technical organization of the work.

Knowing the success of his group is largely dependent upon its internal organization and its relationship to other organizational units, the ideal leader skillfully modifies and improves these organizational relationships. Knowing that the success of his group is dependent upon both the skills and the attitudes of the men in it, he tries to select new men that fit his organization and to train and retain them. He retains them, in part, by being considerate. He knows and likes his followers, gives them the feeling that they are important to the organization, and effectively arranges for the satisfaction of their individual needs.

7

COMMUNICATION

Communication is the giving or exchanging of information, ideas, and feelings through talking, writing, or signs. It is like transportation on a river. The goal of both transportation and communication is to deliver the goods: freight or ideas. Both can use a variety of vessels: motorboats or steamships, telephone calls or letters. The vessels may travel by different channels: they may go by the formal well-marked channels or by channels known only to the local pilots. The vessels may go in dfiferent directions: upstream or downstream, from worker to manager or from manager to worker. Finally, the goods may be accepted or rejected: the receiver may refuse to accept the delivered goods; the worker may refuse to act upon communications received from the manager.

An organization cannot survive without communications; an effective organization must have an effective system of communication. The man-machine system, the man-people system and the leader-subordinate system all require that information, ideas and feelings be exchanged or they cease to function. Within an organization the communication system holds all other systems together.

Effective communication requires clearly defined channels and meaningful content. The channels must be known to everyone, and must be sufficient in number and variety to insure that everyone who needs to get "the word" gets it quickly, clearly, and authoritatively. If workers do not know vacation rosters are posted on the company bulletin board, or if a vice-president issues a policy statement and then receives a poorly written, unsigned memorandum which suggests that the policy statement should not have been issued, communication has broken down.

What goes through the channels must be significant for achieving the goals of the organization. The company newspaper which reports on the social life of the firm's executives is probably regarded by employees as an unimportant channel for communications. The subordinate who spends half of his time with the boss talking about the weather and the other half agreeing with his ideas is filling the communication channel with meaningless trivia.

Communication channels in an organization must be structured carefully. Studies have shown that different communication structures are effective for solving different types of problems (Glanzer and Glaser, 1961). In one study (Leavitt, 1964) each man in a five man group was given five solid-colored marbles. The group's problem was to find out the one color that each member had in common. The method of communication was writing notes, for example, "I have black, white, blue, red, and green." In some groups (restricted) one of the five was the leader and the other four could only send notes to and receive notes from him. In other groups (unrestricted) the members could communicate with each other as well as with the leader. The groups with restricted communication solved the problems more quickly and more accurately, although the members of the group (except the leader) reported that they were bored. When the groups were given marbles that were hard to describe; unusual colors and different colors and shades in one marble, the results changed. With these more complex problems the groups with less restricted communication were quicker and more accurate in reaching solutions and were less bored doing it.

This chapter will examine the seriousness of communication problems in the typical organization and consider principles that lead to their solution.

PROBLEMS IN COMMUNICATION

We all have problems in communication, though we are generally more aware of the failures of others to understand us than of our failures to understand them. Consider, for example, the statements shown in Table 7-1. Undergraduate and graduate students in personnel courses marked each statement true or false according to how they thought that average workers who answered the questionnaire had probably responded. Before reading the results below, you may now wish to look at the table and decide for yourself which answers most workers would give.

The majority of workers marked all the statements true. The majority of personnel students marked all of them false. Among the students, graduate students were more often wrong than undergraduates. For example, 60 percent of the workers answered true to the statement, "The average worker thinks he should be advanced by ability rather than by seniority." Among 332 undergraduate personnel majors, 32 percent answered true; among 21 graduate personnel students, 19 percent answered true. What the "correct" answers really are is a matter for debate. It is not debatable, however, that most of these potential executives did not know what workers *think* are the correct answers to the critical questions in the table.

TABLE 7-1   The attitudes of the average American worker

Several thousand workers in 150 companies completed an anonymous questionnaire on which they indicated whether they agreed or disagreed with statements like those below. How well can you predict what their answers were? If you think a majority of the workers agreed with the statement, answer "true." If you think a majority of the workers disagreed with the statement, answer "false." Answer them not as you think workers really are but as the typical worker would answer them.

T	F	1.	The average worker really enjoys his work.
T	F	2.	The average worker takes pride in what he does on his job.
T	F	3.	The average worker thinks that wages are increased primarily because he is able to produce more and needs more to live.
T	F	4.	The average worker only occasionally worries about being laid off.
T	F	5.	The average worker feels that the company's investment in new labor-saving equipment generally makes it possible for him to earn more money.
T	F	6.	The average worker thinks he should be advanced by ability rather than by seniority.
T	F	7.	The average worker in a plant should turn out as much work as he can.
T	F	8.	The average worker feels that a company's growth and prosperity depend upon whether he does his work well or not.
T	F	9.	The average worker feels that his work is important to the company's customers.
T	F	10.	The average worker believes that everyone on the job would benefit if each worker did the best he could.

SOURCE: Adapted from Bellows (1954), pp. 137–139.

SUPERIOR VERSUS SUBORDINATE

Table 7-2 summarizes data in a study in which workers were asked, "Different people want different things out of their jobs. What are the things you yourself feel are *most important* in a job?" The table shows the percent of 2,499 men who named the listed items as being among their first three preferences. The foremen of the men were also asked to answer as they themselves felt. In addition, they were asked to answer as they thought their men would respond. It is the latter answers by 196 foremen that appear in the table (Kahn, 1958).

The results are clear: Foremen overestimate the importance of economic factors and underestimate the importance of interpersonal relations and morale factors to the worker. The foremen would have been more correct if they had assumed that the workers' ratings would be the same as their own. For example, 39 percent of the foremen and 36 percent of the workers rated "getting along well with people I work with" as among the three most important aspects of the job. Exactly the same proportion of foremen and workers (twenty-eight percent) rated "getting along well with my supervisor" as important, and so on. Since we tend to assume similarity between ourselves and those we like and feel close to, the *dis*similarity between what the men said and what the foremen thought they would say suggests the lack of a supportive relationship between the foremen and their men.

The foremen's mistakes, one might think, would decrease as their judg-

TABLE 7-2 Differences between what foremen think their men will say they want and what their men do say they want

Things that were important on the job	As foremen thought men would	As men actually did	Difference
Getting along well with people I work with	17%	36%	−19
Getting alone well with my supervisor	14%	28%	−14
Good chance to do interesting work	22%	12%	+10
Good chance to turn out quality work	16%	11%	+ 5
Pensions and other benefits	17%	13%	+ 4
Steady work and steady wages	79%	61%	+18
High wages	61%	28%	+33

SOURCE: Adapted from Kahn (1958).

ments increasingly concerned matters in which they had a vital interest and which they had daily opportunities to observe. As Figure 7-1 shows, however, this is not the case. The illustration is based on the records of a large manufacturing company where time standards have been set for most jobs. Actual productivity is expressed as a percentage of each time standard. While the theory upon which these standards is based assumed that workers will reach 100 percent of the time standard, Figure 7-1 shows that the theory did not fit the practice, since on many jobs workers did not reach the standard. Workers were asked to estimate what they thought was "reasonable" productivity for their job. Their foremen were also asked to estimate what they thought their men would give as a reasonable figure.

Each foreman in this company receives a report every morning on what

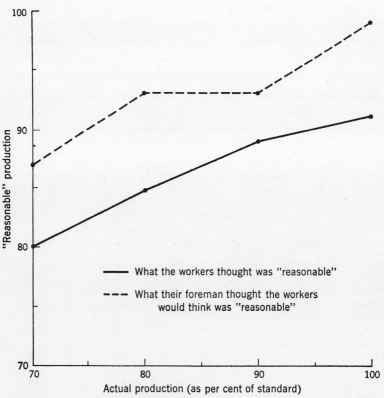

FIGURE 7-1 Errors in the Foremen's Estimates of What Their Workers Would Think Was "Reasonable" Production under Different Conditions of Actual Production. (Likert, 1961, p. 48.)

percent of standard his work group achieved the previous day and what percent of standard each man individually achieved. The foremen also have the responsibility of reporting his productivity to each man and discussing with the men whose productivity was less than 100 percent how to get it up to standard. Here then, if anywhere, the foremen should know what their men think. Yet, as seen in Figure 7-1, they consistently overestimated—in some cases by more than 20 percent—what their men would think was reasonable productivity. The potential conflicts in this situation were exaggerated by the fact (not shown in the illustration) that the men, in turn, consistently overestimated what the foremen would say was reasonable productivity for them.

SUPERIOR VERSUS SUPERIOR

Executives find it difficult to communicate with workers; they also often find it hard to communicate with each other. For example, 23 middle-management executives from the same level of a large manufacturing company read the same 10,000-word case as part of a company-sponsored executive training program. The case concerned the Castengo Steel Company and was written to hold to facts and leave the burden of interpretation up to the reader. It dealt with the poorly defined relations among the factory manager, the metallurgist, and the company president.

After the executives had read the case but before they had discussed it, the instructor asked each of them to assume that he was the top executive of the steel company and to state what he thought was the most important problem facing the company. Ten of the twenty-three executives were in sales or sales-related departments. Eight of these ten mentioned some aspect of sales as the most important problem. Only two of the thirteen executives who were not in sales departments mentioned sales as the most important problem. They mentioned such problems as "employee relations," "teamwork," "organization," etc. The researchers concluded that "each executive will perceive those aspects of a situation that relate specifically to the activities and goals of his department" (Dearborn and Simon, 1958).

The strong executive of the traditional organization is the most selective in his perceptions. His associates describe him in such phrases as "a guy you can count on" or "a guy who won't let you down," as "having a lot on the ball," as "doing what's necessary," and as being "on the beam," "one who really stacks up," "a damn good man," etc. An anthropologist describes him in this way:

The strong have high tolerance for conflict, and unlike the weak, carry little effects of job discords from the plant with them. They flee neither necessary conflict nor responsibility for making decisions. They are able to act quickly and effectively and are skilled in turning ambiguous and contradictory situations to their needs. Where the weak look for protection in the letter of rules, the strong oppose strict interpretations. . . . the weak are prone to lose sight of goals in concentrating on procedures. . . . This, as against the strong, who are so relatively unconcerned with procedure (except as it is a clear aid or can be interpreted to their advantage) and accustomed to moving directly toward goals, that they devise workable methods as needed where situations are doubtful (Dalton, 1959).

The strong generally aid both their superiors and their subordinates by imperturbably resolving ambiguous or contrary demands. Their high speed of perception and firm closure on situations, however, increases the risks of poor communication. The risk may involve millions of dollars, as the following case illustrates.

A CASE STUDY

In 1960 a Federal judge fined 29 firms in the electrical manufacturing industries and 45 executives of the firms a total of nearly 2 million dollars for price-fixing and bid rigging. Seven of the executives received 30-day prison sentences. The sentences were imposed for violation of the Sherman Act of 1890, which declares illegal "every contract, combination in the form of trust or otherwise, or conspiracy, in restraint of trade of commerce among the several States, or with foreign nations" (Brooks, 1962).

The General Electric Company was the largest corporation involved. The price-fixing behavior of some of its executives was in direct violation of a written policy of the company that "No employee shall enter into any understanding, agreement, plan or scheme, expressed or implied, formal or informal, with any competitor in regard to prices, terms, or conditions of sale, production, distribution, territories, or customers; nor exchange or discuss with a competitor prices, terms or conditions of a sale, or any other competitive information." All executives knew of the policy. They were told about it in formal meetings, copies of it were periodically redistributed to them, and they were periodically required to sign a statement saying that they had read it and understood it.

In spite of this apparently clear communication, the government alleged that executives of the company attended meetings with competitors—beginning at least as early as 1956 and continuing into 1959—at which noncompetitive price levels were agreed upon, nominally sealed bids on individual contracts were rigged in advance, and each company was allocated a certain percentage of the available business. The government further alleged that the executives resorted to such devices as referring to their companies by code numbers, making telephone calls from public booths or from their homes rather than from their offices, and doctoring their expense accounts covering their get-togethers to conceal the fact that they had all been in a certain city on a certain day.

Poor communication was apparently responsible. The top executives saw to it that their subordinates knew the policy, they wanted their subordinates to obey it, and they apparently did not know that it was being violated. The implicated executives simply did not *believe* the communication; they thought it was on the books solely to provide legal protection for the company. They interpreted winks from their superiors—or what they construed as winks given when their superiors read the policy aloud—as an instruction to ignore it.

Barnard (1938) recognized this kind of problem many years ago. He stated that effective communication is authoritative, that it should be believed and acted on. He cited four conditions, all of which must be true before a person regards a communication as authoritative. The person receiving the communication must understand its literal meaning, must believe it is consistent with the purposes of the organization, must find it compatible with his interests as an employee, and must be physically and mentally able to comply with it. Obviously one or more of these conditions was not met.

The president of the company tried to explain the situation to the investigating committee in this way:

> When I was younger, I used to play a good deal of bridge. We played about fifty rubbers of bridge, four of us, every winter, and I think we probably played some rather good bridge. If you gentlemen are bridge players, you know that there is a code of signals that is exchanged between partners as the game progresses. It is a stylized form of playing. . . . Now, as I think about this—and I was particularly impressed when I read Smith's testimony when he talked about a "meeting of the clan" or "meeting of the boys"—I begin to think that there must have been a stylized method of communication between these people who were dealing with competition. Now, Smith could say, "I told Vinson what I was doing," and Vinson wouldn't have the foggiest idea what was being told to him, and both men could testify under oath, one saying yes and the other man saying no, and both be telling the truth . . . [they] wouldn't be on the same wave length. [They] wouldn't have the same meanings. I think, I believe now that these men did think that they were telling the truth, but they weren't communicating between each other with understanding (Brooks, 1962).

Communication is a complex process involving the transmission of facts, problems, suggestions, experiences, emotional climates, attitudes, hostilities, loyalties, goals, etc. It is not surprising, therefore, that it often breaks down. Breakdowns may result from people not hearing what is said, not reading what is written, or not understanding or believing what they hear or read. Behind most of these causes lies a still more basic factor: People look at problems from their own special point of view, selecting facts that fit it and forgetting facts that do not. In general, however, making communications easier to understand, stressing upward communication, and recognizing the importance of action as a powerful form of communication will improve communication.

THE USE OF EASY WORDS

We use words in communicating. The easier it is to understand them, the better our communication is likely to be. It is equally important that they be hard to *mis*understand. In one plant, a supervisor asked a female employee "to pull with the team." She was insulted because she felt she was being compared to an animal. In another plant, a superintendent insulted his foremen by telling them that he wanted "to discuss the production problems from your level." He was referring to organizational levels; they thought he was referring to their lack of intelligence. An engineer explaining the operation of a machine to a group of trainees said, "It is really simple; any one of you can learn it in no time at all. We've designed it to be idiot-proof."

In talking to a person, we usually can tell when he does not understand or misunderstands. In writing to him, we may never know whether he understands us or not. As organizations increase in size and complexity, writing becomes more and more the main channel of communication. Consequently, "bafflegab" and "gobbledygook"—the use of pompous, vague, and intangible words to say in a hundred words what could be better said in thirty—becomes an increasingly important obstacle to communication. The following, a mild example, illustrates the point:

> Sick leaves shall be granted to employees when they are incapacitated for their performances of their duties by sickness, injury, or pregnancy and confinement, or for medical, dental, or optical examination or treatment, or when a member of the immediate family of the employee is affected with a contagious disease and requires the care and attendence of the employee, or when, through exposure to a contagious disease, the presence of the employee at his post of duty would jeopardize the health of others.

The employee handbook is one of the most widely used and promising ways of dealing with the common employee complaints that "I don't know what is expected of me" or "I didn't get the word." Yet many of these handbooks are incomprehensible to the employees. For example, an analysis of 11 handbooks from corporations who were in the "Billion Dollar Club" showed that 6 of them were written over the heads of the unskilled non-supervisory employee. At the extreme, the handbook of one company was written in such a way that it would take a college education to understand it, while the typical nonsupervisory employee of the company had a fourth-grade education (Carlucci and Crissy, 1951). A similar analysis was made of the annual reports of 26 large corporations, and the investigators concluded, "On the whole, the general level of reading was *difficult*, and the human interest value *dull.* . . . These reports contain language which is beyond the language experience and fluent comprehension of approximately 75 percent of the U.S. adult population" (Pashalian and Crissy, 1950).

MEASUREMENT OF READING EASE

To evaluate and improve written communication, we first need a reliable and valid measure of the difficulty of written material. The Flesch formula meets the need. It is based on two assumptions: The shorter the words used in a communication, the easier to is is to read; and the shorter the sentences used, the easier it is to read. The formula incorporates these assumptions as follows:

Reading ease = 206.835 − 0.846 syllables per 100 words − 1.015 X average number of words per sentence

The constants are inserted to make the results come out in convenient terms. Thus, a score of zero means that a passage is practically unreadable, and a score of 100 means that it is very easy to understand. Table 7-3 indicates the interpretation given to these and intermediate scores.

The Flesch technique has limitations. It measures readability and human interest *after* something is written. It can only be used effectively in reverse by the exercise of caution and skill: the indiscriminate use of short words and short sentences may communicate nothing. It cannot make the communications of confused people clear. It cannot make simple ideas out of difficult ideas, and it cannot make clear the thoughts of people who do not want others to know what they really think.

TABLE 7-3 Interpretation of reading-ease scores

Reading-ease score	Description of style	Typical magazine
0- 30	Very difficult	Scientific
30- 50	Difficult	Academic
50- 60	Fairly difficult	Quality
60- 70	Standard	Digests
70- 80	Fairly easy	Slick fiction
80- 90	Easy	Pulp fiction
90-100	Very easy	Comics

SOURCE: Adapted from Flesch (1948).

THE IMPROVEMENT OF UPWARD COMMUNICATION

An effective organization requires good communication down from the management, across to people on the same level, and up from the employees. Upward communication is the largest unsolved problem in most organizations, but managers are usually unaware of it. For example, they have been asked, "Consider the most difficult communication problem you have faced in the past six months. Did this problem deal with downward, upward, or sideward communication?" Only one manager in ten answered upward (Likert, 1961). Why are they so little concerned with the problem?

A manager forgets how many ways he has of communicating with his employees and how few ways they have of communicating with him. To begin with, numerous written channels are open to the manager and largely closed to the employee. Practically all managers, for example, use bulletin boards, and most of them send bulletins to employees, insert notices in pay envelopes, distribute employee magazines and handbooks, and write letters to individual employees. They can call meetings, use the public-address system, or ask individual employees to come to see them. Of course, most managers have an "open-door policy" for receiving communications from employees—but few employees go through the door.

The typical manager thinks that his subordinates feel freer to discuss their problems with him than they actually do. For example, 90 percent of the top staff of a company said that their foremen felt free to discuss important things about the job with them. Only 67 percent of the foremen, however, said they felt so free. In turn, 85 percent of the foremen said their men felt very free to discuss important things with them. Only 51 percent of their men agreed that they felt very free (Likert, 1961).

The typical manager thinks he seeks the ideas of his subordinates more often than they think he does. In the study above, 70 percent of the top staff said they always or almost always obtained their foremen's ideas on work problems. Only 52 percent of the foremen agreed. In turn, 73 percent of the foremen said they always or almost always sought their men's ideas. Only 16 percent of the men agreed.

The typical manager thinks he tells his men more than they think he does. Of the top staff of a public utility, 70 percent said they always told their foremen in advance about changes that would affect them. Only 27 percent of the foremen thought that they were kept informed. In turn, 40 percent of the foremen said they always told their men in advance, whereas only 27 percent of their men agreed.

As a result of his misconceptions about the effectiveness of upward communication, the typical superior thinks he understands the problems of his subordinates much better than they think he does. Thus, 90 percent of a group of general foremen said they understood the foremen's problems well. Only 60 percent of the foremen, however, thought that their general foremen understood their problems well. The difference between foremen and men was even greater: 95 percent of the foremen thought they understood the men's problems well, whereas only 34 percent of the men confirmed this opinion (Hamann, 1956).

The superior is confident that he understands his subordinates; his subordinates are eager for him to retain his mistaken confidence. Unless he is quitting in anger, a subordinate does not tell his superior that he is inefficient, is creating unnecessary difficulties for his subordinate, and is unfair and unreasonable. Furthermore, the worse the situation, the harder it is for the subordinate to tell the superior about it. "Yessing" the boss keeps him misinformed, but it also keeps the subordinate out of hot water and increases his chances of being rewarded.

Roethlisberger (1945) explains the situation of the foreman in this way:

> The crux of the foreman's problem is that he is constantly faced with the dilemma of (1) having to keep his superior informed of what is happening at the work level (in many cases so that his superior may prepare in turn for the unfavorable reaction of his superior and so on up the line) and (2) needing to communicate this information in such a way that it does not bring unfavorable criticism on himself for not doing his job correctly or adequately. Discrepancies between the way things are at the work level and the way they are represented to be by management cannot be overlooked; and yet the foreman feels obliged to overlook them when talking to his boss. This makes the foreman's job particularly "tough" and encourages him to talk out of both sides of his mouth at the same time—to become the master of double talk.

THE MEASUREMENT OF EMPLOYEE ATTITUDES

To begin with, what superiors need is an unbiased view of what their subordinates really think and feel. For decades most companies have maintained "suggestion boxes" for getting at least some idea of what their employees are interested in. The detailed and systematic measurement of employee attitudes is of more recent origin. In 1947, only 15 percent of companies reported that they conducted regular attitude surveys; in 1957, more than twice as many (32 percent) reported that they conducted such surveys.

The education and training of the industrial psychologist qualifies him particularly well for planning, conducting, and interpreting the results of these surveys. In addition, if he comes into the company from an outside agency, as he often does, he is more likely to convince the employees that the survey is unbiased and that the confidential nature of their answers will be respected.

The general survey

Suppose the officers of a large corporation want to know how well their organization compares with others and to find out which of its plants have the most serious employee problems. A standardized questionnaire that gives a single index of a worker's job satisfaction is generally the best method. The directions and sample items from one such scale are given below (Brayfield and Rothe, 1951).

Job Questionnaire

Some jobs are more interesting and satisfying than others. We want to know how people feel about different jobs. This blank contains eighteen statements about jobs. You are to cross out the phrase below each statement which best describes how well you feel about your present job. There are no right or wrong answers. We should like your honest opinion on each one of the statements.

My job is like a hobby to me.

STRONGLY AGREE   AGREE   UNDECIDED   DISAGREE   STRONGLY DISAGREE

I feel fairly well satisfied with my present job.

STRONGLY AGREE   AGREE   UNDECIDED   DISAGREE   STRONGLY DISAGREE

Each day of work seems like it will never end.

STRONGLY AGREE   AGREE   UNDECIDED   DISAGREE   STRONGLY DISAGREE

It seems that my friends are more interested in their jobs.

STRONGLY AGREE   AGREE   UNDECIDED   DISAGREE   STRONGLY DISAGREE

The answer to each question is given a score from 1 to 5, and the highest total score for the 18 items is thus 90. The scores are highly reliable; scores on odd and even items agree closely with each other and total scores on the scale agree well with scores on similar scales. The whole questionnaire can be completed in a few minutes, the use of marks rather than writing assures the worker of anonymity, and the answers can be quickly and easily scored (an important point if thousands of employees are to complete the form). Since results from many different types of companies are available, the standing of a particular company can be readily determined. Potentially the most valuable aspect of the questionnaire is that its periodic use permits the analysis of trends in employee attitudes within departments and within plants.

The area survey

Assume that the corporation has now completed its survey. Assume further that while the company stands well compared to other companies, one of its plants has particularly low scores. To take any effective action, the company must know *why* the scores are low in this plant. Is it the way the plant is organized? The kind of jobs that the workers have? The physical conditions of the plant? The leadership?

The results of the general survey provide no answer. To find at least a general answer, the company might well decide to survey the employees in this particular plant again to locate more specific problem areas. A series of attitude scales with statements like the following could be employed. On such scales, the worker is asked to indicate the extent of his agreement or disagreement with each statement, and thus a total score for each area is obtainable.

Leadership

1. Our supervisors are capable men.
2. Most of the supervisors are good men but there are a few who aren't.
3. Our supervisors would be better liked if they didn't act as if they were so much better than anyone else.

Work associates

1. It is a pleasure to be courteous to the kind of employees we have here.
2. Fellow employees here deserve to be snubbed.
3. It is wise to treat fellow employees courteously.

Type of work
1. The work here is very interesting.
2. My work is so trying that I am really glad when it is time to quit.
3. The work here is very monotonous.

Working conditions
1. Our working conditions here are ideal.
2. Working conditions here couldn't be much worse.
3. Working conditions here aren't so bad.

GENERAL MOTORS

The "My Job" contest at General Motors (Evans and Laseau, 1950) was a different, expensive but effective way of answering the two questions we have thus far considered: How do the various divisions of the company compare in overall satisfaction? What factors account for low or high satisfaction in particular plants? Almost 175,000 employees (59 percent of all employees) submitted essays in the contest, where the prizes were numerous and lavish. The essays varied from one sentence to twenty typed pages, and from ordinary letters to sound recordings, movies, and poems. Over 600 were written in foreign languages. The following is one example:

> Dear G. M. C.
>
> I'll write you a few lines two let you know why I like my job. The Forman not all ways coming around saying thing there no need of. I like the good wages I get. Then I like all my fellow workmen. I like name of working for G. M. C. I like the hours I work. I like the two 15 mi. Rest Periods each shift. I like the way we all do are work at G. M. C. I like the job I am doing.

The essays were analyzed by the number of times 58 different themes were mentioned. The above essay, for example, would be counted under "supervision," "wages," "associates," "hours of work," etc. The average results showed the following 10 themes most frequently mentioned: supervision, associates, wages, work type, pride in company, management training, opportunity for advancement, insurance, and security.

The contest was about sources of job satisfaction. Nonetheless, calculating the number of employees who did *not* mention a particular theme was an indirect but good way of measuring *dissatisfaction*. For example, the fact that employees in division 57 mentioned steady work, opportunity for advancement, and supervision more often than most divisions strongly suggested that these job elements were more satisfactory in that division. On the other hand, the fact that the same employees mentioned working hours, safety, and rest periods *less* than employees in most divisions indicated that these elements were less satisfactory there.

Most of the elements indicated as unsatisfactory were within the control of the managers of the divisions. Specifically, of the 58 possible themes, the employees in the average division mentioned 29. Of the themes "under-mentioned," some action on 8 seemed desirable and possible. Eventually, the average division took action on 5 of the 8.

The specific survey
Once the results of a survey pinpoint a problem area in a problem plant, as in the General Motors survey, the local managers can sometimes figure out what is wrong and what should be done about it. Often, however, they are not sure and would like more specific information. Suppose, for example, that area surveys reveal that workers are intensely dissatisfied with the plant cafeteria or with their physical working conditions. The results of specific surveys like the following could define with precision the nature of these problems and suggest concrete solutions:

The cafeteria
Most people are rather fussy about their food. What do you think about the cafeteria?

Have you found the food to your liking?	YES	NO
Is there enough variety?	YES	NO
Are the prices reasonable?	YES	NO
Is the service satisfactory?	YES	NO

Working conditions
Following are items describing working conditions. Check as many items as you wish which you feel are bothering you in your work and need to be improved:

Ventilation	( )	Unpleasant dust	( )
Lighting	( )	Lack of sanitation	( )
Too cold	( )	Too far from rest rooms	( )
Too hot	( )	Unpleasant odors	( )
Drafts	( )	Sun glare	( )

Specific surveys may concern off-the-job matters such as the cafeteria or on-the-job matters such as antagonisms between work groups. Finding the "whys" is generally easier for the former than the latter. For example, the job satisfaction of both production workers and inspectors in one company was reduced by antagonism between the two groups. Why were they hostile and what could be done about it? To find out, production workers were asked to answer the following questions (Dunlap, 1950):

1. Do you always know what quality of work will be passed or rejected by the inspectors? YES NO

2. From day to day, do the same inspectors always require from you the same quality of work? YES NO

3. Do different inspectors always require from you the same quality of work? YES NO

About a third of the workers answered no to each of these questions.

A survey of the inspectors showed that they were as confused as the production workers. They were asked, among others, these questions:

1. Are you uncertain whether an item or tray should be passed or rejected?

2. In your opinion, do other inspectors sometimes pass items you would reject?

Seventy percent of the inspectors said they were at least occasionally uncertain as to whether they should pass or reject! Forty-seven percent believed that other inspectors sometimes passed items they would reject.

The actions required, once the results were known, were clear: Inspection standards needed to be more precisely defined, and inspectors needed better training in applying them. The inspection standards were revised, old inspectors were given a refresher course, and new inspectors were given more rigorous and systematic training. A continuing check system was installed to identify workers who were making inspection mistakes. An effort was made to diagnose the reasons for the mistakes and to take appropriate remedies. Work areas were modified for some, rules and regulations were reviewed with others, and still others were asked to get new glasses. Supervisors reported a marked reduction in friction between workers and inspectors as a result of this remedial program.

Technically the value of the results depends on the skill with which the attitude measuring instruments are constructed and the standards used in interpreting the results. (Wakeley, 1964).

The total value of the results obtained depends upon whether a manager really wants to know what the employees think about a problem. No survey at all is better than one which produces results that the manager cannot or will not use. Unused surveys waste time and money. Surveys that are not used also produce hostility among employees who have been led to believe by the survey that something will be done. In short, surveys are of most value to managers who want to improve upward communication in order to take more intelligent actions.

THE PLACE OF ACTION

Actions speak louder than words—to the worker as well as the rest of us. Mann and Dent (1954), for example, asked supervisors in a large utility, "On what basis do you judge your standing with your immediate superior?" By far the most common answer was, "From the amount of responsibility and authority he gives me." The number of raises and promotions was also often reported as a basis.

When a man's words do not fit his actions, we believe his actions. The supervisor who treats a subordinate with a hearty "first name" informality, expresses a "personal interest" in his family, and yet reduces his job responsibilities, is still communicating that he does not like or respect his subordinate. The reverse is also true. A man's words may suggest a lack of respect while his actions show a good deal. The actions generally win out, as the following case illustrates:

> The mechanical superintendent in a small manufacturing company was the prototype of the "bull of the woods" manager. He swore at his men, drove them, disciplined them, behaved superficially like a Napoleon. He was the despair of the staff group who were carrying on a program of supervisory training in human relations. Yet, oddly, his subordinates appeared to have high regard for him. They said, "Oh, his bark is worse than his bite." Morale and productivity in his department were both high.
>
> Probing revealed some significant facts. He was known as a "square shooter" who dealt with his men with scrupulous fairness. Despite his superficial toughness he was sincerely and warmly interested in his subordinates. When they were in trouble—whether it was a simple matter of a few dollars to tide a man over until payday, or a family crisis—he helped out in a matter-of-fact way that left no uncomfortable feeling of being patronized.
>
> Most important of all, he was known to be ready to go to bat for his men on any occasion when he felt that they had not been accorded a fair break by higher management. The men spoke with awe of two occasions during a ten-year period when he had stormed into the office of the big boss to demand that a decision be altered because it was unfair to "his boys." When he was refused in one of these instances, he resigned on the spot, put on his hat, and left. His superior actually followed him out to the gate and capitulated (McGregor, 1960, p. 134).

The actions of a supervisor may show that he has an effective under-standing of the principles of good human relations though he cannot put his principles into neat sentences. On the other hand, a supervisor may have memorized the principles and still do a poor job of putting them into prac-tice. Effective action is the goal. Still, a knowledge of the principles is at least a step toward the goal. The "foundations for good relations" in the Job Relations Training program developed by the War Manpower Commission during World War II are the most widely known set of such principles. Below are the principles together with discussion from the JRT manual:

LET EACH WORKER KNOW HOW HE IS GETTING ALONG.	Suppose a man goes home and some-one says "How are you doing on your job?" and he has to say, "I don't know—no one's said anything." Do you think that's good job rela-tions if the man feels uncertain about important things like his job?
GIVE CREDIT WHEN DUE.	If a man has been sick but stays on at work to finish an important job, maybe you can't give him a raise, but you can let him know it helped you.
TELL PEOPLE IN ADVANCE ABOUT CHANGES THAT WILL AFFECT THEM.	Suppose someone tells you tonight that beginning tomorrow you're go-ing to transfer to the midnight shift and start work at midnight instead of at 8:00 in the morning? Are you going to like it?
MAKE THE BEST USE OF EACH PERSON'S ABILITY.	Have you ever had a man who went sour just because he felt he could do more skilled work than you gave him to do?

To take effective action on human-relations problems, the supervisor must know the principles of good relations, know how to apply them, and want to apply them. Above all, he must be *able* to apply them. He cannot let a worker know how he is getting along if he does not know himself; he cannot reward a man for a good job if he does not have the rewards to give; he cannot tell people in advance if he does not himself know in advance; he cannot make the best use of a man's ability if he has no authority to transfer a man or to change his job. Little wonder that the amount of worker satisfaction is so closely related to the amount of influence a supervisor has on his superior (Pelz, 1952).

In the end, therefore, the quality of the organizations determines the quality of communication. One of the most desirable features of the group system of organization (Chapter 5) is that it provides an effective system of communication. The quality of *both* the organization and communication, however, are heavily influenced by the broad goals and values that set the climate of the organization, intangible though they may seem. The more the values of the company reflect the values of the worker and of the society of which he is a member, the better both the organization and communication within it will be.

A company duplicates in miniature the social system of the community. Disruptions of the social system within the company, particularly disruptions that represent a loss of social status to its members, may have profound effects, as a study of a strike in a New England shoe factory showed (Warner, 1947). The reason given for the strike was wages; actually, disruptions of the social system and of the communication system seemed a more important cause.

The introduction of modern machinery changed the social system. Before the introduction of the new machinery, the personnel in the factory was a closely knit social group. Each man knew his place and how to work up to the next step. He respected the senior skilled craftsmen. The foreman's role was to teach the men highly regarded skills.

After the machines were introduced, the foreman only had to enforce a set of rules. The craftsmen became mere tenders of machines. The management exaggerated the disruption by increasing the social distance between the top management and the employees in the lowest positions. Previously, the employees and the manager had known each other personally. With the arrival of machinery, however, the owner imported managers from outside the city. This resulted in less and poorer communication between the management and the employees.

SUMMARY

Accurate and full communication—the giving or exchange of information, ideas, and feelings through talking, writing, or signs—is vital to the health of an organization. The measurement of reading ease and the adjustment of the level of reading difficulty to the expected reader is helpful in improving downward communication. Contrary to common management opinion, however, upward communication is a more serious problem. Studies consistently show that managers have a less accurate idea of what workers feel than they think they have. The systematic measurement of employee attitudes through general and specific surveys gives managers more accurate information. In communication, however, actions shout while words whisper. When a manager's words disagree with his actions, workers believe his actions. What actions a manager takes depends upon what actions his organization permits him to take and what actions its values and those of the community encourage him to take.

3
ORGANIZATION
DEVELOPMENT

Organizations are continually changing, and every change offers a possibility for improvement. However, just as not all movement is forward, so not all change is development, and only those changes that increase the productivity, integration and morale of the organization represent an improvement. Every personnel decision made within an organization is an opportunity for positive development. By making better decisions about selection, placement, training, appraisal, and incentives, organizations develop. This section considers the ways in which psychologists help organizations make better decisions in these areas.

8

PERSONNEL SELECTION

When a person joins an organization both the person and the organization are taking risks. The person hopes the job will be a "good" one. A "good" job may pay as little as $75 a week or as much as $500 a week; it may be a temporary position to see one through the summer or a significant career choice; it may permit one to use well-developed skills or provide an opportunity to learn new skills. The organization hopes that the person can do a "good" job as it defines good. A "good" employee will do his present job well, remain with the organization, and learn and change as the organization changes.

Each year, as companies try to hire more capable workers and workers try to find better jobs, millions of people change jobs. The process is expensive to the companies, the workers, and society. Processing an application for employment costs a company from $10 to $50. However, considering the costs of training, lost productivity, and integration, the total cost to the company of replacing a worker is estimated to be ten times the direct costs (Scott, Clothier, and Spriegel, 1961). Accurate calculation of such costs is virtually impossible, but the range is probably from about five hundred dollars for a company to hire an unskilled worker to several thousands to hire a highly skilled production, research, or executive worker.

The cost to the company varies according to the size and stability of the work force. Over a seven-year period, for example, one company maintained its work force at a fairly steady 7,000. To do this, however, it had to hire over 2,000 new workers and interview 20,000 applicants (Uhrbrock, 1948). As another company expanded its work force from 12,000 to 20,000 it had to process nearly 200,000 applicants.

Costs of making a poor selection are high now, and continue to rise. Guarantees of continued employment as a result of union-management agreements are becoming increasingly common. As job guarantees expand, it becomes more attractive for an employee to stay with one company, thus, the longer an unsatisfactory person stays the more it costs the company. The cost of a misplaced employee is less obvious but just as high. His chances of being placed in a job that he does not like and performs poorly are also increasing. The total social costs of poor selection are even less tangible but they too are rising. On September 9, 1968, Mr. Willard Wirtz, then Secretary of Labor, signed a memorandum dealing with the use of selection techniques (most specifically tests) by Federal contractors. In Section 1.(b) the order states:

> "Two matters regarding selection procedures are of foremost concern to the Government: (1) recognizing the importance of *proper* procedures in the utilization and conservation of human resources generally, and (2) pointing out the possible adverse effects of *improper* procedures on the utilization of minority group personnel."

The difficulties involved in making good selections are also increasing. Fewer and fewer workers are needed for simple jobs with obvious requirements, more and more are needed for complex jobs with requirements that are hard to specify and harder to measure. Drucker (New York Times, January 21, 1962) estimates that by 1980, half our workers will be "knowledge" workers: teachers, engineers, accountants, scientists, technologists, market researchers, credit analysts, and so forth. Another fourth will be in sales and clerical jobs.

We will examine the factors which make up the complexities of job selection in the following pages.

THE SELECTION PROCESS

The heart of the selection process is prediction. In general, the more we know about someone the better we can predict his performance in a specific situation. Likewise, the more we know about the situation the better we can predict how a particular person will perform in it. When an organization is selecting someone, it needs to know about the person, the job he is to perform, and the situation in which he will perform it.

Suppose that you are in charge of selection for the split and shave department of a shoe factory. Suppose, further, that you know nothing about the split and shave department and make your selections by randomly sticking pins in a list of names. After you have made a hundred selections, you do a study to see how successful you have been in predicting who would be a good employee for the department. You find that 50 are still with the department and 50 left within two weeks. Your best prediction for the future, unless you change procedures, is that one of every two people you send to the department will leave within two weeks. If 50-50 is not good enough, you will need to find out more about the department *and* about the applicants. If you learn about the department and the kind of people it needs, but still select by pushing pins, selection will not improve. If you know everything about every applicant but nothing about the job, there is no rational basis for using your information and selection is still not likely to improve.

JOB ANALYSIS

Job analysis, the systematic study of the duties, requirements and skills of a job, is the essential first step in the development of a job description. Job analysis is basic to almost all of the activities in personnel work. Unless we know what a job is we cannot hope to select someone to fill it, train someone for it, appraise someone who is doing it, or pay someone fairly for completing it.

Several methods can be used to obtain basic data for a job analysis. Virtually all of the methods require either that we watch people do the job or ask them how they do it. The purpose of job analysis is *not* to find out how a particular person functions, but, by seeing how several incumbents do the job, determine its basic features and write them into a general description.

Observation is one method of getting data for a job analysis. In the simplest form of this method, a job analyst watches a number of people do the same job in their normal manner. As he watches, the analyst systematically records his observations in narrative fashion or by using a prepared check list. Direct observation creates problems because many people change their behavior when they know they are observed. The job analyst may use a movie camera or in some other way try to prevent people's knowing that they are being watched. However, this might be considered unethical. Moreover, observation is useless for establishing the mental content of the job: a man thinking about his job and the same man thinking about his last round of golf may look just the same. Another limitation of the observation technique is that it cannot be used when the job cycle is long or when rare events are an important part of the job. For example, it is impractical to watch a skilled cabinet maker for the two months or more that it takes him to create and complete a new suite of furniture or to watch a truck driver for years waiting to see what he does when confronted with a head-on collision. Observation is thus most useful for short-cycle, physical jobs where the analyst can gain the cooperation of the people being observed.

Morsh (1964) lists other methods for doing job analysis. Most involve asking people to tell how they perform their jobs. Job incumbents can write about their jobs by completing a questionnaire, or check list, or keeping a diary. They can discuss their jobs in individual interviews away from the job, in an interview with a group of several fellow workers, or in an interview held while the job is being performed. In general, these methods depend heavily on people's ability to know their own behavior, remember it, and communicate it clearly.

Other methods may be used. Sometimes a group of experts, supervisors for example, meet with the analyst and specify all job characteristics, or the job analyst himself may perform the job.

The good job analyst knows the advantages and disadvantages of all the methods he may utilize, but he is aware that *some* method must be used before selection can proceed. Any method is better than none, for a poor first effort can be improved on later by experience.

Along with knowledge of job requirements, selection depends on information about those who are applying for the jobs. Such information can be gained through interviews, application blanks, credentials, and various kinds of aptitude, achievement, interest, and personality tests. How good are each of these methods for gathering information about people? How can they be improved?

THE SELECTION INTERVIEW

The selection interview is almost universal. More than 99 percent of firms interview applicants before hiring (Ulrich and Trumbo, 1965). While most firms interview applicants, many spend very little time with each applicant and even less listening to him. Daniels and Otis (1950), for example, recorded a sample of 60 employment interviews from eight companies. The average interview lasted less than 10 minutes. Within that time, the average applicant spoke about three minutes and the interviewer spoke for about six minutes.

Most companies are confident that the interview is a valuable selection aid. Subjective confidence, however, is a dubious measure of value. In a study by Oskamp (1965) psychologists were given differing amounts of information about a person and asked to make judgments about him. They first studied a few general facts about a man and predicted how he would behave in 25 different situations. Afterward, they were asked, "How many of your predictions do you think were correct?" The average psychologist expected 33 percent to be correct; 26 percent were actually correct. Next, they were given increasing amounts of information and were asked to make new predictions after each additional bit of information. They again reported the number of predictions they thought they had made correctly. At the final stage, they read more than a thousand words about the person. The more they read, the more confident they became about the accuracy of their predictions. However, their accuracy did not increase at all. At the final stage, the typical psychologist expected to get 53 percent of his predictions correct; he actually got only 28 percent correct. The study concluded: "The judges' confidence ratings show that they became convinced of their own increasing understanding of the case. . . . Their certainty about their own decisions became entirely out of proportion to the actual correctness of those decisions."

Is the confidence of companies in the selection interview justified? Evidence on the reliability and validity of the selection interview suggests that it is not.

The reliability of the selection interview
The reliability of interview ratings is usually measured by comparing the ratings of applicants made by one interviewer with the ratings of the same applicants made by another interviewer. The following old but well-conducted study illustrates the method (Kenagy and Yoakum, 1925). Three sales executives (A, B, and C) were asked to predict the probable success of 34 new salesmen. The executives participated in devising a rating plan. They agreed upon the characteristics required of a good salesman, decided upon the relative importance of each trait, worked out a rating form, and assigned weights to each characteristic so that their ratings could be combined to

give an overall evaluation of each salesman. Then the executives observed the salesmen during their 2-week training course. Executive A rated each of the salesmen during an initial half-hour interview and revised his ratings after the training period.

The executives knew the requirements of the selling job better than most interviewers, they used a more careful procedure than most interviewers, and had much more time with each applicant than most interviewers. Still, the reliability of their ratings was as low as it is possible to get. There was only a chance relationship between their ratings, and there was no relation between the actual sales made by the applicants during their first 2 months on the job and the ratings made by any of the executives. As this study illustrates, the reliabilities of typical interviewer ratings are discouragingly low.

The reliabilities of ratings can be raised by averaging the ratings of more than one rater. The more ratings we combine, the more likely the combination is to agree with similar combinations.

Combining ratings is sure to increase their reliability; it is not sure to increase their validity, for it is possible for interviewers who agree to be more mistaken in their predictions than interviewers who do not agree. Imagine, on the one hand, that three interviewers sit in on the same 10-minute interview of a series of applicants and then each independently ranks them from the best to the worst. Imagine, on the other hand, that one interviewer interviews each of the applicants and then ranks them; that another interviewer talks only to the former bosses of the applicants before ranking them; and that the third interviewer studies only the application blanks, credentials, and test scores of the applicants before ranking them. It is likely that the interviewers in the first situation would agree in their rankings more than the interviewers in the second situation. It is unlikely, however, that the combined rankings in the first situation would be more valid than those in the second situation.

Ratings of men aboard submarines of the Pacific Fleet show that high reliability is not necessarily an index of high validity (Buckner, 1959). Of 171 men rated on technical competence and personal adjustment by three officers, 25 that the officers agreed on and another 25 that they disagreed on were picked out. The average rating for each of the 50 men was then related to objective measures of their competence and adjustment (class standing in submarine school, etc.) The result was that the ratings of the "high-agreement" group had *less* relationship to the objective criteria than did the ratings of the "low-agreement" group. Why? "Differences resulting from ratings being made in the entirely unstructured on-the-job environment may reflect real differences in ratee behavior." In other words, the fact that a sailor did well at one task under one officer seemed to tell little about how well he would do a different task under a different officer. The high-agreement ratings did not reflect this truth; the low-agreement ratings did. Consequently, the ratings of lower reliability had higher validity, i.e., were more closely related to measures of overall performance.

The validity of the selection interview

The validity of interview ratings are generally lower than their reliability. For example, during World War II, candidates for pilot training schools were being selected by objective tests. Applications below a set score were rejected. In an effort to save the best of the rejected men, a flight surgeon and an aviation psychologist interviewed each of them. The interview lasted for 5 to 20 minutes. From the more than 1,500 they interviewed over a period of six months, they selected 285 whom they thought could make it through pilot school.

These were sent to school. Follow-ups showed that 69 percent of them failed and 31 percent passed. Each of them was then matched with a candidate who had made the same scores on the screening tests but who had been admitted to the school somewhat earlier when the rejection score had been lower. Of this earlier, uninterviewed group, 73 percent had failed and 27 percent had passed. That is, the interviewers did only 4 percent better than chance. Even this difference is doubtful, since the standards for passing had been lowered by the time the interviewed candidates came along. In sum, the selection interview program was a huge waste of time (Meehl, 1954, p. 97).

The information gathered by an interviewer is more accurate than the judgments he makes. Accuracy, however, varies a great deal with the kind of information sought. For example, five trained women in Minneapolis interviewed almost one hundred physically handicapped workers to get information about their marital status, education, previous work history, etc. The accuracy of the information gathered was later checked against the records of previous employers and agency records. Some of the disabled gave invalid information on nearly every item: 10 percent gave erroneous information about the nature of their disability, 15 percent about their previous education, 29 percent about the length of their previous employment, and 55 percent about the type of rehabilitation assistance they had received. In fact, the only information recorded with no error was the sex of the interviewee! Weiss and Davis (1960) conclude: "It is indefensible to assume the validity of purportedly factual information obtained by interview."

Any method of selecting workers is open to some errors; every interviewer has some information about an applicant before interviewing him. The critical question then is: Are the judgments he makes with the interview more accurate than those he makes without it? A classic selection study found an answer: No. In 1946, hundreds of students already admitted to psychology graduate schools throughout the country came to Ann Arbor for a week of evaluation of their probable success by dozens of experienced psychologists. In one part of the experiment, the raters predicted the academic success of the students by answering this question:

> How well will this student: effectively master course work content; successfully complete courses in general psychology, clinical psychology, statistics, and related fields; satisfy language requirements for the doctorate; pass general examinations? (Kelly and Fiske, 1951.)

Ratings were made on an eight-point scale. Sometimes they were based on credentials (transcripts of college grades, references, etc.), sometimes on test scores, sometimes on interviews, and sometimes on a combination of these. The students then returned to their graduate schools. After three years, their professors in graduate school ranked the students on their academic performance from the best to the worst. These rankings were used to test the validity of the ratings made years before.

The results are shown in Table 8-1. The rating psychologist had first studied the file of a student and then rated his academic performance. This rating correlated .26 with the actual performance rank of the student three years later. The same rater had then examined the test scores of a student and ranked him again. This examination increased the validity of his ratings to .36. He had then had a 2-hour intensive interview with the student. After the interview, he had rated him a third time. The correlation of this third rating was .32! The 2-hour interview had slightly *decreased* the validity of his ratings.

The overall picture was not quite so destructive. By the same process that they had used to rate academic performance, the psychologists made 11 other predictions (of research competence, integrity, etc.). The median validity of these ratings based on credentials alone was .22; on credentials plus test scores, .29; and on credentials plus test scores plus the 2-hour interview, .31. In conclusion, a long interview by highly trained interviewers

TABLE 8-1   The validity of ratings

Basis for rating probable academic performance	Correlation with rating of actual academic performance
Credentials alone	.26
Credentials & objective test scores	.36
Credentials, test scores, & 2-hr interview	.32

SOURCE: Kelly and Fiske (1951), p. 168.

added practically nothing to the validity of their judgments about success on a job with which they had had years of intimate experience.

The use of the interview

The interview may not be as useless as it seems; too few interview situations have been explored, too few research studies have been made, and too few have used good experimental methods. We cannot, on the other hand, assume that the interview is useful. The evidence suggests that it should be judged guilty of wasting time and money until it is proved innocent.

How can the validity of the selection interview be improved? The simplest promising possibility is to substitute rankings for ratings. That is, instead of rating each applicant on a scale from poor to outstanding, rank all applicants from the best to the worst. Such a small shift could have large consequences, particularly when different men are interviewing applicants for the same job. Ratings have two serious sources of error that rankings do not. In the first place, some raters habitually rate low and some high, regardless of the situation. Consequently, their ratings are not at all comparable. However, if the same raters rank the ratees, the results are comparable. In the second place, some raters habitually use the middle ratings and some use the extremes. Again, the ratings of these kinds of raters are not comparable, yet their rankings are. Because of these weaknesses in ratings, which have been exactly analyzed by Cronbach (1955), recent investigators have shifted from the use of ratings to rankings. Ranking of applicants is not always possible, for an interviewer may see only one or two applicants. Where rankings are possible, however, they should be used; and where the situation can be changed to make rankings possible, it should be.

A comparison of rating and ranking procedures for selecting managerial personnel revealed the superiority of ranking over rating (Albrecht, Glaser, and Marks, 1964). Two staff members of a firm of consultants used an intensive interview, personal history data, and scores on a variety of ability and personality tests to predict the success of 31 recently promoted managers. On the basis of this information, each consultant rated the probable success of each manager. He also *ranked* the managers from the one most likely to the one least likely to be successful. The ratings of the two consultants were combined; their rankings were also combined. The combined ratings and rankings were then correlated with a composite criterion of actual success on the job. The ratings were not related to success ($r = .09$); the rankings were related ($r = .46$). The authors concluded: "The rating-form procedure, in contrast to ranking, adds the uncertainty of interpretation of a scale with the possibility for central tendency or leniency biases to enter the picture."

Selection interviewing could be improved by improving the selection of interviewers. There are obvious things wrong with many interviewers: some have too little education, some too little experience, some too little understanding of the types of people they are interviewing, and some too little information about the jobs they are selecting people to fill. There are also obvious things wrong with the way interviewers are sometimes picked: A clerical worker is transferred to interviewing because he is a poor clerk, an older shopworker is made an interviewer because he wants the status of a white-collar job, a talkative employee who likes to have someone listen to him is allowed to assume the job, etc. The selection of interviewers with more appropriate education, experience, knowledge, and motivation would increase the reliability of interviews.

The ability to judge people is an essential quality of the good interviewer. Unfortunately, some interviewers with appropriate backgrounds do not seem to be good judges. While most people have confident opinions about who are good judges (namely, themselves), they have little evidence to support their opinions. Nor do psychologists. Better selection of interviewers requires better knowledge of the qualities of the good judge. One suggestive study on this question used filmed interviews to test the differences in the ability of 130 students to judge people. The students were then asked to fill out the following questionnaire (Grossman, 1963):

T F 1. I enjoy being a leader of people.

T F 2. I am sometimes influenced in minor decisions by how I happen to be feeling at the moment.

T F 3. I think it is more important for a person to be reverent than sympathetic.

T F 4. No individual, no matter what the circumstances, is justified in committing suicide.

T F 5. I genuinely like everyone I get to know.

T   F   6. I occasionally act contrary to custom.
T   F   7. The notion of divine inspiration may be mistaken.
T   F   8. I have occasionally felt contempt for the opinions of others.
T   F   9. I would rather grow inwardly than be a success in practical affairs.
T   F   10. I like continually changing activities.

The good judges more often answered false to the first five statements and true to the second five. This and other evidence indicated that the good judge was liberal, nonconforming, sceptical, open-minded, and sympathetic but discriminating about people.

Productivity versus integration and morale

Selection interviews are generally invalid. But invalid for what? Practically all selection interviewing has focused upon predicting some aspect of the productivity of the applicant: his skill in doing the work, his ability to perform at a high level, his merit rating, etc. It may well be, however, that interviewers could predict other aspects of the applicant's contribution to the organization much better: Is this applicant going to quit in a short time? What is his absentee rate going to be? Is he likely to add to or subtract from the cohesiveness of the work group of which he will be a part? Will he be interested in the work he has to do, or will he hate it? Several studies suggest that the selection interview may be more useful as a predictor of morale and integration criteria than as a predictor of productivity criteria.

A trained interviewer, for example, has predicted labor turnover (a criterion of integration) among truck drivers with some accuracy. He independently interviewed 108 men who had already been selected by the employment office and rated them as good or poor risks. At the end of 11 weeks, he counted the number who were still with the company. Table 8-2 shows the relationship between ratings and turnover; more than twice as many of those with high ratings were still with the company.

TABLE 8-2   Turnover among truck drivers in relation to selection interview rating

	Percent who left company	Percent still with company	Total percent
High rating by interviewer	45	55	100
Low rating by interviewer	77	23	100

SOURCE: Adapted from McMurry (1947).

In one company 507 applicants were interviewed over a period of seventeen years using a standard personnel interview guide (Ghiselli, 1966). These applicants had already been screened by the company and were considered good prospects, and 275 were actually hired. To validate the interview, interview ratings were compared to a criterion of staying with the company for three years. The criterion was not a specific one of performance, integration, or morale, but a global one of survival. The ratings correlated .35 with the criterion. This is a modest coefficient, but one that is as good as would be obtained with most tests. In a more direct evaluation of the uses of the interview, psychologists interviewed employees and then predicted their attitudes and job performance (Barrett, Svetlik, and Prien, 1967). The psychologists were most accurate in predicting employees' attitudes toward advancement and general morale. They were much less accurate in predicting attitudes toward supervision and rewards. They were unable to predict employee performance successfully.

Ulrich and Trumbo (1965) end their review of the research on the selection interview by suggesting that the selection interview may be most successful if it is limited to assessment of personal relationships and career motivation. They suggest that the interview may be most useful in answering two questions: What is the motivation to work? Will the applicant adjust to the social context of his job?

Summary on the selection interview
Studies showing the low validity of the interview have existed for decades. In spite of these and in spite of the consistent results of more recent studies, the employment interview continues to be relied on in selecting employees. One reason for the failure to abandon it is the intense faith that many people have in their *own* interviewing skill. The faith persists even though a consistent finding in interviewing research is that judges watching an interview are as accurate about the interviewee as the actual interviewer (Wright, 1969). Another reason is that situations arise where the only alternative to an interview is to pick a name out of a hat, as, for example, when a very few men are quickly needed for so unimportant a job that it is not possible or feasible to set up a different procedure.

The most persuasive reason for continuing the employment interview is that it fills a strong human need. Even if a company knows that the interview is invalid, it still wants to meet its employees before hiring them. Even if an applicant knows that the interview is invalid, he wants to talk to a representative of the company about his application. If he is rejected without an interview, he is more likely to feel deprived; if he is accepted without an interview, he is more likely to feel that the company is an impersonal organization. Furthermore, the unique quality of the interview is that it is an interaction: the company finds out things about the employee that will help it to use him, and the employee finds out things about his future work and his job that will make his adjustment easier. Probably the most neglected value of the interview is that it can help prepare the worker to deal effectively with the *bad* parts of his future job.

The best use of the interview may involve emphasizing its counseling function and deemphasizing its selection function, which in any case it seems to do poorly. Such a shift would make the interview not the first but the last step in the selection process. It is time for a new study of the interview, a study of the differences in productivity, integration, and morale between a group of workers hired with a well-planned orientation interview and a group hired without one.

THE APPLICATION BLANK

Like the interview, the application blank is a part of the selection process in nearly all companies. Like the interview, too, its validity has seldom been tested. Typically, a blank is casually scanned for items that seem important or is used only as a point of departure for interview questions. Yet the application blank can be readily converted into an objective instrument that can improve a company's selection procedures.

The application blank reveals a person's age, education, family status, and work experiences as well as many other aspects of his personal history. Such facts about an applicant's history, it is reasonable to suppose, may be intimately related to his future performance. But what are the relationships? Will the fact that a man has been productive in one job for one company in one city be related to his doing well in a similar job for another company in another city? And if it is related, will the facts that predict his productivity also predict how interested he will be in the work and how long he will stay on the job? Generally, the answers can only be guesses. As the following study illustrates, however, the application blank which is properly checked can be converted into a simple and objective predictor of known validity.

The office manager of a large staff of female clerical and stenographic workers cooperated with Fleishman and Berniger (1960) in developing a system of scoring application blanks that was related to job tenure. From the personnel files, they first picked 60 employees who had been with the organization for at least 2 years and were still on the job. They also picked 60 employees most of whom had left by the end of the first year of employment and all of whom had left by the end of the second year. They then compared the application blanks of employees in the long-tenure group with those in the short. Some results are shown in Table 8-3.

Some items for the two groups were not different. There was, for example, no difference in the salaries that workers in the groups had received in previous jobs. Consequently, previous salary was given a weight of zero and had no influence on an applicant's total score. On some items, however, members of the long-tenured group more often gave a positive answer. Their children, for example, were much more likely to be of high school age or older (weight: +3). On some items, however, members of the long-tenured group more often gave a negative response; for example, they less often fell into the under-twenty age category (weight: −3). Each of the 40 items on the application blank was examined and weighted in this way, and a total score for each applicant in the two groups was obtained by adding up the weights for each answer. The scores ranged from −17 to +27. The short-tenured group's average score was 2.3; the long-tenured group's was 8.9.

On the basis of the analysis, it was possible to draw the following profile of the typical long-tenured office employee in the organization:

> She is 30 years old or over, has a local address rather than a suburban one, is married (but not to a student) or is a widow. Her husband is most likely to be an executive or a professional man. She may have one or two children, but if she does, they are of high school age or over. She herself is not employed at the time of application. . . . Usually, she cannot take shorthand, but if she does, it is at a relatively high rate of speed. She does not list more than one outside interest aside

TABLE 8-3 Comparison of long- and short-tenure office employees

Application blank items	Percentage of short-tenure group	Percentage of long-tenure group	Weight given item
Age of children: high school or older	35	63	+3
Local address: within city	39	62	+2
Previous salary: under $2,000	31	30	0
Age: under 20	35	8	−3

SOURCE: Adapted from Fleishman and Berniger (1960).

from work, and that one indicates that she is more interested in organizations than people. Finally, she spent at least two years at her last job (Fleishman and Berniger, 1960).

To double-check the results, the investigators drew from the files the application blanks of 85 additional short- and long-tenured employees. Their application blanks were scored in exactly the same way as those of the first group. The average score of the short-tenured group was −0.7; of the long-tenured group, 6.3. The investigation recommended that a "cutting score" of +4 be used. That is, applicants who received a score of less than 4 should not be hired. If such a system had been used on the group, four out of five of the short-tenured employees would have been rejected; two out of three of the long-tenured employees would have been hired.

In general, the method is simple and cheap. It has been successful in a variety of companies: a life insurance firm, a mining company, and a university. Schuh (1967) reviewed more than forty years of research concerned with predicting employee tenure. He concluded that intelligence, aptitude, interest and personality tests are not useful for predicting how long an employee would stay on the job. The application blank information *is* generally useful: "Of the twenty-one studies using biographical data, only two failed to find at least one item to be related to the tenure criterion." (Schuh, 1967, p. 145).

The use of the application blank is not limited to labor-turnover criteria; it could be tried as a potential predictor of productivity, accident proneness, etc. And of course, use is not limited to office workers. A caution is in order, however: The items that discriminate for one job in one job in one company may not discriminate for the same job in another company. The weighted application blank should be tailor-made for each job in each company.

REFERENCES

The popularity of written references as a part of the selection procedure has declined. In a survey in 1930, for example, 83 percent of companies reported that they required written references; in 1957 in a similar survey, only 50 percent reported that they required them (Scott et al., 1961). There has also been a shift away from open-ended testimonial letters toward standardized questionnaires. A careful validation study of the references of more than a thousand civil service employees in a dozen trades reached a discouraging conclusion: "Results show that Employment Recommendation Questionnaires had practically no value in predicting later supervisory ratings" (Mosel and Goheen, 1958).

Why should references be of so little value? One reason is that they are highly unrepresentative. Wherever possible, an applicant will list as references people whom he knows have a good impression of him. Further, many who receive requests for a reference do not respond. Mosel and Goheen, for example, found that only 56 percent returned a completed reference questionnaire, 23 percent returned it incomplete, 18 percent failed to return it, and 3 percent returned the reference unopened. Probably those who returned the completed questionnaire were more favorable toward the applicant than those who did not.

References generally do not discriminate very well between applicants. Mosel and Goheen found that considerably less than 1 percent of applicants were given a poor reference on either occupational ability or character. Nearly 50 percent were given outstanding ratings.

Even when they do discriminate, the average reference-giver does not seem to know what he is writing about. On Mosel and Goheen's employment recommendation questionnaire was this question: "Is applicant especially qualified for . . . the trade in which he seeks employment?" The merit ratings for radio mechanics, auto mechanics, and painters who had received an unqualified "yes" answer in their references were compared to the ratings for comparable groups who had received an unqualified "no" answer. There was no significant difference in the rated job performance of the two groups. In fact, the "no" group of painters had slightly higher ratings than the "yes" group.

A telephone checkup is one way of reducing the unrepresentativeness of references. While the caller may not be able to get in touch with all the references, at least those he does locate are not as biased a sample as those who return a written reference. People may be freer in their conversational comments than they would be in their written ones. They may not be much freer, however, if they know their comments are being written down. Furthermore, telephone comments may be made with even less care than written ones.

As with the selection interview, it is possible that references concerned with elements related to integration and morale might prove more valuable than those concerned with productivity. What kind of work is the applicant most interested in doing? Do you think he would be likely to fit into our organization and remain with us? Possibly questions of this sort would also elicit answers that differentiate more adequately between applicants. The somewhat greater validity of personality ratings in the references studied by Mosel and Goheen supports this possibility.

On the whole, the chief present value of references is limited to a minority of applicants. It is of value to know that an applicant has lied about his previous employment. It is of value to have the opinion of a person who knows *both* the applicant and the employer well. And it is of value to obtain the bits of information that occasionally turn up in references.

APTITUDE AND ABILITY TESTS

Awareness of the weaknesses of traditional selection methods has resulted in a rapid rise in the use of tests. In 1947, 57 percent of companies reported that they used tests for selection; in 1957, 80 percent (Scott et al., 1961). The actual number of applicants taking tests has mounted even more rapidly, for not only are more companies using tests, but they are using more of them. The U.S. Department of Labor Memorandum on Executive Order 11246 (1968) mentions specifically in its general section the "decided increase since 1963 in total test usage."

Companies that use any test are almost certain to have a clerical aptitude test. Clerical work, however, is not a task but a group of related jobs that vary from messenger boy to supervisor. To determine the general components of clerical jobs, Chalupsky (1962) analyzed the requirements of a representative group of 192 clerical jobs. He found these independent factors:

Inventory and Stockkeeping: making inventories, issuing parts, counting objects, sending reports, etc.

Supervision: assigning duties, reviewing activities, assigning or issuing, etc.

Computation and Bookkeeping: Keeping payroll records, making profit and loss accounts, operating keyboards, etc.

Communication and Public Relations: receiving customers, handling complaints, composing correspondence, etc.

Stenography-Typing: taking shorthand, spelling and punctuating, operating typewriter, etc.

Considering these different aspects of clerical work, it is not surprising that a variety of tests is used in selecting such workers: finger-dexterity tests, arithmetic tests, typing and dictating tests, vocabulary tests, etc. One of the most widely used is the Minnesota Vocational Test for Clerical Workers. It includes tests of the ability to perceive differences in detail like the following number- and name-comparison task:

```
          79542_____79524
        5794367_____X_____5794367
    John C. Linder_____John C. Lender
  Investors Syndicate_____X_____Investors Syndicate
```

The person taking the test is required to check the pairs that are the same and to leave blank the pairs that are different. Since test scores are almost independent of experience, it is an aptitude rather than an achievement test. The test has the virtue of discriminating between simple and complex clerical jobs, for workers on more complex jobs get higher scores. It also has the rare virtue of providing at least some validity in the selection of workers for almost any clerical job (Hay, 1950).

Seventy-eight percent of companies using tests gave some intelligence tests (Scott et al., 1961). Intelligence testing began in the United States with the translation of the individual test that Binet developed for the schools of France. The Alpha and Beta group tests were used during World War I to select and place recruits. By 1940, Thurstone had introduced the Primary Mental Abilities Tests that measured relatively independent components of general intelligence: reasoning, word fluency, verbal comprehension, number, memory, and space abilities. Today, there are hundreds of different kinds of "intelligence" tests: individual and group tests, short and long tests, tests that emphasize verbal comprehension and tests that deemphasize verbal comprehension, tests for the blind and tests for the old, tests for the feeble-minded and tests for the brilliant, tests for schools and tests for businesses. The Otis Self-Administering Test of Mental Ability, the Wonderlic Personnel Test, and the Adaptability Test are widely used in industry. They are short group tests that are most appropriate for those who have not graduated from high school.

Intelligence tests come as close as any to an all-purpose selection instrument of general validity. They have been used to select candidates for laboring and executive jobs, to predict which candidates will remain in their jobs, to single out people who can be promoted to better jobs, to select people who will be productive, and to decide which people will benefit from training programs. They have some value for all these purposes. Ghiselli and Brown (1948), for example, reviewed 185 studies where intelligence scores had been related to the job proficiency of salesmen, clerical workers, supervisors, and unskilled, semiskilled, and skilled workers. The more demanding the job, the closer the relationships tended to be. In all but a few cases, however, there was *some* relationship; in none were the people with the higher intelligence scores significantly less successful. There is an optimum level of intelligence for most jobs; below the level, workers fail; above the level, they tend to move to other jobs. The rejection of applicants with low scores is almost always a wise move, and particularly so in companies concerned with the growth potentialities of their labor force.

The technical problems involved in the best use of clerical aptitude and intelligence tests are so numerous that professional assistance is generally needed. Assistance is even more necessary for the effective employment of the less widely used dexterity tests, mechanical-aptitude tests, trade tests, performance and achievement tests for particular jobs, and any of the hundreds of other available tests of specific and general aptitudes, abilities, and achievements.

INTEREST TESTS

Aptitude tests measure a worker's potential productivity, interest tests his potential morale. Though it is not clear just how vocational interests develop, it is known that they develop early and have a profound influence on a worker's job success. The Strong Vocational Interest Blank and the Kuder Preference Record—Vocational are two of the most widely used tests of this type.

The Strong Vocational Interest Blank

The Strong test consists of 400 items to each of which the person taking the test answers "Like," "Indifferent," or "Dislike." The items are concerned with vocations, school subjects, amusements, activities, and kinds of people. The test can be scored for more than 40 occupations for men and more than 20 occupations for women. A, B, and C scores are given each person taking the test for each occupation. The score for a particular occupation is determined by comparing a person's answers with the typical answers made by people actively and successfully engaged in that occupation. An A score means that a person's interests are very similar to those in that field; B, somewhat similar; and C, not at all similar.

Vocational interests are generally set *before* a person enters an occupation and change little thereafter. Strong tested 50 men when they were college freshmen and again 20 years later; the median correlation of scores was .72. He tested 228 students when they were seniors and again 22 years later. The median correlation was even higher: .75 (Strong, 1951). While some men change their interests after entering an occupation, the odds are against it. Furthermore, those who change are more likely to become *less* interested in the occupation, not more interested.

College seniors tend to select a vocation in which they get an A score. For example, only 4 percent of college seniors get an A score in dentistry, yet Strong found that 45 percent of students in dental school had such a score (Strong, 1943). On the other hand, 62 percent of college students get a C score in dentistry; only 5 percent of dental students do. People with A scores in an occupation tend to stay in it and to like it.

Even high school students tend to select a vocation in which they get an A score. Campbell (1966), for example, followed up 72 men who had gotten an A in Life Insurance Salesman when they were high school seniors. Ten years later they had the following kinds of jobs:

Occupation	Percent
Life insurance salesman	10
Other sales jobs	32
Public relations jobs	12
Lawyers and ministers	22
Jobs unrelated to selling	24
TOTAL	100

Three fourths of these men were in occupations directly or indirectly related to selling.

The Strong test has a serious weakness as a selection instrument: Scores can be faked (Garry, 1953). That is, if an applicant knows the job he is applying for, he can raise his interest score by trying to. Thus, people with A scores may not be really interested in the job. Still, the test is valuable in that applicants with C scores can be rejected at once.

The Strong test also has a serious limitation: There are no scales for scoring many occupations. The development of an interest scale for an occupation requires testing a sample of hundreds of successful members of the occupation, analyzing their responses, and developing for each of the 400 items a weighted score based on the differences (if any) between men in the occupation and men in general. It is an expensive process. There are scales, however, for many business occupations: production manager, printer, personnel worker, sales manager, real estate salesman, life insurance salesman, advertising man, president of manufacturing concern, etc. The Strong test also has the disadvantage of being hard to score: it takes a skilled clerk half a day to score all the scales for *one* person by hand. Special machine services for doing the scoring are available, however.

Kuder Preference Record—Vocational

The Kuder test is newer and less well validated than the Strong. It has however, great flexibility for industrial applications (Tiffin and Phelan, 1953). It consists of groups of three items, such as the following:

1. Exercise in a gymnasium
2. Go fishing
3. Play baseball
4. Cook for a hotel
5. Cook for people on camping trips
6. Cook for a family

The person taking the test chooses the item in each group which he likes most and the item which he likes least. In contrast to the Strong, the Kuder gives measures of interest in broad areas: literary, scientific, computational, persuasive, artistic, musical, social service, mechanical, clerical, and technical. Selections are made on the basis of a profile of the applicant's scores in these general interest areas. Compared to the Strong, the Kuder is more easily scored but also more easily faked.

In general, interest tests have been extensively studied, possess some validity for predicting immediate productivity and more for predicting successful job tenure, create less anxiety among applicants than most tests, and are less susceptible to misuse than aptitude and personality tests. They could be profitably used in selection and placement much more than they are.

PERSONALITY TESTS

An intensive study of 3,000 English factory workers led to a typical conclusion: One out of ten had a serious neurosis; one out of five, a mild one (Fraser, 1947). The greater the number of maladjusted workers in an organization, the more absenteeism, labor turnover, grievances, and accidents it is likely to have. On the positive side, the greater the number of mature, objective, friendly, and cooperative employees a company has, the better off it is likely to be. As companies have become more concerned about these facts, they have made increasing use of personality tests in selection. The number of companies using personality tests has about doubled in the last 20 years. Today if a company requires any tests at all, it is more likely than not to make some use of personality tests.

By far the most common personality test used is some form of inventory: the Guilford-Martin Personnel Inventory, California Psychological Inventory,

Minnesota Multiphasic Personality Inventory, Edwards Personal Preference Schedule, etc. All contain many items, and some contain hundreds. Sometimes the items are worded as questions: Do you feel tired most of the time? Are your feelings easily hurt? and so on. Sometimes the items are in the form of statements to which the person answers true or false: I am extremely ambitious, I enjoy work more than play, etc. Sometimes the person is given two equally desirable items and forced to choose between them.

Scores on inventories do predict job success. Ghiselli and Barthol (1953) found 113 studies where scores had been related to success in different occupations: supervisors (52 studies), clerks (22), sales workers (20), skilled workers (8), service workers (6), and protective workers (5). For each of these job categories, there was a low but positive median correlation between scores and success. Although inventories have been used most often to predict supervisory success, the correlations were lowest for this group. Inventories were best in predicting sales success.

In using personality tests in the selection process it is important to distinguish between the uncritical use of standard personality tests and the development of a valid inventory. After reviewing the validity of personality measures in personnel selection, Guion and Gottier (1965) concluded that none of the conventional personality measures are really useful as selection tools. They state that when they are done well, personality and interest measures which are developed for the particular situation are better predictors than standard personality measures with standard systems of scoring.

The method by which a car-salesman scale was created illustrates the long process of developing a valid inventory. Kennedy (1958) first collected nearly 300 multiple-choice items covering personality, interest, and attitudes that he thought might be related to success as a salesman. He then sent the questionnaire to a representative sample of General Motors car dealers throughout the country, some of whom were selling a high-priced and some a low-priced car. At his request, the dealers had several hundred of their salesmen complete the questionnaire. The dealers returned the completed questionnaires along with a record of the gross earnings of each salesman.

The salesmen were divided into a successful and an unsuccessful group on the basis of their earnings. The answers of the two groups to each item were then compared. The 40 items that most sharply differentiated the successful from the unsuccessful were chosen for the final form of the scale. This final form was again sent to the dealers, who had over 700 more of their salesmen complete it. They again returned the completed inventories with records of the earnings of the salesmen. The result was that the scores of the salesmen were significantly related to their earnings (correlation: .31).

The scale worked equally well for salesmen selling the low- and high-priced cars.

The use of personality inventories presents many problems that do not arise in the use of aptitude tests: People (particularly when they are applying for a job) try to give what they think is a "right" answer rather than a true answer, some people tend to agree and others to disagree with almost any question, and people often give inconsistent answers. The biggest practical problem, however, is the gullibility of unsophisticated managers who want to use such tests. Stagner (1958), for example, gives the following typical example of a personnel manager being "taken" by an unethical test salesman:

> "Let me give you a real demonstration. You take this personality test yourself, and I'll give you the report based on your scores. If you don't agree that it is amazingly accurate I won't even try to sell it to you." The guillible manager takes the test, reads the report, is amazed by its accuracy, and spends a lot of his company's money for a device not worth the paper and printing.

The salesman can achieve his results by including in his "report" statements like the following:

> You prefer a certain amount of change and variety and become dissatisfied when hemmed in by restrictions and limitations (91%).
>
> While you have some personality weaknesses, you are generally able to compensate for them (89%).
>
> You have a great need for other people to like and admire you (85%).
>
> You have a tendency to be critical of yourself (82%).

The percentages after the statement indicate the proportion of 68 personnel managers who agreed that the statement was either a "rather good" or an "amazingly accurate" picture of themselves. About the same percentage of college students will agree. In fact, few people will choose their own personality diagnosis based on adequate test data when given a choice between it and vague generalities like those above. Of course, such sugar-pill diagnoses are completely useless for any selection purpose.

THE VALUE OF SELECTION

The process of selection involves two major elements: job analysis which establishes what is required to do the job, and personnel assessment which tries to find out which people meet the requirements. Selection, therefore, is a process of prediction, and we say the process is valid when it makes good predictions. The U.S. Department of Labor Memorandum on Executive Order 11246 insists on the central importance of validity in the selection process and is clear in stating that ". . . validity should consist of empirical data demonstrating that the test is predictive of or significantly correlated with important elements of work behavior comprising or relevant to the job(s) for which candidates are being evaluated." (Section 2, para (b)) "Under no circumstances will the general reputation of a test, its author or its publisher, or casual reports of test utility be accepted in lieu of evidence of validity." (Section 6, para (a)).

If the particular interview procedure, test, or application blank assumes that the people in group A will be successful as machine operators, the technique is valid to the extent that this assumption is confirmed. In establishing the validity of a selection device, predictions based on the device are correlated with a specific *criterion* of success, e.g. ratings by supervisors, production records. Thus in the selection process we again find evidence for the importance of the psychologist's task of developing sound criteria. (See Chapter 2) Selection is a process which tries to discriminate those who can do the job from those who cannot; those who can learn the job from those who cannot; those who will have high integration, morale and productivity on the job from those who will not. The success of the process depends upon the goodness of the criteria used and the job analyses which have been performed. If these are not good, the selection process loses any claim to being scientific and becomes institutionalized prejudice.

In general, the more valid a selection device is the more useful it is. For example, assume that the percentage of satisfactory workers selected *without* a particular device is 50, and that 50 percent of the applicants for a job are hired. If the device has no validity, the percentage of satisfactory workers selected by using the device would still be 50. If the device has a validity of .30 (if scores on the device correlate .30 with success on the job), the use of the device would result in 60 percent satisfactory employees; if its validity is .60, in 70 percent satisfactory employees; and if its validity is .90, in 86 percent satisfactory employees (Taylor and Russell, 1939).

Selection devices are often wrongly criticized because they reject a good man or pick a poor one. Note, first, that since any method of selecting employees will result in some good ones, using a method with *no* validity will also result in some good choices. In the case of the device discussed above, for example, it would result in 50 percent good choices. Note, second, that even a good device, unless it has perfect validity, will make some mistakes. For example, even if the device in the case above had the unheard-of-validity of .90, its use would result in 14 percent unsatisfactory employees. The goal in using a device, in other words, is not to achieve perfection but to achieve a better batting average. A device that selects 70 percent satisfactory employees is better than one that selects 60; a device that selects 80 percent is better than one that selects 70.

The usefulness of a selection device also depends on the proportion of satisfactory employees picked without the device. If only 10 percent satisfactory employees are picked without the device, the device has a great deal of room to make an improvement. If 90 percent satisfactory employees are picked without the device, there is little room for improvement. The proportion of satisfactory employees picked without a device actually has a strong impact on management thinking about selection: The more dissatisfaction managers feel with the kind of employees they are hiring, the more likely they are to be interested in improving their selection procedures.

The *selection ratio*, the number of applicants hired divided by the total number of applicants, also determines the usefulness of a device. If a personnel manager must hire five electricians and he has only five applicants for the jobs, a selection device that has high validity will be of no use to him. On the other hand, if he has a hundred applicants for a single opening, even a device of low validity will be of some help. That is, as the selection ratio goes down, the proportion of satisfactory employees picked by a device goes up. Assume, for example, that the validity of a device is .50 and the proportion of satisfactory employees picked without the device is 50 percent. Then as the selection goes from .60 (60 percent of all applicants are hired) to .40 and to .20, the proportion of satisfactory employees selected goes from 63 percent to 69 percent to 77 percent. The selection ratio also has a strong impact on management thinking about selection: The lower the selection ratio, the more interested managers are in improving their selection procedures. It is not an accident that the military services, which have the lowest selection ratio (they can sometimes pick one man for a job from a thousand), make the greatest use of selection devices.

Selection devices are most useful when their validity is high, the selection ratio is low, and the proportion of satisfactory employees picked without devices is low.

PROCEDURES IN SELECTION

Selection procedures can, and generally do, become complex. The basic ideas, however, can be appreciated by considering the process in its simplest form.

Assume that one good criterion has been developed to measure differences in job success. All available personnel assessment techniques can then be tested by relating each, in turn, to this criterion. For example, we might first correlate the criterion with intelligence test scores, then with the results of an interview program, then with personality test results, and so forth, until we had run out of personnel assessment techniques. When we had completed all of these correlations, we would then decide which of the predictors to use in our future selection program. We would most likely select the predictor which had the highest correlation with the criterion (the most valid predictor) but would also give consideration to the cost of the predictors. The industrial psychologist, however, seldom faces such a simple world. Usually there are several criteria and several predictors which must be taken into account.

Psychologists have developed many ways to handle the problem of multiple predictors and multiple criteria (Dunnette, 1966; Guion, 1965). The three most common methods are the multiple regression system, the multiple cut-off system, and the successive criteria system.

Using the multiple regression system, it is possible to construct a formula which will predict a person's score on the criterion measure. Theoretically, there is no limit to the number of predictors which may be used in the formula, and theoretically the criterion measure may be obtained by combining several individual criteria. For the sake of simplicity, assume that all the necessary research has been done and a formula such as this is being used in the selection procedure.

$$y = 2x_1 + 3x_2$$

y is the predicted score on the criterion
x_1 is the applicant's score on an intelligence test
x_2 is the applicant's score on a test of strength of back.

Suppose that a criterion score of 100 is considered satisfactory performance. Then under normal circumstances any job applicant whose criterion score was *predicted* to be 100 would be hired. This procedure is sometimes called the *compensation* model because it assumes that a lot of one factor will compensate for a little of another factor. For example, using the formula above, if one applicant has scores of $x_1 = 50$ and $x_2 = 0$, and another applicant had scores of $x_1 = 0$ and $x_2 = 34$, both would be hired.

The multiple cut-off system assumes that compensation is not possible. Instead, this system assumes that there is a minimum level of each trait which a person must have in order to succeed on the particular job. Using the multiple cut-off system requires that a minimum value, a cut-off, be established for each predictor. In order for an applicant to be hired he must be above the cut-off for every predictor. Referring to the example above, assume that the cut-off for x_1 is 20 and the cut-off for x_2 is 20. If x_1 is 19 for a particular applicant, then he will not be hired, no matter how high his x_2 score may be.

Selection by the successive criteria system differs from the other two systems in that it does not attempt to make a prediction about an applicant's success at the time he is being hired. This system may be compared to a hurdle race. An applicant who meets certain criteria levels is hired and begins his training. If he meets certain criteria as a result of his training, he may go into a foreman's job. If after some time as a foreman he meets certain criteria, he moves to a supervisor's job. The successive criteria do not need to be "higher." They only need to be "different." Thus after training, those who do not meet the criteria to become foremen may become research chemists.

These traditional procedures of selection put most of the emphasis on developing reliable predictors and relating these predictors to sound criteria of job success. These methods have moved selection from a haphazard guessing game toward a scientific status. Now newer models of the selection process are emerging which may eventually displace the older models. The new ideas maintain that emphasis on trying to establish a relationship between the predictor and a measure of job success skips some important intervening steps. Dunnette (1963) presents a model of the selection process which attempts to portray the true complexity of making predictions about people.

Some of the things that Dunnette's model tries to make more clear are the following.

1. Predictors are differentially useful for predicting the behaviors of different subgroups. One study, for example, used the Wonderlic Personnel Test to predict job success. The researchers found the test could be useful for selecting Whites but was irrelevant for Blacks (Ruda and Albright, 1968).

2. Similar job behavior may be predicted by quite different patterns of interaction between predictors and individuals. Gordon (1967), for example, compared different *methods* for predicting the success of people in Peace Corps training. The methods differed in whether the main predictors were *tests, clinical judgments,* or *work samples.* Gordon found that all approaches had significant validity.

3. People who performed the same on a predictor may behave quite differently on the job.

4. All behavior occurs in a particular situation and the interaction between the behavior and the situation can lead to quite different organizational

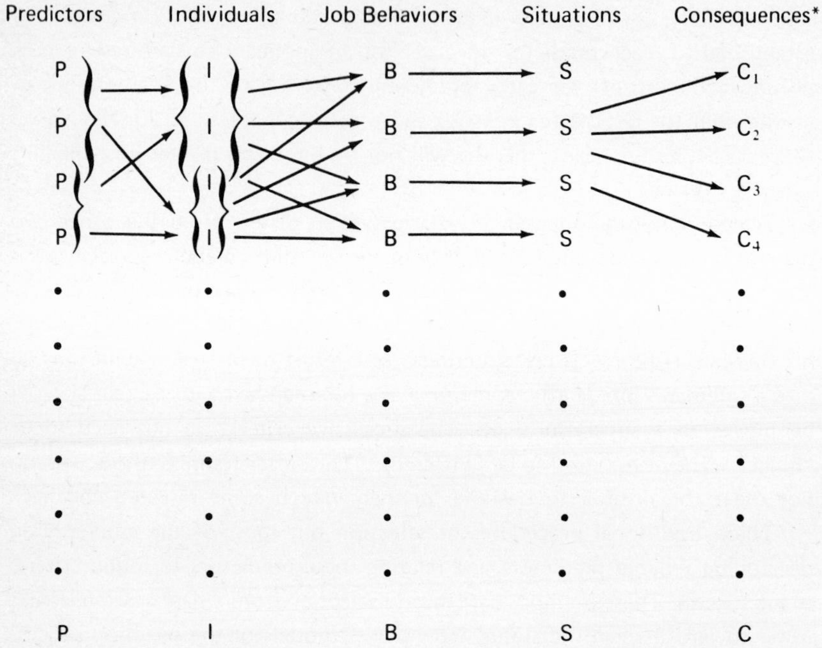

Predictors	Individuals	Job Behaviors	Situations	Consequences*

*Relation to organizational goals.

FIGURE 8-1 Selection Model. (Adapted from Dunnette, 1963, p. 319.)

consequences. The hard-driving, fast-talking, sharp behavior of the car sales-man could have one consequence on the used car lot and another consequence in the foreign sports car show room.

These attempts to portray more accurately the procedures to be followed in selection may help to improve the efficiency and effectiveness of selection. If this improvement does come, then selection procedures may be better able to deal with such special problems as the selection of leaders and the selection of minority group workers (Parrish, 1966).

THE SELECTION OF LEADERS

The selecting of people who will become the managers, supervisors, and executives of companies is a long-standing problem. The virtual impossi-bility of doing a job analysis makes it a peculiarly difficult problem. For most leadership positions, even when an analysis can be completed in some fashion, the description is so general that finding specific predictors is difficult. A well done analysis by Prien (1963), for example, produced only a most general description with the following seven dimensions of a supervisor's position:

1. Supervises the manufacturing process
2. Administers the manufacturing process
3. Supervises employees
4. Coordinates and administers manpower
5. Contacts employees and communicates with them
6. Organizes, plans and prepares work
7. Handles union-management relations

The difficulty of selecting leaders is multiplied because the great man theory of leadership does not work. There simply are no traits which are common to good leaders and separate them from poor leaders or nonleaders.

Based on the previous discussion of leadership (Chapter 6) the following statements appear to form a sound basis for leadership selection. The good leader wants to lead, to be considerate of his followers, and to initiate structure. He also has the intelligence and the knowledge of his work and his subordinates that enable him to make effective use of his motivations. He has qualities which fit the organization of which he is a part and suit the people he leads. In general, leadership is a process involving the man and the group. Consequently, companies cannot select leaders; they can only select potential leaders and try to develop each man's potential.

A formal development program does not guarantee that better potential leaders will be developed. In fact, some experienced observers think that it may have no influence. But whether the developmental program is effective or not, the problem of initial selection remains. How do companies pick their potential executives? The most obvious answer is by education.

EDUCATION AND INTELLIGENCE AS PREDICTORS

Education predicts success. A man who never graduated from grammar school may be a genius, and so also may a college graduate with poor grades. But on the average, education predicts intelligence, and intelligence predicts occupational success.

The value of intelligence tests as an aid in selecting leaders has declined as companies have gone more and more to colleges to find their potential leaders.

The reason is simple: It takes a difference in intelligence to make a difference in leadership. That is, if potential leaders were drawn from the general population, then they would have wide differences in intelligence. When they are drawn from a college population, however, the range of difference is much smaller. At the extreme, if in a group of potential leaders all have the same high intelligence, then intelligence could not account for any differences in their leadership ability. A prominent industrial psychologist who was a college president states the situation in this way:

> . . . there is not much evidence that high academic achievement represents a necessary characteristic for industrial leadership. There may be a positive correlation, but it is not large enough to provide a basis for a recruitment policy. . . . It may be, on the contrary, that the *intellectual* capacity required for effective leadership in many industrial management positions is no greater than that required for graduation from a good college (McGregor, 1960, p. 186).

Typically, companies are selecting their potential leaders from senior classes by means of interviews, references, and occasionally, aptitude and personality tests. The Michigan Bell Telephone Company, for example, has its own full-time recruiter whose job it is to locate college graduates who can become at least middle-management executives in the company. He spends from a half hour to two hours in the initial interview with graduates on their own campus. He has the authority to make on-the-spot offers to graduates. Since other companies within the Bell system also have recruiters, each has agreed that its recruiter will only interview graduates within the area it serves. Still, in one year, the Michigan recruiter interviewed nearly a thousand students to obtain twelve potential executives for the company.

How well does the system work? Graduates, as a whole, undoubtedly have a greater leadership potential than nongraduates. They are brighter, better informed, better motivated, more self-confident, and endowed with the traits that come from higher socioeconomic status. But which graduate should a company pick? Some companies, like Michigan Bell, stress high grades; others are relatively unconcerned about grades.

Practically all companies stress the importance of impressions made in interviews. We have seen that interview impressions are a slender reed to lean upon in the selection of nonsuperivosry employees. In the selection of potential leaders by interview impressions, the reed is even thinner, for the qualities of the good leader are less well known, his work is more complex, and the opportunities for interviewer bias are even greater. All companies have a long list of leaders selected by this method who failed; they also have a long list rejected by this method who succeeded in some other company.

In general, a decision by the superior is inevitable in the selection of any leader. The critical question is: What information can be provided that leads to better decisions by the manager? Better and quicker decisions will be made as the superior improves ways of determining the suitability of a man for his organization, makes more use of fellow workers in judging a man's leadership potential, employs objective measures of the motivation to lead, and develops ways of measuring both the desire and ability of the candidate to be considerate of subordinates and the desire and ability to initiate structure.

MATCHING LEADERS TO THE ORGANIZATION

The "climate" may vary as much from one firm to another as the climate from Maine to California. Leaders in different climates have problems as different as those of the potato farmer in Maine and the vegetable grower in California. How different the leader's problems may be is suggested by the observations of a consultant who visited two companies within a few days:

> The first was a division of a large company which was developing one of the new intercontinental ballistic missiles. The people who make up this organization are young; they are tremendously excited over the challenge represented by their task. The technology of the industry is growing so fast that it is almost impossible to keep up with it. Changes and innovations—some of them revolutionary—take place almost daily. Growth is rapid, and opportunities for advancement and new experience occur faster than people can quite meet them. Almost no one seemed to feel that he was genuinely "on top of his job," and yet it was clear that the organization was doing an effective job, that morale was high, and that people were growing.
>
> I went directly from this company to the headquarters of a major railroad. . . . The managers with whom I talked there showed almost none of the excitement and challenge which had been so vividly demonstrated in the other organization. They expressed generally cynical views about the opportunities for growth and development; they talked about the rigidities of the organization and about the lack of challenge in their work. While there was fundamental enthusiasm among them for railroading, I got the impression that it was focused on the romantic past rather than on the future. Promotions and new job opportunities were seen as depending primarily upon openings created by death or retirement (McGregor, 1960, p. 193).

Leaders that fit one climate may not fit another. Improved selection of leaders in a company, therefore, depends upon finding men who fit its particular climate. The climate of an organization varies with its structure. The flatter it is, the greater the responsibilities its leaders must assume and the more the individual executive is thrown on his own to sink or swim according to his ability. The pyramid organization that does not want to or cannot change does best to select pyramid-type leaders. When the management of a pyramid organization does wish to flatten the structure, the change can only be made slowly. Potential flat-type executives must be recognized and their responsibilities increased, and each small opportunity to flatten the organization must be seen and acted upon.

Measurement of organizational climate

The climate of organizations with the same degree of flatness can vary a great deal, for some have a man-to-man, some a group, and some a bureaucratic system of organization. Each system has its special climate. Flatness can be estimated from a look at the organization chart; the system of organization, however, can only be safely estimated by measuring the attitudes of the leaders in it. Nelson (1950) has measured such attitudes by questionnaires with statements like the following:

A. A new employee should be made to feel that he will get along all right if
    BUREAUCRATIC   1. He follows company rules and regulations and is a reliable worker.
    GROUP   2. He cooperates with the other employees to turn out the day's work.
    MAN-TO-MAN   3. He follows instructions and develops the right work habits.

B. A new supervisor should be recommended mainly on the basis of
    BUREAUCRATIC   1. The candidate's knowledge of, and respect for, company policies and programs.
    GROUP   2. The candidate's reputation among the employees as a natural leader.
    MAN-TO-MAN   3. The candidate's use of practical psychology in getting things done.

C. Departmental discipline can best be maintained by
    BUREAUCRATIC   1. Equal treatment of employees according to clearly written rules laid down by top management.

GROUP 2. Helping the workers develop a common standard of conduct based on company policies.

MAN-TO-MAN 3. The supervisor taking direct action on any serious violation of company policies that may affect production.

The dominant attitude of the organization is determined by giving the questionnaire to all its leaders and finding the average scores. The bureaucratic organization is one in which the leaders generally chose the bureaucratic answers; the group organization, group answers; and man-to-man, the man-to-man answers. Whether a possible leader fits the organization can then be estimated by giving him the same test and matching *his* scores to those of the average leader in the organization.

Sears, Roebuck and Company
Since 1944, Sears, Roebuck and Company has used the same battery of psychological tests as an aid in matching the personalities of potential leaders to its organization. The battery consists of the Kuder Personal Preference Inventory, the American Council on Education Psychological Test, the Allport-Vernon Study of Values scale, and the Guilford-Martin Inventory.

The typical Sears executive is strikingly different in many respects from men in general. A comparison of the scores of 2,500 executives with the scores of men in the general population yields the following picture:

> . . . . the executive group is intellectually superior to the college student, for executives fall at the 65th percentile of general 4-year college norms. . . . He takes criticism more objectively, and shows higher tolerance for different people, ways, and ideas. . . . he places high value on economic considerations and personal recognition . . . and he works toward the achievement of this kind of success. . . . In short, the executive appears to be a goal-oriented person, with unusually fine personal adjustment, and the confidence and ambition which enables him to carry responsibilities (Sears, Roebuck and Company, 1962).

Since the typical executive may not be the best executive, the process of "matching" men to the organization runs the danger of selecting conventional, conservative, and uncreative leaders and rejecting the liberal and creative ones. To avoid this, test scores of typical Sears executives were compared with test scores of seven groups of the company's best executives. In one part of this study, territorial vice-presidents were asked to send to Chicago the kind of men they felt might someday be running the company. When the test scores of this highly mobile executive group of 99 were compared with the scores of typical executives, the analysis yielded the following picture of the most successful executive:

> The Political Values factor is most noteworthy, for without exception these groups score considerably higher than the management average on this scale. It would seem that powerful competitive drive for a position of eminence and authority provides a strong impetus for these men. . . . They are fully confident of their abilities to cope with and control unfamiliar situations, have the facility to deal with problems impersonally, and possess the physical vitality to maintain a steadily productive work pace. . . . They are exceptionally open-minded, tolerant and unbiased in their attitudes; while they prefer a dominant position within a group, they are also cooperative teamworkers who willingly listen to the ideas and suggestions of others. . . . Of all seven groups, only one failed to score significantly higher on at least one measure of mental alertness (Sears, Roebuck and Company, 1962).

Another problem involved in matching men to the organization is that the climates of organizations change. The Sears company does not have the same atmosphere today that it had in 1940, and it will not have the same atmosphere in 1980 as it has today. As climates change, the kinds of leaders who are needed change. Perhaps the wisest moves for progressive managements to make are those that will provide a supply of potential leaders with *varying* attitudes and personalities who can later be matched to the new but unpredictable climates that will develop.

THE USE OF FOLLOWERS TO PICK LEADERS

A supervisor has more knowledge of the men under him than his boss, and his ratings of them tend to be more accurate. The average worker has more knowledge of his coworkers than his supervisors do. Do the worker's ratings of his coworkers tend to be more accurate than the supervisor's? The best simple answer is yes.

Evidence comes from studies of the rating of officer trainees. Ratings by Marine trainees were "a more valid predictor of success in Officer Candidate School and of combat performance" than ratings by superiors. Among Signal Corps trainees, "nominations by class appear to be better measures of the leadership factor than any other variable." Ratings by Air Force trainees were "the most promising OCS criterion found" (Hollander, 1954). Buddy ratings not only predicted success better, but also earlier. For example, buddy ratings predicting which Naval Aviation cadets would complete flight training were as valid as officer ratings that were made a year later. In another study involving military personnel, buddy ratings obtained at an early stage of training proved to be valid predictors of promotion at several successive stages in the soldier's military career. They not only indicated who would be a good non-commissioned officer but also predicted who would be a good officer later on (Amir, Kovarsky and Sharan, 1970).

Buddy ratings are more than a popularity contest. Naval cadets, for example, named both the fellow trainees whom they considered their best friends and the fellow trainees whom they thought had the greatest leadership potential. Only one out of three friends was listed as a potential leader (Hollander and Webb, 1955).

The reliability of buddy ratings is generally as high as, and often higher than, that of ratings by superiors. Marine officer trainees, for example, rated each other after 1 week of training and again after 3 weeks. For such a brief contact, the agreement was surprisingly high (.70s). When they rated each other a third time after longer contact, the agreement was as high as ratings ever go (.90s). The reliability of leadership ratings after 4 months was "outstandingly higher than that of any of the other variables upon which the test was made" (Wherry and Fryer, 1949).

Buddy ratings, however, do not agree well with supervisory ratings. In an aircraft company, for example, Springer (1953) correlated coworker and supervisory ratings of 100 men who were candidates for leadmen (leaders of a group of five to ten men). The coworkers worked closely with a candidate and were not eligible for the leadman jobs. The correlations between coworker ratings and supervisory ratings were as follows:

Job knowledge	.15
Job performance—quality	.25
Cooperation	.29
Job performance—quantity	.33
General fitness for promotion	.39

The agreement between workers and supervisors was low, lower than the agreement between workers or between supervisors. Why? The employees may have been right and the supervisors wrong; the employees may have been wrong and the supervisors right. Most likely, however, the employees and the supervisors saw different aspects of a man's leadership potential. If so, leadership would be best evaluated by a combination of supervisor and employee ratings.

Buddy ratings have more often been used to identify potential military officers than to identify potential business supervisors. The system, however, was successfully tested in a large insurance company as a possible aid in the selection of assistant managers (Weitz, 1958). In another study (Mayfield, 1970) buddy ratings proved to be a valid method for identifying supervisors. This study asked each insurance agent to nominate three other agents in his group for supervisory positions. More than two years later 154 of these agents had been promoted to the position of assistant manager *without knowledge of the nominations they had received.* The researcher then compared the assistant manager's rating after six months on the job with his original score on the buddy ratings. An agent with an A or B buddy rating was almost twice as likely to be a successful manager as one who received a lower buddy rating. (See Table 8-4.)

There have been a few other attempts to use followers to pick leaders (Maloney and Hinrichs, 1959; Roadman 1964). In general, ratings by co-workers or subordinates seem to provide a neglected but valuable aid for improving the selection of potential leaders and for developing present ones.

LEADERSHIP MOTIVATION

A leader must want to lead. Ratings by a man's associates reflect this desire more quickly than ratings by his superiors. Still, it would be better if the motivation to lead could be assessed *before* a man is hired. The leaderless group discussion method and the use of personality inventories are ways of accomplishing this.

Leaderless group discussion

The basic scheme of the leaderless group discussion (LGD) is to have a group of potential leaders confer on a given problem. No leader is appointed. Raters who do not participate in the discussion observe the performance of each member and rate his effectiveness. As yet, there has been no final standardization of the size of the group, length of testing time, type of problem presented, directions, seating arrangement, number of raters, and rating procedure.

TABLE 8-4 Comparison of buddy ratings and success on the job

Buddy rating	Number receiving rating	Number considered successful	Percent successful
A or B	101	66	65
C, D, or E	53	19	35

SOURCE: Data from Mayfield (1970).

Typically, however, pairs of raters agree very well with each other (the median correlation in 12 different studies is .82).

How valid is the method as a way of assessing leadership ability? Bass (1954) found 17 correlational analyses between ratings in LGD and ratings on leadership performance on the job. Samples of these correlations are shown in Table 8-5. They indicate both the wide variety of settings in which the method has been used and the consistently positive results.

LGD ratings are not as easy to get or as cheap as test scores. Tests can be given by clerks; LGD requires trained observers. Tests can be given to a large group at one time; LGD is generally given to small groups at different times. And tests can be mechanically scored; LGD must be scored by hand. If buddy ratings are substituted for observer ratings, these administrative difficulties can be considerably reduced.

Scales to measure leadership motivation

A man's LGD rating is indirectly related to his success as a leader. It is *directly* related to his desire to lead, since only the man who wants to lead will try to lead a discussion. Trying means talking, and talking generally means a high LGD rating. Time spent talking correlated .65 with rated success among management trainees, .77 among sorority girls, and .96 among college men (Bass, 1960, p. 116)!

Participation is related to many desirable leadership qualities. People high in participation, for example, tend to be high in dominance, self-confidence, independence, intelligence, critical thinking ability, and knowledge of the

TABLE 8-5   The relation between LGD ratings and leadership ratings

Men rated by LGD	Nature of rating of leadership performance	Correlation
100 Army ROTC cadets	Rating by superior officer 6 months later	.51
65 fraternity pledges	Nomination for positions of leadership 6 months later	.47
202 civil service administrators	Rating on general merit as an administrator 2 years later	.36
123 foreign service personnel	Rating on "suitability for foreign service" by their superiors 2 years later	.33
84 shipyard foremen	Rating on adequacy as a foreman by their superiors	.29

SOURCE: Adapted from Bass (1954).

topic being discussed (H. C. Smith and Dunbar, 1951). Still, wanting to lead and being successful in leading are different things. LGD ratings reflect both desire and success.

The *desire* to lead can be most conveniently assessed by a personality scale. Scales measuring the strength of the desire to influence others are variously called "dominance," "ascendency," "aggressiveness," "assertiveness," etc. They include statements like the following:

> I enjoy taking responsibility for introducing people at a party.
> I have criticized workmen who fail to have work done for me on time.
> I enjoy making a speech before a large crowd of people.
> I enjoy being a leader of people.
> I like to talk about myself.

As the statements indicate, the dominating person exercises social initiative, maintains his rights, does not mind being conspicuous, acts as a leader, and is frank rather than reticent. Social boldness rather than timidity is a central quality in this pattern of behavior.

The value of personality inventories as a method of picking leaders is viewed with wide and justifiable scepticism. Although they are extensively used, their merit has rarely been checked. Typically, scales that have been proved to be of value in one company in one situation often turn out to have little value in another company. Of all scales, those measuring some aspect of dominance seem to have the greatest general applicability. Of 17 studies where dominance scores were related to leadership, 11 showed a significant correlation. Two, however, showed no relationship, and four showed that dominating persons were rejected as leaders (Stogdill, 1948).

In the selection of potential leaders, dominance scores provide a quick way of eliminating those who do not like to dominate and do not really want to be leaders. An applicant must have some taste for leadership in order to succeed. Too big an appetite, however, may create hostility and resistance among those to be led. Willingness to lead is only one requisite; other necessary attributes may have no relationship, or even a negative relationship, to dominance. Intelligence and knowledge, for example, have a slight negative relationship: the smarter and better informed a person, the less likely he is to be dominating (Guilford, 1959).

Personality scales at present have only a modest contribution to make to the selection of potential leaders. Unquestionably, however, they will be improved and their use expanded.

LEADERSHIP ATTITUDES

As discussed previously, the best leaders are both considerate of their subordinates and effective at initiating structure, although the two attributes are unrelated. Two possible ways of measuring where a leader stands on these dimensions is to have him rated by others or to have him rate himself. Both methods have been tried, and both have value as devices for selecting leaders (Fleishman, 1953; 1955; Dore, 1960).

SUMMARY ON SELECTING LEADERS

Practically all companies now use, and some probably overuse, educational achievement and intelligence test scores in the selection of potential leaders. Beyond these devices, companies and psychologists are exploring the possibilities of matching leaders more carefully to the jobs they will do, using followers to help select leaders, and measuring leadership motivation, attitudes, and skills. As we develop better models and procedures we should do a better job in the selection of leaders.

Improving selection of leaders and other workers is only one way of improving a company's goal achievement. Productivity, integration, and morale are the outcome of interaction between the man and his job situation, but good people at any level of the organization, if the job situation is poor, may not be productive. Poor workers, if the job situation is good, can be productive. Training, incentives, appraisals and counseling are other methods of improving the interaction between the worker and his job. The following chapters consider these methods.

SUMMARY

Both the costs of poor selection and the difficulties of making good ones are mounting. Selection is not a cut and dried procedure of passing a test and getting a job. It requires job analysis, the careful study and evaluation of the job for which people are being chosen. Selection also requires assessment of the people who wish to get jobs. Interviews, application blanks, references and tests all are commonly used to assess people and improve selection. All these techniques have weaknesses; all have strengths.

In general the effectiveness of any selection device depends on its validity, on the proportion of satisfactory employees picked without the device, and on the proportion of applicants who must be hired regardless of their probable success.

Recently the procedures for combining the information from job analysis and people assessment have been the subject of fresh thinking and research. The results of these new approaches indicate that the quality of selection can be improved and that selection may become increasingly useful for dealing with special problems, such as the selection of potential leaders.

Selection is a basic area of industrial psychology. It combines an emphasis on the practical problem of getting people who can work in organizations with an emphasis on the scientific problem of how to measure human abilities, skills, personality, and performance.

9

TRAINING

Selection procedures bring people into an organization and match them to certain jobs. However these procedures do not ensure that the people will do the jobs well. In the area of leadership, for example, better selection is only one way of improving the effectiveness of company leaders. Improvement through selection is limited by the imperfections of the selection devices; by the scarcity of leaders, which limits the amount of picking and choosing that a company can engage in; and by the probability that the difference in the *potential* effectiveness of the best and poorest candidate is not very great. Improvement through training has none of these limitations. In comparing the overall improvements to be made through selection with those to be made through training, Haire (1956) concludes, "It does not seem at all out of line to hope for something on the order of eight or ten times as much improvement from leadership training as from selection."

Training activities try to ensure that people can do their jobs and can take on new jobs as the occasion arises. A person's job-related experiences shape his job behavior. The purpose of training is to guide a person's experiences so that the changes in his behaviors, abilities, and attitudes make him more interested in his work, more loyal to the organization, and more productive. Training is an attempt to control learning, since new learning can lead to new behavior.

How do organizations train people—shape their behavior in ways that make it easier to accomplish organizational goals? How can training be improved?

A GENERAL MODEL FOR TRAINING

Almost all learning theories make use of four basic terms (Bass and Vaughn, 1966). In order for learning to occur the necessary (but not sufficient) conditions are a motivated learner, a stimulus, a response, and feedback.

Motivation is basic to learning. If the potential learner is not motivated, little if any hope exists that learning will occur. Most of us need only to review our own experiences to confirm the essential quality of motivation. Teachers are always delighted to work with motivated students and expend great effort to ensure that students are motivated to learn.

In order for learning to begin there needs to be a stimulus. The stimulus is an occasion for a response. This stimulus may be internal, i.e., contractions of the stomach or a rapidly beating heart, or it may be external, i.e., a ball coming toward one's chest or rain running down the back of one's neck.

The response made to the stimulus may be any behavior that the learner is capable of showing.

Feedback is some indication of the relationship between the stimulus and the response. When the feedback indicates the response is an appropriate one, it reinforces the response, i.e., it serves to increase or maintain the strength of the response. When cold rain runs down the back of your neck you may say, "Oh, pshaw!" You find that the water is still running down the back of your neck. This wet feedback does not reinforce your response. You turn up your coat collar. Feedback now tells you that the water is no longer running down your neck, and the coat-collar-turning-response is reinforced.

The general model of training is an attempt to arrange the conditions of learning—motivation, stimulus, response, feedback—in such a way as to ensure that the goal of the training program is achieved. Three phases make up the general model: preparation for training, exposure to training, and transfer of training.

PREPARATION FOR TRAINING

Preparation for training consists of getting the learner ready to learn, i.e., motivating him, and getting the organization ready to train. To prepare the learner it is necessary to answer two questions for him: What is to be learned? Why should he learn it? The same questions are the basis for getting the organization ready to train. The organization needs to specify the goals of the training as concretely as possible. If the people administering the program cannot say what it is designed to accomplish and for whom the training is intended, they cannot answer the trainees' questions. An organization which undertakes a training program because "everyone else is doing it" or because "it sounds like a good idea" will waste time, money, and the good will of employees.

After a training program is designed for a specific group of people and to accomplish specific goals, the next task is to answer trainees' questions about it. "Am I going to learn a new skill, refresh an old skill, improve a present skill? Am I supposed to change my attitude about something? What am I supposed to get from this training? Why should I take this training? Am I being considered for a promotion; am I going to get a new machine; am I going to be transferred? Am I taking this training because I have been doing a poor job, because I have been doing a good job, or because nobody knows what kind of job I have been doing?" The answers to these questions prepare the trainee for the training experience and should provide him with incentives to learn.

EXPOSURE TO TRAINING

For learning to occur, the trainer, the material to be learned, and the trainee must come together. Stimuli are presented to the trainee through a lecture, a teaching machine, a demonstration, or a discussion. As a result he makes a response: he thinks, or turns left, or is nicer to people, or bends his knees when he lifts a box. Some of his responses are reinforced and some are not. He learns. Depending on the purpose of the training program the stimulus-response-feedback cycle is repeated few or many times. Each time the cycle is completed the trainee has practiced the appropriate pattern of behavior and established it more firmly as his own. Within the program the trainee must have time to practice the new pattern of behavior and to digest it and make it a part of himself. "Learning based on repetition tends to be mechanical and barren till the participant ceases to be self-conscious about it and uses it routinely as a part of his habitual pattern of behavior." (Lynton and Pareek, 1967, p. 21).

TRANSFER OF TRAINING

Learning new behavior within the training situation does not complete the process. In order for the training to be useful to the organization, the trainee must show the results of his training when he returns to the job. Ensuring that the new behavior is used on the job is difficult.

On-the-job training may avoid the problem. If the job itself presents a challenge that requires new learning, then learning is quite likely to occur and be apparent in later performance (Berlew and Hall, 1966). In other cases, the training situation can be made such a close simulation of the actual working situation that the problem of transfer of training is lessened (Wakeley and Shaw, 1965). In all cases the training program should be designed to facilitate the transfer from the training situation to the job situation.

A classic study that illustrates problems of transfer of training concerned a human relations training program.

The International Harvester study

Since 1947 the International Harvester Company had been sending its supervisors from various plants in the United States and Canada to Chicago to attend a 2-week training course that lasted for eight hours each day. During the period of the study, classes were conducted at a hotel in which several floors were set aside to accommodate the men. The major stress in the program was on principles of human relations. Instructional techniques ranged from the extensive use of visual aids to textbook materials, and from role-playing and group discussion to conventional lectures. During the evenings and after classes, the instructors and students held frequent informal discussions of problems the supervisors faced on the job. While the trainees were overwhelmingly favorable in their reactions to the training, the management wanted to know the impact of the training on job behavior (Fleishman et al., 1955).

The criteria of effectiveness used through the study were the consideration and initiation-of-structure scales which have already been discussed in Chapter 6. Scores on these scales at the beginning and at the end of training showed a *rise* in consideration scores and a *fall* in initiation-of-structure scores. No control groups were used in this part of the study.

The study's primary purpose, however, was to evaluate the long-range impact of the program. To this end the scales were given to (1) 32 foremen who had had no leadership training at the company's central school, (2) 30 foremen whose training had occurred from 2 to 10 months before, (3) 31 foremen whose training had occurred from 11 to 19 months before, and (4) 29 foremen whose training had occurred from 20 to 39 months before.

The design would have been more exact if the *same* men had been tested before training and at various intervals after training. Analysis, however, showed that the various groups averaged about the same age (forty-four), about the same education (11 years), and about the same number of years with the company (16 years).

The foremen were then divided into those whose *superiors* had high consideration scores and those whose superiors had low ones. As Figure 9-1 shows, in the long run it was the considerateness of his superior rather than anything related to training which had the most influence on a foreman's score. That is, foremen who had supervisors with high consideration scores tended themselves to have high ones. The authors offer the following explanation:

> With reference to training in human relations, our study yields one clear implication. . . . Our foremen developed a point of view in school but lost it on their return to the plant if their superior had a different point of view . . . this suggests that to improve social relations almost anywhere, it is important to work on the whole social setting. It is not possible to pull people out of this setting, tell or teach them some ideas,

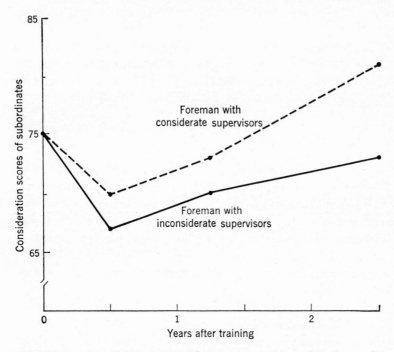

FIGURE 9-1 The Influence of Considerate and Inconsiderate Superiors on Subordinates Trained to Be Considerate. (Adapted from Fleishman et al., 1955.)

and then return them to the setting and consider everything fixed . . . (Fleishman et al., 1955, p. 101).

CURRENT PRACTICES IN TRAINING

In the past what a worker learned about his job was largely uncontrolled: he was put on the job and left to pick up what he could. Times have changed. In 1930 only 38 percent of companies had special classes for employees; in 1957, 62 percent did. In 1930, 24 percent of companies paid part of the employees' expenses in furthering their education; in 1957, 61 percent did. In 1930, 34 percent of companies had foremanship training classes, in 1957, it was 71 percent (Scott, et al., 1961). American industry now spends about $3,000,000,000 each year on formal training programs (Lynton and Pareek, 1967). When the expenditures for all management development activities and those of the training programs of non-industrial organizations are added, the total annual expenditure for training of all kinds exceeds $10,000,000,000. Perhaps the one statistic which best shows the growth in importance and sophistication of training is the membership of the American Society for Training and Development. In 1943 the membership was 15; today it exceeds 5,500.

Training is a large and a growing part of the work of industrial psychologists. Current practices in this area vary in three ways: with whether the training emphasizes general human relations skills or more specific job skills, with where and when it is conducted, and with what techniques.

THE EMPHASIS OF TRAINING

Training activities are as old as the existence of jobs. Even formal programs have a long history. For example, apprentice training and instruction in the guild halls centuries ago. However, it is only in relatively recent times that employers have taken the responsibility of providing training for employees. The shortage of skilled workers, for example, during war time periods or during periods of the rapid emergence of new industries requiring new skills, such as the computer industry, has often forced companies to begin teaching their own employees.

The earliest and still the most common kinds of training programs emphasize specific job skills. Companies are interested in training riveters, or lathe operators, or office machine operators, as well as providing skill training for supervisors and managers. Among the earliest programs of this sort was the Job Instruction Training program (JIT) developed during World War II. This program attempted to train supervisors to become trainers so that they could effectively pass along their know-how to the expanding numbers of people in the defense industry.

While the emphasis on skill training has moved from non-supervisory workers to supervisors and managers, human relations training has moved from supervisors to workers. It emerged as a training emphasis thirty years ago. These early programs were heavily influenced by the JIT programs and were intended mainly for foreman and other first line supervisors. During the period from the middle 1940's until the middle 1950's human relations training became a fad. The lack of positive results from these early programs helped bring the fad to an end. But training in human relations did not end; human relations training programs for supervisors and managers are still widely used and new techniques of instruction are developing rapidly. Most human relations training is still directed at supervisory personnel. There is, however, a trend for nonsupervisory workers to become involved.

LOCATION AND TIME OF TRAINING

Training is increasingly being viewed as a continuous activity that is required if members of the organization are to keep up with the rapid changes in technology and thinking.

On-the-job training

About nine out of ten companies report that they train their new employees on the job. It is still the most common location for management training (Foreman, 1964). Most of the time, the training is done by the individual's supervisor; some of the time, by special instructors. On-the-job training has many advantages: It is realistic, it is easily organized, it stimulates high motivation, it speeds the worker's adjustment to his supervisor and fellow workers, and its direct costs are small. It also has weaknesses: The trainer may be a good worker but a poor teacher; the trainer may be antagonized by being given an unwanted additional assignment; the worker, by poor instruction and in his haste to gain immediate productivity, may fail to learn the best way of doing his job. Consequently, the total costs of training (time of trainer + wasted material + damaged equipment) may be very high.

On-the-job training does not just happen. Like any training, it must be planned. Just being on a job and getting "experience" does not necessarily improve performance. One study examined the hypothesis that there is a positive relationship between years of supervisory experience and leadership performance (Fiedler, 1970). After examining data from three experiments involving 385 managers and supervisors in five different organizations, the researcher concluded that there was no support for this hypothesis. He said, "Leadership experience and leadership performance—another hypothesis shot to hell."

Orientation training

Orientation training, sometimes called "indoctrination" or "induction," aids the new employee in his initial adjustment to the company and to his job. The objectives of such programs may be to:

1. Increase the employee's knowledge of such matters as company rules, wages, insurance, and products
2. Develop the skills involved in safe working habits and quality production
3. Develop confidence in the company and pride in its products

Practically all companies have some training aimed at the first objective; few have programs aimed at the last. The orientation may be only a brief talk with the employee's supervisor, concluding with the presentation of an employee handbook. Or it may include a guided tour of the plant, formal orientation classes, and a careful introduction to the supervisor, work associates, and the details of the particular job.

Little can be accomplished in developing confidence unless the attitudes encouraged by training are supported by the employee's job experiences. A company cannot gain acceptance of substandard working conditions by propaganda in an orientation course. But the company which is an innocent victim of public or worker mistrust can hope for real success in proclaiming its assets through orientation programs.

Vestibule training

About one in ten companies have some form of "vestibule" school, a school within the company with its own quarters and equipment. Their general aim is to teach the operation of a few machines rather than to develop craftsmen. They can provide excellent conditions for learning. Instruction is better under a full-time instructor than under a foreman with many responsibilities. In a relatively quiet, unhurried atmosphere trainees are taught approved methods rather than the unauthorized short cuts of the older workers. The progress of the trainee can be followed more closely and evaluated more accurately. His motivation is also likely to be high, for he is going to school on company time, he is working on the same type of machine he must operate on the job, and he may have the opportunity to try out for more than one job.

The most common argument against vestibule training is its cost: special quarters, a special training force, and duplicate machines must be provided. This argument has little weight in periods of rapid expansion which call for a large number of workers to be trained in a short time. Under such circumstances, the training costs per man are small. Even in normal times vestibule training is probably not so expensive as it appears to be. Its costs are all obvious and measurable, whereas the costs of on-the-job training, for instance, are largely hidden. Furthermore, such schools have advantages beyond providing optimal learning conditions. Instructors have an excellent opportunity to evaluate the trainee for placement purposes, new employees can be tried on a variety of different machines at little cost before final placement, and an efficient way of retraining displaced older employees for new jobs is provided.

Apprentice training
An apprentice is a worker who is learning a trade but who has not reached the stage where he can work without supervision. In the Middle Ages, a young man was bound over to his employer by his parents through a contract which required him to spend a number of years working for the employer in exchange for the training he received in the trade. Today, one out of two companies have some form of apprentice training. Less than one worker in a hundred, however, is an apprentice at any given time. Most apprentice training programs are in the metalworking trades. The Allis-Chalmers Manufacturing Company of Milwaukee, the Ford Motor Company, and the General Electric Company have well-organized and well-known programs.

Formal training and job training are sometimes both within the company and sometimes both outside the company. The smaller the company, the more likely training is to be conducted outside. A common compromise is for a company to cooperate with a vocational school, the school providing the formal training and the company providing the job training, a minimum wage during training, and a job at the completion of training.

Apprenticeship training generally takes much longer than necessary. Better selection of trainees, more effective training, and, above all, more freedom to progress according to demonstrated ability would result in considerable savings of time and money in most such programs. Many apprentices who are now required to put four years into the training could easily finish in half the time.

Off-the-job training

On-the-job training develops the skills required to perform specific tasks. Companies are becoming rapidly aware, however, that training should not end here, for a company's greatest competitive advantage lies in the fullest development of its human resources. A survey by Scott et al. (1961), for example, shows that in 1947 only 25 percent of companies paid part of their employees' expenses in furthering their education; in 1953, 44 percent paid part; and in 1957, 61 percent. Off-the-job training covers a wide range of educational activities: night school classes, correspondence courses, university extension programs, graduate work, etc.

Combining locations

Many training programs will use more than one location in order to achieve results. In one factory turnover was very high. Thirty percent of the employees left in less than one month; 40 percent left in less than two months; and 68 percent left within one year. The researcher (Lefkowitz, 1970) examined three different training programs which attempted to reduce turnover. In one of these employees received one day of vestibule training, in a second there were two days of vestibule training, and in a third three days of vestibule training. Results showed that the longer the training program the lower the turnover rate. However, the results also demonstrated that the longer the training period the lower the productivity rate. Guided by this information a fourth training program integrating vestibule and on-the-job training was established. In this manner, the best balance between staying on the job and high productivity resulted.

TECHNIQUES OF TRAINING

The trainer is guided in his selection of methods by the aims of the training session and the place where it is conducted. A lecture is a good technique for presenting new information to a group in a classroom setting. It is a bad one for convincing people that they can depend on the other members of a group in the work setting.

Some common training techniques are presented briefly in the following pages. A much more complete discussion of these and other techniques is presented in *Training and Development Handbook* edited by Robert Craig and Lester R. Bittel.

The lecture

The lecture remains one of the most important techniques of instruction. "The lecture is a prepared presentation of knowledge, information, or attitudes for the purpose of having others understand or accept the speaker's (instructor's) message." (Zelko, 1967, p. 141). The key word in the definition, the word that makes the difference between excitement and boredom, is "prepared." When the lecturer is prepared he can control the training situation and present material more clearly and in less time than is possible with virtually any other technique.

Lectures are not a good way of presenting human relations training programs. The lecture approach assumes that knowledge gained from talks and books will be applied to everyday problems. Some of the reasons for doubting this assumption are suggested by the following comments of a foreman:

I've been a foreman in this shop for over ten years, and so far as I know I've been doing a good job. Why do you suppose management has asked all of us to attend these conferences, to listen to all this new talk about human relations dished out by those fellows in the training section of the personnel department? Hell, not one of them has even known what it feels like to be a foreman and be caught in the squeeze all the time between front office people and the men. Now with a union it's even worse.

We've known for years that in order to avoid being pushed around by the union and the men you have to exert your authority and maintain your position so they'll know who's boss. This "soft" approach they want us to learn may work in some places. I even doubt that. But I've never seen a boss who could get away with it and run a successful department.

My last ten years as a supervisor have taught me, what for me at least, is the best way to get results in my shop. My men are used to the way I run the place and we get on pretty good. It's my way, and it's best for me. Why should I waste my time learning new ways to supervise when the boss seems perfectly satisfied and we've got no friction here? Besides, even if I did learn something new, I couldn't apply it with the boys. They'd think I got religion or something. Sure, I'll go over and listen to what they've got to offer, but I have my doubts about applying any of it around here. It takes too much of my time (Saltonstall, 1959, p. 236).

The conference

The aim of conference training is to encourage intensive participation by trainees. Consequently, the groups are small. The size best suited to gain optimum participation varies with the physical facilities, the skill of the conference leader, and the purpose of the meeting. A group sometimes has as few as five, typically has twelve, and rarely exceeds thirty.

A conference without a plan might seem the best way to encourage full participation. Such conferences, however, typically become aimless conversational boat rides that waste time, frustrate the participants, and are dominated by a few. Obviously, some planning and structure are needed.

THE HARVARD CASE STUDY METHOD

Case studies provide an increasingly popular way of focusing conference discussion. The method, as it has been developed by the Harvard Business School and used by hundreds of universities and business firms, employs cases that are taken from actual business situations. Some are more than ten thousand words in length and contain a mixture of facts, opinions, assumptions, attitudes, and feelings which the trainees in the conference are expected to evaluate in reaching decisions and recommending actions.

Conference leaders who have had considerable experience with the method make the following suggestions:

As you look at these cases focus more on "what is going on and why?" in the relationships that you find in the case, rather than "who is the culprit?" The latter approach is likely to lead to negative criticism which is seldom as productive as positive understanding and creative analysis of human relationships. Your case analysis will lead you to your decision and action. Make sure that the analysis is done thoroughly, taking into account all the pertinent elements, before you decide what to do. Avoid premature conclusions based only on your personal experience. There will seldom be unanimity among the participants as to the definition of major problems found in the case. Each person seeing the case from his particular point of view will seldom agree with everyone else in the analysis phase of case discussion. Different alternative decisions or workable solutions will occur to different members. They should be asked to defend their decisions, while maintaining an open mind by listening to the alternative solutions suggested by others. When dealing with human affairs, with so many unpredictable factors involved, we can seldom say that there is one perfect solution which all can agree upon. It is through the process of analysis itself and the weighing and evaluating of different assumptions, viewpoints, and interpretations that people gain the deeper understanding which enables them to make better decisions and take more responsible actions. Your objective through case discussions should be to cultivate for yourself a useful approach for understanding and dealing skillfully with the variety of human problems that will confront you as an executive (Saltonstall, 1959, p. 462).

As these suggestions imply, the cases are long and complex, and participants frequently have violent disagreements about them. As there are no
"right" answers, the participants find no easy way to resolve their differences objectively. "Critical-incident" cases (Champion and Bridges, 1963)
attempt to resolve this difficulty in two ways. First, the cases focus upon
a single critical situation involving a single principle of management. Consequently, they are much shorter and simpler. Second, the comments of several
experts in the area of human relations are appended to each incident as guide-
lines for participants discussing the cases.

CASES WITH RIGHT ANSWERS

The Case of Bill, shown in Table 9-1, illustrates a variation of the case method,
both brief and quite flexible, that uses actual cases, and provides "right"
answers (H. C. Smith, 1961). Ways in which the approach may be used are
indicated by the following suggestions for conference leaders:

1. Give the trainees 10 minutes to read the case and answer the statements.
2. While they are completing the case, write the numbers 1 through 15
on the blackboard with columns headed "true" and "false." When the trainees
have finished, poll the group to find the number answering true or false to
each statement and write the results on the board.
3. Starting with the first statement, ask those who answered true and
those who answered false to give reasons for their answers. If time is short, it
is best to concentrate on those questions in which there was the greatest difference of opinion. The conference leader's role at this stage is the nondirective one of clarifying and restating the reasons.
4. After the discussion (but still without reference to the correct answers)
ask the group to answer the statements again in the light of the discussion.
5. Read the correct answers and have the trainees check the number
they got correct.
6. Tally the distribution of correct scores on the board and the gain
(or loss) from the discussion.
7. At this stage "why" questions are common. The leader may choose
to contrast the reasoning of the most accurate with that of the least accurate
trainees, give his own comments on the case, or relate the case to general
principles involved in understanding people.

In large groups the conference leader may simply ask the trainees to complete the case, then give the answers and tally the results on the blackboard.
He may then proceed with a lecture that uses the case as a starting point. A

TABLE 9-1 The case of Bill

Bill, a man with a fourth-grade education, is a 10,000-dollar-a-year traffic manager for a Milwaukee brewery. While working in the ranks before his promotion, he gained the reputation of being the hardest-working driver. He is a big man and maintains that "Hard work never hurt anyone." Bill is very loyal to the company and has high moral standards.

Which of the following statements are true of Bill and which are false?

T F 1. He readily accepts drivers' excuses as to how they lose time during the day.

T F 2. He believes in trade unions.

T F 3. He feels that "trouble-making" shop stewards should be undermined in the eyes of their fellow workers..

T F 4. He works 10 to 12 hours a day and six to seven days a week.

T F 5. Like other members of management, he drinks Scotch when out with his friends.

T F 6. He wants his sons to go to college.

T F 7. He knows that he has proved himself, so he has no fear of losing his job.

T F 8. He tries to promote his company's product at all times, even to the point of losing friends.

T F 9. He feels that the union's seniority rule is as good a basis as any for promoting helpers to drivers.

T F 10. He believes that his employees should be paid on a commission basis.

T F 11. He believes that his employees should be glad to work overtime for extra money.

T F 12. He loves to play golf.

T F 13. He requires his drivers to be dressed neatly and always to look presentable in public contacts.

T F 14. He associates socially with other members of the company management.

T F 15. He will pay any worker overtime if he puts his time in, even though his sales or stops do not merit it.

Correct answers:

1. F	4. T	7. F	10. T	13. T
2. F	5. F	8. T	11. T	14. F
3. T	6. T	9. F	12. F	15. F

---

more involved but workable scheme is to divide the large group into small discussion groups after step 1 and let the groups discuss the questions and arrive at a group answer to each. The average scores of the discussion groups may be compared. Some zest can be added by dividing the groups according to level of supervision, departments, etc., and having the groups compete. The method also provides a convenient way of demonstrating the relative effectiveness of various sizes of groups, and styles of group leadership.

JOB RELATIONS TRAINING

The ultimate goal of human-relations conferences is to have trainees apply the principles they learn to problems on their own jobs. The case study methods thus far discussed neither state clear principles nor give trainees practice in dealing with their problems. The JRT program does both. It is one of the three supervisory programs developed by the War Manpower Commission during World War II, the other two being Job Instruction Training and Job Methods Training. The program, which consists of five 2-hour meetings, has been completed by millions of supervisors in the United States and foreign countries.

The trainer follows a detailed manual. During the first session, he develops a four-step procedure for handling personal problems. A card passed out at the end of the session has this outline:

1. GET THE FACTS
   Review the record.
   Find out what rules and plant customs apply.
   Talk with the individuals concerned.
   Get opinions and feelings.
   Be sure you have the whole story.

2. WEIGH AND DECIDE
   Fit the facts together.
   Consider their bearing on each other.
   What possible actions are there?
   Check practices and policies.
   Consider objective and effect on individual, group, and production.
   Don't jump at conclusions.

3. TAKE ACTION
   Are you going to handle this yourself?
   Do you need help in handling?
   Should you refer this to your supervisor?
   Watch the timing of your action.
   Don't pass the buck.

4. CHECK RESULTS
   How soon will you follow up?
   How often will you need to check?
   Watch for changes in output, attitudes, and relationships.
   Did your action help production?

In the next four meetings, the supervisors bring in problems from their own jobs. These are discussed and criticized by the other supervisors, using the four-step method.

Role-playing

Lectures and conferences develop the leader's knowledge of human-relations principles. They may also develop his understanding of how these principles *should* be used in dealing with his own personnel problems. Still, it has often been observed that the trainee's behavior on the job does not change, for the training has taught him how to think about his problems but not how to act. Role-playing gives him an opportunity to learn how to act in applying what he has learned.

In using the role-playing method one trainee pretends he is a worker, for example, and another trainee pretends he is a supervisor. The following outline suggests how role-playing is typically used in leadership training:

1. Begin with a short discussion of the general area in which lie the problems to be taken up.
2. Select and send out of the meeting room two of the trainees.
3. Describe to the group the problem situation which will be played out. Give enough background material so that the problem becomes alive.
4. Select a member of the group to play the role of the worker.
5. Ask the group if there are any questions—if the problem under consideration is clear. Suggest or, better, obtain from the group, possible lines of action that the foreman might take, and orient the group toward watching the ensuing play with the set, "How could it be done better?"
6. Set before the group a table and two chairs and furnish enough "props" to make the situation quite realistic.
7. Call in one of the men waiting outside. Have him take his place at the desk and explain the problem to him. Make sure he understands the setting, and then start the action: "The problem is clear? Very well. You are in your office and you had asked Jack to come in. Here he is. He walks in and says, 'Did you want to see me, Mr. Frank?' "
8. Decide when the play has gone on long enough for the purpose in mind and arbitrarily end it.
9. Have the primary player take his place with the group. Sum up the action that took place. It is helpful to outline the events of the first play briefly on a blackboard, and cover it before the next man comes in.
10. Call the second player and repeat instructions. The man taking the role of worker essentially repeats his previous behavior.

11. When the second play has ended sum up the action of the second play and review what happened in the first.
12. Ask all three of the actors for their reactions. This gives the players a chance to "save face" by themselves pointing out the errors that they may have made, and serves to give the group additional information.
13. Open the meeting to general discussion. Try to get a third column on the blackboard indicating what the group now feels would be the preferred foreman behavior.
14. Select a member of the group who has not yet played a role and have him act out the foreman's role along the lines indicated by the group. Instruct the group to watch carefully for flaws in what they have set up as "preferred" behavior (Bavelas, 1947).

The goal of role-playing is to increase the realism, sensitivity, and flexibility of the participants. These, then, are the questions before the observers as they view a man's role-playing: How well did his behavior fit the role he was playing? How often and how well did he alter his behavior to fit the reactions of his partner? How much and in what ways did his behavior change from one role to another? The best answers to these questions can generally be obtained from conflict situations rather than from well-structured ones, because the former are more likely to involve the players emotionally. Consequently, the assigned roles are often not routine ones, such as a supervisor introducing a new worker to his job, but more like the following:

Participants: Mr. Thomas, Superintendent of Schools
Mr. Green, a high school teacher

DIRECTIONS FOR MR. THOMAS: You are the Superintendent of Schools in a community with a population of five or six thousand. Mr. Green is a teacher in your high school. He is about 35 years of age and a bachelor. You have heard so many rumors concerning his sexual misconduct that you now feel it necessary to talk to him about the matter.

DIRECTIONS FOR MR. GREEN: You are a public high school teacher in a community of five or six thousand people. You are about 35 years of age and unmarried. You have just had word that the Superintendent of Schools would like to see you in his office (Bronfenbrenner and Newcomb, 1948).

Role-playing often puts the participant on the defensive if he feels that he is in a threatening environment. To be fully effective, therefore, the method requires an atmosphere of security and cooperation, an atmosphere that often does not exist in management conferences.

MULTIPLE ROLE-PLAYING

Role-playing in pairs before the training group not only makes the participants self-conscious but also can be quite time-consuming. Multiple role-playing reduces self-consciousness and takes less time for the trainer. In this type of role-playing all the members of even large groups can participate simultaneously. The large group is first subdivided into subgroups of five or six persons each. The trainer presents a problem which each of the subgroups is to solve by role-playing. For example: "How can a supervisor most effectively assign a new truck to a member of a five-man group, all of whom have trucks of varying ages and conditions?"

Typically, the trainer issues a written set of instructions to one person in each group, who becomes the foreman of the particular group. The "foreman," in turn, passes out written instructions to each member of his group. For example: "John, you have to do more driving than most of the other men because you work in the suburbs. You have a fairly old truck and feel you should have a new one because you do so much driving." After 20 to 30 minutes, during which each member of the subgroup plays his assigned role as the foreman attempts to solve the problem, the discussion is halted. Each foreman is asked to report the solution for his subgroup, and then the group as a whole discusses the effectiveness of the solutions and of the methods used to reach them. While multiple role-playing has many advantages, it requires considerable time in the preparation and pretesting of the problems and the roles assigned.

Sensitivity training

Lectures and conferences on human relations, and even role-playing, aim at getting trainees to think differently about their day-to-day human problems. It is well known, however, that many people can talk the "human-relations language" who cannot practice what they preach. Many of these people, do not hear as well as they think they do—do not really listen, constantly interrupt, impose their ideas on others, and do not understand what other people think and feel. Fully effective human-relations training requires trainees not only to think differently about human problems but to feel and behave differently. *Sensitivity training* is the name which has been used since 1954 for a training program that aims to change behavior and feelings.

Sensitivity training has grown from the work of applied group dynamicists, of members of the National Training Laboratory in Group Development, and of group psychotherapists and nondirective counselors (Tannenbaum et al., 1961). While the method is still in the process of change, it does have certain essential elements. To begin with, it is limited to small groups, for it requires high participation, involvement, and communication. For example, one especially effective training technique which is only practical in small groups is to make a rule that when anyone wants to contribute to the discussion, he must first repeat what was said and felt by the person who spoke just before him. "For the first time in my life I find that I am *really* listening to what others say" is a comment frequently made by trainees after some experience with sensitivity training.

Since the training stresses learning by feeling and doing, it is "process-oriented" rather than "content-oriented." That is, while some reading and occasional lectures are used, the stress is on emotional rather than conceptual learning. At one training session, for example, Paul, a sales manager of a large firm, was considered boastful by his group because he constantly made comments like "as division head," "as sales manager," or "at our last convention." After much discussion of this behavior, one thoughtful member of the group said:

> I have done a great deal of thinking about Paul. Contrary to what others have said, I don't think he alludes to himself to impress us as a person of supreme self-confidence. I feel he needs to reassure himself to remain comfortable in this group. I no longer resent all these references to himself and his position. I bet Paul doesn't have a college degree; he probably came up the hard way and really made good. Now he has to show his title to himself to see that it's for real. After a long silence, Paul agreed (Tannenbaum et al., 1961).

The training is "trainee-centered" rather than "trainer-centered." The trainer has many vital functions to perform in the group: he provides the initial organization; he establishes a model of behavior by his acceptance of criticism, his nonevaluative comment, and his willingness to yield his authority; and he facilitates communication by raising questions, clarifying issues, and encouraging participation. The focus, however, is upon the trainees. They are given the opportunity to decide what they want to talk about, what kinds of problems they wish to deal with, and what means they want to use in reaching their goals. As the trainees concern themselves with these problems, they begin to react in characteristic ways: some participate, some remain silent, some dominate the discussion, and some become angry. These reactions become the content of the course. One trainee, for example, wrote in a diary after an early session:

> It seems to me that this afternoon we were each intent on getting over our own ideas and having the group accept them. I now know that I wasn't listening closely to what others were saying, for I was busy

formulating my answers to what I thought they were saying. . . . I am sure this is progress. . . . If the other members were doing the same, no wonder we couldn't reach any conclusions!

Some frustration seems essential to the success of the training. To be effective, the trainee must be motivated to evaluate himself and to make changes, when he feels these would benefit him. He is unlikely to do these things unless he is jarred out of his complacency. One trainee, for example, confides in his diary:

Today I was on the "hot seat." I felt quite tense and uncomfortable when the group started to talk about me, and I was glad when we later shifted to someone. . . . Still, I knew they were on the right track. They were getting at the truth. . . .

Some resistance to the training process seems inevitable, for changing oneself is disturbing. It is natural, therefore, for people to defend the notion of themselves with which they feel most secure. The following are some common statements of resistance to the training process: "You can't change human nature," "I know myself better than anyone else ever will," "If there is one thing I know, it's how to deal with people," "Let's stop getting personal—let's be mature and look at the facts!" "What do you expect us to do—psychoanalyze everybody?" "I think this is great—I'm learning a lot by sitting back and watching all the others," "We run a business, not a nursery school," and "I don't know what you are doing to us, but I don't like it."

The expression of unkind, impolite, and ridiculous attitudes and feelings is basic to the training process. In order to overcome resistance to expressing these kinds of feelings, the group must remain basically friendly. Atmospheres are *not* necessarily friendly when attitudes of "let's-all-join-in-the-fun" or "let's-be-a-happy-family" are expressed. Atmospheres are considerate and helpful only when the stress is upon understanding rather than criticism, so that people feel free to speak frankly and to listen with understanding to what others are saying.

Is sensitivity training effective? First it should be stressed that even if the trainess do not change at all, the *group* may change dramatically. If a group of coworkers comes together to improve its human-relations skills, it is probable that the members will learn to trust each other more, learn to be more open with each other, and make some progress in solving their common problems. All these things can happen without any member of the group changing his personality in the slightest or becoming generally more understanding of people. Undoubtedly, many human-relations programs are set up with just such group changes as their primary goal.

Trainees are generally enthusiastic about their T-group experiences. They report that their self-perceptions, understanding of others, and interpersonal effectiveness improved as a result of their training. Between 1963 and 1968, the number of participants in T-groups conducted by the National Training Laboratory doubled. The method is not only used in executive development programs but also in police training, in marriage counseling, in church services, and in group psychotherapy. In short, the method is growing, is popular, and is commercially successful.

Trainees feel that training improved their understanding of themselves and others. However, the empirical evidence on this has not firmly established that it does (Campbell and Dunnette, 1968). Twenty college students did not understand their trainer any better after 30 hours of training than they did at the end of the first session (Lohmann, Zenger and Weschler, 1959). A dozen members of another group did not understand each other any better after four months of training than they had at the beginning (Bennis, Burke, Cutter, Harrington and Hoffman, 1957). Two National Training Laboratory Groups had no better idea of the attitudes of the typical member of their group at the end than they had at the beginning of training (Gage and Exline, 1953). If training does not improve their understanding of their own leader and their own group, it is hard to see how it could improve their understanding of people outside the group.

Some more recent studies show that the T-group experience produces measurable impact. Danish and Kagan (1971) studied changes in the sensitivity of 51 participants in six T-groups that lasted for ten days. Overall, there was an improvement in affective sensitivity. However, only two groups improved significantly. Two did not change and two declined slightly. The authors conclude: "This raises a question about whether or not people can be 'taught' to improve their affective sensitivity. Possibly some individuals are strongly resistant to change and the kind of experience used to improve affective sensitivity may actually encourage such people to defend even more tenaciously. . ." (p. 54).

Still, a company probably will benefit when its employees attend a T-group together, if they remain enthusiastic about the shared experience. If the employees increase their liking and trust for those with whom they work, this is likely to improve their cohesiveness, their interest in the work they do together, and, consequently, their productivity. They are also likely to look upon the organization which provided them with a personally stimulating and satisfying experience in a favorable light.

Coaching

A superior is in an advantageous situation for teaching his subordinates. He is in a position to know more about them than anyone else, to reward them effectively for learning, and provide them with a wide range of learning opportunities through the delegation of authority and through counseling.

College students, badgered almost daily by information from instructors about their performance, find it hard to appreciate how little information of this kind a typical employee on the line, in the office, or executive board room gets. The situation of a division sales manager in a major oil company is common: "During the 20 years I was in India, not one person from the higher echelons of management ever discussed with me how I, as an individual, could do a better job." Of 100 managers interviewed, 35 reported that they had *never* had a formal interview concerning their overall performance. The majority reported that superiors were vague in their evaluations and that they did not make specific suggestions for improvement (Mahler, 1958).

The principles of coaching are relatively few and simple. The coach must listen to what the subordinate has to say, find common goals with him, discuss the subordinate's present activities, and stress strengths rather than weakness. His attitude should be one of trying to help the subordinate improve himself. It is difficult, however, to get superiors interested in doing any systematic coaching. Unless the superior appreciates the importance of coaching and is rewarded by the organization for doing it, he is unlikely to give serious attention to his role as a trainer.

Position rotation

Position rotation has been called the merry-go-round system. Essentially, it consists of rotating people from one position to another in the organization for relatively brief periods of time, but it takes many forms. In the Procter and Gamble Company, for example, trainees enter a department as assistant foreman—the understudy of the foreman. One by one, the foreman delegates his responsibilities to his assistant. When the delegation is complete, the foreman himself is rotated to another position, where *he* becomes the assistant foreman and has responsibilities delegated to him. The United States Rubber Company has used the "flying squadron" approach, where trainees are rotated for relatively brief periods of time into a variety of jobs. The job experiences alternate with classroom instruction.

The Consolidated Edison Company of New York has had a job-rotation plan since 1943, with April 1 and October 1 marked as "moving days." The following are given as the advantages of the program:

1. It provides a well-rounded training and a background of experience for the individual, familiarizing him with many phases of the company's operations.
2. It streamlines the organization through periodic introduction of new managerial viewpoints, eliminating practices or operations which may have been carried on unnecessarily over a period of years.
3. It eliminates the assumption by an individual of any "vested right" in a particular job.
4. It tests the individual.
5. It improves any situation where the efficiency of the organization is being impaired by lack of cooperation.
6. It widens the trainee's circle of acquaintance among company executives (Sargent, 1958).

Learning programs

A learning program is the systematic application of learning principles to a task so that the trainee quickly and completely masters it. For example, JIT is a program for teaching supervisors how to teach. As far as it goes, it is an effective learning program. From the supervisor's point of view, since training is only one time-consuming part of his job, the less of his time the program takes, the better. Ideally, it would take no time. It is toward this ideal that psychologists strive in their development of automated learning programs.

In automated learning, the trainee learns by interacting with the program without a trainer being present. In effect, however, a learning program is much like a private instructor. Like a good instructor, a program keeps the trainee alert and busy. It insists that a point be thoroughly understood before moving on. It presents just that material for which the trainee is ready. It helps the trainee come up with the right answers by hinting, prompting, and suggesting. And it holds the trainee's interest by telling him when he has made the right response.

Table 9-2 shows some elements of automated learning programs. The program consists of a series of "frames" (10 in this case, although even brief programs have hundreds). The learner is led so slowly from what he knows to what he does not know that he seldom makes a mistake. Technical terms are introduced slowly and repeated often (note "filament"). The "vanishing" technique (the slow withdrawal of the number and strength of the cues to the right answer) is frequently employed. The finished program is so easy to follow that it runs the risk of boring the more able learners. The development of an effective program, however, is a long and hard undertaking. It requires a person who is an expert in programming and, more important, an expert in the task being taught.

TABLE 9-2 Part of a program in high school physics

The machine presents one item at a time. The student completes the item and then uncovers the corresponding word or phrase shown at the right.

Sentence to be completed	*Word to be supplied*
1. The important parts of a flashlight are the battery and the bulb. When we "turn on" a flashlight, we close a switch which connects the battery with the _____.	bulb
2. When we turn on a flashlight, an electric current flows through the fine wire in the _____ and causes it to grow hot.	bulb
3. When the hot wire glows brightly, we say that it gives off or sends out heat and _____.	light
4. The fine wire in the bulb is called a filament. The bulb "lights up" when the filament is heated by the passage of a(n) _____ current.	electric
5. When a weak battery produces little current, the fine wire, or _____ does not get very hot.	filament
6. A filament which is *less* hot sends out or gives off _____ light.	less
7. "Emit" means "send out." The amount of light sent out or "emitted" by a filament depends on how _____ the filament is.	hot
8. The higher the temperature of the filament the _____ the light emitted by it.	brighter, stronger
9. If a flashlight battery is weak, the _____ in the bulb may still glow, but with only a dull red color.	filament
10. The light from a very hot filament is colored yellow or white. The light from a filament which is not very hot is colored _____.	red

SOURCE: Skinner (1958).

How does automated instruction work out in business? IBM has a central training center where employees from all parts of the company are sent for instruction (Hughes and McNamara, 1961). One course given at the center is a 16-week course for computer servicemen concerning the IBM 7070 data processing system. In March, 1960 an instructor in the course and a psychologist began preparing programmed textbooks for the introductory section of the course. By September they had prepared 719 frames covering the first 15 hours of conventional instruction (the equivalent of the first 5 weeks of a 3-hour college course).

Seventy trainees using only the programmed textbooks were compared with forty-two trainees attending the conventional classroom course. The two groups were similar in age, education, previous computer experience, and aptitude for learning the type of material given in the course. The time that the two groups spent in learning, their learning achievements, and their attitudes toward the two types of instruction were then compared.

The automated-instruction group spent 27 percent less time working through the frames than the other group did in attending classes: 11 hours versus 15 hours. The automated group also spent less time in outside study. Yet on the same objective achievement test given at the end of the training, the automated group did much better. None of the automated group had a score below 80, whereas 16 percent of the classroom group did. More than five times as many of the automated group obtained scores of 95 or higher (12 percent versus 67 percent). Students in the automated course who had had other conventional company courses were asked which they liked better. Eighty-seven percent said they liked the automated course better.

In summary, trainees in the automated program spent less time learning, learned much more, and enjoyed the learning more. The benefits to the company are clear: The use of automated instruction resulted in better-trained and better-satisfied employees at lower instructional costs. The potential financial savings are also high: With automated instruction trainees could be taught in their local divisions, and thus the company would be saved the expense of maintaining them while they attend the central training school.

THE IMPROVEMENT OF TRAINING

Improvements in training are made by doing a better job of specifying training goals, by making use of sound principles of learning, by improving the learning situation, and by evaluating training.

SPECIFYING TRAINING GOALS

What is the best way to go about improving training? A learning theorist who has had wide experience with military training programs has this to propose:

> If I were faced with the problem of improving training, I should not look for much help from the well-known learning principles like reinforcement, distribution of practice, response familiarity and so on. I should look instead at the technique of task analysis, and at the principles of component task achievement, intratask transfer, and the sequencing of subtask learning to find those ideas of greatest usefulness in the design of effective training (Gagné, 1962).

To learn, a person must know what he is supposed to learn. To train, an instructor must know what he is supposed to teach. The clearer the goals of training the better the training. Yet the goals of many industrial training programs are not even stated. When they are, they are usually general rather than specific: "to make the trainees better truck drivers" rather than "to develop the ability to back into an alley with not more than 6 inches clearance on either side and to park in a space not longer than the truck plus 7 feet." Job analysis, an essential first step in personnel selection, is also essential for training. Job analysis, the systematic study of the duties, requirements and skills of a job, is the first step in the development of more specific and realistic goals for training.

A "job" is the set of activities to be performed by one person in one particular company. In the technical vocabulary used to describe and analyze the work men do, a *job* (for example, "zinc etcher in the Rose Company") is more specific than a *major occupational group* ("skilled workers"), an *occupational field* ("printing"), an *occupation* ("photoengraver"), or a *job category* ("photoengraving etcher"). On the other hand, a job is more general than a *task* ("removes plate from machine before acid starts to eat under printed design"). A task is the smallest part of a total operation which is assigned to a man to complete as a step in that operation. That is, a job is made up of many tasks; a job category, of many jobs; an occupation, of many job categories; an occupational field, of many occupations; and a major occupational group, of many occupational fields.

The first phase of a job analysis is a *job description*: a detailed outline of the materials and tools used and the operations performed on a job. A careful job description includes the following kinds of information:

A. Methods and procedures of work
 1. Duties that the worker is expected to fulfill
 2. Materials and supplies that the worker uses
 3. Tools, machines, and equipment that the worker uses
 4. Methods and procedures used in carrying out the duties

B. Nature of the work
 1. Mental and physical characteristics needed
 2. Repetitive aspects
 3. Dangerous aspects
 4. Unhealthful aspects

C. Relation of this job to other jobs
 1. Helpers and assistants
 2. Coworkers
 3. Coordination of the work of the job with that of other jobs

D. Physical conditions of the work environment
   1. Inside or outside work
   2. Illumination, ventilation, and noise

E. Conditions of employment
   1. Methods of selecting employees
   2. Length and hours of work periods
   3. Amounts and methods of pay
   4. Permanency or seasonality of the job
   5. Opportunities for promotion and advancement

For training purposes, job descriptions do not tell us enough about what the trainee must do to perform the job or what abilities and skills he needs to have in order to perform it. For training purposes, therefore, a detailed description of the tasks that make up a job is required.

TASK ANALYSIS

A task is the basic unit in a job description. A task description tells one thing that a worker does, what he does it to, what he uses as tools, and what he needs in the way of skills to do it. A typical statement of a task would be the following:

Activity	Performed on	Tool used	Specific skills
Inspects shaft of assembled motor to measure 1.25 inches ± 0.05 OD	Assembled motor	Micrometer	Rules for micrometer reading and for subtraction Skill in manipulating micrometer Ability to discriminate pressures

A job description tells about the job; a task description tells about the behavior of the worker who does the job. These behavior descriptions are often given in detailed *subtask* descriptions: "Turn setscrew of micrometer to fully expanded position, hold shaft of motor in position, tighten setscrew, turn on counter switch," etc.

Informal task analysis was the key to the success of JIT (Job Instruction Training), the most massive industrial training program ever attempted. The Bureau of Training of the War Manpower Commission set it up during World

War II to meet the critical problem of thousands of untrained new supervisors faced with millions of untrained new workers. Although the Bureau of Training was discontinued in 1945, the JIT program has continued as a part of the training programs of many companies. Well over ten million industrial, governmental, and union supervisors have completed the program.

The program consists of five 2-hour meetings of the conference type designed to teach supervisors how to teach a man to do a task. Each conference normally includes 12 supervisors and a trainer and never includes more than 20. The first session stresses the importance of training to production, the value of the superior's training skill, and the right way to instruct. It concludes with the presentation and demonstration by the trainer of the following four-step method in how to instruct:

Step 1
PREPARE the worker
Put him at ease.
State the job and find out what he already knows about it.
Get him interested in learning job.
Place in correct position.

Step 2
PRESENT the operation.
Tell, show, and illustrate one IMPORTANT STEP at a time.
Stress each KEY POINT.
Instruct clearly, completely, and patiently, but no more than he can master.

Step 3
TRY OUT performance.
Have him do the job—correct errors.
Have him explain each KEY POINT to you as he does the job again.
Make sure he understands.
Continue until YOU know HE knows.

Step 4
FOLLOW UP.
Put him on his own. Designate to whom he goes for help.
Check frequently. Encourage questions.
Taper off extra coaching and close follow-up.

In the following four sessions each participant brings in a task of a worker he is supervising and tries to instruct another participant in the task by using the four-step method. The other supervisors criticize his training demonstration.

The demonstration typically reveals weaknesses in the supervisor as a trainer: He rambles, he talks all the time while the trainee listens, he uses incomprehensible technical language, he takes far too much time, etc. Generally, his weaknesses can be traced to failures in his preparation for instruction. Specifically, his weaknesses are caused by a failure to analyze the task that he is trying to teach.

At the end of the second session, after the demonstrations of several supervisors have revealed the errors arising from an inadequate task analysis, the trainer introduces a sheet for making a simple task analysis. He demonstrates how to use the breakdown sheet by applying it to the task of tying a fire underwriter's knot, as shown in Table 9-3. He stresses that finding and teaching the trainee the key points are the most essential things in good instruction. He illustrates key points in different kinds of work:

When using a knife, a key point is to cut away from you.

When lifting a load with an overhead crane, a key point is to pull the chains or cables up taut, then *hesitate* for a moment to check the hitches before lifting the load.

When riveting, an important point is to know when to remove the pneumatic riveter. The key to this point is to *listen* to the riveting. The sound will change when the pieces are solidly together.

TABLE 9-3 Breakdown sheet for training man on a new task

Part: Twisted lamp cord	*Task: Tie fire underwriter's knot*
IMPORTANT STEPS IN THE TASK	KEY POINTS
Step: a logical segment of the task when something happens to ADVANCE the work	*Key point:* anything in a step that might injure the worker or make the work easier to do, i.e., "knack," "trick," special timing, bit of information, etc.
1. Untwist and straighten lamp cord	Hold 6 inches from the end
2. Make right-hand loop with right-hand-strand	Put stub in *front* of main strand
3. Make left-hand loop with left-hand-strand	Pull the strand *toward* you, then *under* the stub of the left-hand, and make loop *behind* the main strand
4. Put left-hand-strand through the right-hand loop	
5. Pull knot taut	Make ends *even* before pulling and pull until knot is *snug*.
6. _____	
7. _____	

SOURCE: War Manpower Commission (1945).

In mines, the strength and safety of the roof is determined by tapping the roof rock with a steel bar. The sound as the bar strikes the roof tells the story: Judging the sound is the key point.

When welding, there are two main points: (1) Apply the flame *ahead* of the weld, and (2) get the metal to the right heat, a matter of observing the color and behavior of the metal.

What are the benefits of JIT? In 1945, at the request of Congress, the War Manpower Commission sent more than 600 companies using the JIT program a questionnaire asking them to report any improvements they had noted. A large majority of the companies reported considerable reduction in training time as well as increases in productivity. In general, they were enthusiastic about the program (War Manpower Commission, 1945).

Effective training begins with clearly specified goals. Where job analysis can be used it is a valuable tool. However, even in human relations training programs where job analysis may not be helpful, goals should be stated as clearly as possible.

IMPROVING THE LEARNING SITUATION

Specifying and communicating the goals of training to the trainees helps produce motivated learners. Other improvements are also possible.

Feedback is central to the learning process. A learner must know the effects of his responses. Imagine trying to learn how to putt a golf ball if you are never permitted to see the ball after you hit it. Imagine trying to learn how to be a supervisor if you are never permitted to see, touch, or hear your subordinates. To improve the learning situation feedback should be as fast, accurate, and specific as possible. What a person learns is controlled by his knowledge of how well he is performing. *As knowledge of performance increases, both the speed and level of learning increase.*

While the stimulus-response model is a great aid in understanding the basic forms of learning, much of human learning is more complex than the simple "one stimulus-one response" model. Much of human learning involves verbal behavior, ideas, and the relationships among abstractions. Training which creates an environment where learners can discover relationships on their own initiative, have insights, and remain stimulated fosters understanding and improves the learning situation. The understanding of what is learned is important in most human learning and of central importance in the field of human behavior and relations.

Improvement in the learning situation can be obtained by proper selection of trainees. Instead of involving all personnel in the same training program an effort can be made to match trainees and programs. Selection procedures can be used to ensure that trainees have the background, intelligence, previous training, and motivation to benefit from the particular program. This would seem to be an easy task, but it is one which is frequently overlooked.

Finally and obviously, training can be improved by improving the quality of trainers. Men and women who know the value of job analysis, specification of goals, feedback, understanding, selection of trainees, and so forth are the key ingredients in improving training. Principles do not work by themselves; they require skilled and trained people to administer them.

THE EVALUATION OF TRAINING

Two psychologists who have devoted much of their professional lives to training have this to say about training in business and industry:

> Much must be done in implementing training before it can become a well-established, valuable management tool. Training has been taken on faith (as has much of general education), and little or no demands have been made to evaluate it in a rigorous fashion. Until training is submitted to systematic and carefully controlled research and evaluation, management will continue to use (or discard) a tool of unknown worth, or, worse yet, jump from bandwagon to bandwagon as training fads skip from the case method to role playing to brain storming and back again. These techniques *may* have merit. We do not know, and the research which will tell us remains to be done. The evidence submitted thus far raises more questions than it answers (McGehee and Thayer, 1961).

Other industrial psychologists also agree that much more research is essential for the significant improvement of industrial training. Yet managements generally take little note of this agreement, nor do they seem to remember it for long when they do. It is quite possible that all companies might most profitably spend 50 percent of their training budget in training research; it is unlikely that any spend as much as 1 percent. Companies find it easy to relax with their traditional training programs and difficult either to believe in the value of training research or to assemble the instruments, ideas, and skilled people necessary to conduct it.

Traditional training does *not* continue because of its proved effectiveness. Quite the contrary. On-the-job training, for example, is the most widely used, although a large-scale study by the Navy shows that it is not the most effective. The Navy has used two methods of training apprentices for its more than 60 occupations: (1) on-the-job training aboard ship or at a station where learning by doing is stressed but supplemented by informal class training; (2) formal training at Navy schools where both theory and job applications are taught. To test the relative effectiveness of the two training methods, Merenda (1958) obtained more than 3,000 pairs of apprentices, of whom one in each pair had gone to formal school and the other had had on-the-job training. The pairs were matched for general aptitude by their scores on the Navy General Classification Test. Training effectiveness was measured by comparing average scores obtained on the advancement examinations that are part of the promotion process. These examinations are made up without consultation with the schools and vary a great deal from one test administration to another. The results were decisively in favor of the formal school training: In nearly all the 30 occupations studied, the formally trained did better, and in two-thirds of them the differences were large.

Research results throw serious doubt on such small matters as details of the JIT program as well as on such large matters as on-the-job training. Lawshe and Cary (1952), for example, checked the value of the principle in step 3 that the supervisor should have the trainee "explain each KEY POINT as he does the job again." They gave 52 college students a pretest requiring the assembly of various types of levers, gears, and shafts. Pairs of individuals who had the same scores on the pretest were selected, one being assigned to the experimental group and the other to the control group. The experimental group was required to "talk back" the instructions given on the assembly of a different set of gadgets. The control group was not required to "talk back" but was required to do everything else in the same way. When the results were compared, the control group had made no more errors and had learned just as rapidly to assemble the gadgets as the experimental group. The tasks were learned as well without the application of the JIT principle as with it.

THE CRITERION PROBLEM

A company may be convinced of the value of training research, assign competent people to conduct it, and support it enthusiastically, but serious problems still remain. The greatest of these is the criterion problem. Solving it requires the development of reliable and valid measures to determine whether the training actually does what it is supposed to do.

The most common and the most useless criteria are the casual opinions of those who pay for the training. We have seen, for example, that the companies using the JIT program were enthusiastic about it and reported considerable reductions in training time, savings in manpower, increases in production, etc. Yet few had any records to support their assertions, and none had records that would permit them to separate the influence of training from the influence of engineering improvements. In general, management opinion is useful in identifying worthless programs but useless in separating the programs that seem good from those that are good.

The opinions of trainees are based on more direct experience with training than those of management. Still, their opinions are also of dubious value as a criterion. Satisfaction with a training program is often determined more by the trainee's interest in the kind of work he is learning to do and by his satisfaction with the conditions that surround the training than by the amount that he has actually learned.

The use of achievement tests at the end of training provides a better criterion than the opinions of either the sponsors or the trainees. Criteria of this type are illustrated by the objective achievement test given at the end of the IBM learning program and by the advancement examinations used to evaluate the effectiveness of on-the-job training in the Navy study. Fryer and Edgerton (1950) also used this kind of criterion in evaluating three different methods of training Air Force gunners. They used four groups: (1) one viewed a 15-minute animated humorous film, (2) one read for 30 minutes from an illustrated manual, (3) one was given a 30-minute illustrated lecture, and (4) a control group had no training. The criterion was an objective examination given after each type of training session. Although the film session was only half as long as the reading and lecture sessions, the trainees in the film session made significantly higher scores.

Achievement test results, although they are generally better criteria than trainee opinions, are still not ideal, for the aim of training is to improve performance not on achievement tests but on the job. The two kinds of performance are seldom closely related and sometimes are not related at all. Severin (1952), for example, summarized 10 studies relating training performance to later supervisory ratings of job performance. The median correlation was practically zero (.11). He also summarized the results of 58 studies in which training performance was compared with later productivity records. While some correlations were as high as .50, some were as low as zero. The median correlation was only .24. He concluded that it is not safe to assume a relationship between training performance and job performance. The assumption should be checked.

Job performance measures come closer than test scores to the ultimate goal of training. Job performance criteria, however, have seldom been used, for getting any such measure is always hard, and getting a good one is still harder. They are especially difficult to obtain in a service industry. Yet even here they can be found. Casbergue (1961) used a performance criterion to evaluate the success of a training program for waitresses from a hotel restaurant, a restaurant and bar, and a coffee shop. The criterion was the waitresses' sales checks. He compared the average size of the checks per customer for the 2 weeks before training with the average size for the 2 weeks after. The 15 waitresses showed gains from 0 to 19 percent, the average gain being 7.8. The measure was hard to get, because the checks of some restaurants did not show the number of guests served, some did not show which waitress did the serving, and some were destroyed at the end of each day.

Multiple criteria are better than single criteria. A trained waitress, for example, might sell more food in 2 weeks but irritate customers in doing so, become dissatisfied with her job and fellow waitresses, and quit. The Prudential Insurance Company set up multiple criteria to evaluate three widely accepted methods of training their debit agents (Baxter, Taaffe, and Hughes, 1953). The *individual training* method (used with 99 trainees) consisted of 1 week of prejob training by the local sales manager. The *individual training + conference* method (96 trainees) involved the same week of pretraining plus a week of conference training at the home office after 6 months of actual job experience. The *conference* method (80 trainees) involved 2 weeks of prejob training at the home office conducted by its training consultants. Agents trained by all three methods also had on-the-job training by their immediate supervisors.

The following criteria were used to evaluate the three methods at the end of 12 months:

Knowledge test: A 100-item objective examination covering the material taught in the training course.

Job satisfaction: A 43-item questionnaire covering all major aspects of the job.

Labor turnover: The percentage of trainees who had quit the company by the end of their first year.

Supervisory rating: The rating of each agent by his immediate supervisor in the nine areas of work that had been stressed in the training course.

Productivity: A composite figure for each agent which included all the types of insurance sales he had made during the year.

Cost of training: A cost figure including all direct training expenses: agent's compensation while in training; agent's meal, hotel, and traveling expenses while attending conferences; and the salaries of the training consultants. The time spent by local supervisors in training was not included.

The results of the evaluation are clear-cut: None of the training methods was significantly better on *any* of the criteria. The costs of the conference method, however, were more than five times the costs of the individual training method. The difference for the company as a whole could run into several hundred thousand dollars per year. The home office management decided to spend this difference on better supervisory training for district and staff managers.

Comparisons of training methods lead, more often than not, to similar negative conclusions. Consequently, training people often have a natural reluctance to evaluate their pet programs. Yet the measurement of the success of training is never the only, and seldom the most important, outcome of training evaluation. The development of more clearly defined training goals, more realistic instructional procedures, and better ways of giving trainees knowledge of results are normal by-products of an evaluation. In fact, much of the best training research is directed at just these questions: With which of several possible goals is it best for a particular program to concern itself? Which sequence of instruction is most effective? How much and what kind of feedback to the trainee regarding his progress is most beneficial?

Above all, every evaluation has the exciting possibility of turning up unexpected results that shed an entirely new light on the problem. Even the goose-egg results of the training of insurance agents led to an unanticipated action—a decision to train the supervisors of the agents rather than the agents themselves. Like research in the physical and biological sciences, psychological research may reap benefits from a surprising quarter.

Training is expensive, and so is research. If a less expensive program produces the same results as a more expensive one, obviously the cheaper program is to be preferred. But this raises the old question, What is the difference between the cost of training and the savings from it? Greenly (1941), for example, trained operators who had been on a job for years in a new way of changing knives on a flying shears. Was the training worth the expense? An evaluation of the training revealed that the average time for changing the knives was reduced from over 30 minutes to less than 20 minutes, at a saving to the company of more than $20,000 per year. Whether training is worth the cost can best be determined by training research. Companies are beginning to realize that paying for training without paying for an evaluation of the training means taking a costly risk.

THE EXPERIMENTAL DESIGN PROBLEM

A relevant measure of success is necessary in order to evaluate a training program. The presence of such a measure, however, is not sufficient; the experimental design must also provide assurance that the changes were actually due to the training. Some designs are listed below. They are arranged from the one giving the least to the one giving the most assurance that any results obtained could only be due to the influence of training.

1. Measures after training without a control group
2. Measures before and after training without a control group
3. Measures after training with a control group
4. Measures before and after training with a control group

A control group is a group which does not receive the training program or which receives a different kind of training from the one which is being evaluated. Below are examples of each of these designs used in the evaluation of actual human-relations programs.

1. Measures after training without a control group

Taking measurements after training is the easiest method of evaluation. It is nearly universal in all parts of our educational system. For example, students attend a course in the psychology of human relations in industry. At the end, they take a test covering their knowledge of the facts and principles of human relations. From their test scores, what can be realistically concluded about the effectiveness of the training? The answer is: almost nothing. While the test scores report how much different students know about the course content, they tell nothing for certain about when, where, and how they learned it. It is thus theoretically possible that the students learned all they knew *before* they took the course. In general, this method of evaluating a training program is the most naive and the least defensible.

The weaknesses of this evaluation method were demonstrated following a course in personal factors in management taken by more than a hundred supervisors of the Bell Telephone Company of Pennsylvania (Stroud, 1959). After the course, the supervisors were given a measure of consideration: the Leadership Behavior Description Questionnaire developed at Ohio State. The superiors of the supervisors also filled out the questionnaire as they felt the supervisors behaved. The average supervisor who took the course had a high consideration score (31.5), and his superiors gave him a still higher one (34.6). One might conclude that the training was successful, but it was not. A control group of supervisors who did not take the training also filled out the questionnaire and were rated by their superiors. The average supervisor in the control group had a consideration score practically as high as the average supervisor who took the course (30.9), and the control supervisor was rated almost as high by his superior (31.0).

While measures after training without a control group are the weakest of all designs, they are often all that is available. They are still much better than none, particularly when they supplement information obtained by more elaborate methods. For example, in one evaluation of the impact of a sensitivity training program on organizational effectiveness, various comparisons were made between executives who had taken the training and those who had not. Nine months after the training, 10 of the trained executives were also asked to indicate in a group discussion whether they felt that the training had had a positive impact upon their work life and, if so, what the impact had been. All 10 of the executives said they thought the impact had been positive. In their recorded comments one of them explained it in this way:

> Well, I would say that my job has been made easier by a magnitude of five. One way that I see the impact is to compare my relations with the individuals outside the division. God, what a mess! I feel completely frustrated. I go to meetings and it is clear that no one is levelling. Finally, I decide to say what I believe all of us are feeling. Well, it falls flat on its face. It is as if they say: "Look, we're in a swamp and we want to stay there."

Another of the executives said:

> You know, funny thing, if you ask me if I have changed, I guess I would say, "I hope so." I feel much less tense with this group around the table. My answer would be that I believe all of you had made great improvements! (Argyris, 1962).

2. Measures before and after training without a control group

The use of "after" measures alone does not show how much change, if any, took place during the period of training. The use of before and after measures does reveal changes. It does not show, however, whether the changes were due to the training. For example, the War Manpower Commission (1945) attempted to evaluate the effectiveness of its JRT and other J programs by asking 600 companies who had used them to estimate what changes had occurred in various areas since the programs had been installed. Table 9-4 gives the overall improvements which, if they are taken at face value, suggest that the programs were sensationally effective. This assumes, however, that nothing but training was responsible for the improvements. In reality, many things may increase effectiveness—improved equipment, better scheduling, improved supervision, better materials, better selection of employees, etc.

TABLE 9-4 Changes after the J programs, as reported by 600 companies

Area of change	Percent of companies reporting improvements of 25 percent or more
Reduction of grievances	96
Reduction in training time	92
Savings in manpower	73
Increase in production	63
Reduction in scrap	53

SOURCE: War Manpower Commission (1945).

The design for evaluation of the J, or Training Within Industry, programs was poor; the criterion also was poor, for it was based upon the opinions of the involved companies. It is unlikely that many of the companies had and used good records of grievances, training time, production, and scrap in reporting their opinions. Even with a good criterion, however, we could not know whether the changes were due to the training given.

The weaknesses of the before-after design without a control group can be seen by considering a before-after study which did include a control group. The 48 "trainees" were students in a general psychology class (H. C. Smith, 1955). The criterion instrument was objective and reliable: 90 multiple-choice questions covering facts, principles, and applications of psychology. The same test was given the first day of the course and again at the time of the final examination. The difference in the scores was the measure used to evaluate the effectiveness of the training.

Since one purpose of the study was to test the effectiveness of group discussions, the class was divided into five groups to work on group projects during class meetings. The students were told that their individual grades would be determined in part by the average improvement made by their group. At the end of the course, test scores showed that the average student in the discussion class had improved 24 points from the initial to the final test. Was this good or bad? The students did learn something about psychology during the course. Did they learn more than they would have learned in a lecture class?

An answer required a comparison of group discussion classes with lecture classes. Each student in the discussion class was matched with a student in a lecture class who had the same initial score and the same attitude toward participating in class. When the test scores of this control group were examined, it was found that the average student in the lecture class had improved 22 points from the initial to the final test. The small difference of two points (24 — 22) was insignificant. Overall, then, the discussion class was no better than the lecture class.

A secondary purpose of the study was to test the idea that students who like to participate do best in a discussion class. To measure attitudes toward participation, each student answered 10 questions like the following on a five-point scale from strong agreement to strong disagreement:

1. Do you like to participate in class discussions?
2. Do you think that class discussions are valuable?
3. Do you volunteer ideas to start discussion in class?

On the basis of the results of the scale, the five discussion groups were organized so that all the members of three groups had intermediate attitudes, all the members of the fourth group had very favorable attitudes, and the members of the fifth group had very unfavorable attitudes toward participation. The groups were also matched so that they had the same average score on the initial achievement test. At the end of the course, the members of all five groups filled out a "course satisfaction scale." The group with the most favorable attitudes toward participation reported the greatest satisfaction with the course. This group also had an average gain on the achievement test of 19 points. Was this good or bad? Again, an answer can only be found by comparison. Since the group with the least favorable attitudes toward participation gained 21 points, two points more than the most favorable group, it is clear that those who were most enthusiastic about participation learned no more from the discussions than those who were least enthusiastic.

Training evaluations should not only describe what happened but also, and usually more important, *explain* what happened. Measures after training without a control group usually give only a few descriptive clues and fewer explanatory ones. Before and after measures without a control group give more clues. As the number of controls increases and the overall design of the study is improved, describing and explaining become easier.

For example, Table 9-5 summarizes the results of the experiment in discussion and lecture training methods. All the groups were matched in achievement, but their initial attitudes toward participation varied from very favorable to very unfavorable. The left-hand column shows that enthusiasm for participation is no sign that the discussion method will be effective: those most favorable toward participation *learned more in the lecture* than in the discussion class. On the other hand, those with moderately favorable attitudes

TABLE 9-5 Before-after gains for groups in lecture and discussion classes

	Attitude toward participation			
Type of training	Very favorable	Intermediate	Very unfavorable	Total
Group discussion method	19	27	21	24
Lecture method	26	21	23	22
Difference between methods	−7	+6	−2	+2

did *significantly* better in the discussion class. Those unfavorable toward participation did about the same under both methods. How can these results be explained? It seems likely that people who have an urgent need to talk (the high participators) or not to talk (the low participators) do not benefit from the group discussion method. People who can talk *and* listen (the intermediate participators) do benefit.

3. Measures after training with a control group

After-training measures with control groups represent better design than before and after measures without controls. In fact, an after-training measure with a control group can give trustworthy evidence about both the impact of training and the reasons for the results. For example, one good study of this type evaluated the effectiveness of three training methods to improve listening and to increase skill in getting people to "open up" (Maier, Hoffman, and Lansky, 1960).

The three groups trained were three successive psychology classes. The first class (group 1) heard a series of lectures on causation and attitudes as they influence group behavior. The second class (group 2) heard the same lectures as group 1 as well as additional lectures on democratic leadership. The group 2 students also participated in weekly role-playing sessions. The third class (group 3) had all the training given to groups 1 and 2. In addition, group 3 had lectures on nondirective counseling and special sessions of practice in reflecting feeling.

The criterion of success was the quality of performance in a role-playing scene at the end of training. Each student was asked to play the role of Mr. Jones, a personnel manager, interviewing Mr. Smith. The following information was given to Mr. Jones:

You have a persistent problem with Mr. Smith, the manager of a large office group in the company. He objects to older employees and refuses to accept transfers. . . . You can't understand Smith's position and, therefore, you have decided to talk to him to see if you can't give them a better deal. Here are some things you should know about the behavior of the older girls: . . . (Maier et al., 1960).

There followed a list of 10 facts about the older girls. Some were favorable (absences lower, less tardiness), some were ambiguous, and some were unfavorable (more time in rest rooms, less willing to do unpleasant jobs). The measure of listening skill was the number of these facts introduced into the interview by the trainee. The lower the number the better his score, since it was assumed that the fewer the facts he introduced, the more he was listening to what Mr. Smith said. Conversely, the greater the number of facts introduced by Mr. Smith, the better the trainee was rated in the skill of getting people to open up.

Results showed that the training given group 3 was most effective in improving skill in listening; that given group 2, next; and that given group 1, least effective. That is, the average number of facts introduced by group 3 members was only 27 percent of the 10 facts available; by group 2 members, 35 percent; and by group 1 members, 41 percent. Skill in getting others to talk, however, was not increased by any of the training methods. That is, regardless of the kind of training, Mr. Smith introduced about the same percentage of facts. Taking the study as a whole, the impact even of group 3's training was small in spite of the large amount of time devoted to the development of these quite specific skills of listening and getting people to open up.

After-training measures with control groups have a big weakness: It is hard to make sure that the experimental and control groups are the same at the beginning of training. One way of overcoming this is to match the experimental and control groups on all important variables before training begins. Even when extremely careful matches are made, however, some critical initial difference in experience or intelligence may be overlooked and may bias the results. Another way of overcoming the weakness is to assign trainees to experimental and control groups in a random fashion. This solution requires large groups in order to reduce the influence of chance factors. The above study used such a method. It assumed that students from the same college taking the same course in different quarters were random samples. To reduce the influence of chance factors, it employed large groups: 275 students in group 1, 246 in group 2, and 145 in group 3.

The reader should be reminded that the design and criterion problems are quite separate. Thus, one might view the design of the above study as satisfactory but question the adequacy of role-playing performance as a criterion of listening skill. On the other hand, one might view the criterion as adequate but question the adequacy of the experimental design.

4. Measures before and after training with a control group

This method succeeds better than any other in avoiding the common pitfalls of training evaluation.

    1. Matching experimental and control groups on the before-training measures avoids the danger that the groups may not be comparable at the beginning.

    2. Taking the difference between before and after measures in the experimental group pinpoints the changes that occur during the training period.

    3. Comparing these changes with those that took place in the control groups isolates the changes caused by the training itself and allows comparison of it with other influences creating change.

Wherever the method can be used, therefore, it should be.

THE BELL TELEPHONE STUDY

The precision in results which is possible with this method means that confident conclusions can often be reached on the basis of a small training group. In 1953, for example, the Bell Telephone Company of Pennsylvania sent 17 of its executives to the University of Pennsylvania for a special 10-month program. The following year it sent 19, and a year after that, 21. The executives took courses in history, science, philosophy, and the arts that required an unusual amount of reading. The aim of the program was to meet the need of business for managers "with breadth and depth, with a broad knowledge of the world in which business exists and operates, with a sensitivity to the forces that affect our business system, and with an understanding of people and their motivations."

    The measures used to evaluate the effectiveness of the training included two standard achievement tests (The Graduate Record Test and the Cooperative General Culture Test) and measures of artistic, economic, and liberal values (Viteles, 1959). The tests were given at the start and at the end of the 10-month training. They were also given to 16 carefully matched executives of the company who did *not* participate in the training program.

    In spite of the relatively small number of trainees involved, the results were clear. All the trained groups made much higher scores on the achievement tests at the end of the training than they had at the beginning. They also made much higher scores in artistic and liberal values and much lower scores on economic values at the end of training than at the beginning. The changes were clearly greater than the changes in the control group during the same period. For example, 53 percent of the control group disagreed with the liberal statement, "Individual liberty and justice are not possible in socialistic countries." At the end of the program, 95 percent of the trained executives disagreed. In addition, 94 percent of the control group agreed with the statement, "Democracy depends fundamentally upon the existence of free business enterprise." Among the trained group, only 67 percent agreed with the statement.

It is clear that the executives changed a good deal as a result of their training; it is *not* clear that these changes had any beneficial influence on their job behavior. This is not a weakness of the experimental design but of the criteria, for no measures of job behavior were used in evaluating the effectiveness of the program. The absence of such measures is a serious limitation.

SUMMARY

Formal training programs are coming into wider use as companies become more conscious of the potential benefits of a better trained work force. Greater emphasis on motivating trainees, specifying training goals, using sound methods and principles of learning in training results in improved programs. The true value of training, however, remains more a matter of faith than of established fact, and companies often skip from bandwagon to bandwagon searching vainly among the methods that *may* be effective for those that truly are. Research is essential if the benefits of training are to be confirmed and if present training is to be improved.

Evaluation of training requires both good criteria and sound experimental design. From the least to the most satisfactory, the four major types of designs are as follows: (1) measures after training without a control group, (2) measures before and after training without a control group, (3) measures after training with a control group, (4) measures before and after training with a control group.

As criteria for evaluating the effectiveness of training, the opinions of management or of trainees are a poor substitute for realistic before-and-after measures of job performance. Better performance measures not only permit better evaluation; they also permit implementation of the most basic of learning principles: As knowledge of performance increases, the speed and level of learning increase.

10

WORK INCENTIVES

A man works only to satisfy his needs. Some needs are satisfied without work: He needs oxygen to breathe, and he has it. Some needs are satisfied by the work itself: He may like what he is doing so much that he works for the sake of working. The critical conditions for need satisfaction, however, are those that sometimes are and sometimes are not provided. These vary for the same worker from time to time, from one worker to another on the same job, and from one job to another. In general, an *incentive* is any condition that will satisfy a need. More specifically, it is any critical condition that causes a man to behave in a certain way. Most specifically, it is any critical condition that is *deliberately controlled* in order to get a man to behave in a desired way.

A company desires its employees to be more productive, more loyal, and more interested in their work, and it therefore attempts to control the conditions that increase productivity, integration, and morale. Broadly, anything that it deliberately does to achieve these ends is an incentive. Such an incentive, however, may be weak or strong and may or may not gain the desired end. The more we learn about men at work, the more effective incentives we find, and the greater becomes the number that a company can use. This chapter will first examine the best-known, oldest, and most widely used production incentive: money. It will then take up less well-known integration and morale incentives.

PRODUCTIVITY INCENTIVES

Money satisfies needs. Even so, using money to get men to do more work is a complicated task. For one thing, any company has a limited amount of money and for a second thing, very little is known about what money means to people and about the relationship between money and effective performance. After reviewing the research on the role of financial compensation in motivation Opsahl and Dunnette (1966) concluded that,

> . . . there is probably less solid research in this area than in any other field related to worker performance. We know amazingly little about how money either interacts with other factors or how it acts individually to affect job behavior . . . . Speculation, accompanied by compensation fads and fashions, abounds; research studies designed to answer fundamental questions about the role of money in human motivation are all too rare (p. 94).

Many people find it difficult to talk about what money means. Most of us treat matters of salary and wages in a highly secretive fashion, being reluctant to tell anyone how much we make, and being equally reluctant to ask others how much they make. Money comes close to being a taboo subject. Lawler (Dunnette, et al., 1967) argues strongly that organizations should adopt more open and public policies about pay. He stresses that it is hard to be rational about money matters when basic facts are unknown.

Opsahl and Dunnette (1966) list five theories about how money may operate as an incentive.

1. Money may be a *Generalized Conditioned Reinforcer*. Money is often associated with basic need satisfiers, such as food and drink. Consequently, we may eventually generalize the relationship. That is, we come to accept money as a way of satisfying needs, a so-called secondary reinforcer.

2. Money may be a *Conditioned Incentive*. Money is commonly associated with other more basic incentives. As a result, we may eventually generalize the relationship and accept money as an incentive. This theory can be

demonstrated under laboratory conditions. However, it is hard to demonstrate in real work situations for it is hard to find an incentive that is more basic than money.

3. Money may be an *Anxiety Reducer*. Most of us feel anxious when we do not have money. Somehow as we grow up in this culture we learn that we feel "bad" when we do not have money and that we feel "good" when we do have money. Money reduces our anxiety and makes us feel better.

4. Money may be a *"Hygiene Factor."* One general theory of what motivates people at work states that there are certain features of a job, such as a person's autonomy and responsibility that are "motivators" (Herzberg, Mausner and Snyderman, 1959; Herzberg, 1966). Increases in these features increase job satisfaction and performance. Other features of the job are "hygiene factors." These need to be maintained and occasionally increased in order to prevent dissatisfaction. They do not, however, increase satisfaction. Money is such a "hygiene factor." Some money keeps us from becoming dissatisfied. More money, however, does not make us more satisfied. This theory has generated more research than any of the others. However, results are still inconclusive (Whitsett and Winslow, 1967; House and Wigdor, 1967).

5. Money may be an *"Instrument"* for gaining desired outcomes. Vroom (1964) believes that the meaning of money as an incentive in any particular situation depends on two conditions: Can money be used as an instrument to attain some desired result? Is there a high expectation that by behaving in a certain way monetary reward will follow? For example, money will be an incentive for a person if he thinks that money will lead to a goal he values, say security, *and* if he expects that working harder will give him more money. If he does not see money as an instrument for attaining what he wants, say watching the sun set, or if he does not expect to get more money for working harder, then money will not be an incentive for him. Locke, Bryan, and Kendall, 1968, recognize that as an incentive money may have many different effects; but they conclude that

> "It must be stressed that whatever the effects of monetary incentives on performance, their *ultimate* impact should be a function of the degree to which the individual *values* money as compared to other incentives and his perception of the degree to which a given course of action is seen as a *means* of attaining this value. . ." (p. 120).

In addition to these five theories, an increasing amount of research is being done on *equity theory*. This theory holds that the worker is satisfied with his pay when he perceives that it is equitable or fair. In order to be considered fair, what the worker gets out of the job (pay, fringe benefits, status, etc.) must be in balance with what he puts into the job (hard work, skill, training, education, etc.). Deviations above or below what the worker sees as the balance point result in changes in his attitudes or his performance (Smith and Cranny, 1968). The equity point that a person sets is entirely subjective. He does, however, have an objective guide for his judgment. He may compare his ratio of inputs and outcomes to the input-outcomes ratio of some other person. This relationship is expressed in the formula

$$\frac{\text{my inputs}}{\text{my outcomes}} \quad \text{compared to} \quad \frac{\text{his inputs}}{\text{his outcomes}}$$

An example of the kinds of studies which equity theory produces is the following (Adams and Rosenbaum, 1962). Students were hired as part-time interviewers. One half of them were told that they did not really have the qualifications for the job but that since the work needed to be done quickly they would be hired. They were also told that because of a technicality they would be paid the same hourly rate as people who were fully qualified for the job. The other half of the students were told that they were fully qualified for the job and were hired. All students then went to conduct interviews for two and one-half hours. None of the students suspected they were taking part in an experiment. The results of this study showed that those students who believed they were not qualified worked harder than the other students. The "inadequate" interviewers conducted significantly more interviews than the "fully qualified" interviewers. Why? Equity theory would say that the students who thought that they were being paid too much in relation to their skill level did more interviews so that the combined skill-hard work input would balance the high pay outcome. Students who felt that their skill (input) justified their wage (outcome) did not feel that they had to work so hard.

Inequity thus may occur in two ways. The outcomes (wages) may be too low compared to input (effort). In this case, the worker is dissatisfied. The outcomes (wages) may be too high compared to input (effort). In this case, the worker feels guilty. People can apparently tolerate guilt better than dissatisfaction (Jacques, 1961; Pritchard, 1969).

Equity theory is not a refined theory that can answer many questions with confidence (Weick, 1966). It does meet one vital test of a good theory. It has produced a great deal of research and provided some answers while generating many interesting questions.

Every company has limited money and limited knowledge about how money operates. Still, a company must decide how it will use money as an incentive. Our economic system is based on monetary rewards. The two most generally accepted incentive principles are (1) the more important the job a man has, the more money he gets, and (2) the more a man produces, the more money he gets.

THE MORE IMPORTANT THE JOB, THE MORE PAY

Straight time is by far the most common method of paying workers. That is, companies pay their workers not for the work they do, but for the hours they spend at work. The typical time worker also gets other kinds of payments: paid vacations, sick leave, pensions, paid rest periods, and so on. These fringe benefits continue to climb: in 1947 they averaged 15 percent of payroll costs; in 1957, nearly 25 percent. Time payments and fringe benefits are not direct incentives to produce. They are, however, indirect ones, for the worker who does not produce may lose his job. Furthermore, the poor producer will lose his chance to gain a better job with higher pay.

Before workers can be paid according to the importance of their jobs, the relative importance of their jobs must be known. *Job evaluation* is a systematic method for determining the relative value of jobs. The relative value of some jobs is easily agreed upon: the job of president is more important than the job of washroom porter. The relative value of other jobs is not so easily agreed upon. Is the job of supervisor more important than the job of a chemist? Is the job of a zinc etcher more important than the job of a lathe operator? As the number and complexity of jobs have increased, the demand for a systematic method of evaluating their importance has risen. About three out of four companies now have a formal job evaluation system.

The ranking of jobs from the least to the most important is the simplest systematic method of job evaluation. Using this method, job evaluators typically study the descriptions of a group of jobs and then rank them from the least to the most valuable.

The *point system*, the most popular method of job evaluation, is more complicated than ranking. The first step under this system is to select factors that can be used to compare all jobs: the education necessary, experience necessary, physical demands, responsibility involved, etc. Then each job is rated on each factor. For example, a job may be rated as requiring "little," "some," "average," "considerable," or "great" education, experience, responsibility, etc. Then points are assigned to each rating on each factor. For example, "little" may be 1 point; "some," 2 points; "average," 3 points, etc. The same rating on different factors may have the same number of points. For example, average education and average working conditions both may count 3 points. Usually, however, the same ratings on different factors are given different weights. That is, while average physical demands are given 3 points, average education may be given 6. Whatever the number of job factors and however the points are assigned, the evaluator eventually totals the number of points for each job. The larger the total, the more important the job is judged to be.

Evaluations by the point system have the virtue of being quite reliable. For example, Harding, Madden, and Colson (1960) had five evaluators rate 50 representative Air Force jobs using 10 factors: knowledge, physical skill, adaptability and resourcefulness, responsibility for money and materials, responsibility for directing others, responsibility for safety of others, physical effort, attention, job conditions, and military combat. Even though the supervisors and craftsmen who did the ratings were given no opportunity to discuss them with each other, the total points the different raters assigned the different jobs were in very close agreement (overall correlation: .95).

How many factors is it desirable to use? Essentially, the ranking method uses one factor (the overall value of the job) in evaluating jobs, while the point system may use as many as 20. The best present answer seems to be much closer to 1 than to 20. Myers (1958), for example, evaluated 82 jobs in the home office of a life insurance company by the use of 17 factors: mental requirements, frequency of decisions, difficulty of judgment, constant attention to details, education, experience, effect of inaccurate work, review on work, persuasion, confidential nature of work, physical demands, etc. He then analyzed the results to find out what was really determining the ratings of different jobs. A single factor accounted for about 90 percent of the differences in points: overall value of the job. That is, if the raters had been asked to rank the jobs, the rankings would have been in close agreement with the results of the 17-factor point system. And, of course, a great deal of time would have been saved.

Job evaluation is a necessary first step in applying the principle that the more important the work a man does, the more money he should get. The results of the point system, however, are too cumbersome, for the range from the lowest to the highest job generally runs into the hundreds of points. To meet this problem, the wide range of points is converted into a much smaller range of *labor grades*. A labor grade, in other words, is simply a range of points. For example, the National Metal Trades Association uses the system shown in Table 10-1 for converting job points to labor grades. Any job that was assigned total points between 360 and 381 would fall into labor grade 1, etc. Of course, the range of points for a labor grade varies from one situation to another depending upon the number of labor grades used, the number of factors rated, and the number of points assigned to each rating of

TABLE 10-1 An example of the relation between job points and labor grades

Labor grades	Range of job points
1 (highest)	360–381
2	338–359
3	316–337
4	294–315
5	272–293
6	250–271
7	228–249
8	206–227
9	184–205
10 (lowest)	162–183

each factor. The total number of points for the most valuable job may go into the thousands.

Finally, a pay range is assigned to each labor grade. For example, the hourly pay for the man in a labor grade 1 job may range from $9 to $10; in labor grade 2, from $8 to $9; in labor grade 3, from $7 to $8, etc. Thus, paying men according to the importance of the work they do requires, in turn, descriptions of the jobs they do, evaluations of the jobs based on the descriptions, assignment of labor grades based on the evaluations, and determination of a pay range for each grade.

THE MORE PRODUCTION, THE MORE PAY

When a worker is paid for his time, it is understood that he is actually being paid for his production. Production incentives make the understanding explicit. The variations in such systems are almost endless. Straight piece rates, piece rates with a guaranteed minimum, differential piece rates, group piece rates, group bonuses, premium plans, task and bonus plans, and measured day rates are among the most popular. Still, three out of ten companies in 1957 had other plans. Some of the plans are simple and some are complicated, some require careful time studies and some do not, some require efficiency ratings by supervisors and some do not, some reward the individual and some reward the group, and some guarantee a minimum wage and some do not. All, however, aim to pay the worker for his production and to pay him more for more production.

The *straight piece-rate* system is the simplest. The formula for figuring earnings under this system is:

Earnings = rate per piece X number of pieces

The rate per piece may be established on the basis of the past performance of workers or on the basis of carefully established time standards. Without the use of established time standards, workers are likely to restrict production for fear of rate cutting by the management, and managers are likely to be tempted to cut rates. While no minimum wage is required by the logic of the system, *piece rates with a guaranteed minimum* are much more common than piece rates without a minimum. In fact, the former is the most popular of all incentive systems; more than one in five companies make some use of it.

The *differential piece-rate* system was the idea of Frederick W. Taylor, who fathered scientific management early in the century. Under his plan, a worker is paid a lower rate per piece when his total production is under the standard set and a higher rate when it is at or above the standard. For instance, if the standard calls for 100 pieces per day at 20 cents per piece, a worker's rate in case he failed to make the standard would be less, say 19 cents. At the extreme, a worker could earn $20 for making the standard (.20 X 100) but only $18.81 for making one under the standard (.19 X 99). The system gives the worker a strong incentive to make the standard. However, it places a heavy burden on the management to keep working conditions standard so that a worker's low production is not due to things beyond his control. The system has never been widely used.

The *group piece-rate* system is nearly as popular as the individual one. It is simpler to run, for instead of keeping track of the productivity of the individuals in a group, the company need only keep track of the productivity of the group as a whole. The Scanlon plan, a company-wide *group bonus* system, illustrates the advantages of the group system. However, the presence of too many beginners or loafers in a group can disrupt its efficient operation.

The various *premium plans* have as their distinctive ingredient the saving of production time. The formula for computing a worker's earnings under the Halsey plan (the oldest plan of this type) is as follows:

$$\text{Earnings} = \text{rate per piece} \times \text{actual time} + \frac{\text{rate per piece} \times (\text{allowed} - \text{actual time})}{2}$$

Suppose, for example, that a worker is paid $2 to produce a piece and is allowed 2 hours to produce it. Actually, however, he finishes it in 1 hour. By substituting in the formula, it can be seen that he would be paid $3 for producing the piece. The plan is simple and easy to introduce, and it requires no great change in normal working conditions. Its weakness is that it encourages the worker who has different kinds of work to spend his time on the kind he can produce the fastest, for by doing so he can make more money. It is most often used when a company is in the process of changing from a straight-time system to some other system based upon carefully established standards.

The *task and bonus plan* was devised by H. L. Gantt, an associate of Taylor. It pays on the basis of standard time. If a worker produces less than the standard set for the day's work, he is paid a guaranteed minimum. If he produces at or above the standard set, however, he is paid according to the formula.

Earnings = 1 1/3 X rate per piece X standard time

Suppose, for example, a worker is paid $1 for each piece and the standard time for completing it is 1 hour. If he produces less than eight pieces in an 8-hour day, then he is paid the minimum wage of $8. If he produces eight pieces, however, he is paid 1 1/3 times $8, or $10.67. If he produces sixteen pieces, then he is paid 1 1/3 times $1 times 16 hours, or $21.33. The system is equivalent to a high piece-rate system with a minimum guaranteed wage.

Under the *measured day rate* system a worker earns his base pay on a system. Beyond this, however, he is given bonuses according to his versatility, quality of work, dependability, quantity of production, and other factors. The system is comprehensive. It does, however, require detailed and repeated ratings of the worker by his supervisors. There are numerous serious problems involved in the rating of workers, as we shall see in the next chapter.

THE MORE PAY, THE MORE PRODUCTION?

Naturally, companies who use incentive systems think they work well. For example, 117 companies surveyed by the Dartnell Corporation in 1948 were of the opinion that their systems were resulting in higher productivity, lower unit costs, lower absenteeism, higher morale, etc. A similar but larger survey in 1953 asked for and got a more quantitative picture. The average company reported a 39 percent increase in production, a 12 percent increase in take-home pay, and a 12 percent decrease in labor costs as a result of its incentive system.

Fewer and fewer companies, however, seem to think well of incentive systems. They have declined in popularity over the past 40 years in both the United States and Great Britain. Hunt and Turner (1967) point out that the enthusiasm for using wage incentives apparent in the 1940's decreased greatly in the 1950's and continues to decrease today. Table 10-2 shows the percentage of companies in this country in 1930, 1940, 1950 and 1957 using the systems that were discussed in the last section.

The 1930 figures are based on the mailed questionnaire replies of 195 companies employing over 2 million workers; the 1957 figures are based on the replies of 852 companies employing over 6 million workers. The figures

TABLE 10-2   Percent of companies using various wage incentives

Type of incentive system	Year			
	1930	1940	1950	1957
Piece rate with minimum	21	39	33	23
Group piece rate	29	22	18	16
Group bonus	10	12	9	7
Measured day rate	—	10	6	6
Premium plan	18	7	7	6
Straight piece rate	50	35	7	5
Task-and-bonus plan	9	11	6	4
Differential piece rates	6	3	2	2

SOURCE: Data from Scott et al. (1961), p. 572.

must be viewed with some reservations: the companies selected were more personnel-minded than the average, and the validity of mailed questionnaire replies is always somewhat doubtful. Yet the trends are consistent and large. Compared to the 1957 companies, for example, twice as many of the 1940 companies reported using one or more of these incentive systems. Between 1930 and 1940 there was a large shift from straight piece-rate systems to piece-rate systems with a guaranteed minimum. Except for this shift, however, the decade-by-decade decline for all systems is remarkably consistent. Why?

More and more companies are finding it difficult to devise incentive systems to fit the kinds of work created by modern technology. Bricklaying is ideal for an incentive system: Bricks are laid by a single man, the number he lays can be easily measured, and his productivity is the result of the energy and skill he applies. Jobs are moving away from this ideal. More and more of them produce a service rather than a material product. Material production is, more and more, the result of group rather than individual effort. The production of an assembly line is hard to put on an individual incentive system; the production of an automated factory is impossible.

Many observers now believe that individual incentives are devices left over from an earlier age. Katz (1964), for example, states:

The traditional philosophy of the free-enterprise system gives priority to an individual reward system based upon the quality and quantity of the individual effort and contribution. This type of motivation may operate effectively for the entrepreneur or even for the small organization with considerable independence of its supporting environment. It encounters great difficulty, however, in its application to large organizations which are in nature highly interdependent, co-operative structures (p. 139).

Incentive systems can be devised to fit the most unlikely situations. The more unlikely the situation, however, the higher the cost of an appropriate incentive system tends to be. Cost alone is not a sound basis for rejecting an incentive system, for it is the earnings of the system minus its costs that determines its value. Still, more and more companies seriously doubt that the earnings outweigh the costs.

One reason for their doubt is that a company, before putting a job on an incentive system, is almost certain to study it with care. The study is likely to result in better methods of doing it. The better system, companies are beginning to believe, accounts for most of the gains made. Some evidence supports the belief. For instance, extensive studies of English boot and shoe workers under day-rate and piecework plans showed that the pieceworkers were producing about twice as much as day workers. The same study, however, made a comparison of the way the jobs of English and American boot and shoe workers' jobs were organized. The American jobs were more efficiently organized, and the American day workers were producing nearly as much as the English pieceworkers. The greater productivity of English pieceworkers over day workers might well have been the result of the better organization of the piecework jobs (Rothe, 1960).

The most serious doubts grow out of an increasing awareness that the most ingenious incentive system is a poor substitute for the solution of the human problems faced by particular workers on a particular job. There is an increasing awareness that there is no magic wage formula which always works, that a formula is a symbol of a way of organizing human beings to satisfy human needs, and that the same formula can symbolize quite different ways with quite different effects. How the worker—rightly or wrongly—sees the incentive in relation to his own needs, and how he perceives the intentions of the managers, are the important determinants of a successful system.

Some companies have learned that workers may not see more money as providing them with more need satisfaction. Young girls in an English factory, for example, threaded needles for older girls to use. Under the day-rate plan, they threaded an average of 96 dozen per day. The management devised a piecework plan to increase productivity: The more they threaded the more they were paid. The average dropped to 75 dozen. They were then put on a task plan: When they threaded 100 dozen, they could go home with a full day's pay. This plan worked, for the girls finished on an average of 2 1/2 hours earlier. Why did the second plan work and not the first? More money was no incentive for the girls, because their parents were taking all they earned. More free time, however, was something the girls wanted and would work for.

Other companies have learned that while workers generally want more money, they often don't want it badly enough to do an unpleasant job faster. In an English candy factory, for example, 10 girls wrapped pieces of candy, unwrapped poorly wrapped pieces, and packed the finished pieces in boxes. They rotated on these operations. On a day-rate basis, they produced a fairly constant rate of 100 units per week. The company first put them on a competitive bonus system and then on an individual piecework system. Under the bonus system, the girls nearly doubled their speed of wrapping; under the piece-rate system, they nearly tripled it. Under the bonus system, the girls improved their speed of packing; under the piece-rate system, they improved their speed of wrapping still more, nearly doubling their rate. Their speed of unwrapping the poorly wrapped pieces, however, did not increase under either the bonus or the piecework system. The unwrapping was apparently such an unpleasant task that it remained uninfluenced by the system.

A study in a large Middle Western manufacturing plant showed the variety and the power of the impact that the same incentive system had on 300 skilled machinists. Dalton (1948) found that only 3 percent of the men were responding to the system with enthusiasm, 20 percent were fighting against it, and the remaining 77 percent were making some compromise with it. Jerry Bates, the informal leader among the fighters, said:

> The incentive is just a trick to beat the working man. They didn't put it in here to make us rich. We know that. That's why we try to stick together—so we can use them some while they're using us. This slowing up is just like holding back butter and shirts to get high prices. You know yourself that the big factories, farmers, and producers of all kinds always lay down when prices begin to fall or when they see a chance to push 'em up. Well, in a way, we're doing the same damn thing—and we got just as much right to do it.

Of the nine men who were responding enthusiastically to the incentive system, Jim Watson was outstanding in producing more than twice the normal rate. He was fifty years old, a strong family man who ran a small farm on the side and had little interest in community or factory social life. He said:

> When them sons-of-bitches start buying my groceries they can tell me how much bonus to make. Until then, I'll make as much as I can. I want to send my girl to school and as long as I can make the money to do it, I'm not letting a damn union stop me. A lotta these guys think a union will get them big money for doin' nothing. Well, I joined to shut them up. So I'll make as much as I can. They're always puttin' pressure on the inspectors to get my work rejected, but I'll get by. Sometimes I think this is the damndest country in the world. If you need a little help,

everybody runs from you. If you make a little money everybody's down on you. Well, they can stay down on me. If I can run 400 percent, by God, I'll do it.

Companies are also learning that even an effective individual incentive system may be a mixed blessing, for it weakens essential cooperation between workers. In a steel mill, for example, one shift was breaking all production records, and the pay envelopes of the workers were bulging. The workers on the second shift, however, were disgruntled, for the employees on the high-producing shift were skipping the housekeeping duties. This left the second shift with clean-up work that reduced its tonnage. Individual incentives tend to create resentment among workers not on the system, among workers on jobs with more difficult standards, and among workers who suffer from the skimping on needed cooperative effort.

In general, companies are learning that efforts to motivate men by paying them according to their productivity are sometimes successful but are almost as often unsuccessful. Money is *one* potent incentive, for it not only provides a worker with the means of satisfying his needs but also gives him a knowledge of results, a measure of how well he is doing. Still, unless the system promotes integration and morale as well as immediate productivity, it is likely to do as much harm as good. The nearly universal hostility of unions toward incentive systems is only the most obvious signs that such systems often do not promote integration and morale.

INTEGRATION INCENTIVES

Money as a production incentive is of uncertain value. As an integration incentive, as a way of keeping a man tied to the organization, it has a much more certain value. Increasing wages reduces the chances of a man quitting and increases the chances that he will be loyal to the company. Companies, consequently, try to pay higher wages in times of full employment and to pay higher wages to their best men at all times in order to hold them.

In using money as a production incentive, a company relates money to a worker's productivity. In using money as an integration incentive, a company pays him well to stay a week, better to stay a year, and best to stay a lifetime. Money works better as an integration incentive because it better fulfills the basic desire of the worker for job security. The typical worker wants sure money before more money.

The particular incentive which is seen as providing security varies. Nealey (1964) obtained from over 1,000 members of the International Brotherhood of Electrical Workers their preferences for six different employee benefit programs. Each of the plans would cost the company approximately the same amount of money. The six plans were:

1. The company will pay the cost of an additional $50.00 a month pension to be added to my retirement benefit.
2. I will get a six percent raise.
3. The normal workweek shall be cut to 37 1/2 hours without any reduction in weekly earnings.
4. The company will pay the entire cost of full hospital insurance for myself and my family.
5. It will be agreed that all regular employees must be members of the union. (The union shop will be put into effect.)
6. I will have three weeks' paid vacation a year in addition to my present vacation; the extra vacation to be taken when I choose.

For the total group of over 1,000 workers the hospital insurance option was the one most preferred. The shorter work week was the option least preferred. Preferences, however, varied with age: Younger people preferred more hospital insurance. Older people were more interested in pensions. Table 10-3 shows how important the various benefits were to people in different age groups.

The strength of the need for security varies. Low-status workers value it more than high-status workers, old workers value it more than young workers, and the uneducated value it more than the educated. Overall, however, the average worker ranks job security as the most essential aspect of his job. Herzberg et al. (1957), for example, have summarized the results of 150

TABLE 10-3   Preference for benefits related to age

Benefit	Order of preference by age				
	Under 30	30–39	40–49	50–59	60–65
Hospital insurance	1	1	1	2	2
Union shop	3	2	2	3	4
6% raise	4	3	4	4	3
3-week vacation	2	4	5	5	5
Pension	5	5	3	1	1
37.5 hour week	6	6	6	6	6

SOURCE: Data from Nealey (1964).

studies in which different job incentives, including job security, were ranked by various workers. Leading the list was job security. Employment and the money it brings are the basic requirements for need satisfaction; unemployment is the most basic source of frustration. Yet statistics on unemployment consistently show that between three and six percent of workers are out of jobs. Among women, young workers and minority group workers, as many as twenty-five percent are without jobs. Little wonder, therefore, that workers rank job security high and like companies that provide it.

The income of a worker and his family may be threatened by unemployment, ill health, retirement, or death. As Table 10-4 shows, practically all companies provide some security in some of these areas. They are providing more all the time. Between 1930 and 1957, for example, the percentage of companies with group life insurance plans, health insurance plans, and private pension systems doubled. Such plans enhance company integration. They not only increase the chances that an employee will stay with a company but also increase his cooperativeness. Of all areas of management action, for example, workers are likely to be most resistant to technological innovations, for they see them as a threat to their job security. The more secure in his job a worker is, the more cooperative about such changes he is likely to be.

When activity decreases to the point where it is necessary to reduce the force, all employees on a *plant-wide* basis *within each occupation* shall be considered on the *basis of service*, and those having the least accredited service shall be selected for layoff.

TABLE 10-4 **Percent of companies using various integration incentives**

Type of integration incentive	Percent of firms providing the incentive *
Insurance coverage for	
Doctors' bills	94
Hospitalization	93
Retirement plan (other than Social Security)	70
Group life	70
Disability income	54
Accidental death and dismemberment	53
Major medical	46
Other incentives	
Free medical examinations	30
Paid sick leave	26
Layoff allowance	11

*Based on 111 firms surveyed.

SOURCE: Data from Greene (1964).

The statement is a modern form of the oldest type of job security, a seniority system of layoffs. Under this system, if it becomes necessary to lay off half the electricians, for example, all of them would be considered as an occupational group. Then, starting with those that had the shortest employment with the company, the required number would be laid off. Often the decline in activity requires laying off more in some occupations than in others. Under such circumstances, the system generally allows workers of greater seniority in one occupation to displace workers of less seniority in another *if* the worker with greater seniority can learn to do the work without an extensive retraining period.

The seniority system lets the men know where they stand in relation to each other; it does not decrease the chance that many of them will be unemployed and unpaid for long periods. Guaranteed minimum employment systems do. They guarantee work for a minimum number of weeks per year (19 of 32 companies reporting such plans in 1957 guaranteed 52 weeks of employment). The Procter and Gamble Company has such a plan that was begun in 1923. The Nunn-Bush Shoe Company and George A. Hormel Company also have well-known guaranteed employment plans. Most of the companies originating such plans already had well-established work loads to begin with: banking and insurance companies, public utilities, mail-order houses, etc. The plans, first introduced by managements with some union resistance, are now being strongly advocated by many unions. These plans, along with private and public unemployment compensation arrangements are steadily raising the level of integration incentives offered by companies competing for loyal workers.

Integration of the work force is also achieved by providing salaries for all workers. Companies that have salaries for all workers report good experiences. The Gillette Safety Razor Company, for example, began its plan in 1955 and after several years of operation reported a decrease in absenteeism (Kaponya, 1962). Salaries give workers a feeling of job security. Salaries also indicate that the company trusts the workers. If a man can be hired as a manager and trusted to earn his salary, why not trust people at other levels of the organization?

MORALE INCENTIVES

A company's incentives are the conditions that it controls in order to increase productivity, integration, or morale. Morale incentives are the most comprehensive. Conditions that increase productivity may actually decrease integration and morale, conditions that increase integration may increase or decrease productivity and morale, but the conditions that increase the worker's intrinsic interest in his work also increase productivity and integration.

The more careful selection of workers, in order to hire those who are not only capable of but also interested in doing a particular job, is one obvious way to improve morale incentives. We are, however, so used to thinking of an incentive as something tangible that we give a worker for working that it is hard to think of improved selection as an improved incentive. Yet it is one, for selection is a critical condition that a company can control in order to get a worker to be more productive, more loyal, and more interested in his work. In fact, better selection may be a more effective incentive than more money or a bigger pension, since it may well have a more significant effect on productivity, integration, and morale.

Companies, of course, try to control the conditions of selection even though they do not think of the process as an incentive. Still, they are more likely to use selection as a production rather than a morale incentive. For example, they make heavy use of intelligence, aptitude, and dexterity tests that predict the ability to produce, and light use of tests that predict interest in the job. One reason is that ability tests are generally more reliable and valid than interest tests. This is true, however, partly *because* management's concern with ability tests has led to greater effort being put into their development.

THE DEVELOPMENT OF UNINTERESTING JOBS

Morale depends upon getting an interested worker on a job. It also depends upon having an interesting job to give him. Almost everyone accepts the idea that some kinds of work are more interesting than other kinds. Nonetheless, it is a strange and uncomfortable idea to most managers that they can *control* the interest of jobs, that they can make jobs more interesting and they can make them less interesting. Many, however, have succeeded so well in making jobs less interesting that they appear to have had an effective course in principles for manufacturing dull jobs. Following are a few of these principles.

The introduction of *mechanical pacing* on a job is one of the surest ways to make it not only less interesting but actually painful. Being paced by a machine so that every few seconds or minutes there is the same operation to do again is one of the hardest things for most workers to bear. On an automobile assembly line, for example, workers say:

> The job gets so sickening—day in and day out plugging in ignition wires. I get through with one motor, turn around, and there's another motor staring me in the face. It's sickening.

> The work isn't hard, it's the never-ending pace. . . . The guys yell "Hurrah" whenever the line breaks down. . . . You can hear it all over the plant (Walker and Guest, 1952).

The workers generally reported that their previous jobs had been more interesting, but the pay and security provisions on the assembly-line jobs were better. Job interest is expendable; the hungry man will perform dull work to get food, the lonely man to get friends, and the family man to provide better for his children.

Even on mechanically paced jobs, workers are different: most dislike them but some like them. Among assembly-line workers, for example, some said:

> I like doing the same thing all the time. I'd rather stay right where I am. When I come in in the morning, I like to know exactly what I'll be doing.
>
> I repeat the same thing day in and day out. I like it—I can do it fast.
>
> I like to repeat the same thing, and every car is different anyway. So my job is interesting enough (Walker and Guest, 1952).

Some managers see in these differences a way to avoid having bored workers on repetitive jobs. If they can select more effectively those who like or at least can tolerate such jobs, they will reduce the problem of boredom.

There has developed a widely held stereotype of the kind of person who does not suffer from boredom: he is an inferior and insensitive type—placid, extroverted, happy, unable to daydream, uncreative, and above all, unintelligent. Unfortunately for those seeking the selection way out of the boredom problem, the results of psychological research do not support the stereotype. P. C. Smith (1955), for example, studied 72 women workers doing light, repetitive work in a small knitwear mill in northern Pennsylvania. She measured their level of boredom by objective and subjective means; objectively, by such indicators of boredom as talking, frequency of rest pauses, average working hours, and the shape of the output curves; subjectively, by asking the women such questions as "Do you often get bored with your work?" "Is your job too monotonous?" and "How well do you like the work that you do?" She also determined their age, education, ambition, tendency to daydream, restlessness, leisure-time activities, and extroversion by the replies to an anonymous questionnaire.

The results showed that the most bored workers were *not* more intelligent, more ambitious, more extroverted, or less inclined to daydream than the least bored workers. The most bored *were* younger, more restless, and less satisfied with the personal and home lives they led. The conclusion was that "satisfaction with repetitive work does not necessarily reflect insensitivity and stupidity, as the more romantic textbooks seem to imply."

It still may eventually be possible by improved selection and more judicious exposure to develop workers who are better adapted to repetitive jobs. The price, however, for the community as well as the company would be high. Wyatt (1929), who has made some of the most extensive and careful investigations of boredom and repetitive work, stresses the costs:

> Unless operatives are able to find facilities for development outside the factory, it seems probable that long and repeated exposure to monotonous conditions of work will have a dulling effect on mentality, and lead to the formation of habits which may impair their value as members of the community. . . . Although in many individuals the natural tendency is to behave in accordance with lines of least resistance, repetitive work seems to accentuate this tendency, instead of stimulating thought and action along original paths. It is probable, therefore, that the unfavorable effects of repetitive work are not confined to the industrial environment but extend to activities outside the factory and have a detrimental influence on thought and behavior in general. The provision of attractive educational and cultural facilities is accordingly of the utmost importance, if the repetitive worker is to take her place as a harmoniously developed and worthy citizen.

The introduction of *surface-attention requirements* into mechanically paced jobs makes them even more uninteresting. A moronic girl working on a punch press told an experienced interviewer that she had had the same job for ten years. The interviewer expressed disbelief because all the old operators he had known had lost at least one finger. By way of explanation, the girl replied, "Only them that thinks loses their fingers." Surface-attention jobs are those that urgently require a little, but not much, attention: jobs on punch presses, buzz saws, etc. Repetitive jobs without this requirement at least leave the worker free to think about something else. A short-story writer, for example, planned his stories in detail while working as a house painter. On surface-attention jobs, however, the worker for his own safety must give a constant small bit of his attention to the job. It is generally painful for him to do so.

Making simple jobs even simpler makes them even less interesting. Whether studies have been concerned with egg packing (Peach, 1946), handkerchief folding, soap packing, cigarette making, or car assembling (Walker and Guest, 1952), the findings are consistent: The simpler the job, the more boring it is to the typical worker. No principle of making jobs uninteresting has been pursued with more vigor. Industrial engineers have long and conscientiously striven to make jobs ever simpler and to lay out work in ever greater detail.

Making jobs meaningless makes them less interesting. A legendary ditch-digger was asked to dig a 5-foot hole in a vacant field, and having dug, was asked to fill it up again. After repeating the process several times, he threw down his shovel and started walking from the field. He returned with enthusiasm to the job when he was told that the purpose of the digging was to locate a vital pipeline. The principle, if carried to the extreme, makes the worker not only uninterested in what he is doing but *unable* to do it, as the following experiment by Karsten (Lewin, 1935) showed.

College students were instructed to draw vertical lines on sheets of paper and to group the lines in a fixed pattern, such as two lines close together, followed by three lines close together, then back to two lines, and so on. They were not told the purpose of the effort nor were they told how long they would be expected to continue. They were never told to stop. When they finished one sheet, they were given another and told to continue. As the sheets filled up, the students struggled to vary the job: they shifted from large to small lines, from heavy to light strokes, from downward to upward strokes, from straight to curved lines, from fast to slow rhythms, and so on. The quality of their work gradually declined. Eventually, it became difficult to make out from the sheets what they were trying to do. At the end of 4 hours, the average subject was unable to continue. He was psychologically satiated.

Workers rarely become as satiated as the student line drawers, for they, at least, have the goal of getting paid. When Karsten paid unemployed workers by the hour to draw lines, they continued to draw them neatly and accurately through an 8-hour day. Still, some workers on simple and mechanically paced jobs who are given no say in what they do or how they do it, who are not told why the work is important, and who are frequently interrupted as they work, come close to the same satiation point.

THE DEVELOPMENT OF INTERESTING JOBS

How can more interesting jobs be provided? This is a difficult question because what is boring to one worker may not be to another. Hulin and Blood (1968) suggest that some workers may be "pulled along" by a mechanically paced operation and not find it a "bad job." Or a worker may see his job as a safe rather than a boring job. Still, there are ways to make more jobs more interesting for more people.

Herzberg (1966) suggests that jobs in industry need to be enriched. He argues that instead of giving a man fewer and fewer tasks to do, a man should do as many tasks related to his job as he can. A person's job should allow him opportunities for achievement. It should be complex enough so that he can demonstrate that he can accept responsibility. The job should not be completely defined but should have an open end to its description so that the person doing it has an opportunity to show his creativity. It should be of direct interest to the person. These are difficult criteria to meet.

Enriching a job is more than just enlarging it. Enlarging may just mean "more of the same old thing"—tripping three foot pedals instead of one. Enriching involves more tasks to perform and more of the total person involved in doing them. For example, enriching a machine job would mean that the person not only tripped the foot pedal on his machine. He would also set it up for operation, take responsibility for short-term and long-term maintenance, make sure that he had the proper material to machine, and inspect and take responsibility for the material as it left his work station.

Some people believe that while enriching jobs might make workers feel better, it would make production less efficient. There is very little research to confirm or refute this belief. However, there are cases where job enrichment has been accompanied by an increase in productivity. In a study reported by Biggane and Stewart (1963), the job of assembling a waterpump was redesigned. Originally a 26-part washing machine waterpump was assembled by five men working on an assembly line. In the redesigned job each worker assembled the entire pump by himself. Quality improved with rejects going down from five percent before the redesign to five tenths of one percent after the job enrichment program was completed. The average cost of producing a waterpump was lower, and the rate of turnover was lower.

Another way to make work more interesting is to encourage members of the organization to participate more in job planning and operation. When all employees in an organization participated in bringing about change on their jobs, morale improved and production goals were met (French, Ross, Kirby, Nelson and Smyth, 1958). In this study the management of a men's clothing company wished to make major changes in production methods. The objective was to shorten the time necessary to produce a garment and thus reduce the in-process inventory, to provide more flexible control of the production process, to reduce costs, and to improve the quality of the product. The company had a general plan for re-engineering the production lines but the specific details of the changes had not been worked out. Since the company had two small plants and one large plant, they planned to introduce the changes at the small plants first. At each of the small plants the plant management conducted a series of meetings with workers to introduce the plans and explain them. During these meetings workers asked questions and offered suggestions, and afterwards the changes were introduced gradually.

The new system was eventually completed. After it had operated for a long enough time to become stable, management initiated another series of meetings. In these, management and workers discussed revisions in the wage rates and tried to insure that the earning opportunities of all workers were protected and no one suffered any economic loss as a result of the new methods. Workers also had a chance to make known any complaints or suggestions about their equipment and other features of the changes. All complaints were investigated and corrected. As a result of this careful planning and participation the new system was fully developed and refined in the small plants and later successfully introduced into the large plant. The outcomes desired by the management when they introduced the change were achieved with very little employee dissatisfaction.

In general, efforts to build participation into the day by day activities of on-going companies have not been successful. One exception is the Scanlon plan (Chapter 3). The Scanlon plan does provide a financial incentive by paying a bonus based on money saved as a result of cost reduction. At the heart of the plan, however, is a system of committees which encourages participation among all members of the organization in day by day activities as well as in special circumstances which arise in the company. Production committees of workers and their supervisor meet once or twice a month in each department to discuss and review all suggestions for departmental changes. If the changes can be made without great expense and without involving other departments, they are made immediately. In addition to these production committees there is a screening committee. Once each month the screening committee, composed of elected representatives of the workers and of top management, meets to review all changes and to discuss changes which do cost large amounts of money and do involve more than one department.

Most reports about the Scanlon plan have been of the case study variety. Few well-controlled studies have been made. Lesieur and Puckett (1969), after reviewing the thirty-year history of the Scanlon plan, conclude that it has proved itself. They particularly stress the benefits of the participation basis of the plan:

> In applying a Scanlon plan, a company says to its employees, "Look, we can run the company—we have run it for a number of years—we can run it well. But we think we can run it much better if you will help us. We're willing to listen." (p. 118)

Job enrichment and participation in decisions about the job are ways of making jobs more interesting to more people. In general, morale incentives —the deliberative control of the critical conditions that make for interested workers and interesting work—are the most potent of all incentives. Productivity incentives are often so in name only, actually resulting in no increase in productivity. When they do succeed, it often seems as if the human energy available for achieving company goals is a constant, for increased productivity tends to result in a decline in integration or morale. Integration incentives likewise, while generally more effective than production incentives, seem to succeed at the cost of productivity or morale. Effective morale incentives, however, seem to make new energy available for achieving company goals: the bored worker who becomes excited about his job pours fresh effort into it. Sometimes his energy is wasted; most of the time it leads to increased production and increased loyalty to the company that has involved him.

The typical manager and the typical industrial psychologist see the same picture—a company with the need to increase the productivity, integration, and morale of its workers. The manager, however, sees productivity in the foreground, integration and morale in the background; the psychologist puts morale in the foreground. Increasing morale seems to him the best way to increase productivity and integration also.

SUMMARY

A work incentive is any critical condition that a company deliberately controls to get its workers to be more productive, more loyal, or more interested in their work. Companies have long but mistakenly assumed that financial incentives could satisfactorily achieve all these ends. In using money as a production incentive, companies have generally followed the principles that the more important a man's position and the more productive he is in it, the more money he should get. The sharp decline in the number of companies using money as a production incentive reflects the increasing doubt about its value for this purpose. The sharp rise in the number of companies with group life insurance, health insurance, pension systems, and private unemployment insurances reflects increasing confidence in money as an integration incentive. There is no evidence that money has much value as a morale incentive, i.e., as a way of increasing the worker's intrinsic interest in the work that he is doing.

The preoccupation of companies with financial incentives has led them to neglect other work conditions that they can deliberately control for the purpose of increasing productivity, integration, or morale. In fact, their tendency to increase the number of even simpler mechanically paced jobs with many surface-attention requirements is a *negative* morale incentive. The industrial psychologist stresses positive morale incentives, for increases in morale lead to both increased productivity and increased integration.

11

APPRAISAL AND DEVELOPMENT

Two out of three companies have a formal program of employee appraisal. Organizations grow and develop by selecting good people, providing training and ensuring that there are appropriate incentives for moving individual employees and the total company toward the goals of productivity, integration, and morale. Information about how people are functioning is necessary if the company is to measure the validity of its selection programs, to evaluate the effectiveness of its training and incentive programs, and to assess the different ways of organizing work and styles of leadership.

Much of the work in employee appraisal focuses on present performance, and terms such as merit rating or efficiency ratings are used. Increasingly, though, the idea is growing that appraisal should be both an evaluation of present performance and a guide to personnel development. Other terms such as personnel review, performance appraisal, and development appraisal that reflect this shift in emphasis are becoming more common. Industrial psychology once focused on immediate performance and its value to the organization; now it stresses the development of the individual employee. How appraisal is done, how it can be improved, and how it is used in personnel development are the questions treated in this chapter.

TECHNIQUES OF APPRAISAL

The goal of appraisal is to find how a person measures up when compared to some standard of performance. To achieve this goal it is necessary to observe the individual and to make systematic comparison of these observations to similar observations for a specific group.

OBSERVATION OF PERFORMANCE

The best rating methods cannot eliminate errors due to ignorance. A supervisor must know an employee to rate him. The better he knows an employee, the better he can appraise him. This obvious principle is often neglected. Supervisors, managers, and executives make ratings of subordinates they cannot remember; they cannot support their vague impressions with facts; and they do not record observations that would be helpful in making and supporting their evaluations. The most basic improvement which can be made in appraisals is the improvement of the observations upon which they are based.

Employee performance records
A potential appraiser who keeps daily records of the performance of his people has more facts than those who do not. For example, supervisors of the Delco-Remy Division of General Motors were asked to record incidents of effective and ineffective performance among their men after different intervals. Twenty-five recorded them daily, twenty-five recorded them each week, and twenty-five recorded them every two weeks. The supervisors who kept daily records recorded twice as many incidents as those who kept biweekly ones.

Supervisors rarely have time to keep such detailed performance records, but at the Delco-Remy Division Flanagan and Burns (1957) developed a system for it that took the average supervisor less than 5 minutes each day. The first step in its development was the collection from supervisors of several thousand incidents of effective and ineffective performance like the following:

> I observed an employee looking through the scrap tub. Shortly after, he came to me stating that someone had thrown a large piece of

cast-iron piston into the scrap tub. We salvaged this piston and a short time later used the piece to make a pulley for a very urgently needed job.

This man was operating a trim press and was having considerable trouble with the magazine. He failed to see that all that was needed was to increase the clearance. This was a very simple adjustment—one he had often done.

The thousands of incidents were eventually classified into the following 16 critical job requirements for hourly-wage employees:

Physical and mental qualifications

1. Physical conditions
2. Coordination
3. Checking and inspecting
4. Arithmetic computation
5. Learning and remembering procedures and instructions
6. Judgment and comprehension
7. Understanding and repairing mechanical devices
8. Improving equipment and showing inventiveness

Work habits and attitudes

9. Productivity
10. Dependability
11. Accepting supervision and organizational procedures
12. Accuracy of reporting
13. Response to departmental needs
14. Getting along with others
15. Initiative
16. Responsibility

These requirements were included in a manual together with examples of each which illustrated behavior showing a need for improvement and behavior showing outstanding performance.

The supervisor used a performance record sheet for each employee. The sheet listed the requirements and provided a red side for noting effective and a blue side for noting ineffective performance. In using the form, the supervisor recorded the date and a phrase opposite the relevant requirement that would help him recall the details later. For example, on the sheet for John Henry opposite "physical condition" he might write "1/14 Needed ladder." This would recall later that "Henry had to get ladder to reach raw stock near machine. Time wasted getting and returning ladder each time." Opposite "checking and inspecting" he might write "1/14 Good decision on bolts.

1/20 Accurate dial reading." This would later recall that "Henry quickly decided on the best size of bolts to use on new part; read dials, gages accurately and quickly, thus permitting best timing and control on job we were running."

Practically all the foremen participating in the program reported that they thought it was valuable. A number of less direct measures supported their report. Over a 4-year period the ratio of effective to ineffective incidents rose, the number of employees turning in suggestions doubled, and the number of disciplinary warnings was reduced by half.

RATING SCALES

Appraisals are universal. We appraise doctors, grocers, and barbers and act on our judgments of their effectiveness. Managers appraise their supervisors, engineers, and production workers and act on their appraisals. Most appraisals are informal, unguided, and communicated by word of mouth. A first step toward a more formal appraisal is to put these informal and unguided evaluations in writing. For example, commanding officers throughout the military each year have been required to write 50- to 100-word assessments of their subordinates. Here are excerpts:

> A quiet, reticent, neat appearing officer—industrious, tenacious, diffident, careful, and neat. I do not wish to have this officer as a member of my command at any time.
> Is keenly analytical, and his highly developed mentality could best be used in the research and development field. He lacks common sense.
> He needs careful watching since he borders on the brilliant.
> Of average intelligence except for lack of judgment on one occasion in attempting to capture a rattlesnake for which he was hospitalized.
> Never makes the same mistake twice but it seems to me that he has made them all once.
> Recently married and devotes more time to this activity than to his current assignment (Richardson, 1950).

While this free-written method is simple, it has many drawbacks: It encourages the appraiser to interject his personal values and opinions, it is too dependent upon writing skill, it is time-consuming and therefore too dependent upon the willingness of the appraiser to take pains, and it cannot be used to put men in rank order for promotion or other purposes. These weaknesses led to the widespread use of rating scales, that reduce these drawbacks.

All ratings are quantitative rather than qualitative. The quantification ranges from crude to fine. At the crudest level, the rater may be asked to check an item if he has observed it in an employee and to leave it blank if he has not. Here, for example, is part of a checklist for a short-order cook:

_____ Gets orders confused

_____ Spills grease and food

_____ Arranges orders neatly for delivery

_____ Remembers several orders in sequence

The next step in quantification is the use of three rather than two categories. Here, for example, are items from the scale of a large electronics firm, where the rater is asked to check the employee as below average, average, or above average on each:

Below	Average	Above	
_____	_____	_____	General dependability
_____	_____	_____	Knowledge of job duties
_____	_____	_____	Application of time and energy

Five is the most common number of categories employed. Here are items used in the rating scale of a mining company:

Poor	Below average	Average	Above average	Excellent	
_____	_____	_____	_____	_____	Quality
_____	_____	_____	_____	_____	Quantity
_____	_____	_____	_____	_____	Versatility

Ten is near the limit for the number of categories. For example:

1	2	3	4	5	6	7	8	9	10	Cooperativeness
Low			Average				High			

In a graphic rating scale, a straight line represents a trait, and the rater is asked to check anywhere along the line. For example:

0	50	100	Cooperativeness

Theoretically the graphic scale permits an infinite number of categories. In practice, however, the number of categories used is rarely as high as ten. Generally, the quantitative categories have a qualitative label. For example, in the rating of "safety" the labels might run from "careless of his own and others' safety" through "protects others, allows for unusual incidents," to "quick to sense possible hazards and takes steps to get them corrected." Such verbal labels, however, are eventually translated into ratings of 1, 2, 3, 4, etc. Often a total rating score is obtained by adding the ratings on all traits.

The number of traits rated may vary from one to dozens, and the traits themselves are extremely varied. Some of the variety is related to the kind of work done. A manufacturing plant is likely to pick such traits as quality of work and quantity of work; a bank, neatness and memory; and a department store, knowledge of merchandise and customer contact. On the whole, however, the variety has more to do with biases of those who make up the scale than with the kind of work.

Where there is a choice of raters, the one who has the most chance to observe a worker should do the rating. For example, 100 flight mechanics at Bolling Air Force Base were rated by 3 commissioned officers and 14 non-commissioned officers (Whitla and Tirrell, 1954). The noncommissioned officers supervised the work of no more than 8 men, whereas the commissioned officers supervised much larger groups. The commissioned and noncommissioned officers rated the mechanics on a six-point scale from poor to superior on three questions: How well does he get along with others? How much does he know about his job? and How well does he do his job? The ratings were related to the mechanics' scores on the Flight Mechanics Job Knowledge Test. In every comparison, the ratings of the noncommissioned supervisors were more valid than those of their superiors.

Regardless of who does the rating, the use of scales escapes the frying pan of formless casual appraisals but lands in the fire of rating errors. The nature of some of these errors and the methods that psychologists have developed for reducing them are examined below.

The level and spread of ratings

Assume that we are rating the same person on the same traits and that we have the same information about him. Still, our ratings will differ because of differences in our rating habits. Some of us are habitually strict in our ratings and some are lenient; some rate everyone about average and some rate everyone either low or high. Habits of strictness or leniency create errors of *level*; habits of rating at the middle or at the extremes create errors of *spread*. Teachers of different sections of the same course, for example, often give the same examination, and their students often get very similar scores. Still, teacher ratings of students differ in level and *spread*. The average grade given by some teachers will be lower than that given by others, and some teachers will give many more Fs and As than others. Similar differences in level and spread occur in supervisory ratings. The average ratings of some supervisors will be higher than those of others, and some supervisors will rate everyone as about average while others will rate many as being poor or outstanding.

Failure to correct these differences in rating habits results in serious errors. Suppose, for example, company policy declares that all employees who are rated outstanding will be given large wage increases or will be eligible for immediate promotion. The workers who have supervisors with high-level and wide-spread rating habits will have a substantial advantage over those who have supervisors with low-level and narrow-spread habits, an advantage that has nothing to do with actual differences in work performance. The ranking technique eliminates these sources of error.

THE RANKING METHOD

In using the ranking method, the supervisor ranks his men in order of merit: (1) Tom Jones, (2) Dick Thomas, (3) Harry Smith, etc. Most commonly, he ranks them in their overall performance. He may, however, be asked to rank them on such separate traits as quantity of work, initiative, etc. These separate rankings can then be converted into an overall ranking by adding the rankings on separate traits and finding the average.

The ranking method eliminates leveling errors, for all raters must use all ranks. Consequently, it is impossible to have "low" or "high" rankers. It also eliminates errors of spread, for every rater must use every rank once and not more than once. In addition, ranking a dozen or so men on their overall performance is the simplest and quickest method of appraisal. It is also the most natural method, for people in general tend to make judgments of the overall performance of a worker that dominate their more specific judgments. Finally, rankings have the most direct relation to personnel actions: the man in the first rank in a department is the most eligible, and the man in the last rank the least eligible, to get a raise.

One weakness of the ranking method is that it may divide men who are good performers from those who are about as good. It forces the supervisor who regards several men as being of equal ability to rank them from the "most equal" to the "least equal." The weakness is not too serious, however, since supervisors generally do not regard many employees as being equal. Their greatest difficulty in making discriminations is with the men in the middle, and this is the group least likely to be affected by rewarding or punishing actions.

Another built-in weakness of ranking is that it makes comparisons between men in different groups uncertain. Suppose the head of a department wishes to promote his best employee and he has four subordinate supervisors who have each ranked the men under them. He then has a choice among four men ranked first. Are they equally good performers? Probably not. It is even quite possible that a man ranked second by one of the supervisors is better than three of the men ranked first. Regardless of the method used, however, such fine discriminations are always uncertain.

Comparisons of men in different groups become more certain as the number of men ranked increases. Unfortunately, as the number of men ranked increases, the practical problems of ranking them become greater: it is easy to rank 5 men, difficult to rank 25. The *paired-comparisons* method, a variation of the ranking method, makes the comparison of 25 men more reliable and easier (but not quicker). The supervisor is given a series of cards on each of which are the names of two of his men. He checks the name of the better man in the pair. The cards are made out so that the name of every man appears once on a card with the name of every other man. A man's rank is determined by the number of pairs in which he has been chosen as the better. The method quickly becomes tedious and time-consuming: in rating 20 men, he must make almost 200 comparisons; in rating 100 men, almost 5,000 comparisons!

The *forced-distribution* method modifies the ranking principle so that it can be conveniently used with large groups. Like ordinary rating scales, it may be used to rate men on one or many traits and to put them into few or many categories. The key difference is that the rater is forced to assign a definite percentage of his men to each category. Assume, for example, that a supervisor using an ordinary scale is asked to rate his 100 men on their overall performance on a five-point scale: (1) poor, (2) below average, (3) average, (4) above average, and (5) excellent. He can, and generally does, rate few men below average and many men above average. Using a forced-distribution system, he would also have five categories: (1) lowest, (2) next lowest, (3) middle, (4) next highest, and (5) highest. However, he is now required to put an arbitrarily assigned percent into each category, for example: (1) 10 percent, (2) 25 percent, (3) 35 percent, (4) 25 percent, and (5) 10 percent. That is, instead of ranking the men individually, he assigns them to ranked categories. It is desirable to avoid adjectives like "poor" in describing these categories, for supervisors resist putting their men under unfavorable labels.

Rankings are simpler to make, more likely to be valid, and easier to use in making practical decisions than ratings. If rankings are so superior, why do ratings still dominate the appraisal scene? Answer: Appraisers do not *like* to rank. The "low-leveller" does not like to put anybody at the top; the "high-leveller" does not like to put anybody at the bottom. The "narrow-spreader" does not like to put anybody at the bottom or top; the "wide-spreader" does not like to put anybody in the middle. To replace ratings with rankings, these resistances must be overcome.

THE HALO EFFECT

Whether we like a person or not has a great influence on our judgments of him. If we like him, we tend to rate him high on desirable traits, low on undesirable ones. If we dislike him, we do the reverse. That is, we tend to put an angel's halo around those we love, a devil's horns on those we hate. The halo effect accounts for some differences in level and spread: those who generally like people use a high level and those who do not, a low level; those who see people as much alike use a narrow spread and those who see them as either angels or devils use a wide spread. While ranking methods eliminate these differences in level and spread, they do not eliminate likes and dislikes.

Ratings are intended to be as valid a measure of a worker's performance as possible. If a supervisor's liking for a worker were determined solely by his work performance, then the liking would not lower the validity of the rating. To an extent, this does happen: some supervisors remain aloof from their subordinates so that they have *no* likes or dislikes which are not based on work performance, and all supervisors are influenced somewhat in their likes and dislikes by work performance. Likes and dislikes, however, are determined by many factors. For one thing, they are determined by perceived similarity; the more we think a person is like us, the more we tend to be attracted to him. Many of the similarities and differences between a supervisor and a worker, of course, have nothing to do with work performance.

Not only their likes but also their personal needs influence supervisors' ratings. Tannenbaum, Weschler, and Massarik (1961) wrote personality evaluations of 11 supervisors based on interviews with their subordinates. Here, for example, are some of the comments made about one supervisor:

> I don't think he knows my name.
> I talk to him as little as possible.

> I'm not sure he really knows what we are doing.
> He may know his job, but we pay a high price to get it done.

The investigators concluded that he was primarily concerned with the promotion of his own ideas, discouraged initiative, was unaware of his effect upon his subordinates, and bolstered his own insecurities by maintaining rigid control. The following are comments made about another supervisor:

> It's a real pleasure working for him.
> He doesn't always do the things I like, but I respect his judgment.
> He is the best man around.
> I think other people may know more than he does, but he knows how to help you think through a problem.

It was concluded that he was concerned about maximizing the performance of each subordinate, promoting cooperative effort, delegating responsibility wherever possible, and learning about the needs of his subordinates.

On the basis of such evaluations, the investigators then filled out detailed performance ratings for each supervisor's subordinates as they thought the 11 supervisors themselves would fill them out. The guessed ratings were compared with the actual ratings, and the investigators concluded, "The interviewer was able to account for a significant portion of the variance of performance ratings on the basis of his clinical evaluation of personal, interpersonal, and situational factors." That is, if different supervisors had evaluated the same group, their evaluations would have been quite different.

THE FORCED-CHOICE METHOD

In the rating-scale method, the rater indicates how little or how much of a characteristic a worker has. In the ranking method, the rater lists the men from the one who has the most to the one who has the least of the characteristic. Unlike either the rating or ranking methods, the forced-choice method presents the rater with sets of favorable or unfavorable phrases. In each set, the rater is forced to choose from equally favorable (or unfavorable) phrases the ones that are most descriptive and least descriptive of the man he is rating. This method, therefore, reduces the halo effect, for it forces the rater to choose between apparently equally desirable (or undesirable) characteristics in describing a man he likes.

Here is one set or "block" of phrases used in the forced-choice rating of Air Force technical instructors:

    a. Patient with slow learners
    b. Lectures with confidence
    c. Keeps interest and attention of class
    d. Acquaints classes with objective for each lesson in advance (Berkshire and Highland, 1953)

The rater of an instructor was asked to pick from this block of favorable phrases the two that he thought were most descriptive of the instructor. There were 30 additional blocks of four phrases. While all the phrases in each block sound favorable, some discriminate poor from good instructors and some do not. For example, good and poor instructors (determined by independent rankings by their supervisors) were equally often described as lecturing with confidence and acquainting classes with objectives. On the other hand, good instructors were more often described as being patient with slow learners and keeping the interest of the class. Total scores were found by adding weights assigned to checked items according to their discrimination value. That is, instructors described by items that did not discriminate poor from good instructors got the lowest scores; those described by items that *did* discriminate got the highest scores.

Forced choice is used in a variety of forms. The above form presents four statements in each block; some offer as few as two and some as many as five. The above form has all favorable phrases in a block, and all 31 blocks consist of favorable phrases. Some forms, however, have used favorable and unfavorable phrases in the same block, while others have an equal number of blocks made up of favorable and unfavorable statements. The above form instructs the rater to pick the two most descriptive statements, while others instruct him to pick only one, and still others instruct him to pick both the most and the least descriptive. The above form also has a scoring key based upon item analysis, but other forms have scoring keys developed in other ways.

WHICH IS THE BEST FORM?

Berkshire and Highland compared many variations of the forced-choice form for their resistance to halo effects, their reliability, their validity, and their acceptability to the raters. They concluded that the form illustrated above (four statements per block, all favorable, in which the two most descriptive statements are chosen)" . . . was most bias-resistant, yielded consistently higher validities under various conditions, was one of the two best-liked forms, and had adequate reliability. It seems reasonably clear that this method of constructing forced-choice forms is superior to the other methods tested in this experiment."

Of all methods, forced-choice ratings seem likely to give the most valid results. Like the ranking method, they eliminate errors due to level and spread; unlike rankings, they reduce errors due to the halo effect. Though hard to develop, they are easy for raters to use.

Zavala (1965) in his critique of the forced-choice method makes the specific point that in most studies which have compared the method with other more conventional rating methods, forced-choice has demonstrated its superior validity.

Some authorities, however, question the superiority of forced-choice ratings. Cozan (1955), for example, reviewing the results of forced-choice appraisals of Army officers, personnel counselors, retail store managers, production foremen, pharmaceutical salesmen, physicians, and research personnel, concludes that such ratings, although they can result in more valid appraisals, do not always do so. The development of good forced-choice scales takes time, money, and skill. Failure to pay these developmental costs accounts for most of the cases where the method has failed to show a clear-cut advantage over other methods. Whether the higher validities are worth the higher costs depends on the kind and amount of use made of the ratings.

THE USE OF APPRAISALS

Employee ratings are almost indispensable to the industrial psychologist. His daily work involves the development of more effective selection procedures, training methods, incentive systems, etc. To evaluate these, measures of success are essential. Ratings are the most convenient, and often the only, available criterion. The more valid they become, the more useful they are. For example, in the evaluation of the reference letters of applicants for Federal civil service jobs, the psychologist found that they had no relation to later supervisory ratings. The conclusion is of some value. It would have been more valuable, however, if the supervisory ratings had been more valid. In the long run, it may be recognized that the greatest value of appraisals is as a measure against which to check other company programs.

Ratings were first developed and at first exclusively used as a part of wage and salary plans. Their use has dropped sharply in this area. Brown and Larson (1958), for example, examined trends in rating practices in 23 governmental and industrial organizations in California: state agencies, utilities, aircraft companies, oil companies, and manufacturing concerns with a total of more than 300,000 employees. They found performance appraisal programs almost completely separated from salary administration. Increases in a worker's pay were determined by many elements: his seniority, time since his last increase, the pay range for his job, morale of the work group, budgetary allotments to his department, profits of the organization—and his work performance. Where work performance was a factor determining pay, its evaluation was generally separated from the performance appraisal program.

The decline of merit ratings as a part of an incentive system has many causes. Union resistance to their use has intensified, managers have become more sceptical of the validity of the ratings, and supervisors have become more concerned about their negative effects on productivity, integration, and morale. McGregor (1957) suggests that there is an even more potent reason for the manager's resistance to such uses of appraisal:

> The conventional approach, unless handled with consummate skill and delicacy, constitutes something dangerously close to a violation of the integrity of the personality. Managers are uncomfortable when they are put in the position of "playing God." The respect we hold for the inherent value of the individual leaves us distressed when we must take responsibility for judging the personal worth of a fellow man. Yet the conventional approach to performance appraisal forces us, not only to make such judgments and to see them acted upon, but also to communicate them to those we have judged. Small wonder we resist!

Most managers, like most people, would rather help than judge.

Merit ratings are now often unused and useless. A supervisor may rate each of his workers once a year and send the completed forms to the personnel office. A clerk may then file them in the appropriate folders, and no one may ever tell the workers how they were rated or look at the ratings in the folders. The ratings, in fact, may not be worth looking at. The United States government, for example, designed the most extensive appraisal program in the world as an aid in determining salary increases, promotions, and other actions under civil service. The Second Hoover Commission concluded that the processing of papers required for the program was "a burden far beyond any benefits it produced" (U.S. Government, 1955).

Employee progress report, employee counseling program, employee appraisal and development plan, development guide—these are the kinds of names that are now being used by progressive companies as titles for their appraisal programs. The titles reflect the increased stress on improving the work performance of both the supervisor and the employee. The programs themselves stress discussion of the appraisal report with the employee, planning with the employee for his progress and development, and following up the appraisal and plan with specific action. Encouraging the growth and development of people, long a core value of our educational and governmental institutions, is becoming respectable as a principle of management.

PLANNED PERFORMANCE APPRAISAL

What is a person supposed to do? How well is he doing it? What should be done about him? The second question concerns appraisal; the third, the use of appraisal. Good answers to the second and third questions require a good answer to the first, but poor answers to the first are typical when it is executives who are being appraised. The goals of a production worker and the tasks he must perform to achieve them are fairly easy to specify, but the tasks that an executive must perform to do a good job are hard to pin down. *Planned performance appraisal* programs answer this problem by first spelling out overall goals for a company and then formulating goals for each group within the organization that must be met if the overall goals are to be obtained. The executive of a group is then appraised in terms of his group's success in achieving the performance planned for it.

Assume, for example, that the president of a company manufacturing washing machines decides to increase unit volume in the next year by 15 percent. In consultation with others, he then determines what each group in the organization must do in order to achieve this overall goal. The goals for a particular group are its "planned performance." The executive in charge of the group is eventually appraised in terms of the relationship between the performance planned for the group and its actual performance.

The division manager, for example, may have the quantitative goals of increasing overall profits by 35 percent and expanding the company's share of the market from 21 percent to 25 percent, and the qualitative goals of developing a new line of motors and starting a weekly department meeting. In turn, the targets for the personnel manager may include increasing the typing pool from 25 to 30 workers, reducing cafeteria costs by 60 percent, developing a safety training program for the operating divisions, etc. And the director of manufacturing may have such targets as cutting lead time of component purchases from 120 to 100 days, reducing the spoilage ratio by 2 percent, speeding up the utilization of suggestions, etc.

How successful is this system of management by objective? Patton (1962), who has made extensive use of the system, has this to say:

> Only a handful of companies have seriously attempted to set up such a programmed approach to performance appraisal. . . . However, the top

executives of companies that have tackled task planning are almost uniformly enthusiastic with results achieved so far. The principal accomplishment, in their view, is the establishment of a task-oriented way of life. Job objectives are more clearly defined and, therefore, better coordinated. Individual executives know what is expected of them and can target their activities more effectively. Last but certainly not least, the annual review of "hits and misses" between superior and subordinates becomes more realistic and more productive of improved performance.

Appraisals under this or any other system are not an end but a means to the end of making more effective use of human resources.

THE DEVELOPMENTAL INTERVIEW

The performance appraisal of an employee is best used as an aid in improving his work performance. Of course, to have any chance of improving, the employee must be told how he has been appraised. Yet about half the companies who have a formal appraisal program do not make a policy of telling their workers. Even where there is a policy, the supervisors of many workers still either do not tell them or tell them in such a way that the workers do not realize they have been told. If they do realize it, they often react in a hostile way. How can the supervisor make more effective use of the interview in which he informs a worker how he has been appraised?

FINDING A COMMON GOAL

The first step in a constructive interview requires that the supervisor and the employee reach an agreement about the quality of his work performance and his developmental goals. Meyer et al. (1965) point out that just participating in performance appraisal interviews is not likely to improve performance. Specific improvement goals must be set as a part of the interview. This is a difficult step, for the two people are rarely in agreement at the start. To begin with, the employee commonly has a better opinion of himself than does his supervisor. In a study by Parker et al. (1959), for example, 117 clerical workers rated themselves, and their supervisors also rated them. The clerks rated themselves higher on all eight of the rating scales used. The disagreements were greatest in the ratings of "leadership potential" and "ability to work with minimum of supervision" and least in "amount of work done" and "quality of work done." The clerks were also asked to estimate how they thought their supervisors would rate them. Their estimates were lower than their own self-ratings but higher than the ratings the supervisors actually gave them.

Employees, like most people, want to think well of themselves. Consequently, they find it hard to accept, or even to hear, criticism. Employees *say* they want to know where they stand. What they mean, however, is more like, "I think I am doing all right, and I would like to know that the boss thinks the same way," or "I know I am doing well, and I would like more recognition from the boss," or even "I know I am not doing well in certain respects, but I don't think the boss knows it, and I would like to be sure this is the case." As a result, the supervisor who offers a criticism finds himself in an uncomfortable dilemma. He offers general criticism and is asked for specifics; he gives specifics and receives a long list of extenuating circumstances. Furthermore, the more an employee needs to be criticized, the less willing he is to listen.

Even when allowances are made for the employee's greater leniency toward himself, he still disagrees with his supervisor. Correlating self- and supervisory ratings reduces the influence of leniency. In spite of this, Parker and his colleagues found generally low correlations, as shown in Table 11-1. The supervisory ratings of a worker's ability to work with others and his leadership potential had practically no relation to the worker's self-ratings. On the other hand, there was a fair degree of agreement about conscientiousness and amount of work done. A supervisor and his subordinates often disagree about facts. Even more often, they disagree about what is important and what is unimportant for good job performance. The clerks, for example, gave a great deal of weight to their ability to work with a minimum of supervision. The supervisors gave it little weight.

An employee and his supervisor see his work performance in different ways; they also work toward quite different goals during the developmental interview. Kellogg (1962) divided General Electric managers attending a series

TABLE 11-1 Correlation between supervisory and self-ratings

Scale	Correlation
Ability to work with others	.13
Leadership potential	.19
Ability to do complicated jobs	.28
Ability to work with minimum supervision	.30
Overall performance	.35
Quality of work done	.37
Conscientiousness	.41
Amount of work done	.53

SOURCE: Parker et al. (1959).

of small conferences into a "John" group and a "Manager" group. Both groups were given the following information:

John

John Jones is a young man in his thirties, with a liberal arts degree, and a law degree. He was in the top fifth of his class in arts, but only in the top half in law. He was originally hired on a relations rotating program and was placed in union relations for his first job. After about a year there, he went into salary and wage administration and has been in this field for about three years. He is bright, quick, outgoing; he is quite a leader; he is persuasive both orally and in writing. He is not very detail minded, dislikes routing and records very much. He wants to be eventually at least a relations manager and possibly a general manager. He had some assignments in manufacturing and he liked them very much, so that he is torn between relations and manufacturing and would welcome advice on this point.

Manager

John's manager is about fifty years old. He has been in the salary and wage field all his life. He would like to be promoted but has been passed over twice, so that he feels it is not very likely. He is personally very methodical, detail minded, and a little withdrawn and reserved. He feels that John's records are not as accurate as they could be and that John does not spend enough time at his desk doing his paper work. He does recognize some excellent results—John has won the confidence of managers, his advice on pay levels and rates is frequently asked, and better understanding about pay administration has been achieved.

The Manager group was asked to pretend that it was the evening before a discussion with John to help him make a plan for his development. In addition to the above descriptions the group was given details about his education, work history, past performance appraisals (average or better), and a few test results. The John group was asked to pretend that they were John, faced the next day with a discussion of his development needs and plans. After the two groups had discussed the situation and made their plans, a chairman of each group presented them to the class.

In 11 different conferences, the Manager and John groups invariably saw the situation in quite different ways. The managers saw John as a below-average employee even though they knew he had received above-average ratings from his former supervisors. The Johns saw the manager as a person impossible to work for who blocked his advancement and failed to give rewards for good work. The managers and Johns set widely different aims for their discussion. The managers planned to get John to be more exact, keep his records better, and develop more self-discipline. The Johns planned to get out from under the manager without making him an enemy.

How can a supervisor best go about reconciling these differences with his subordinates? A chief engineer in a large manufacturing company approached it in this way. His company had a typical appraisal program that required him to fill out the form for each of his subordinates every 6 months. He passed the forms on to his subordinates with the instruction, "Why don't you fill this out on yourself from your knowledge of how you have performed during these few months. I'll fill one out on you independently. If we agree, we won't need to worry about much of an appraisal interview. If we disagree, we can get together and thrash out our differences." The method prevents an immediate open conflict between the supervisor and the employee. It does not, however, resolve the conflict.

An appraisal program at the Detroit Bank (Hall, 1951) was designed to reduce the conflict. Its four-step method included a self-appraisal by each employee, an appraisal by his immediate supervisor and by the branch manager, and a three-way interview between the employee and two management representatives. Finally, a panel composed of the manager and three other management representatives reviewed all the appraisals and gave the employee an overall rating from 1 to 7, 1 indicating that he should be promoted immediately and 7 that he should probably be replaced.

The supervisor who confronts an employee with his evaluation of what the worker is doing is generally facing only the easier part of the problem. The worker's major question is "What *should* I be doing and how can I do it?" Formal job descriptions are only a partial answer. These satisfy management's need for order and for reassurance that everyone has a piece of paper telling him what to do. Each supervisor, however, has his own ideas about what he wants his subordinates to do and how he wants them to do it. In turn, each subordinate has *his* ideas that are based on his own work experiences, his interests, his perception of what his boss wants, and the demands made upon him by his fellow workers. A supervisor should find out what these ideas are.

In discussing his subordinate's views, the supervisor might best begin by asking him what he thinks his major responsibilities are. In some cases, he may ask him to list them before the interview. A natural part of such discussions is the consideration of better ways of meeting these responsibilities. In the process, the supervisor can ask the employee to suggest goals for himself in relation to the job. These are more likely to be too general rather than too specific, too many rather than too few, too high rather than too low. When the supervisor and employee have agreed upon a few specific and realistic goals to be achieved by a definite time, the major work of the developmental interview is over.

The only constant for successful goal setting is that the particular supervisor must *relate* effectively to the particular subordinate. Most subordinates like to participate in setting their own goals, but some like to be told. Some supervisors are loud and dominating, and some are quiet and reserved. Employees expect their supervisor to behave in ways consistent with his personality, and they become suspicious and distrustful when he does not. In general, therefore, a technique that can be used by some supervisors cannot be used by others, and a technique that can be used with some employees cannot be used with others. There is no substitute for sensitive adaptation by the supervisor to the particular employee and the particular situation.

STICKING TO THE PRESENT

The development of an employee involves adding to his job knowledge, improving his skills, and extending his capabilities. The developmental process can be oriented toward better performance on his present job or better performance on future jobs, but it is more effective when directed toward his present job. In the first place, the employee is likely to be motivated to try harder. He is rewarded for his present work, he knows that it matters to him how well he does it, and he sees his personal worth as determined by his present performance. In the second place, the chances for feedback, so critical for effective learning, are here most numerous and specific.

The experienced worker, however, may well see his job as an exercise in doing the same old thing in the same old way. The problem can be solved by adding a new element to it—a new piece of work, a new standard, a new customer, a new application, etc. The new element should require him to add to his knowledge in certain areas or to develop skills which he has not previously needed.

The more detailed the knowledge a supervisor has about an employee's present performance, the more effective his feedback to the employee will be. Often, however, a supervisor's knowledge is vague and impressionistic. For example, he may start the interview by saying that he had to rate the employee low on both quality and quantity of production during the past 6 months and that he was sometimes lazy and careless. The employee is likely to conclude that the supervisor doesn't like him and has it in for him.

On the other hand, he may tell the employee that on the first of March when a pan of parts was accidentally spilled and the assembly line had to be shut down until more parts could be obtained, the employee was the only one who sat down and waited until the parts were available without making an effort to help pick up and sort the spilled parts. The employee is more likely to agree with such specific feedback and to respond favorably to it.

LEADING FROM STRENGTH

In antediluvian times, while the animal kingdom was being differentiated into swimmers, climbers, runners, and fliers, there was a school for the development of animals. The theory of the school was that the best animals should be able to do one thing as well as another . . . . No one was allowed to graduate from school unless he could climb, swim, run, and fly at certain prescribed rates; so it happened that the time wasted by the duck in an attempt to run had so hindered him from swimming that his swimming muscles had atrophied, and so he was hardly able to swim at all; and in addition he had been scolded, punished, and ill-treated in many ways so as to make his life a burden. He left school humiliated. . . . The eagle could make no headway in climbing to the top of a tree, and although he showed he could get there just the same, the performance was counted a demerit, since it had not been done in the prescribed way. An abnormal eel with large pectoral fins proved he could run, swim, climb trees, and fly a little. He was made valedictorian (Burnham, 1919).

As the fable suggests, strengths rather than weaknesses should be stressed in development. Of course, an employee cannot do some things because he has never tried, and he does some things poorly because he thinks no one cares. If he tries hard and fails, however, he will view continued attention as a criticism and feel resentful. Even if he is not resentful, his lack of talent will set a low ceiling to his achievement. Besides, the same general results can often be achieved as well through using his strengths as his weaknesses. Like the animals in the antediluvian school, a company that stresses weaknesses will end with everyone working hardest at the things he does poorest.

Stress a person's strengths. It is difficult to take our eyes off a person's weaknesses. Kellogg (1962), for example, found that *all* the groups playing the part of John Jones's manager stressed some plan to overcome his weakness for routine and detailed work. Even those who were playing the part of John generally recommended such a plan.

Emphasizing the strengths of a subordinate is hard to do. An employee's work failures are more likely to require the supervisor's attention than his successes. Consequently, if a worker knocks over a stack of boxes and spills their contents, the supervisor is likely to remember it; if a worker quickly decides on the best size bolts to use on a new part, the supervisor is likely to forget it. The supervisor who habitually jots down examples of strengths corrects the tendency and provides, as well, a start toward stressing an employee's good points. Once started, it is likely to grow.

LISTENING

The developmental interview aims to set the employee's performance goals, to examine the problems involved in reaching them, and to find solutions for the problems. If the supervisor is to succeed, he must relate effectively to the employee, stick to the employee's performance on his present job, and stress the employee's strengths. It might seem, then, that the supervisor would need to do a great deal of talking and to exercise close control over the course of the interview. Nothing could be further from the truth. Basing it on the extensive findings of the Hawthorne studies, the Western Electric Company (1938) prepared a manual to guide its supervisors in conducting employee interviews. The recommendations were clear:

1. Listen—don't talk.
2. Give full interest and attention.
3. Never argue.
4. Do not listen exclusively to the manifest content of the expression.
5. Listen for:
   What the worker wants to say.
   What he does not want to say.
   What he cannot say without help.
6. As you listen, plot out tentatively and for subsequent correction the pattern that is being set before you. To test, summarize what he has said and present for comment. Always do this with caution— that is, clarify but do not add or twist.

The same advice has since been often repeated. For example, Maier (1958), in discussing the appraisal interview, says of the role of supervisor:

> Since the objective is employee development, the interviewer cannot specify the area for improvement, because this would be making a judgement. He must limit his influence to stimulating thinking rather than supplying solutions, and be willing to consider all ideas on job improvement that the employee brings up. His function is to discover the subordinate's interests, respond to them, and help the employee examine himself and the job. He must forget his own viewpoint and try to see the job as the employee sees it.

To "forget his own viewpoint" is as hard for the supervisor as for the rest of us. If he has ever done the employee's job or even seen it done, he is likely to have a confident idea of the "right" way to do it and is likely to find it difficult even to think of any other way. Yet there are almost always alternatives that are as good or better. Generally, the best way is the one that best fits the man doing it. The supervisor should encourage the employee to ask himself, "What is the best way for me to tackle my job in order to get the best possible results in the shortest possible time?" When he has answered this question, the supervisor should help him to evaluate and apply the answer.

A supervisor often does not think he should listen. He thinks he should "tell and sell"—tell the employee what is wrong with his performance and sell the employee on a specific improvement program. This method has some advantages in dealing with employees who feel insecure and respect the greater knowledge and experience of the supervisor. With most workers, however, it is likely to produce resentment and strained job relations. Also, and more important, it produces yes men who concentrate on pleasing the supervisor instead of getting the job done.

Burke and Wilcox (1969) surveyed 323 girls in six offices of a large public utility in order to specify the characteristics of an effective development interview. They found that a girl felt satisfied with the session, wanted to improve her performance, and did improve her performance when her supervisor did a good job in the appraisal interview. A good interviewer gave the girl a chance to present her own ideas and feelings, was helpful and constructive, tried to clear up present job problems and cooperated with the girl in setting some future goals. The study also found that girls who were more satisfied with the day-to-day behavior of their supervisors were more likely to think their supervisor did a good job in the development interview.

There are many ways to conduct a good developmental interview. As on other jobs, the most effective way for a supervisor is one that best fits him. Still, there are sound critical guides for all. The effective supervisor helps the employee set his own goals and does not set them for him; he encourages the employee to think about his performance on his present job; he stresses the employee's strengths, not his weaknesses; and above all, he listens—even when he would rather talk.

THE DEVELOPMENT OF SUPPORTIVE RELATIONSHIPS

In a successful developmental interview, the worker feels supported by his supervisor—feels that his supervisor understands and likes him, is trying to help him to do a good job, and generally approves of and respects the importance of his work. The supervisor, however, is unlikely to give support unless he gets it in turn. That is, effective employee development depends on the quality of the relationship between the employee and his supervisor. The quality of this relationship, however, is largely determined by the general quality of *all* relationships within the organization.

Supervisors can easily be trained to express more considerate attitudes toward their subordinates. However, if the general climate in which they work is not supportive, they can just as easily *un*learn their consideration. The International Harvester Company, for example, sent most of its foremen to the company's central school in Chicago to participate in a 2-week course in human relations that stressed the importance of consideration. An attitude scale measuring consideration was given before and after the course, and scores rose sharply. After a few months back on the job, however, some supervisors became *less* considerate than supervisors who had no training. Overall, the average score was about the same after a few months as it had been at the beginning of training.

Next the consideration scale was given to the foremen of the trained supervisors, who were then divided into those who had considerate foremen and those who had inconsiderate ones. The differences were striking: Supervisors of considerate foremen had higher scores before training began and retained their higher scores after they were back on the job. The conclusion was that considerate leaders develop considerate subordinates and that an organization with a supportive climate develops members with supportive attitudes (Fleishman, Harris, and Burtt, 1955).

How can a company develop a more supportive climate? To begin with, the psychological climate is influenced by the physical climate—consideration or its lack is most obviously reflected in the physical conditions of work. The nature of the company's small work groups, however, is the key determinant of climate. Leaders exercise their most helpful or most harmful influence through their impact on the work group. The effectiveness of communication, a potent determiner of the organizational climate, is heavily dependent upon the way work groups are organized.

THE PLACE OF THE PROFESSIONAL COUNSELOR

A worker's boredom with his job, his difficulties with his teammates, his fights with his supervisor, his disagreements with his nagging wife, his worries about his sick children, and countless other personal problems seriously affect his productivity, loyalty, and morale. Every worker sometimes faces such problems, and an understanding supervisor and a supportive environment is of great help to him in dealing constructively with them. Some problems, however, are so serious and so much a product of the worker's own background and personality that he needs professional assistance. The effective supervisor needs to know what these problems are and when to seek help in solving them.

THE PSYCHOTIC WORKER

Virtually everyone at times feels tense and unhappy. Some people, however, exhibit such intense and prolonged unhappiness and behavior so dangerous to themselves or to other people that they need hospitalization. *Psychosis* is the term used to describe this most serious form of mental illness. At any given time, roughly 1 percent, or about two million, of the people in the United States are suffering from some form of psychosis. The majority of them improve or totally recover. Since about one out of every twenty persons is hospitalized for mental illness sometime during his life, large companies must fairly regularly deal with such individuals.

All people suffering from a psychosis have one element in common: a severe disturbance of their contact with reality. They may have an inadequate contact with the world of physical reality, with the world of social reality, or with their own inner psychological world—and often with all three.

> Thomas Bryan, a thirty-seven-year-old unmarried carpenter, was admitted to the hospital on the complaint of his mother. "He doesn't shave and lets his beard grow. He won't circulate with anyone. He lies in bed. I've been bringing him his meals. I am afraid he will go away and get caught in a snowstorm."
>
> William Oslo, a fifty-eight-year-old race-track petty official, lost his job as a result of his belligerency. He was constantly criticizing his working wife, calling up his friends in the middle of the night to give them tips on the races, sending radiograms about purchasing horses which he could not pay for, and attempting to organize large political rallies. When asked how he felt, he said: "I never felt better in my life."
>
> Howard Dennis, a forty-five-year-old unmarried employee of a board of education, was admitted to the hospital after he had scratched his neck with a piece of broken china in a suicidal attempt. In explanation he said: "It's depression from living an abnormal life. I spend too much money. I had another personality in my waking hours" (Smith, 1961).

The behavior of most psychotics is *disorganized:* they respond to situations in a fragmentary and haphazard way. During attacks of delirium, for example, the alcoholic is completely disoriented, is incapable of remembering what happens, and is continuously experiencing a wide variety of hallucinations. Yet in the illness which is often most difficult for a company to handle, *paranoia*, little or no disorganization may be present. On the contrary, the person with paranoia may seem well organized and technically competent, have a good grasp of correct conduct, and lead a farily well-adjusted life. The disorder is characterized by fixed and sometimes dangerous *delusions*. For instance:

> An expert tool and die maker had made a real name for himself in a large steel plant. When he reached about fifty years of age, he began to be very critical of the work of others around him and suspicious of his supervisors and the company as a whole. He told fantastic tales about the way he was being treated and, in spite of his good record, the company was forced to let him go. The medical department recommended that he get psychiatric treatment, but after one appointment with a specialist, he refused to go back. He went to work for a smaller company, but in only two or three months the same pattern began to repeat itself. Even though he had no supervisory responsibility, he insisted on instructing and criticizing other workers. This company also had to discharge him. His family too was aware that something was wrong, for at home he spent most of his time brooding about the "injustice" of the way he had been treated (Gilmer, 1961, p. 472).

The behavior of most psychotics is *desocialized*; they become more and more completely detached from people and society. This is the central characteristic, for example, of *schizophrenia*, which accounts for about half the people in mental hospitals. Yet some psychotics are not socially withdrawn. *Manic-depressives*, for example, in their manic phase are generally extremely eager to be with people. The speeded-up, overdriven, and overexpansive executive who is on the brink of a manic-depressive breakdown presents a dangerous and difficult situation for a company to handle.

The behavior of most psychotics shows some *deterioration*: a general, severe, and relatively permanent drop in the effectiveness of behavior. For example:

> A traveling salesman employed by a paint company lost his position through inefficiency. He secured employment with a rival firm, but when calling on old customers, he made no mention of his new connections. He showed curious lapses when sending orders, and wrote "two quarts" or "three gallons" but failed to specify what was wanted. When his superiors called his attention to these discrepancies, he argued and became enraged. Soon the difficulties and complications became intolerable and he was discharged. He then wrote letters to other firms asking for employment, but although he began with a request for work, he usually ended with some irrelevancy such as ordering cherry trees.

At this juncture the patient went through his old check-books and happened to find an entry of two thousand dollars. He immediately concluded that this money had remained in the bank and had increased at compound interest for many years. Promptly he entered upon an orgy of spending. He promised his niece a $5,000 string of pearls. He talked of building a large and expensive home with a basement full of maids (Bluemel, 1938, p. 396).

Deterioration is often the result of physical damage to the nervous system. The forgetfulness, mental rigidity, and untidiness that accompany *senility*, for example, are the products of permanent damage to brain cells. Other types of brain damage, however, may not be permanent. The traveling salesman above, for example, was suffering from *general paresis*, which is caused by a syphilitic infection and which can be cured. Some instances of deterioration, such as that which generally accompanies schizophrenia, may have no apparent physical basis.

A company can only be alert to possible psychotic symptoms and the need for expert advice. Diagnosis and treatment invariably require professional psychiatric and psychological aid.

THE NEUROTIC WORKER

Like the psychotic, the neurotic is extremely tense and feels unhappy. Unlike the psychotic, he is generally able to adjust fairly well to normal life, does not require hospitalization, and can establish some rapport with those around him. A neurosis, then, is not a specific mental illness but a certain range of maladjustment—less severe than in a psychosis, more severe than in the normal personality. It is hard to set the exact limits of the range and to count the number of people in it. A variety of studies, however, points to the general conclusion that at least one worker in ten is sufficiently impaired by neurotic symptoms to be in need of professional help.

Neurotic anxiety

All of us become anxious in certain situations, displace our anxieties to other situations, or repress our anxieties. All of us, that is, would answer yes to some statements like the following:

I worry quite a bit over possible misfortunes.
I am troubled by attacks of nausea.
My sleep is fitful and disturbed.
Life is a strain for me much of the time.

The more such statements we honestly have to answer yes to, the more anxious we are. Anxiety is a vague but enduring fear. In some dangerous situations, anxiety is natural and also useful in leading a person to deal constructively with the danger. In some safe situations, however, some people still become extremely anxious. There, anxiety is *disproportionate* to the objective threat. The more disproportionate the anxiety, the more neurotic the person.

Whether anxiety is proportional or disproportional sometimes depends on who is deciding. The owner's anxiety about the security of his business may seem neurotic to the worker. In an anxiety *attack*, however, there is no question. For no apparent reason, the suffering person's heart begins to pound, his breathing becomes difficult, vomiting is not infrequent, he feels caught in the grip of gigantic circumstances, and he is overwhelmed by feelings of terror and despair.

The most common source of neurotic anxiety is chronic and severe punishment, deprivation, rejection, or disapproval by a parent:

> I always had a fear of my father which it is no exaggeration to call desperate. There was constant and serious trouble between him and my mother, although I had no comprehension of this. I assumed that all fathers were brusque, profane, given to heavy-handed punishment and intermittent drunkenness—that they were due various services with no obligation in return. My father often laid the weight of his hand on my mother in the presence of the children. Once, when displeased with me, finding no switch at hand, he beat me with a stick of stove wood. Strangely, I felt much more abused and afraid when my mother flew to my defense and sympathized with me. At this time (the preschool stage) and later, I can remember that my father often ridiculed me for wordlessness. His physical presence paralyzed me. From my earliest recollection, I was timid and diffident (Wallin, 1939, p. 100).

As such a child grows, these feelings generalize to other human relations. The son of a harsh father may be neurotically anxious in the presence of the most considerate boss. In general, he sees the world as a harsh and hostile place and himself as incapable of dealing with it. Phobias, obsessions, compulsions, and hysteria are inadequate methods that the neurotic has learned for dealing with his anxieties.

Anxiety as a creator of anxiety

Anxiety produces physiological symptoms. These symptoms, in turn, often make the person even more anxious. For example:

An ambitious but overdependent patient developed a typical anxiety attack in which gastrointestinal symptoms were prominent. One day at work, just after his convalescence from a severe attack of "grippe," he learned that he had not been granted an expected salary increase. To this information, which he angrily considered evidence of unfair discrimination, he reacted characteristically with nausea and diarrhea. Shortly afterward he had another attack of nausea and diarrhea, which he attributed to food poisoning; and because of his heightened anxiety, the gastrointestinal symptoms persisted. The patient then became greatly concerned over the possibility that he had a gastric ulcer, or perhaps cancer of the stomach. He consulted one physician after another, tried innumerable sorts of medication, and insisted upon repeated gastrointestinal investigations, in spite of the discomfort they entailed. The consistent medical reassurances he received that there was no evidence of organ pathology gave him no lasting relief. Finally, he left work and stayed home in bed for a period of nine weeks, convinced that he was suffering from an obscure but fatal illness. . . . Therapy aimed, not at the symptoms of anxiety, but at the conflict between passive and aggressive reactions which had induced them, brought him eventually to full social recovery (Cameron and Margaret, 1951, pp. 311–312).

The generalization of anxiety

Anxiety, like all intense emotional states, tends to *generalize*: the person who is made anxious by one situation tends to be made anxious by similar situations or by anything that happened to be a part of the original situation.

A recent graduate of an engineering college was hired by one of the industries in his home town. In spite of his mild protests, he was asked to assist two other employees with some rather complicated mathematical calculations. His desk was crowded into an already small office where the other two men were working. After a few months, he began to complain that the office seemed stuffy and that he felt as if the walls were closing in on him. He would frequently go off on errands or just go outside to get a breath of fresh air. After a period of about six months, his feelings became so intense that it was necessary to change his assignment. In the conversations that took place at this time, it became obvious that he felt very unsure of himself whenever he was dealing with mathematics. His reactions toward the work he was doing generalized to the room itself, and claustrophobia was the result (Gilmer, 1961, pp. 469–470).

It has been customary to label these chance stimuli that become associated with anxiety as *claustrophobia* (fear of closed places), *agoraphobia* (fear of open places), etc. This is not a useful custom, however, since any chance or incidental stimulus present at the time of an anxiety attack may later provoke anxiety.

Incomplete repression

Repression is the "forgetting" of things that are painful. We tend to remember triumphant moments, to repress embarrassing ones; to remember the times we have been intelligent, to repress the times we have been fools; to remember our altruistic decisions, to forget our selfish ones. We "forget" what makes us feel inferior, ashamed, guilty, and anxious. Neurotics also "forget" things that provoke anxiety. Among neurotics, however, the repression is so extensive and so unsuccessful that their behavior becomes disorganized, eccentric, and ineffective.

Obsessive-compulsive acts are one way of keeping anxieties repressed. At times of death, for example, mourners protect themselves from their anxious fantasies by meticulously following the funeral ritual. The neurotic person, who is chronically under trying circumstances, is often preoccupied with obsessive thoughts (persistent ideas that he himself regards as false, useless, or annoying) or with compulsive acts (acts that he himself regards as unnecessary or absurd). Preoccupation with these ideas and acts helps him to keep his anxieties repressed.

Obsessive-compulsive acts tend to develop in people with compulsive personalities. Such people are excessively clean, orderly, obstinate, and stingy in their habits; pedantic, scrupulous, and hairsplitting in their arguments; introverted and egocentric in their thinking; and aloof in their interactions with others. Because of these deep roots, such reactions are often extremely difficult to change.

Hysteria is a quite different reaction to incomplete repression. It is a broad term that covers the *creation* of physical symptoms that have no organic base, the *exaggeration* of symptoms that have some organic base, and the *development* of organic pathology as a result of stress. The tendency to exaggerate normal sensations or discomforts produced by the heartbeat, gastrointestinal motility, or noises in the ear are a common example of a hysterical reaction. From such minor difficulties, hysterical reactions range through tremors and tics or stammering and stuttering to hysterical paralyses like the following:

> A workman attempted to throw an electric switch which was supposed to carry several thousand volts. He believed he had received a shock which had gone through his left leg and hand. However, after the accident he walked almost a mile, got into a friend's car, and was taken home. All at once he discovered he could not use his left leg and had a

loss of sensation on the left side. He was bedfast for two months, apparently paralyzed in his left leg and thigh. Later, he walked with the aid of crutches and a brace. He believed that the electricity had destroyed a nerve in his leg. Since the incident had occurred while he had been working, he asked 50,000 dollars as compensation. The case was eventually diagnosed as "industrial shell shock" because of these facts: (1) the switch did not carry as much current as he thought, (2) it was so well protected that it was almost impossible to receive a shock, (3) electricity burns flesh but does not paralyze nerves, (4) his symptoms were not the kind he would have shown if the nerve had been injured, and (5) his muscles did not shrink as they would have if the muscle had been paralyzed. He was awarded 3,500 dollars and reported to be perfectly well (Menninger, 1945).

It is often difficult to assess the relative importance of organic and psychological factors in such cases. Sometimes, as in this instance, it is difficult to distinguish such cases from pure malingering. People who develop hysterical reactions tend to be extroverted in their thinking, immature in their social reactions, and relatively disorganized in their behavior.

THE ALCOHOLIC WORKER

People often see a gulf between the normal and the neurotic or psychotic person. No such gulf actually exists, as the transition, usually gradual, of a man from normal drinking to neurotic and finally psychotic drinking illustrates. Some consumption of alcohol is normal human behavior—unless we wish to call most of the human race abnormal. Thus, a large majority of Americans report that they have at least an occasional drink (Bacon and Straus, 1953). Some of these show the signs of a neurotic drinker: blacking out, drinking alone, drinking before or instead of breakfast, and displaying aggressive behavior when drinking. A few show the lack of contact with physical, social, or personal realities that is the mark of the psychotic. The movement from normal to psychotic behavior and back again is suggested by the following case of a forty-year-old executive who had been drinking to excess for 13 years:

On admission he was anemic and undernourished and showed marked tremor of his tongue, lips and hands. He was unsteady and uncertain in his bodily movements and in his speech. He talked of scenery moving by on the ceiling, snakes crawling around, of a wolf biting at his chin. "I can't sleep—there are two snakes crawling around on my pajama coat. I gave it to one of them (slapping bedclothes). My, what a lot of flies in this room! (none present). Guess I'll wear these trousers (bed sheet). Here, Joe, leave those papers alone. I'll take this voucher along with me (takes hold of blanket)." He picks at pajamas and says, "Oh, there I've got you, you rascal." He also picked an octopus off the floor and alligators out of his vest pocket.

During the first four days his condition remained stationary. He saw brown cats, red canaries, bugs, dogs and goats in his room. At various times he said he was in a hotel, a club, a friend's home, and aboard a ship. He carried on conversations with people not present. He talked as though his wife were in bed with him and he was apprehensive that she might be harmed. . . .

During the first few weeks of hospital treatment the patient's condition improved rapidly. The hallucinations disappeared but he continued to be troubled with visual distortions for three months. Objects seemed to be either too large or too small. He became apprehensive that his own voice was peculiar or that he was not acting normally. After five months he was discharged much improved with a diagnosis of delirium tremens. He continued to improve and returned to his work. A year later he reported that he was living amicably with his wife and that they had a healthy child. He had solved most of his difficulties by total abstinence . . . (Henry, 1938, pp. 157–159).

Considering the gradations in drinking behavior, it is not surprising that there are wide disagreements about the number of alcoholics in the United States: some say less than a million and some say more than seven million. Probably about one in twenty workers has a drinking problem. At any rate, an increasing number of companies are finding the problem too big to be dealt with by cover-up or discharge methods. The Consolidated Edison Company of New York, for example, has an excellent alcoholic rehabilitation program (Franco, 1954).

Early diagnosis is vital to the success of a rehabilitation program. Consistent tardiness or absence on Monday morning, frequent occurrences of leaving early on Friday afternoon, unexpected disappearances from an assigned post during a tour of duty, recurring excuses for absence due to minor illnesses, and frequent off-duty accidents, especially with assault as a factor, are all clues to a possible alcohol problem. Drinking well beyond allowable limits, the hiding of drinking, temporary amnesia as a result of drinking, and an unusual amount of time spent in justifying drinking are sure signs that there is a drinking problem.

Supervisors are in an especially favorable position to observe these clues and signs. They will not report what they see, however, unless they feel that the employee as well as the company will benefit. The company, therefore, has the responsibility for developing a climate where the alcoholic is viewed as being ill and where his coworkers think he is as much entitled to help as the man who breaks his leg on the job.

AID FOR THE DISTURBED WORKER

The development of a supportive company environment helps reduce the anxieties of the disturbed employee. It also helps speed his diagnosis, for his supervisor often has an intimate knowledge of his problems. In an unsupportive climate, however, the supervisor may fail to use his knowledge because of his fears that his own superiors will interpret the situation as a reflection on his supervisory abilities, that his subordinates will interpret it as a form of ratting on a fellow worker, and that the employee will blame him if he is demoted or discharged. The more supportive the environment, the less foundation for such fears the supervisor will have, and the more likely he will be to use his knowledge for the benefit of his subordinates.

Since psychological disturbances frequently involve physical disturbances, the company physician is often the first to identify and to provide some help for the disturbed employee. Some companies now have a psychiatrist or psychologist on their staff to help them deal with such problems, and many more have a part-time consultant. Many companies also have psychological counselors who, although they do not hold a psychiatric or psychological degree, are trained to provide therapy within the industrial setting.

The goal of the counselor is to help the neurotic person to recognize his anxieties, to uncover their origins, and to deal with them in a more effective way. The therapist's first and probably most important step toward this goal is to establish a good relationship with his client. It is only then that he can help him to recognize his defense mechanisms, to put his anxieties into words, and to solve the problems which have created them. To accomplish these ends, he may offer support and reassurance, indicate his understanding and acceptance of his client's feelings and problems, probe for facts and feelings, clarify and interpret what the client says, or evaluate what the client says, proposes to do, or does.

THE NORMAL WORKER

Normal workers have personal problems too. One company tabulated over a 3-year period the kinds of problems brought to its counselors. In order of frequency they fell into the following categories: housing, financial and budgetary, vocational and educational guidance, information, health, group health and group hospitalization, adjustment to the community, adjustment to the job, family, emotional or personality disturbances, adjustment to human relations on the job, marital, legal, mental illness, maternity leave, and insurance (Dreese, 1942). The solution of some of these problems requires only accurate information; some, only expert advice; and some, psychotherapy. The divisions, however, are shadowy. The man who asks for a loan may need therapy more than money; the man who asks for therapy may need money to pay the rent more than therapy.

Many managers are uneasy about, or actually opposed to, the "fad" of counseling, at least of relatively normal people. Some think that there are too many little "tin Freuds" and "amateur psychiatrists" who are "picking at the scabs of psychic wounds." Others argue that it constitutes an unwarranted invasion of the privacy of individuals and that "we should be able to take a man at face value and not always fret about what he really means." Still others feel that it is positively dangerous for a company to overstress the irrational aspects of human behavior and to understress the rational ones (McNair, 1957).

Many who oppose industrial counseling are counselors without knowing it. For example, one psychologist spent a day studying the activities of a supervisor as part of a job analysis program. He reports:

> During the day, along with giving orders, making inspections, and planning for the next day's work, this particular supervisor helped six of his employees to work out solutions to individual practical problems. The six problems involved such diverse activities as listening to grievances about working conditions and handling a telephone call from the wife of a worker who wanted advice on a domestic problem (which wasn't given, by the way!). I mentioned to the supervisor that he was carrying out a good load of counseling during the day. His reply was to the effect that he didn't do counseling because this wasn't part of his job. He did not regard the six individual problems he gave his time to as counseling. The writer would, however, for in each instance the foreman let the employee unburden himself by talking through his problem. In three of the cases, I received the impression that the employee *himself* worked out a solution to his problem as he talked and responded to the supervisor's questions (Gilmer, 1961, pp. 165–166).

The question, then, is not whether a company should provide counseling for its normal workers. It does. The question is whether it should provide a formal counseling service. Nor is it a question of whether *all* the counseling should be done by a formal counselor. Under an extensive counseling program, most of the counseling is still done in an informal way by a worker's supervisors and fellow workers. The question is: Are there any advantages in having *some* formal counseling?

The problem of evaluating the benefits of formal counseling in an objective and convincing way is still largely unsolved. It is hard to measure the amount of improvement realistically. It is harder to measure whether improvement in a particular situation has generalized to other situations. It is still harder to determine how much of the improvement would have occurred without the counseling. One of the few efforts which have been made to evaluate industrial counseling illustrates some of these difficulties. A control group of employees with personal problems was not counseled at all. A second group was counseled, but the counseling was judged to be unsuccessful. A third group was counseled, and the counseling was judged to be successful. The control group remained on the job an average of a little over 2-months, the unsuccessful group remained an average of a little over 3 months, and the successful group averaged over 10 months. Unfortunately, the results cannot be accepted at face value, for it was not clear that the problems of the successful group were as severe as those of the control and unsuccessful groups (Weider, 1951).

Some counseling, as we have seen, is an almost inevitable function of a supervisor. It can take a great deal of time that he does not have or does not want to give to this activity. A formal counseling program provides a solution for him. As counseling is organized in the Western Electric Company, for example, an attempt is made to have one full-time counselor for every 300 employees. At the request of an employee or his supervisor, the counselor has the authority to take the employee from his job (without loss of pay) to discuss personal problems.

Even if he makes the time available and has the interest, a supervisor may have little skill as a counselor. After all, he has been selected and trained not as a counselor, but to get a production job done. Some counselors are selected for the job more because they seem to have a knack for it than because of their formal education. Still, a full-time counselor quickly accumulates more experience in dealing with disturbed employees than the most seasoned supervisor. As companies have become more sophisticated about counseling, the educational and experience qualifications have risen.

Regardless of a supervisor's interest in and competence as a counselor, he has a serious disadvantage in the role: He is the boss as well as the counselor of his subordinate. The dual roles are almost certain to conflict at times. What does a supervisor do if an employee tells him he has cheated the company? If an employee tells him he is secretly drinking on company time? If an employee calls him a poor supervisor? These are somewhat unrealistic questions, for even the disturbed employee knows that problems of this sort should not be discussed with his supervisor. He may not be able to turn to his fellow workers either, for his behavior may be of personal concern to them, or he may fear that they will tell someone who would be concerned. He does need to talk his problems over with somebody, however. The formal counselor who is known to keep confidences provides him with an answer. In the Western Electric program, for example, the counselor is trained to keep confidences, and the counseling department makes no reports to the management which would permit identification of an individual or group. Records are kept by means of an elaborate code, and both the employees and the managers are constantly instructed in the confidential nature of the counseling relationship and the importance of keeping it that way.

THE SUPERIOR WORKER

An influential and growing number of consulting psychologists offer professional counseling service to the top executives of companies. One consultant firm, for example, has more than a hundred psychologists providing such a service through its regional offices throughout the country. The general aim of this counseling is to make the most effective men in the organization even more effective.

An executive has personal and organizational problems that he hesitates to discuss with other executives of the company because they have a high stake themselves in the same problems. Yet he wants to discuss his problems with someone and can benefit from doing so. Ideally, he needs a counselor who will not be helped or harmed by the way he handles the problem, who knows the organization and its people intimately, who knows the human side of enterprise, and who is trained as a counselor. The clinical psychologist acting as a professional consultant to the firm approaches this ideal.

The consultant helps executives to understand themselves and their organizational problems. His procedures are variable but include making written appraisals of individual executives based on interviews and tests, conducting developmental interviews with individual executives, counseling them and sometimes their families, and leading group meetings where the executives discuss their mutual problems. A common by-product is the employment of psychologists as full-time employees of the company to perform specific tasks that grow out of these discussions.

SUMMARY

Two out of three companies have a merit rating or performance appraisal program. The programs are most often used as a part of wage and promotion plans based on merit. They are best used as a part of employee development programs.

If appraisals are to serve a useful purpose in the development of employees, they must use raters who know the people they are rating, rating forms which are appropriate, and procedures which result in meaningful interviews with employees.

The keeping of a daily performance record by a supervisor ensures that he will have detailed and objective knowledge of each person's performance. It enables him to produce evaluations that can be accepted and used by subordinates to improve their performance.

The rating forms used may be quantitative or nonquantitative; they may be short or long. All forms must deal with the problems of *level* (the tendency of some raters to rate higher than others) and of *spread* (the tendency of some raters to distribute their ratings over a wider range). The techniques of ranking, paired comparison, and forced distribution can solve these problems satisfactorily but cannot solve the problem of *halo* (the tendency of raters to rate those employees whom they like personally higher than those whom they do not like regardless of their work performance). The forced-choice method is less subject to this problem because it forces the rater to choose between what seem to be equally desirable descriptions of the ratee.

The developmental interview is designed to encourage the growth of the individual employee. Its effectiveness is dependent upon the supervisor's success in finding common goals with his subordinate, in sticking to the employee's present job performance, in stressing his strengths rather than his weaknesses, and in listening to what he has to say. In turn, whether the supervisor succeeds in playing his part depends upon the company's success in creating a generally supportive organizational atmosphere.

Companies are making increasing use of psychiatrists and clinical psychologists in their development programs. Such professional help is imperative in dealing with psychotic workers and is desirable in dealing with many neurotic workers. The most frequent use of professional counselors, however, is not to make sick employees better, but to make healthy employees healthier.

12

ORGANIZATIONAL CHANGE

The preceding chapters on selecting, training, appraising, and rewarding are oriented toward improving the organization by developing individuals to fit its needs. The organizational orientation, on the other hand, strives to improve the organization by changing its system to better fit the individuals who work in it. This orientation is more complex and less well understood than the individual orientation. Its potential for improving the organization, however, is greater. There is even greater potential in combining the individual and the organizational perspectives.

Planned organization change is a frontier region of thinking and research for industrial psychology and other social sciences. As the science and art of planned change progresses, assumptions about what improves an organization are being tested. Some have been tested in laboratory situations, some in actual organizations, and some in both. All of those below have shown enough promise to keep researchers busy with further studies, but none has been completely demonstrated:

1. Trust is better than power in integrating individuals with organizational goals.

2. Assuming that people will be responsible and considerate is better than assuming that they will not.

3. Creating conditions in which individuals and groups are responsible for their own performance is better than trying to control performance by external means.

4. Overlapping responsibility is better than non-overlapping responsibility.

5. Decisions based on participation by many people are better than those made by a few.

6. Shared leadership is better than centralized leadership.

7. Supervision that stresses communication and facilitating group activities is better than supervision that acts as the agent of higher authority.

8. A wide span of control and many chains of command are better than a narrow span of control and a single chain of command.

9. Job enrichment is better than job simplification.

10. Working to change individuals as members of face-to-face groups is better than working to change individuals apart from their work groups.

This chapter explores the implications of these assumptions for the setting of organization goals, for theories of change, and for ways of applying the theories in practice.

THE GOALS OF CHANGE

All companies accept the general desirability of increasing integration, morale, and productivity in their organizations. However, different individuals and groups within the organization often have conflicting ideas about the *relative* importance of these goals and about the best ways of measuring progress toward each of them. These conflicts can only be resolved when the goals are translated into concrete and measurable form. It is the central task of the psychologist working in the area of organizational change to develop realistic measures of these goals that the company will accept and act on. It is vital, therefore, that he understand as well as he can the different ways in which decisions about goals are made in organizations and the different ways in which organization change can occur.

Bennis (1966) developed a table (see Table 12-1) in which he describes the ways organizations change based on how they establish and pursue goals.

TABLE 12-1 Classification of change processes

Power ratio change agent/ organization	Mutual goal setting		Goals set by one side or neither side	
	Pursued		Pursued	
	deliberatively by one or both sides	*not deliberatively by either side*	*deliberatively by one side*	*not deliberatively by either side*
50/50	PLANNED CHANGE	Interaction	Technocratic	Natural
100/0	Indoctrination	Socialization	Coercive	Emulative

SOURCE: Adapted from Bennis (1966).

He believes that change results from the interaction between a *change agent* and the organization. The change agent is very often a consultant from outside the organization, but it may be a new accounting system, a new production process, or any innovation. The kind of change process that occurs depends on three features. *What is the power ratio between the change agent and the organization?* Does each party influence the other with equal power, do they share power in some other ratio, or does one party do all of the influencing? *How are the goals of change established?* Is there collaboration in setting goals or does only one party, or neither party, set goals? *How are goals pursued?* Are they pursued deliberately by one or both parties or without deliberative intention by either party?

Examples of the kinds of change mentioned in the table are:

Indoctrination. While each party has goals (mutual but not necessarily identical) and pursues them deliberately, there is an imbalance of power. Mental hospitals might fall into this category.

Coercive. In practice this is an extreme form of indoctrination, e.g., so called brainwashing in war time prison camps.

Socialization. This change process is best observed in the relationship between small children and their parents.

Emulative. This is the well known "copy cat" process, e.g., the subordinate changes to become more like the superior in a formal organization.

Interaction. This process is much like socialization except that the power ratio is more nearly equal. It might be observed between older children and their parents or in married couples.

Technocratic. In this process one party sets the goal and pursues it but seeks information from an "expert" (who may or may not give it), e.g., a CPA advises on setting up an accounting system.

Natural. In this process "things just happen," e.g., an accident.

This table is a rough approximation, of course, and not a finished product. The table does make clear that change can occur under a wide variety of conditions. It also makes clear that *planned change* involves equal power of the change agent and the organization, collaboration in setting goals, and deliberativeness by both parties in pursuing goals. No other form of change calls for such a close working relationship between the two parties.

THEORIES OF CHANGE

Every answer to a serious question about organizational improvement implies a prediction about how the organization is expected to behave under some imagined circumstances. A company that is in doubt about the answer becomes confused and indecisive. An organizational theory, a set of concepts and assumed relationships between them, serves the essential purpose of providing predictions about how the organization will behave under different circumstances. Any theory that a company actually uses has the value of reducing confusion and indecision and making the organization more confident, comfortable, and willing to act. But the more explicit, the better tested, and the more widely accepted a theory, the more valuable it will be. It is a major task of the psychologist to develop such theories.

At present, there is no single well-developed and generally accepted theory of how to change organizations. In this regard, Katzell (1962) has said:

> Whereas scientific theory is positive or descriptive in formulation, organization theory has tended to be normative or *prescriptive*; whereas scientific theory is largely developed by induction from the facts, organization theory has relied heavily on deduction from *assumptions;* and whereas scientific theory is proposed as valid for a specific universe, organization theory is often promulgated as *general truth*. (p. 104) (italics added)

Sensitivity training, System 4 (Likert, 1967), and Managerial Grid (Blake and Mouton, 1964) theories focus upon different aspects of organizational change: sensitivity training on individual changes that will cause system changes; System 4 on changes in the organizational structure itself; and the Managerial

Grid on the interaction between individual and organizational changes. These different theoretical approaches do not necessarily conflict but complement each other.

In this section, we will consider the theories that exemplify, in turn, the individual, organizational, and interactional orientations to organization change. In the next section, we will examine applications of each of these orientations in the creation of change.

SENSITIVITY TRAINING

In Chapter 9 sensitivity training was discussed as a method for improving the skills and performance of individuals. Sensitivity training can also be used as a method for improving organizations. The theory behind the use of sensitivity training as a change technique is: If enough people in an organization hold new values in common and behave in ways consistent with these values, then the structure of the organization will change to fit these values.

Bennis (1967) believes that the new values and behaviors represented in sensitivity training are a requirement of our age. They must bring about change in organizations because the present, largely bureaucratic, structures cannot continue to exist. The bureaucratic model for organizations is highly vulnerable. It cannot keep up with the rapid and unexpected growth in population, with the increased size of organizations, with the improved educational level of people, or with the complexity of modern technology. The major problems facing organizations between now and the year 2000 will be how to integrate human needs with organizational goals, how to distribute power within organizations, how to promote cooperation, and how to adapt to increasingly rapid changes. The bureaucracy will fail to meet these problems. Very few people have taken a position as extreme as that of Bennis. However, most of those who use sensitivity training for organization change would agree with the direction of his thinking.

What are these values and behaviors which are the goals of sensitivity training? In their review of the affectiveness of sensitivity training, Campbell and Dunnette (1968) list six objectives.

1. *Increased self-insight or self-awareness concerning one's own behavior and its meaning in a social context.* Learning how others see and interpret our behavior and gaining insight into why we act in certain ways in different situations.

2. *Increased sensitivity to the behavior of others.* Developing an increased awareness of the full range of communicative stimuli emitted by

other persons (voice inflection, facial expression, bodily position, in addition to the actual choice of words) and developing our ability to infer accurately the emotional bases for interpersonal communications. What is the other person feeling?

3. *Increased awareness and understanding of the types of processes that facilitate or inhibit group functioning and the interactions between different groups.* Why do some members participate actively while others retire to the background? Why do subgroups form and wage war against each other? How and why are pecking orders established? Why do different groups, who may actually share the same goals, sometimes create seeming insoluable conflict situations?

4. *Increased diagnostic skill in social, interpersonal, and intergroup situations.* Achieving the first three objectives should provide us with a set of concepts we can use in diagnosing conflict situations, reasons for poor communication, and the like.

5. *Increased action skill.* Very similar to number 4, but refers specifically to our ability to intervene successfully in intergroup or intragroup situations so as to increase the satisfactions, effectiveness, or output of group members. The goal of increased action skill is toward intervention at the interpersonal rather than simply the technological level.

6. *Learning how to learn.* This does not refer to our cognitive approach to the world, but rather to our ability to analyze continually our own interpersonal behavior for the purpose of helping ourselves and others achieve more effective and satisfying interpersonal relationships.

The basic learning experience takes place in a training group (T-group) of 10 to 15 people. Usually there are no planned activities, no agenda to be discussed and no discussion leader. The T-group attempts to focus on the "here and now" by encouraging people to discuss themselves and their relations to the group. By dealing with the emotions and feelings which are a part of the here and now, the group moves toward realizing the above goals.

There is no standard method of using sensitivity training to accomplish organizational change. However, the following steps might be followed. In the first stages key members of the organization including top management might go away for a week or two of sensitivity training. In this first stage probably no two members of the same company would be in any one T-group. The purpose of this step is individual development and awareness that the total organization might benefit if more people were exposed to such training. Step two might involve a larger group of people from the organization going off-the-job for sensitivity training. In this case the T-groups might be made up entirely of people from the same organization. The groups would be so arranged that no person would be in a group which included his immediate superior. At this step people would experience individual development and would learn that others in their "back-home" company also recognize the value of the training. Step three in the process would involve actual work groups participating as a unit in off-the-job T-groups. Here the idea would be that individuals would learn the value of the training in dealing with actual work problems. The final step would be to have work groups use their knowledge in actual, on-the-job work situations as a basis for working together and not just as a training exercise.

These steps might take years to accomplish in an ongoing company. In a large company the first two steps alone could take several years. In any except the smallest company, steps three and four might require additional years of practice and new learning.

The effectiveness of sensitivity training in contributing to organizational change is unknown. One of the main problems in determining the effectiveness of sensitivity training is that it is usually only a part of a larger program so that the particular influence of the training is hard to separate from the influences of other parts of the program. There seems to be little doubt that most people do change their attitudes and behaviors after T-group experiences. There is also evidence that people show these behavioral changes in the work setting. Does the changed behavior actually help the company? Could the same change be produced by other means? There are still no confident answers to these questions.

SYSTEM 4

The System 4 theory of Rensis Likert (1961) defines four systems by which companies are actually organized and managed: exploitive authoritative, benevolent authoritative, consultative, and participative. In his more recent work (Likert, 1967), these are called Systems 1, 2, 3, and 4. The numerical identifications are helpful because they replace words difficult to define—words that interfere with accurate communication. They also represent more clearly the idea that the systems merge into one another rather than being completely separated. The System 4 theory assumes that as an organization moves from System 1 to 4, its integration, morale, and productivity rise. An outstanding virtue of the theory is that the dimensions along which the systems change from one to another have been carefully defined and can be measured. Consequently, System 4 can be readily applied to a particular company.

Systems 1, 2, 3, and 4 differ from each other on eight major variables.

1. The leadership processes used.
2. The character of the motivational forces in the organization.
3. The character of communication processes.
4. The character of the interaction-influence process.
5. The character of the decision making process.
6. The character of the goal setting process.
7. The character of the control process.
8. The performance goals sought and the training provided.

For example, in System 1 superiors do not trust their subordinates and seldom get the ideas or opinions of subordinates regarding job problems; in System 2 superiors have some trust in subordinates and sometimes get their ideas; in System 3 superiors have substantial trust in subordinates and usually get ideas from them; and in System 4 superiors trust their subordinates completely in all matters and always get their ideas and opinions and try to make constructive use of the information obtained in solving job problems. Table 12-2 shows in a brief form how the systems differ on each of the variables. The purpose of organizational development is to change from a position close to the System 1 end of the continuum to a position close to the System 4 end.

Companies near the System 1 position are characterized by high performance goals and a high degree of pressure on individuals and groups to meet performance standards. High pressure leads to compliance with company goals based on fear and produces unfavorable attitudes, poor communications, restrictions of output, and other effects which prevent the company from reaching its goals. When people have these unfavorable attitudes and behaviors the end result is that absenteeism and turnover are high and productivity which may be high for a short period will be low over the long run. At the other end of the continuum companies which are closer to the System 4 position perform quite differently. High performance goals are characteristic of System 4 also, but instead of the high pressure of System 1, the principle of supportive relations, the principle of responsibility, and the principle of group system of organization are used in organizing and managing. These principles of System 4 lead to favorable attitudes among the people within the organization, excellent communications of significant information, high trust and loyalty, and other effects which assist the company in reaching its goals. The end result of this system is that absenteeism and turnover are low and productivity and earnings are high.

In order to bring about organizational change a company must know

TABLE 12-2 Management systems 1, 2, 3 and 4

	Management system characteristics	
Variable	1	2
Leadership	Superiors and subordinates do not trust each other and display no supportive behavior.	Superiors are condescending and subordinates are subservient. Supportive behavior displayed in condescending manner.
Motivation	Fear and threats used to appeal to economic motives. Organization marked by hostile attitudes and dissatisfaction with membership in the organization.	Rewards and punishment used to appeal to economic and some ego motives. Attitudes toward company are sometimes hostile sometimes favorable, moderate satisfaction with membership in the organization.
Communication	Very little upward communication, usually inaccurate. Communication from the top viewed with great suspicion by subordinates.	Limited upward communication. Communication mostly downward and sometimes believed, sometimes not.
Influence	Subordinates exert no influence on activities in their units. No teamwork. Little interaction and always marked by fear and distrust.	Subordinates exert almost no influence on activities in their work units. Relatively little teamwork.
Decision-making	Most decisions made at top of organization and based on inadequate and inaccurate information. Subordinates never involved in decisions about their work.	Some decisions made at lower levels but always checked with the top before action is taken. Subordinates occasionally consulted about decisions.
Goal-setting	Orders issued. High goals sought by top and generally resisted by subordinates.	Orders issued with some opportunity to comment. High goals sought by top and moderately resisted by subordinates.
Control	Concern for the control function exists only at the very top.	Concern for the control function exists primarily at the top.
Performance-training	Training resources are fairly good. Organization seeks average performance goals.	Training resources are good. Company seeks high performance goals.

SOURCE: Adapted from Likert (1967).

3	*4*
Superiors and subordinates have substantial trust in each other and generally display supportive behavior.	Subordinates and superiors have complete trust in each other and display supportive relations in all situations.
Reward, punishment, and involvement used to appeal to economic and ego motives. Attitudes toward company are usually favorable and there is moderately high satisfaction with membership in the organization.	Participation and involvement used to appeal to full range of motives. Organization marked by highly favorable attitudes and high satisfaction with membership in the organization.
Some upward communication, some downward communication. Communication usually accepted but sometimes questioned.	Accurate and accepted communication flows upward, downward, and to the sides.
Subordinates exert a moderate amount of influence on activities in their work units. A moderate amount of team work.	Extensive, friendly interaction with substantial teamwork and substantial influence by subordinates on activities in their work units.
Policy decisions at top but more specific decisions at lower levels. Subordinates usually consulted about decisions.	Decision-making done widely throughout the organization, using full and complete data. Subordinates fully involved in all decisions related to their work.
Goals set by top after discussion with subordinates. High goals sought by higher levels and only occasionally resisted by lower levels.	Goals set by group participation. High goals sought by all levels.
Concern for the control function shared by top and middle levels and to a small extent at lower levels.	Concern for the control function felt throughout the organization.
Training resources are very good. Organization seeks very high performance goals.	Training resources excellent. Organization seeks extremely high performance goals.

where it stands and where it wants to go. Likert (1967) presents several questionnaires that provide the appropriate information to the company. While the questionnaires may differ in form, they are all based on the four systems and the seven or eight organizational variables mentioned above. (Questions about performance and training are sometimes omitted.)

People within the organization fill out a questionnaire that asks a large number of questions about communication, motivation, leadership and the other variables. For each question the person is asked to say where he thinks his organization is between System 1 and System 4. A typical question is: What is the direction of information flow in your organization? The person indicates his answer by marking on a scale like this:

Downward	Mostly downward	Down and up	Down, up, and with peers

Another question might be: To what extent are managers aware of problems, particularly problems at lower levels in the organization? and the scale would be:

Unaware or partially aware	Aware of some, unaware of others	Moderately aware of problems	Generally quite well aware of problems

An answer at the left end of the scale indicates System 1 organization and an answer at the right end of the scale indicates a System 4 organization.

After people in the organization have completed the questionnaire, those who administered it combine the answers and construct a profile of the company. The profile shows the company's position between System 1 and System 4 on each question asked. Profiles may also be prepared for different groups within the company. These profiles permit the answers of top management to be compared with the answers of their supervisors or the answers of one department to be compared with those of another. This information then becomes the basis for planning organization change. Information is returned to the company in feedback sessions and groups within the company identify and try to solve specific problems of communication, performance, leadership, or whatever is appropriate. The specific actions taken vary widely. They most frequently include management development activities and attempts to implement the principles of System 4. The questionnaire is readministered regularly to measure progress toward the System 4 goal.

The total plan for organization development requires that the company select System 4 organization and management as a goal, find out where it is in relation to the goal, develop and carry out specific plans to reach the goal, and periodically measure progress toward the goal.

MANAGERIAL GRID

Sensitivity training approaches organizational change from an individual point of view; System 4, from an organizational one. Managerial Grid Theory (Blake and Mouton, 1964; Blake and Mouton, 1968) is more comprehensive than either of these, for it focuses on the interaction between the individual and the organizational views. It accepts the theory of sensitivity training that the personalities in a company influence its structure and systems. It also accepts the theory of System 4 that the organization molds the personalities within it. It stresses, however, the interaction between these views: organizations influence employees; employees influence organizations. Consequently, from the interaction view, organizations deserve the employees they have, and employees deserve the organizations they get.

In the Managerial Grid system for changing organizations there are six phases.

1.   Basic training in grid theory.

2.   Development of work teams in the work situation.

3.   Development of cooperation between and among the work teams in the organization.

4.   Development of a strategic model for organization change.

5.   Development of a plan and methods of implementation for specific changes in particular units of the organization.

6.   A systematic critique to review progress and initiate new plans.

The purpose of step one in the system is to teach individuals theories of behavior and their application in working organizations. In particular, individuals learn about the Managerial Grid Theory (see Chapter 9) and the importance of considering both people and production. To attain this knowledge people go to a one or two week training session. Usually there are five or ten people from a company in a study group. Participants are selected so that there are several different hierarchical levels in any one group but no one is in a group with his boss. Several study groups from the same organization go through training at the same time. Within each study group individuals complete questionnaires and do team problems which help them to understand their managerial style and the kinds of results achieved by it. Members of the study group help each other to gain better insight into the importance and usefulness of various styles of management.

The purpose of step two is to bring the new knowledge of behavioral theory back to the organization and put it to work. It is not enough for an individual to have learned about his style in the training situation. He must learn what style he uses when he is on the job and dealing with real problems. Nor is it enough for a man to try to change his behavior when the work group makes no change. In developing teamwork each work group explores its usual "normal" way of dealing with problems and tries to effect whatever changes are necessary in order to develop a "problem-solving culture." Each team works toward setting standards and establishing specific objectives for team and individual achievement. Each team continually evaluates its performance to determine if it is becoming more effective.

Intergroup conflicts may occur between union and management, staff and line, division and plant management, or between other groups in the company. The purpose of step three is to locate intergroup conflicts and bring about intergroup cooperation. Resolving an intergroup conflict may take weeks, months, or years but is worked at systematically for as long as it takes. The process of resolving conflict requires that each side, independently, define and state specifically its present relationship with the other group and what relationship it would like to have. Then in a series of gradual steps, representatives from each group and finally the complete groups meet to examine and resolve the differences between their views.

The purpose of step four is to have top executives develop a strategic model that specifies the intellectual foundations of the company. This step requires explicit statements about six key areas. (Blake and Mouton, 1968). The statements must define financial objectives, describe the activities of the organization, define the customers and markets, specify organization structure, provide the basic policies to guide decision making, and state what must be done to promote growth in the company.

In step five the various divisions and departments of the organization make specific plans and implement them within the strategic model developed in step four. The activity is aided by the previous work in steps one through three since these steps should have resulted in better management of work groups, better cooperation and work within work groups, and more cooperation among work groups. All planning and implementing activities are coordinated by the top managerial team.

Step six, systematic critique, attempts to identify problems and their causes as the organization changes. The review also provides a basis for improving the quality, direction, and rate of progress for the individual plans and for the total plan. The specific form of critique varies with the organization. In general, however, the evaluation will make use of quantitative measures to assess performance, productivity, integration, and morale. Before starting the change program, the company agrees on which measures should be taken. Then, from the first day of step one, appropriate information is gathered and appropriate surveys are administered throughout the total effort.

Managerial Grid Theory has been presented briefly. When put into practice in a company, however, it may take years to complete the cycle of six steps. Parts of the cycle may need to be repeated as new people, processes, or functions are added to the company. The theory may become an integral part of the company and gradually become the company's basic operating style and not a program for change.

The authors believe that the six phases are in a logical sequence. They point out that applying the sequence to a particular organization is not a mechanical process. The sequence is designed to deal with two kinds of problems—those of communication and those of planning. The first three steps in the process are aimed at improving communication within and among work groups. Steps four and five are aimed at solving problems of planning. Thus all steps in the process are necessary. However, the rate of application, amount of overlap between phases, specific points of application, and other considerations will depend upon the particular communication and planning situation the organization faces. Much of the timing will also depend upon the skill and art of the change agent working with the company.

The Managerial Grid system has had wide publicity and application to organizations in this and other countries. To this time, however, there have been no published studies establishing the effectiveness of the program in bringing about organizational improvement. Beer and Kleisath (1967) did study the results of applying the first step and found significant improvements. But, partly because it takes so long to complete the full cycle of steps, there have been no thorough reports of the application of one full cycle. Still, the Managerial Grid system of organization change is the best presented, most detailed, and most thoroughly developed of the techniques for changing companies.

METHODS OF CHANGE

How do companies try to improve their organizational structures? This section considers actual programs of change instituted in three companies which evaluated the results. The first illustrates an individual approach; the second, a systems approach; and the third, an interactional approach. Only the last was a deliberate effort to apply an explicit theory of change. All, however, are based on the assumptions listed at the beginning of the chapter.

PLANT Y: AN INDIVIDUAL APPROACH

The individual approach is the simplest method of trying to improve an organization. At the extreme, it only requires the selection of a man to head an organization whose leadership attitudes and behavior are the attitudes and behavior that are wanted throughout the organization. Guest (1962) has described a company that successfully applied this method.

The six plants of an automotive assembly division were almost identical in organizational structure, technology, and product. However one of them, Plant Y, was performing so badly that the division's top management was considering drastic action, perhaps even closing the plant. Three years later, Plant Y had become the most efficient of all six plants. During its period of improvement Plant Y kept virtually all of the same supervisory personnel, the same formal structure of organization, and continued to produce the same line of products.

Plant Y made one change; it got a new top manager. Guest's report is an effort to understand why attitudes and performance improved so much after the introduction of the new manager.

Under the former manager not only was performance poor but employees at all levels of the plant expressed their discouragement and hostility. With things going badly in the plant, division management frequently gave orders to the plant manager to improve conditions and usually accompanied the orders with implied or actual threats. The plant manager did not attempt to persuade the division management to change orders. Instead, he passed along the orders and threats to his own subordinates who passed the same messages on down throughout the organization.

Under the new manager the style of life within the plant changed. The new man took several different steps which had a definite order but which overlapped in time. The key ingredient in the change seemed to be that special orders and threats from the division management stopped. The new manager reassured people in the plant by word and action that they did not need to fear losing their jobs. He talked frequently and widely with employees in order to become informed about the problems and needs of the organization. He introduced regularly scheduled meetings with his immediate subordinates in which they participated freely. They expressed ideas and suggestions to the manager and to each other. (This style of meeting was gradually adopted by all levels of the organization.) The manager involved his people in planning and gathering information before requests were made to divisional management.

A few comparisons of specific measures at the beginning and end of the three-year period show how the plant changed. At the beginning the ratio of interactions originated by superiors to interactions originated by subordinates was five to one. Three years later the ratio was two to one. Giving orders had apparently been replaced in large part by discussion. At the beginning of the change period production supervisors showed resentment and suspicion toward staff men, such as engineers and accountants, and felt that they were a threat and not an aid in getting the job done. Three years later staff members were seen as valuable; they were seen as having and giving information useful to the foremen. On the measures of direct costs for labor, Plant Y went from 16 percent above standard which was the worst of the six plants, to two percent above standard which was the best of the six plants. On the measure of indirect labor cost, Plant Y went from poorest in the division to tied for best in the division. Absenteeism decreased from a rate of 4.1 percent to a rate of 2.5 percent, and turnover dropped from 6.1 percent to 4.9 percent. Measures for labor grievances, quality, and safety likewise showed marked improvement.

Table 12-3 shows what happened on a number of measures following the change of leadership in Plant Y.

Clearly the new manager and the changes he introduced were accompanied by improved productivity, integration, and morale. The question of how much of the change was the result of the leader and how much was the result of the new climate of the plant cannot be answered by this study. However, it is significant to note that after three years the new manager was promoted to a higher position in the division and left Plant Y. During the next two years, Plant Y continued to be the best plant in the division and performed better than it ever had before. Thus, even when the leader left, the changes which he had built into the organization continued to function effectively.

THE WELDON COMPANY: A SYSTEMS APPROACH

Another study of organization change is reported by Marrow, Bowers, and Seashore in their book *Management by Participation* (1967). Marrow is president of the company which changed, and Bowers and Seashore are organizational psychologists responsible for the change program. Unlike Plant Y, the method used in the Weldon Company focused primarily on changes in the organizational system.

TABLE 12-3 Changes in Plant Y between 1953 and 1956

Measure	Result
General efficiency	Went from poorest in division to best in division
Ability to return to normal after a schedule change	Best in the division in 1956
Manufacturing costs of introducing a new model	Lowest in the division in 1956
Indirect labor costs	Went from poorest in division to tied with one other plant for best in division
Quality performance	Went from one of the poorest to first or second best in division
Safety performance	Went from consistently poor to top position in division
Labor grievances	Went from second highest to lowest number of grievances in division
Absenteeism	Rate dropped
Turnover	Rate dropped
Present performance compared with past performance	Improved
Performance compared with other plants	Improved
Number of superior-originated interactions (orders)	Decreased
Communication up, down, and laterally	Improved
Communication-production to non-production groups	Improved
Attitudes toward goals and people in the organization	Went from generally negative to generally positive

SOURCE: Guest (1962).

Early in 1962 the leading company in the pajama industry, Harwood Manufacturing Company, purchased the Weldon Company, which had the second highest volume of production in the pajama industry. During the several years preceding the purchase, Harwood was a profitable company and Weldon an unprofitable one. The new owners decided to keep the entire management group of Weldon in order to maintain continuity in the operation. Originally the only changes contemplated were to improve the facilities and work methods and install work systems modeled after those existing at other successful Harwood plants. After a short time, however, it became clear that more complete and far reaching changes were necessary.

The plan for a more thorough change program included three main features. First, as many Weldon people as possible were to be retained and "things were to be allowed to quiet down." Second, the physical plant, work methods, equipment, and production systems were to be modernized. Third, a new style of company life, participative management and leadership, which encouraged employees to become involved in the decision-making process, was to be introduced. The goals were to improve productivity, integration, and morale. While the three main features guided the efforts to bring about change, the idea was not to complete one step before going to the next. Instead, a time table of change was developed which called for the various activities to be overlapping. A few examples will illustrate the specific steps used to implement the change.

While "things were quieting down" two steps were taken—a personnel department was established and employee attitudes about a number of aspects of the company were measured. In the area of plant and process improvement, the shipping department was reorganized and an incentive pay system was introduced. The basic production system was changed from a mixed batch approach to a single (unit) batch approach. In their attempts to introduce a new style of leadership to the company, the new owners and the consultants tried to demonstrate participative management by example. In addition, all plant managers and supervisors participated in sensitivity training groups. The new owners also made a concerted effort to distribute responsibility widely throughout the organization.

In 1964 Weldon looked at various measures to see what effects the changes had made (Table 12-4). Return on capital investment went from −15 percent in 1962 to +17 percent in 1964. The monthly turnover rate among operators went from 10 percent to 4 percent during the same period. The daily rate of absences from work went from 6 percent to 3 percent. Production efficiency went from −11 percent to +14 percent. Comparable records for Harwood plants also showed improvement, but the improvements were far less dramatic.

When the attitudes expressed by workers in 1964 were compared with those expressed in 1962, the evaluators found that attitudes were only slightly more positive toward the company. The answer to one question, however, indicated that the future looked good. In both 1962 and 1964 people were asked what their personal plans were regarding staying with or leaving the company. In 1962 about one-half of the Weldon employees said they were definitely planning to leave or would leave when the right op-

TABLE 12-4 Changes at Weldon (1962–1964) compared with changes at Harwood

Measure	Harwood	Weldon
Return on capital investment	Increase	Greater increase
Production efficiency	Increase	Greater increase
Operator turnover rate	No change	Decrease
Absences from work	No change	Decrease
Attitude toward company	Not measured	Slightly more positive
Attitude toward staying with company	Not measured	Increased number planned to stay
Attitude toward unionization	Not measured	Improved greatly

SOURCE: Marrow, Bowers, and Seashore (1967).

portunity came along. By 1964 a large majority planned to stay indefinitely. One final example of change—unionization of the Weldon plant, was accomplished peacefully even though for several years before Harwood made the purchase attempts at unionization had aroused bitterness and contention.

THE SCANLON PLAN

In Chapter 10 the Scanlon plan was discussed as a group incentive system. It is also a program for organizational change and is a good example of the system approach that has been used in a variety of organizations.

The basic Scanlon plan has two main features. It is an incentive program that pays a bonus to all members of an organization based on improvements in productivity. It also involves forming a committee of subordinates and a supervisor in each unit of the company and a central committee of top management and elected representatives from the ranks. The purpose of the committees is to identify and solve problems that prevent increasing productivity.

The incentive feature of the plan provides management and workers with the common goal of improving productivity. Two-way communication is fostered by the committee structure. Further, the committees attempt to make use of the principle of supportive relations and the principle of responsibility by encouraging superiors and subordinates to work together on common problems. Unlike the other programs for changing organizations, the Scanlon plan does not involve any specific management training off the job nor does it involve any feedback of special information to the organization. An outside change agent may or may not be involved in helping the company establish and maintain the plan. If a change agent is involved, he may help to train the committees to work together. He may train various people within the organization by counseling with them and by providing them with information and data based on research in the behavioral sciences. Finally, he may suggest that the organization explore the usefulness of special training and other programs of organizational change.

Companies using the Scanlon plan as the basis for a program of change assume that desirable change will occur as the committees work toward solving day-to-day problems which impede productivity, integration, and morale. They also assume that, as the people within the company develop trust and confidence in each other by working together toward a common goal, interest in long range planning will develop. Not only will there be greater interest in long range planning, but the committee structure will provide a mechanism for participation in planning and in executing plans.

As with the other programs for organizational change the effectiveness of the Scanlon plan program is supported by no convincing research data. Some companies have developed remarkably well under the plan. On the other hand, some organizations which tried to use the Scanlon plan gave up because the desired changes were not occuring. Why attempts to use the plan fail, or succeed, is not known. Failure may occur because the principles of the plan are unsound or at least inappropriate to the particular company. It may be that the principles are sound but that the company is not skillful enough in applying them. With successful applications, the soundness of the principles and the skill of the company in applying them are impossible to separate. Perhaps if the company needs to change badly enough, because of market conditions or internal inefficiencies, almost any "reasonable" set of principles would serve to bring about change and growth.

SIGMA PLANT: AN INTERACTION APPROACH

In the interactional approach, a simultaneous effort is made to change both the system and the individuals in it. Thus, the Managerial Grid theory involves training individuals to understand and to apply the Managerial Grid theory of organizational systems. Blake, Mouton, Barnes, and Greiner (1964) report on the success of this approach in one plant that completed the first stages of the change program.

Sigma Plant of the Piedmont Comapny was a large plant of about 4,000 employees, 800 of whom were managerial and technical staff people. The plant was considered by company top management to be technically competent and had consistently been able to meet production goals.

Two major problems suggested that change should be planned and carried out. One of these concerned relations between the division management and the plant management. Division management was trying to delegate to the plant management many decisions which for some years had been made almost exclusively by division headquarters. The attempts at delegation were failing. The other problem existed within the plant. Relationships between different departments and levels within the plant were in bad shape and rumors and suspicions about "empire building" by various groups were common.

The change program began with training in the Managerial Grid (Chapter 9). Beginning in November of 1962 the first group of forty managers participated in one week of training. During the week each man examined his managerial style, practiced his style in a variety of simulated problems, and received feedback and criticism from others who were in training with him. The purpose of the training was to demonstrate the superiority of a managerial style (9-9) which brings a combination of high concern for people and high concern for production to the solution of organizational problems. Other groups of about forty each participated in the week's training until by the summer of 1963 all 800 managerial and technical people had participated. By the time the last groups finished training, the first groups were taking systematic steps in the plant to put into practice what they had learned during the training sessions. An evaluation of results of the first stage of the change program was made at the end of 1963 (see Table 12-5).

More than 600 people completed a questionnaire which asked what changes they had observed in a variety of areas within the plant. The results indicated that people felt that their own boss's work effort had increased, the work effort of the group had increased, and the quality of decisions made by the individual work groups had improved. Results showed that 49 percent of those who completed the questionnaire felt that they improved in the way they worked with their boss, 55 percent felt that they had noticed improvement in the way people in their work group worked together, and 61 percent had noticed that the work groups had improved in the way they worked with each other.

Measures of production and productivity also showed improvement. For all measures 1960 was used as the base year. The actual values of the measures for the year 1960 were assigned a value of 100 and later years were compared as a percent of the 1960 year. Productivity increased from 103.2 in 1961 to 103.9 in 1962 and increased again to 131.3 in 1963. Net profits before taxes were 229.0 in 1961, 118.0 in 1962, and 266.0 in 1963. Thus, even in the area of production where the plant already had good performance, substantial improvement occurred.

TABLE 12-5 Changes in Sigma Plant, 1960 to 1963

Measure	Result
Gross revenue	Increased
Raw material costs	Increased
Non-controllable operating costs	Increased
Controllable operating costs	Decreased
Number of employees	Decreased
Net profit before taxes	Increased
Productivity	Increased
Opinions of people in the organization	
indicated that they felt:	
The boss's work effort	Increased
The group's work effort	Increased
The quality of decisions made in groups	Improved
The ease of working with the boss	Improved
The ease of working with others in one's own work group	Improved
The ease of work groups working with other work groups	Improved

SOURCE: Blake, Mouton, Barnes, and Greiner (1964).

THE STATE OF THE ART

At this stage of research and practice those who are active in the field of changing organizations are much like architects. The architect combines a knowledge of the physical sciences with artistic and creative skills and brings this combination to bear on a complex problem. In both his planning and execution the architect may try to do things that have not been done before—to do things which neither theory nor practice has solidly established as "the way it should be done." The organization change agent combines knowledge of the social sciences with skills in working with people and brings this combination to bear on a complex problem. Not all change is planned, nor does all unplanned change lead to bad results. Planned change involves deliberately changing people and their relationships with each other. It is the focus of these change agents.

Change must precede improvement, but change is not always improvement. While this has been general truth for many years, it has been often ignored. Frequently those who could not see the merit of a particular change were cast in the role of the villain and accused of "standing in the way of progress" or of "being resistant to change." As more research has accumulated and especially as the kind of change desired has not occurred (failure), the resisters have helped to bring about more carefully planned, more systematically applied, and more carefully evaluated change programs. The rational resister has shown the validity of the position that the inevitability of change does not mean that his organization needs to change at this time in the direction that someone else thinks it should. Advocates or resisters may advocate or resist with rational and objective reasons or they may do so with emotional, subjective, and nonrational ones (Barnes, 1967).

If a company is to improve by change, there must be real and recognized reasons for change. These reasons may be generated either by internal conditions (high turnover, low productivity, high absenteeism) or by external conditions (loss of markets, inability to provide necessary services, higher costs of materials). If a company is to improve, the goals it hopes to attain by a change must be concrete, and specific actions must be taken to bring about the change. Finally, if a company is to improve, the results of the change must be measured to see if the company is actually moving closer to its goals.

Developing the appropriate criteria is here as everywhere the hardest task and evaluation is the most crucial process. If the change program is not getting results, other changes should be tried. The important task is attaining the goals, not sticking with unworkable methods. The "trapped" administrator sticks with unworkable methods while the "experimental" administrator keeps his eye on the goal (Campbell, 1969, p. 428):

> *Trapped administrators* have so committed themselves in advance to the efficacy of the reform that they cannot afford honest evaluation. *Experimental administrators* have justified the reform on the basis of the importance of the problem, not the certainty of the answer, and are committed to going on to other potential solutions if the one first tried fails.

SUMMARY

Building on a base of early and long-term interest in improving organizations by processes of selection, training, appraisal, development, job design, and incentive systems, industrial psychology is now involved in planned change programs which take the face-to-face work group rather than the individual as the unit of the organization.

There is as yet no one generally accepted theory of change or even well developed competing theories. However, present theories share common assumptions:

1. Trust is better than power in integrating individuals with organizational goals.

2. Assuming that people will be responsible and considerate is better than assuming that they will not.

3. Creating conditions in which individuals and groups are responsible for their own performance is better than trying to control performance by external means.

4. Overlapping responsibility is better than non-overlapping responsibility.

5. Decisions based on participation by many people are better than those made by a few.

6. Shared leadership is better than centralized leadership.

7. Supervision that stresses communication and facilitating group activities is better than supervision that acts as the agent of higher authority.

8. A wide span of control and many chains of command are better than a narrow span of control and a single chain of command.

9. Job enrichment is better than job simplification.

10. Working to change individuals as members of face-to-face groups is better than working to change individuals apart from their work groups.

The goals of change for an organization may be set by chance, by indoctrination, or by coercion. Planned change, however, necessarily involves collaboration in the setting of goals and in pursuing them. Theories of change may reflect an individual orientation (Sensitivity Training), an organizational orientation (System 4, Scanlon plan), or an interactional orientation (Managerial Grid). The different methods of instituting changes reflect similar differences in orientation. Each of these theoretical and methodological orientations has had some successes and some failures.

The essential ingredients of successful change are the setting of realistic and measurable goals, a commitment to achieving them rather than a commitment to defending one way of achieving them, and frequent evaluation of progress.

4

PROBLEMS AND SOLUTIONS

13

THE JOB OF THE INDUSTRIAL PSYCHOLOGIST

We have now seen the personnel, organizational, and leadership problems of companies from the point of view of the industrial psychologist. It remains to examine in more detail who he is, where and how he works, and why more and more companies are seeking his help in solving their specific problems. We shall first consider the historical development of industrial psychology and the educational development of the individual psychologist. We shall then discuss the organizations that employ him and the steps that he follows in solving their problems.

THE DEVELOPMENT OF INDUSTRIAL PSYCHOLOGY

On December 20, 1901, young Walter Dill Scott, associate professor of psychology at Northwestern University, said to the Agate Club in Chicago:

> Psychology is, broadly speaking, the science of the mind. Art is the doing and science is the understanding how to do, or the explanation

of what has been done. If we are able to find out and to express the psychological laws upon which the art of advertising is based, we shall have made a distinct advance, for we shall have added the science to the art of advertising.

In the audience was the head of a large advertising agency, who offered to start a monthly magazine if Scott would prepare a series of articles showing how psychology could be used in advertising. Scott agreed, wrote the articles, and thus became America's first industrial psychologist (Ferguson, 1961).

Scott achieved many firsts during his professional life. In 1915, he became the first professor of applied psychology. In 1916, he became director of the newly formed Bureau of Salesmanship Research, the first organization whose psychological research was paid for by private firms. In 1917, he and his associates published *Aids in the Selection of Salesmen*, which set the pattern for selection research and practice that was followed by the Army during World War I and later by the U.S. Civil Service Commission. In 1919, he established the Scott Company, the first personnel consulting organization. In 1922, with Clothier, he published *Personnel Management*, a book that has remained an authority in the field and whose sixth edition was published in 1961.

THE HAWTHORNE STUDIES

In 1924, discovery of the "Hawthorne effect" changed the course of the developing applied science. The Hawthorne plant of the Western Electric Company in Chicago began an apparently simple experiment to answer the question: What is the best work lighting? The results, however, were hard to understand. For example, workers in an experimental group had their illumination increased from 24 foot-candles to 72 foot-candles. Their production increased significantly, but so did the production of a control group whose illumination remained at 24 foot-candles.

The final illumination experiment led to the conclusion that a new approach was necessary. In this experiment, a group of workers was asked to comment on different intensities of illumination. An electrician came in daily to change the bulbs to increase the illumination. The workers commented favorably on the changes. Experimenters then instructed the electrician to act as if he were changing the bulbs, but actually to put back the same bulbs. The girls commented as favorably on the *apparent* change.

The puzzling results, the persisting desire of the experimenters to solve the puzzle, and the support of the Western Electric Company's management led to a series of experiments lasting more than 10 years. In the relay assembly-room experiments, the work behavior of 6 girls was intensively studied for several years. Several more years were spent in conducting, recording, and analyzing more than 20,000 interviews with employees and supervisors. For 6 months a single observer recorded the activities of 14 workers in the bank-wiring room as they wired, soldered, and inspected electrical connections. And over a period of years, a personnel counseling program for the plant was planned, developed, and installed.

In 1939, Roethlisberger and Dickson published *Management and the Worker*, the major report of results. It had been preceded by Mayo's *Human Problems of an Industrial Civilization* in 1933 and by Whitehead's *The Industrial Worker* in 1938. All were long and detailed reports. In general, however, the experiments showed that (1) an increase in favorable attitudes of employees had a greater influence on production than any increase in light, (2) increasing the employees' personal recognition had a greater influence on production than increasing their wages, and (3) more employees were influenced by their own informal organization than were influenced by the formal organization set up by the management. Since these books were published, experimenters have become wary of the "Hawthorne effect": increases in productivity that seem to be due to objective changes (in lighting, incentive systems, leadership, etc.) but are actually due to changes in the general attitude of the employees.

Before the Hawthorne studies, the industrial psychologist had stressed the individual worker; that is, he had concentrated on developing better tests and better interview procedures for selecting good workers and better methods for training them for their work. After the Hawthorne studies, the stress shifted to the problems of the work group: How can better work teams be developed? What type of leadership is most effective in dealing with groups? How can a more efficient organizational structure be developed? The Hawthorne studies broadened the field of industrial psychology to include not only personnel psychology but also industrial social psychology. These studies remain the most influential experiments in the history of industrial psychology.

THE PRESENT ERA

As Figure 13-1 shows, the number of psychologists in the United States grew rapidly in response to the demands of World War II. In 1940 there were less than 3,000 members of the American Psychological Association;

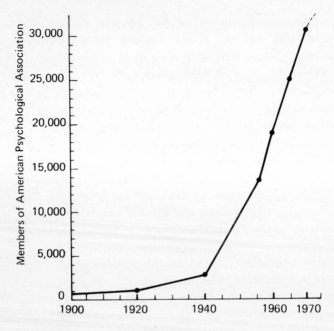

FIGURE 13-1 Growth in the Number of Psychologists in the United States.

in 1960, more than 18,000; and by 1970, more than 30,000. During World War II, several thousand psychologists helped establish and expand selection, training, and other programs for military personnel. Most of these programs had applications to industrial problems. Tests developed for the military were used for industrial purposes, the applications of learning principles to military training were utilized in industrial training, studies of reaction to combat stress had implications for vocational guidance, and studies of the design of airplane cockpits opened up the field of engineering psychology. Psychologists came into the war effort from varied fields of psychology: clinical, experimental, social, and educational. After the war, some remained in military service, and many went directly into industrial work.

The growth of industrial psychology gained formal recognition with the establishment in 1945 of the division of industrial and business psychology of the American Psychological Association. The growth has led to the expansion of college courses in this area. The first text was written by Viteles in 1932; since that time well over one hundred texts for courses in industrial psychology have been published.

THE EDUCATION OF THE INDUSTRIAL PSYCHOLOGIST

The education of the typical industrial psychologist begins with an undergraduate major in psychology. In 1959, more than 7,000 students were graduated with a major in psychology. This figure represented about 2 percent of all graduates—a percentage which had not changed much since the middle 1940's (Recktenwald, 1957). By 1967 almost 20,000 students were graduated with a major in psychology and this figure represented over 3 percent of all graduates. What do most of these students do? Barnette (1961) asked 375 such former majors, graduates of the University of Buffalo, what they were doing and found that about one in three was working in business or industry. He also asked them what, if anything, they felt their psychology training had lacked. The most common answer, particularly among those who had gone into business, was that they wished they had had more work in social, applied, and industrial psychology. Among the positions most commonly filled by psychology majors who go into industry are jobs as interviewers, counselors, management trainees, statistical analysts, and assistants to professional psychologists (King and Kimble, 1958).

While a course in industrial psychology is a normal part of a psychology major's program, only a few students who take such a course are planning to major in psychology. Most students elect it as one part of their general preparation for a business career. One of the authors, for example, found that 55 percent of his students at a Midwestern university gave reasons such as these for taking the course:

> To increase my understanding of problems I may come in contact with during my life in business.
> To assist me in my career as a business administrator.
> As psychology is an integral part of decision making at all levels, it should help me in dealing with both employees and consumers.
> Though I am an electrical engineering student, I want to gain some understanding of the human problems I may meet in my work.
> I'm an interior design major and since I will be in the business world and will be working with all kinds of people, I felt that this course would benefit me.
> I am majoring in restaurant administration and after exposure to the industry this summer I feel that I need to understand people better in order to be a successful restaurant manager.
> After working in business for three years, I have learned something of the value of psychology in managing men. I hope the course will add to my knowledge of this area.

Thirty-four percent of his students saw a more specific relationship between the course and their planned career. Of this group, many expressed an interest in personnel work as a career:

> I understand that courses like this one are basic background for a career in personnel work, the field that I plan to enter when I graduate.
> As a personnel major, the reason is obvious: to learn more about human relations.
> After graduation, I plan to do graduate work in the personnel area. I consider this course a foundation for my later training.

Others, while they had not decided exactly what kind of work they eventually wanted to do, were certain that it would be directly related to the course:

> Although I am a social science major, I am not sure what I will do with it. Personnel administration, labor and industrial relations, and law are among the possibilities. This course may help to crystallize my aspirations.

Eleven percent of the author's students were planning to major in psychology. Of these, 2 percent were seriously planning to do graduate work in psychology—a necessary step toward a professional career. The number but not the percentage of students who are taking this step continues to rise. While the percentage of undergraduates who major in psychology has grown in recent years, the percentage of graduate students in psychology has remained fairly constant. In 1959, 7 percent of those who were granted a Ph.D. received it in psychology; in 1967 the percentage was about 6.5.

Of those who receive a Ph.D. in psychology, only about 1 in 20 specializes in industrial psychology. About half specialize in counseling and clinical work and are employed by an agency: a mental hospital, an institution for the retarded, a prison, a juvenile court, a mental-health clinic, or a university health service. Others specialize in educational and school problems, in animal behavior, in statistics, or in the development of psychological tests. Some psychologists are interested in several of these areas and many shift from one to another during their careers. Consequently, psychologists may and do enter industry from jobs in clinics, in school systems, or in computer laboratories.

The easiest way of establishing the professional status of an industrial psychologist is through his membership in the American Psychological Association. The organization publishes a widely distributed directory, which gives not only the education but also a summary of the experience and professional interests of each of its members. Quacks and unqualified men claiming to be psychologists—and these are many—will not be in the directory. Psychology departments of colleges and universities are usually able and willing to help find qualified psychologists for interested persons.

THE EMPLOYMENT OF INDUSTRIAL PSYCHOLOGISTS

The one psychologist in 20 who does specialize in industrial psychology works for a company, a consulting firm, a university, or a government agency. About 35 percent of the members of the APA's division of industrial and organizational psychology are working in industry, 25 percent in consulting firms, 26 percent in colleges and universities, and 11 percent in governmental agencies (Sawyer, 1960).

Universities interested in the effectiveness of training programs for industrial psychologists, therefore, seek information about the work situations, experiences, and reactions of people from all these different job areas in order to improve training and keep it up to date (Campbell, 1970).

THE COMPANY PSYCHOLOGIST

In 1934 Bills gave the following account of a typical day in the life of an industrial psychologist. At 9 in the morning he met with other personnel people to decide on the placement of an employee for a 2-month period. This employee was mentally ill, but the company was attempting therapy by a psychiatrist rather than immediately discharging him. The conference over, he turned to the problem of deciding whether a person's ability to punch Hollerith cards could be determined in 3 weeks. Before lunch he also gave attention to a problem concerning the transfer of two employees to fill two vacancies and to the general problem of salary levels and rating scales. After lunch, he met with the loan fund committee to discuss a problem arising from the misapplication of some funds. Later, he talked to a cleaning woman who felt that the supervisor was not giving her a fair deal. He also talked to an employee who had been secretly married for 6 months and had to inform her disapproving parents.

Fifteen years later, the accent had shifted somewhat away from day-to-day service and toward research. In 1948, Canter asked more than a hundred psychologists working in industry to describe the kinds of activities they were performing. Only a minority reported that they were carrying out administrative duties, interviewing, or handling personal problems. The majority were involved in some kind of research activity: constructing tests, conducting questionnaire surveys, improving job analysis methods, etc.

The trend has continued. Today, not only are more psychologists doing research for their companies, but also the focus is shifting from short-range to long-range research—from applied research to basic. That is, psychologists are becoming more concerned with fundamental research on individual and group processes rather than with the quick application of already developed social science techniques to management problems.

The General Electric Company's recently organized behavioral research service is in the forefront of the trend. (Hovland, 1961). The company specifies that the service will "undertake experimental studies pertaining to employee effectiveness within normal General Electric working-life situations" and will "encourage and assist social scientists in universities to undertake behavioral research relevant to situations found in the business world in general and in the General Electric Company in particular."

One of the four psychologists in the General Electric service was concerned with studies of the supervisory or managerial function in industry; another, with conditions that inhibit or stimulate creative problem solving among the company's 22,000 scientists and engineers; another, with the use of survey techniques for the study of employee attitudes and attitude change; another, with a program of laboratory and field experiments concerning job satisfaction among hourly employees; and still another, with the satisfaction a worker gets from different ways of arranging work. All the psychologists were working, not on pressing managerial problems, but on basic human problems of men at work.

THE CONSULTING PSYCHOLOGIST

About one out of four industrial psychologists works for a consulting firm. The size of these firms ranges from an office consisting of a psychologist with a clerical staff to an organization employing hundreds of psychologists and maintaining many regional offices. Their working territories may be limited to a single city or may be national and sometimes international. They may be made up exclusively of psychologists providing only psychological consultation, or they may also include engineers, accountants, lawyers, and other professional people providing a wide range of consulting services. The psychological consultant himself may specialize in a single service such as testing or counseling, or he may offer many psychological services. In all cases, however, he has companies rather than individuals as his clients and therefore deals with individuals only in their work-life situations. As the following example illustrates, often his most valuable service is not to solve the problem as the company sees it, but to *define the problem* in a better way.

One of the clients of a firm of consulting psychologists was a large rubber company. The firm's psychologist working with the company was asked by the sales division manager to evaluate the training director in one department to find out if this man was well qualified for his job.

> Instead of immediately accepting this assignment, the psychologist explored the reasons for being uncertain about his subordinate's qualifications. This led to a discussion of the Manager's general dissatisfaction with the selection and training of salesmen. Upon the psychologist's suggestion, it was agreed that it might be of more value to focus on the general problem of the department's seemingly poor performance rather than merely to evaluate the Training Director. The consultant therefore was made available to the Salesman Selection and Training Department to help develop a program designed to reduce personnel turnover and raise sales productivity. Subsequent interviews with the Training Director revealed that he felt most of the high turnover and low productivity of the salesmen were attributable to the field training and supervision they received after they left the home office training school. At this point, with the prior approval of the Training Director, the consultant recommended to the Sales Division Manager and the Executive Vice-President a plan incorporating the following procedures:
>
> 1. Obtain active participation of all departments concerned with recruiting, selecting, training, compensating, or supervising salesmen.
> 2. Involve people at all levels with each of these departments; meet with these people in groups so constituted that no person would be in the same group as his immediate superior.
> 3. Conduct these group meetings as "brainstorming" sessions to get ideas for lowering turnover and increasing productivity. The group should agree to abide by a rule for these meetings prohibiting any criticism of persons or any immediate evaluation of ideas in order to permit maximum flow of thinking.
> 4. Collect, classify, and tally ideas.
>
> Five meetings were held, involving 40 people who produced 151 ideas. After the ideas were classified, the consultant recommended that the decisions on evaluating and implementing ideas with merit be assigned to a special task committee consisting of appointed representatives from every level. As an immediate result of the project, radical changes were made in almost every phase of the sales program, i.e., recruitment, selection, home office and field training, compensation rates, forms and procedures, sales techniques, and methods of supervision. Other positive effects were: increased sales, a significant reduction in time required

for salesmen to get into production, more effective communication among the different levels of the sales organization and especially between home office and field. Finally, many people reported that they felt much more motivated as a result of seeing so many needed changes put into effect (Glaser, 1958, pp. 487–488).

THE UNIVERSITY PSYCHOLOGIST

Teaching is the task which industrial psychologists in academic settings have in common. The other tasks that they perform, however, are widely variable. For example, five of the thirty psychologists in a large Midwestern university are specialists in the industrial area. All teach undergraduate courses (introduction to industrial psychology, psychology of advertising, personnel interviewing, etc.). All are advisers to graduate students planning to become industrial psychologists (more than half the Ph.D.s in industrial psychology are granted by Midwestern universities). In addition, each has a special area of interest.

One of the five works half-time as a consultant to local companies. Much of this time is spent in helping interested firms set up programs modeled after the Scanlon plan. He is able to choose as clients those that he feels are most likely to benefit from his services. In his consulting activities he frequently takes graduate students with him as intern assistants, and many of them base their thesis research on data gathered with the cooperation of the client companies.

The second of the five has spent much of his time in governmental overseas activities. He has been in Korea as a personnel consultant for the Army, in southeast Asia as a training consultant to the local government, in Africa as an evaluator of United States educational and technical assistance programs, and in Washington as an adviser to the Peace Corps in its selection program. As both the American government and American industry have become more involved in international programs, so also has the industrial psychologist. In turn, as underdeveloped countries have become more industrialized, they have become more interested in sending students to the United States to be trained as industrial psychologists.

The third of the industrial psychologists is interested in test construction and human engineering. The fourth is involved with problems of large-scale organizations, and particularly with the human problems the organization faces because of the introduction of automated processes. The fifth is primarily concerned with the development and evaluation of sensitivity training programs for supervisors.

THE GOVERNMENT PSYCHOLOGIST

That government agencies, like private companies, have personnel and organizational problems is reflected in the fact that more than one in ten industrial psychologists works for a government agency. Some work for city and state civil service commissions, aiding in the selection, training, and appraisal of employees. Many more work for a wide variety of agencies of the Federal government: the Defense Department, Bureau of Public Roads, Forest Service, etc. Many also work for private organizations (e.g., the Systems Development Corporation and the Human Resources Research Organization) whose sole customer is the Federal government.

The Federal government has become an increasingly large supporter of psychological research both in and out of government agencies. In 1953, it gave 10 million dollars to 149 institutions outside the government for research projects; in 1959, it gave three times as much to three times as many institutions (Young and Odbert, 1960). Inside the government, agencies are employing more psychologists to work on problems like the following: the development of tests for the more effective selection of military officers, the study of driver behavior for the purpose of developing better highway transportation systems, and the evaluation of the effectiveness of a wide variety of training programs.

STEPS IN SOLVING A PROBLEM

Whether he works for a company, a consultant firm, a university, or a government agency, the industrial psychologist is concerned with helping to solve the human problems created by an industrial civilization. In the process, he tries to formulate a given problem as precisely as possible, to review what is known about it, to explore it as first hand, to make as good a guess as he can about the answer, to set up a procedure for testing his guess, to select a group on which to carry out the test, to analyze the results of the test, and finally, to interpret and apply the results.

His efforts to solve a problem may stop at any point along the way. He may find that the problem has already been solved by someone else, or he may feel that he has a good answer after only a preliminary survey. He may decide that the problem is not important enough to justify setting up a test of the guess he has made, or he may find that no adequate procedure or no adequate group is available for testing his guess. Or if he makes the test, he may find that the results are too inconclusive to provide an answer to the problem. To illustrate these steps, the solution of an actual problem, the constructive use of work music (mentioned in Chapter 2), will be described in the following sections. At the same time, some of the psychologist's general problems in dealing with each phase of the process will be discussed.

FORMULATION OF THE PROBLEM

A psychologist in a company employing over 100,000 employees was asked by the management to aid in the solution of the problem of work music in the company. This company had 12 different plants.

The central management had felt it would be desirable for all plants to have the same policy in regard to the use of music. It had, therefore, appointed a central committee composed of representatives from each plant to decide on such a policy. Most of the committee members were in favor of having music. Some, however, were opposed, claiming that it would be an expensive headache which eventually would be harmful to efficiency. In an effort to reconcile these conflicting opinions, the committee reviewed studies dealing with the question. Although it found many eloquent accounts, there was not enough evidence to base a decision on. Finally, the committee asked the psychologist to consider the feasibility of conducting an experiment within the company to obtain more conclusive evidence.

The psychologist felt that the influences of music might be so complicated that they would be difficult to study. Does music produce any changes in the attitude or behavior of employees? Such changes, if any, might be varied and hard to measure. The difficulties involved in designing a study which would isolate the effects of music from the many other factors influencing attitudes and behavior would be considerable. Still, the company was interested and cooperative. It was willing to allow one of its new plants to be employed for the experiment, to provide the psychologist with sufficient authority to control the experiment carefully, and to assign him sufficient personnel to complete it. The answer to the problem seemed to have considerable importance for the company as well as potential value in many industrial settings outside the company. The psychologist therefore suggested that an experiment be conducted and outlined a tentative plan, which was accepted by the committee (H. C. Smith, 1947).

Even to be *aware* that a problem exists is an achievement. For example, it was only after considerable discussion and search that the members of the music committee realized that they had a problem—that music might influence their goals in a way that they did not understand but wished to discover. Awareness that there is a problem, however is not enough; people may look in the wrong direction for an answer, or more commonly, they may state the problem in such a muddled way that they can never get a clear answer. Often, the psychologist's most basic contribution is to help a company become aware of its human problems and to help it clarify them.

REVIEW OF KNOWLEDGE

When the company's psychologist had formulated the music problem and the committee had accepted his tentative plan, he spent several days in the library. He started with the *Psychological Abstracts*, a periodical which has been published by the American Psychological Association since 1927. The monthly journal has paragraph summaries of psychological studies that have been published in United States and foreign journals, and the bound annual volumes have an elaborate index.

Looking under "music" in each of these volumes, the psychologist found the following abstract:

1321. Kerr, W. A. *Experiments on the effects of music on factory production*. Appl. Psychol. Monogr., 1945, No. 5, Pp. 40. Studies were made in an industrial plant of the effects (quantity and quality of production, and net good yield) of the presence of different kinds of music and, in one instance, of the absence of certain kinds of music from a music-adapted group. While none of the differences were statistically significant, the consistency of the workers' being in favor of the presence of music is taken as in itself significant. Results were more favorable under hourly-pay-rate conditions than in incentive-pay situations. There was no marked superiority of any one music type. T. E. Newland (U.S. Naval Reserve)

He then located the *Applied Psychology Monograph* referred to and studied the 40-page report in detail. In addition, he found an earlier report of an experiment by an English industrial psychologist that related music to productivity. Although many articles were listed which reported opinions about music and productivity, there were no other experimental studies.

The results of the two experiments, while generally favorable to music, indicated that the problem could not be considered solved. Nonetheless, an examination of the methods previously employed and the difficulties encountered allowed the experimenter to profit from previous difficulties and mistakes. One experiment, for example, had failed because the attempt to have music one week and no music the next week had made the employees so indignant that the management forced the termination of the experiment. In planning his own experiment, therefore, the psychologist decided to have only one no-music day per week and to prepare the workers by informing them in a letter that the music program was in the process of development.

Individuals and committees in industry sometimes spend many hours discussing and attempting to find the answers to problems which have already been solved by someone else. One difficulty lies in their ignorance of where to look. They do not know, for example, of the general availability and convenience of the *Psychological Abstracts*.

A more basic difficulty is that many industrial studies are never reported. Companies tend to feel that the publication of research on which they have spent a good deal of money is too generous a gift to possible competitors. Sometimes a company merely lacks interest in making a general scientific contribution. Sometimes a study is concerned with problems that the company prefers to keep confidential. In the long run, of course, there would be a general gain to all if more industrial studies were published and more psychologists tried to encourage such publication. Certainly the situation is improving: Between 1925 and 1930, an average of 200 industrial psychology studies were published; between 1955 and 1960, there were three times as many (Meltzer, 1960).

PRELIMINARY OBSERVATIONS

After reviewing the literature, the psychologist working on the music problem visited the plant where the experiment was to be conducted. He inspected the recording equipment available and acquainted himself with the work schedule. He also visited several plants of other companies that used music programs and heard about the problems they had encountered. These visits supplemented the literature in giving him a concrete idea of the practical problems concerned with a music program and the kind of difficulties he was likely to have. The importance of adhering rigidly to a definite time and program of music was thoroughly discussed with the management of the plant in order to enlist its cooperation. The necessity of keeping the fact that a study was underway a temporary secret from the employees was also thoroughly talked over with the plant and personnel managers.

Often an industrial psychologist's attack upon a problem may be terminated as a result of his preliminary observations, for these may strongly indicate that a particular solution is the best. Or at the other extreme, it may be terminated because the practical difficulties in conducting a worthwhile experiment may prove to be too great. The psychologist may decide that his own judgments will be as sound without any experiment as with the results of an inadequate one.

THE HYPOTHESES

The psychologist formulated hypotheses that he planned to test in his music experiment. Among these were:

1. Most employees like music while they work.
2. Productivity increases with the use of music.
3. Productivity varies with the type of music played.

A hypothesis is a guess about the answer to a problem. It may be a confident guess: the hypothesis that employees would like music, for example, was supported by the results of many earlier studies. It may be a wild guess: in the case of the hypothesis that productivity would increase with the use of music, the psychologist felt that the results of previous studies lent it only mild support. Confident or wild, however, a hypothesis *must* be stated in such a way that it can be tested; otherwise it is useless. Thus, the experimenter as he formulated hypotheses tried to plan how he would measure music, productivity, and type of music, and how he would relate these measures to each other.

A REPRESENTATIVE SAMPLE

The psychologist picked the employees on one small assembly line for his production experiment. Many factors entered into this selection. There were enough employees (21) so that the gross effects of chance would be greatly reduced. More important, the job operated on two shifts, day and night, so that the results obtained from one shift could be checked against the results from another. The psychologist also found that there were unusually good records of the productivity of each girl and the group as a whole. (The lack of such records is a frequent obstacle to good industrial experiments.) Finally, the work of the group was highly repetitive, which would make it representative of many factory jobs.

In order to have data for interpreting the results of the study, the experimenter gathered detailed information about the group: age, sex, education, years of experience with the company, and the exact nature of their jobs. In addition to an intensive study of this group, information was obtained from more than 700 shop and office employees in regard to attitudes toward music. This number represented a relatively wide sample and was large enough to permit detailed analyses according to type of work, age, etc.

The main reason why the selection of the sample is so important is that the results of a study can be confidently applied only to groups *like* the one studied. Thus, the workers sampled in the music study were all women; the results apply most dependably to women. The workers sampled in the study were all relatively inexperienced; the results apply most dependably to inexperienced workers. The workers sampled in the study were all engaged in highly repetitive jobs; the results apply most dependably to workers on such jobs. The point is not a minor one. Uhrbrock (1961), summarizing this study and the ones completed in the 15 years since it was done, concludes that *only* "young, inexperienced employees engaged in doing simple, repetitive, monotonous tasks increased their output when stimulated by music." In general, then, the ideal sample should faithfully represent the groups that the results will be applied to.

THE TEST OF THE HYPOTHESES

By this time, the psychologist had formulated the hypotheses, selected the setting, and picked the subjects. He was ready to test his hypotheses. Testing the hypothesis that workers like music presented no great difficulties. A questionnaire was designed to ask them how they felt about music before this program began, and interviews were conducted near the end of the experiment to see how they felt after having been exposed to the music for several months. An analysis of the results showed that 98 percent were at least mildly in favor of having music while they worked.

Testing the hypothesis that music increases productivity was much harder. Productivity is influenced by many factors: the interest, health, and experience of the workers as well as the tools, flow of work, and type of supervision. In the ideal test, all factors influencing productivity would remain the same except for music. The psychologist attempted to approach this ideal by using the following controls:

1. A large enough sample so that chance variations in productivity would be minimized

2. A pattern for playing music that would cancel out the influence of technological variations on productivity

3. Statistical controls that would reduce variations in productivity due to the day of the week, to improvements in production over time, and to absenteeism

4. Repetition of the study with a second group to reduce the possibility that some unknown nonmusic condition had affected the results in the first group

The girls on the assembly line were exposed to a carefully scheduled pattern of music for 12 weeks. During these weeks, the productivity of the individuals was measured hourly, and the productivity of the line as a whole was measured for each shift. At the end of the experiment, variations in music (the independent variable) were related to variations in productivity (the dependent variable). An analysis of the results led to the following conclusion: "Production under varying conditions of music increased from 4 to 25 percent. The average increase on the day shift was 7; on the night shift, 17 percent" (H. C. Smith, 1947).

Experiments are not the only way to test hypotheses. They may be tested by consulting expert opinion, by making a careful case study, or by making systematic observations. None of these methods, however, is as convincing as an experiment; no psychologist would question that, other things being equal, an experiment is the best way to test a hypothesis. But other things are not equal, for an experiment is the most difficult and expensive method to employ. In each case, therefore, the investigator decides what method he will use by balancing the precision of the experimental approach against the greater time and effort required.

THE REPORT OF RESULTS

As the experiment progressed, the psychologist made regular reports to the management. Soon after the completion of the study, he made a complete report to the music committee. At his request, the committee authorized the publication of the results as an *Applied Psychology Monograph*.

USE OF THE RESULTS

On the basis of the findings, the psychologist prepared a series of specific recommendations for the use of music. They covered technical matters of equipment, programming, and the times, places, and manner in which music should be employed in the company. They stressed that the wishes of the workers were a good, though not infallible, guide in when and how to use work music. The positive results of this and similar experiments have led about one company in three to install some form of work music program.

Managements are sometimes distressed by the large amounts of money and the small amounts of certainty involved in psychological experiments. Yet it is the very nature of experimentation that this should be so. Since it is the purpose of an experiment to learn something new, it is a poor experiment whose results can be confidently predicted, for in such a case little that is new is being learned. On the positive side, like experiments in any field of science, the process of testing for the truth of an uncertain guess about human behavior often results in new, unexpected, and highly useful information.

SUMMARY

The Hawthorne studies of the 1930s and the extensive military work of psychologists during World War II were turning points in the history of industrial psychology, a field which came into existence at the turn of the century. Today, 1 in 30 new college graduates is a psychology major; 1 in 15 new Ph.D.s is a psychologist; and 1 in 20 of the more than 30,000 psychologists in the United States is primarily interested in industrial psychology. About one-third of industrial psychologists are employed by companies; one-fourth, by consultant firms; another fourth, by colleges and universities; and one-tenth, by governmental agencies.

Wherever he is employed, the industrial psychologist is concerned with solving the human problems created by an industrial civilization. In the process, the psychologist (1) formulates problems, (2) reviews previous knowledge, (3) makes preliminary observations, (4) states hypotheses, (5) finds representative samples, (6) tests hypotheses, (7) reports the results, and (8) uses the results.

14

THE JOB OF THE EXECUTIVE

Throughout the past thirteen chapters, this book has been examining new ways of dealing with old problems. In thirteen sections named and numbered for the previous chapters, the following pages will present a bird's-eye view of these problems. Here they will be discussed from the standpoint of present and future industrial leaders, since the executive has the greatest opportunity, and therefore the greatest responsibility, for solving them. He cannot succeed in this by doing the same old things in the same old ways; he needs to do new things in better ways. More and more, companies are looking among graduating seniors for leaders who have learned these new ways.

1. THE ORGANIZATION

An executive works in an organization. He must be constantly aware that his success and the success of the organization depend upon how well the goals of the organization are achieved. Frequently he plays the leading role in establishing and monitoring the formal structure to ensure that the ways people are relating to each other and to their jobs is helping to accomplish organizational goals. As he goes about his job, the executive knows that the principles for organizing his company are always a subject for review. The formal organization may be sound, it may require some minor adjustments, or it may need major adjustments based on changes in technology, changes in the make up of the work force, improved education level, or new information about how people work and what work means to them.

The executive is also aware that informal organization within the formal structure is a fact of life. He recognizes that the informal organization may hinder or help in achieving goals. Part of his job is to make sure that it helps. An executive understands and tries to communicate to others that the ways in which people group themselves and behave are just as important as the formal structure, rules, and policies of the organization.

As Figure 14-1 suggests, the job of the executive is (1) to increase the output per unit of input in his organization (productivity), (2) to build its capacity to maintain itself under stress (integration), and (3) to get his employees more interested in their work (morale). It is no small part of his task to become and to remain aware that *all* these goals are important. Often he is acutely conscious of the production goal, but only dimly aware of the integration goal and entirely unaware of the morale goal. Consequently he may be taking pride in temporary increases in productivity while, un-

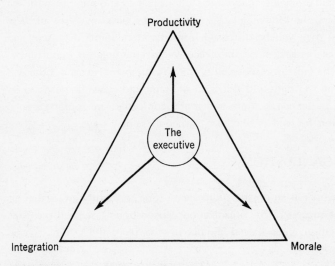

FIGURE 14-1 The Goals of the Executive.

known to him, his methods of gaining the increases are dangerously lowering both integration and morale.

2. THE MEASUREMENT OF GOAL PERFORMANCE

Before he can know whether the organization is achieving its goals, the executive needs to have criteria—measures of goal performance. The criteria need to be as reliable, free of contamination, relevant, and comprehensive as possible.

Incomplete criteria are the prime reason for the executive's neglect of integration and morale. The first maxim of an old statistics book was "Anything that exists can be measured." A better maxim for the executive is "Anything that can be measured is overemphasized." Since a worker's production is easier to measure than his feelings about the company and his job, his production is likely to be stressed and his feelings neglected.

An executive typically has many good measures related to economic efficiency and productivity: investment in plant and equipment, production, sales, costs, earnings, percentage of net earnings to sales, etc. He has few and poor measures of worker loyalty and motivation. The discrepancy leads him toward two kinds of mistakes: (1) faulty conclusions about what type of management leads to the best results; (2) faulty conclusions about the value of specific programs and techniques. For example, since pressure-oriented and threatening supervision can often achieve impressive *short-run* increases in productivity, he often concludes that this is the best type of leadership because he cannot see its disastrous long-run effects upon integration and morale. On the other hand, he may retain unwarranted confidence in such expensive procedures as the selection interview, an incentive system, or a human-relations training program because he has no measures of integration or morale to use in testing their effectiveness.

The better and more complete the measures available to the executive, the better the job he can do. Also, the *sooner* he can get the measures, the better; measures for last month are more useful than measures for last year. A short "feedback cycle," for example, is a valuable resource for making technological changes. As the changes are introduced, frequent measurements permit rapid adjustments. In this way improvements can be achieved smoothly and efficiently with a minimum of adverse consequences. In general, short feedback cycles can save a great deal of time and money by providing a check on new ideas at an early stage in their application. New ideas are not always better ideas.

Better and faster measures are most useful when an executive makes them available to everyone involved. For example, if a group is responsible for planning its own work, it has as much need for measures as the supervisor of the group. Furthermore, if the group does not get the measures, the measures the executive gets from the group are likely to be inadequate, for distortion of measures for self-protection is nearly a universal practice at every level of a firm. Here is a typical example:

> One of the departmental Production Committee's most vigorously-pressed suggestions concerned the scheduling of jobs. Workers complained that they often set up their equipment as scheduled, only to find that the particular paper needed for that job was not yet on hand. Though paper for other jobs was apparently available, they could not make a switch since setup time was generally great. This complaint involved people outside the department, however, so the Production Committee could do little about it themselves. They passed it on to the top Screening Committee, a group which included the company president.
>
> The head of the scheduling department, of course, felt particularly concerned with this complaint, and so he did some "homework" in preparation for the meeting. For each job, the worker turns in to the scheduling department a time slip on which is tabulated the total elapsed hours in terms of "running time," "delays," and so on. The department head examined the file of these slips thoroughly and found that there was actually very little delay due to "insufficient paper." When the question came up in the meeting, he triumphantly produced these "facts" and discounted the complaint as of minor importance. This disclosure was greeted with an embarrassed silence. After a long half-minute, one of the workers spoke up: "Those time slips are way off. We fill them out. We were told by the foreman that he would get in trouble if we showed that delay time, so we usually added it to the running time. We've been doing it that way for years. We had no idea you were using the slips as a basis for planning" (Schultz, 1951, pp. 209–210).

3. WHY PEOPLE WORK

People work to satisfy their needs. Most executives would *say* that they believe this and would *say* that they believe that people's needs include status, understanding, and autonomy as well as food and shelter. Many executives, however, do not *act* as though they agree. Few executives would *say* that they believe the average worker has an inherent dislike of work, must be threatened with punishment to get him to do a fair day's work, dislikes responsibility, and has little imagination. Many executives, however, *act* as if they believe these things. The best translation of the executive cry, "Let's be practical," is often, "Let's accept these beliefs of mine about why men work." However, contrary to traditional management beliefs, work is as natural as play or rest, and the average worker likes to exercise self-direction, responsibility, and ingenuity in the service of goals to which he is committed. *How* to get his subordinates committed to company goals is the basic task of the executive. The principles of common goals, supportive relationships, and employee responsibility provide general guides for sound executive action.

The principle of common goals states that an executive should take actions which lead most directly to the setting of goals that involve both company and worker. The most common violation of the principle is the unstated but deep-seated assumption that the goals of the company are more important than those of the workers. Thus, both executives and workers are promoted or transferred with little or no consultation, on the assumption that what is good for the company is good for the employee. Full application of the principle of common goals requires instead a deep-seated feeling that the goals of the worker are as important as the goals of the company, and that the company can gain the maximum benefit only when both company and employee agree about what is the best thing for him to do.

The principle of supportive relationships states that an executive should take those actions that are most likely to build the worker's sense of personal worth and importance. Actions leading the employee to feel that he is not understood, not liked, and not respected as a worker violate the principle. Supportive actions are those which make him feel that he is understood, accepted, and liked; that his work is generally approved and respected; and that others are trying to help him do a good job and satisfy his needs.

The principle of responsibility states that an executive should take those actions that are most likely to lead the worker to seek and accept more responsibility for his own work and for the work of the organization. Actions that permit and encourage the worker to participate in decisions that he feels are important to him and his work fulfill the principle.

These principles do not provide solutions; they do provide a constructive way of looking at human problems. The average worker will enjoy his work, enjoy directing his own activities, and exercise ingenuity in solving his work problems *if the executive takes the actions that lead to the creation of the proper working conditions.*

4. THE ENVIRONMENT OF WORK

The technological changes that began with the slow substitution of mechanical power for muscle power have been accelerated over the past few decades by the substitution of mechanical senses for human senses and mechanical brains for human brains. Technological change is essential for the survival of many companies. Yet it is complex and expensive, and it sometimes fails to produce the expected results. Consequently, the executive is relying more and more on the human engineer to improve man-machine systems. In the process of making improvements, the human engineer designs equipment displays and controls as well as modifying the physical working environment. He sees people, machines, and the environment as parts of a system designed to achieve certain goals. Each part must be as good as it can be and all the parts must work together effectively and efficiently.

Union and government leaders as well as executives approve the trend toward automation, although they make the reservation that "It should be planned for and introduced with sensitive regard for any adverse impact upon individuals." Some workers are adversely influenced by being changed to automated jobs: some dislike the change, many are disturbed by the increase in night-shift work which automation usually demands, and most feel an increase in tension and pressure. Overall, however, most workers would like to have at least some parts of their jobs mechanized, and the typical worker is likely to be happier on an automated than on an unautomated job. The executive can avoid many of the problems that arise with automation by giving workers advance notice of planned changes, by discussing with them the transitional problems, and by providing adequate training for the new jobs.

The major problem created by automation is displacement. Automation continually creates new jobs and destroys old ones. On balance it adds to the total number of jobs. While the process of creation and destruction is going on, however, individual workers may be displaced. The worker is equipped to do a job which no longer exists and is not trained to do the job that does exist. The capable executive can usually plan automation so that few, if any, workers employed by a company need to be laid off. However, even when the individual company can solve its problems of automation, the national problem remains. Large percentages of young workers, undereducated workers, and minority group workers find that the old jobs which they might have had no longer exist. These workers remain unemployed.

Displacement is a national problem. Its solution must be on a national scale, rather than on the level of the individual firm. The problem remains as yet unsolved. A shorter work week will be of some benefit. The general solution lies in the training of "present and future members of the labor force so that they will have the capacity to be fully productive members of

society under the new conditions laid down for us by automation" (Killingsworth, 1962). The executive must become more aware of the national problem and play his full part in helping to solve it.

5.   GROUPS IN THE ORGANIZATION

A worker is a part of a man-machine system. He is also a part of a man-man
system: he works with other men in a social setting. The executive's greatest
responsibility is to organize the men in this social setting in the most effective
way. If it is done ineffectively, he and his men are destined to fail; done
effectively, they are on the way to success. Yet no one really knows just
what a good human organization is and how to create one. The research of
social scientists is now providing some guides to the answers. Below is a
summary of various actions an executive can take to create a poor or a
good organization.

To create a poor organization, centralize as much power as possible at
the top. Insist that all decisions be made there, and punish those who make
their own decisions or fail to follow out your decisions. Create a tight span
of control by having a pyramid organization where each man is closely supervised by the man above him and closely supervises a handful of men below
him. Specialize the organization so that each group has a single simple thing
to do. Specialize the work of the individual so that he also has a single—and
even simpler—thing to do. Spell out in detail what each man is responsible
for, and hold him tightly to his responsibilities. Let the worker decide nothing
you can decide for him, tell him nothing you can avoid telling him, dis-
courage workers from becoming friendly with each other, and in general,
make it clear that you do not trust them and that you are watching them
like a hawk. The larger the company, the better all these ideas will work
to make it a poor organization.

To create a good organization, focus on creating great teams rather than
great individuals or a great bureaucracy. Delegate as much responsibility to
these groups as you feel you safely can—then delegate a little more. Flatten
the organization to the point where so many men report to a supervisor
that he *must* delegate authority. Generalize the organization so that each
part of it has many things to do. Enlarge the jobs of workers so that each
man has many different things to do. Stop assignments at the group level;
hold the group responsible for results, but give it freedom to decide the best
way of achieving them. Fit the members of the work groups together carefully, encourage them to interact with each other, give them as much informa-

tion as you can, interact with them as much as they want, and let them decide for themselves about as many things as possible. Provide for linking-pin teams to tie the overall organization together. Do everything possible to convince each worker that he has a real stake in the achievements of the organization, that the organization needs his best contribution, and that you are interested in developing his maximum potentialities.

An organization's success depends upon the development of (1) common goals among all members of the organization, (2) a supportive social environment, and (3) people who seek and effectively carry out responsibility.

6. LEADERSHIP AND SUPERVISION

It is well for the executive to understand that his functions are more important than he is. If his subordinates fully grasp the importance of the executive's job to them, he can be stupid, ignorant, or even nonexistant, and yet they can effectively achieve their objectives. An authoritarian and masculine executive can be a success in one situation and a failure in another. The ideal executive is best viewed not in terms of his personality but in terms of his *relationship* to the particular group he is leading.

The ideal executive understands he has a part to play which is different from that played by his subordinates, and he knows that the success of his group depends upon his playing this part well. He is ready and eager, but not too eager, to assume his role. He is accepted, liked, and respected by his subordinates as well as by his superiors. He has enough intelligence and knowledge to understand the particular job he is doing and to make improvements in it. He knows that the success of his group depends upon how it is organized, and he is skillful in modifying and improving its organizational relationships.

Since he is acutely aware that the success of his group depends upon the skills and attitudes of the men in it, he tries to select new men who fit his organization and to train and retain them. He knows and likes his subordinates, gives them the feeling that they are important to the organization, and effectively arranges for the satisfaction of their individual needs.

The ideal executive knows that leadership is doing. Thinking should guide his actions and thoughtfulness should set his style, but he must act.

7. COMMUNICATION

The communication system determines the effectiveness of all the other systems within the organization. Effective executives recognize the importance of communication and help establish channels which are numerous, clearly defined, and carry meaningful content. Communications must be received quickly, clearly, and authoritatively. Those who receive communications must understand them, believe them, find them compatible with their own interests, and be physically and mentally able to act on them.

An executive often fails to communicate because his communications are too dull or too hard to understand. The measurement of reading ease and reading interest gives him a quick check on whether his letters, his bulletins, his policy statements, and the publications of his organization are interesting and simple enough to be understood. If they are not, the trouble may be due to his carelessness, his style of writing, the fuzziness of his ideas, or his unwillingness to say what he really thinks.

Communication may fail because subordinates do not understand the executive. It may also fail because the executive does not understand his subordinates. Although the typical executive generally feels quite confident that he understands his men, one of the best-established facts in the area of communication is that he does not. General and specific surveys of employee attitudes can remedy this weakness. Attitude surveys also provide much-needed criteria of integration and morale to aid in the evaluation of past executive actions and the planning of future ones.

The most common and serious communication problem is not that of misunderstanding what is wanted but that of not doing what is wanted. That is, the subordinate may understand what his superior wants, but he does not want to do it—and therefore often does not do it. The executive is too likely to view communication failures in the agreeable (to him) master-servant framework and to try to solve them within that framework. The "servant," however, is a citizen in a democracy and reflects its values. In the end, the effectiveness of communication depends upon how well what is communicated to him fits the values of a democratic society.

8. PERSONNEL SELECTION

Executives have to maintain and often to expand their work force. This can be a time-consuming and expensive process. Over a period of years one company found that simply to maintain its force, it had to interview every year one applicant for every two men on the payroll. In the process of doubling its force, another company found that it had to interview ten applicants for every man on the payroll. The direct and indirect costs of replacing an employee are increasing.

The use of application blanks, references, and selection interviews helps maintain the right *number* of employees. Most companies, however, have no evidence that the quality of the employees hired by their selection process is any better than chance. They have no evidence, either, that it is *not* better; that is, they have no evidence at all. The executive who wants to hire better employees cannot count on doing so by using the latest test or hiring the closest consultant. The only guides he can truly rely on are the results of evaluations conducted in his company.

The essential first step in the evaluation of a selection device is the same as that in the evaluation of *any* device: obtaining a reliable and valid measure of job success. The next step consists of recording the predictions made with the device: the ratings of the selection interviewer, scores on tests, or scores on the application blank. The final step is validating the predictions against the measures.

The development of "keys" for scoring application blanks illustrates the essentials of the validation procedure. A convenient measure of success is job tenure: the longer the worker stays on the job, the better the initial selection. Applying this criterion, the investigator pulls records of short- and long-tenured workers from the files and analyzes each item on the application blanks of the two groups. He then weights the items so that those which do not discriminate between the two groups have no weight and those which discriminate most sharply have the most weight. Thus the predictor of the job success of an applicant becomes his total score on the weighted application blank. The investigator then validates this predictor against a new set of applications drawn from the file.

A valid key for an application blank can be developed in a day. While the essentials of validation are the same for any selection device, the process is normally much longer and more complicated. Most executives, therefore, cannot conduct their own evaluation study, but at least they can know what it takes to do one and can recognize the importance of doing it. Evaluation cannot improve the selections made tomorrow; they can improve those made next year.

The selection of leaders and potential leaders presents special problems to the executive. The devices available for selecting leaders are the same as those available for the selection of other employees: application blanks, educational records, intelligence test scores, personality scores, interviews, and references. Selecting good leaders, however, is more difficult in many ways. Less is known about the critical requirements of a good leader than of a good worker, the devices available for measuring the known requirements are less adequate, and these requirements vary from one leadership job to another and from one period in a company's existence to another.

Many of the difficulties in improving a selection program involve technical problems such as the reliability and validity of the selection devices and the measures of job success. The executive may need to make selections, especially of potential leaders, without the aid of validated devices. He can help himself by asking not only whether an applicant has potential to be a good worker but also how interested the applicant is in doing the work and how he will like the working conditions. The executive can also help himself by taking his personal impressions less seriously than his fellow executives generally do.

Executives determine the policies of selection programs. It seems clear that the best policies are those that stress developing sound measures of job success and using proven selection devices.

9. TRAINING

Executives recognize the need for training, and they support programs—sometimes very elaborate and expensive ones—to meet the need. Billions of dollars are spent each year to provide training for people at all levels of organizations. People receive training on-the-job and off-the-job, in lectures and workshops, to operate machines and to improve human relations. How well does all this training work? Nobody really knows, and almost nobody is trying to find out.

Industrial psychologists are generally agreed that more research is needed to evaluate present training programs and is essential for the significant improvement of traditional training programs. Yet executives as a rule take little note of this, nor do they seem to remember it long when they do. It is quite possible that executives might profitably spend 50 percent of their training budget in training research, but it is unlikely that any do spend as much as 1 percent. They find it too easy to relax with their traditional programs, they find it too hard to believe in the value of research, and they are too busy to assemble the instruments, ideas, and skilled people necessary to conduct it.

Is on-the-job or off-the-job training better? Executives act as if the former were, for it is much more popular. Research evaluations, however, clearly indicate that it is not. For example, a study compared 3,000 pairs of Navy apprentices, of whom one in each pair had gone to formal school and the other had received on-the-job training (Merenda, 1958). The results were decisively in favor of the formal school training: In nearly all the 30 occupations studied, the formally trained performed better; and in two thirds of them, the differences were large. Since on-the-job training in the

Navy is more systematically and carefully carried out than in most companies, it is likely that the differences in favor of off-the-job training would be still greater in the typical firm.

At the present, more executives are becoming seriously concerned about human-relations training and are trying hard to develop long-range programs devoid of fads. Their programs may still fail because they are based on the wrong assumptions. Human-relations training, for example, stresses the importance of personal feelings and emotions in behavior, but the typical organization stresses an impersonal and rational approach to all problems. If the training program emphasizes the rational approach, it may do more harm than good. In any case, no matter how sound the emphasis may be, no one can be sure that it is effective until its effectiveness has been actually demonstrated.

As in other types of evaluation, obtaining the criteria of training success is the most basic and difficult problem. How can we measure human-relations skill? How can we measure leadership effectiveness? How can we measure performance in any area? The executive who develops a good criterion may get immediate and substantial benefits, as in the following case where the criterion itself became an excellent training device.

> In a Pittsburgh public utility, furnace stokers had no indication of how well they were doing. Gages were installed to show the efficiency of the individual boilers and the data from these gages were plotted to show individual improvement in the technique of firing the boilers. The result was an annual saving of $333,000 in coal (Mosel, 1958).

The example illustrates a basic learning principle: As knowledge of performance increases, both the speed and the level of learning increase.

10. WORK INCENTIVES

Men work only to satisfy their needs. An incentive is a condition of need satisfaction that is deliberately controlled in order to increase the productivity, integration, or morale of workers. Thus, what an executive does to foster the goal achievement of his workers is *his* incentive system, and its success is *his* success.

All executives use money as an incentive. Its use is guided by two general principles: The more important the job a man has, the more money he should get, and the more productive a man is on his job, the more money he should get. Job analysis and job evaluation are employed in putting the first principle into effect. Straight piece-rate, differential piece-rate, and measured day-rate systems are among the many systems used in putting the second principle into effect.

In the past, executives have often viewed money as the *only* incentive to work. Times are changing. The percent of companies using various wage incentive systems has steadily declined over the past several decades. Some of the decline results from the difficulty of setting up financial incentive systems for the increasingly complex and interrelated jobs of modern industry. Much of the decline, however, results from growing doubts about whether giving men more money for more work actually gets any more work done.

More and more executives are wondering whether their preoccupation with money as an incentive has not led them to neglect other more potent types of incentives. Conclusions from research on industrial behavior justify their doubts. Table 14-1, for example, lists the various types of incentive systems and gives rough ratings of them in terms of how much, at best, can be expected from each in a typical company. Thus, the best kind of comprehensive security provisions can only ensure the loyalty of workers. On the other hand, the best kind of organizational improvements can increase productivity and morale as well as integration. Realizing the potentialities of the nonfinancial incentives requires that we know more about them than we now do and that we put what we do know to better use.

11.   APPRAISAL AND DEVELOPMENT

Useful measures of job performance are vital to the development of employees and to the efficiency of the executive and his organization. The most convenient and popular measure is some form of merit rating or

TABLE 14-1   The potentialities of incentives

Type of incentive system	Potentialities for increasing:		
	Productivity	Integration	Morale
Job evaluation	Low	Moderate	Low
Security provisions	Low	High	Low
Financial rewards for production	Moderate	High	Low
Selection procedures	Moderate	Moderate	Moderate
Training and development	High	Moderate	Moderate
The redesigning of jobs	Moderate	Moderate	High
Organizational improvements	High	High	High

performance appraisal. Yet such ratings have many pitfalls. Raters are unduly influenced by their personal likes and dislikes, some rate low and some rate high, and some spread their ratings while some do not. Although the use of rankings, forced distributions, and forced choices can reduce these sources of error, it cannot compensate for an executive's lack of detailed knowledge about the performance of his subordinates.

The executive may eventually find that appraisals are of most benefit as a guide in taking organizational actions. His daily work involves the development of better selection procedures, training programs, incentive systems, etc. To evaluate these actions, he needs measures of performance. Ratings are often the only available measure. The more valid they are, the more useful they can be as a criterion.

The practical problem with appraisals is that executives, like most people, would rather help than appraise. Consequently, the typical executive avoids making merit ratings, and those he cannot avoid making are often unused and unusable. The best solution seems to be to separate the adjustment of salaries from the appraisal of performance. Salary adjustments are influenced by many elements having nothing to do with merit: seniority, the time since the last increase, the pay range for a job, budgetary allotments, and the profits of the organization.

The executive can best use appraisals exclusively as an aid in helping his subordinates understand how they are doing and how they can do better. If this is the honest intent, then he will not avoid making the ratings or make meaningless ones. Encouraging the growth and development of people, long a core value of our education and governmental institutions, is becoming a sound management practice.

An executive gets results through people. Consequently, the better his relationships with his subordinates and the more he contributes to their development, the better the results he gets. The developmental interview is the formal name for what is, at best, an informal conversation with a subordinate about his present work and his future plans. For such a conversation to be successful, the executive must *relate* successfully to his subordinate.

To relate successfully to others, there is no substitute for adaptation to the particular employee in the particular situation. Most subordinates like to participate in setting their own goals; some, however, like to be told. Some executives are loud and dominating; some are quiet and reserved. Employees expect their supervisor to behave in ways that are consistent with his leadership role and his personality, and they become suspicious when he does not. Thus a technique that one supervisor can use successfully cannot be used successfully by others, and a technique that can be used in dealing with some employees cannot be used in dealing with others.

Most executives think that they relate well to their subordinates. The test, however, is what the subordinate thinks. Does he feel that the executive is relaxed when he is talking to him? Does he believe the executive understands his feelings and problems? Does he think the executive likes him? If so, the relationship is a successful one. The answers, however, are unlikely to be yes if the executive believes he is cleverly concealing his true feelings from the subordinate.

There is little an executive can do, in the long run, to conceal from a subordinate the fact that he does not like him. He can, however, learn to like and trust his subordinates by giving them additional responsibilities, by concentrating on their day-to-day work, by remembering good performances more than bad, and by *trying* to understand. That is, regardless of an executive's personality or his feelings about his subordinates, he can best proceed by (1) trying to develop common goals with them, (2) sticking to the present, (3) leading from strengths, and (4) listening.

12. ORGANIZATIONAL CHANGE

People are selected, trained, and paid to fit the organization. The executive understands that when these processes are done well the organization is improved. More and more executives realize that planned change which focuses on the face-to-face work group as a basic unit of the organization can also lead to improvement.

In any organization changes are inevitable. The question for the executive, therefore, is not whether to change but *how* to change. Increasingly, executives are planning and controlling change so that the organization will better fit the people who work in it. The worker of today is not the same as yesterday's worker. He is better educated, more complex in his motivations, and more likely to understand democratic principles and expect them to be practiced on the job as well as in his civic and political activities.

The executive knows that there are new findings and new assumptions that imply new organizational systems. If he tries to enrich jobs rather than simplify them, the organization changes. If he stresses that supervisors are to facilitate group activities rather than just give orders, the organization changes. No generally accepted theory can explain how the changes will come about and no methods can ensure that the changes will in fact be improvements. While there are no sure answers to the question of how to do it, there are three general approaches to organization change that the executive can consider. He may emphasize the individual approach which assumes that as more people in the organization adopt new attitudes their behavior will change and thus improve the organization. He may emphasize the organizational approach which assumes that as the organization's systems are changed, the behavior and attitudes of people will improve. He may emphasize the interaction approach which assumes that changing individuals *and* the organizational systems is the best way to produce improvement.

Whatever his approach the executive must combine three ingredients to produce successful change:

1. He must seek the cooperation of as many people as possible within his organization in setting realistic and measurable goals of productivity, integration, and morale.

2. He and the others must have a commitment to achieving these goals rather than a commitment to defending a particular way of achieving them.

3. He must ensure that the organization's progress toward its goals is evaluated carefully and frequently.

13. THE JOB OF THE INDUSTRIAL PSYCHOLOGIST

The job of the psychologist is to help the executive solve his human problems. The psychologist, however, is often reluctant to offer ready-made solutions, for human problems are more complicated than technical ones and have been studied for a much shorter time. He tries to avoid the difficulties implicit in this situation by persuading the executive to conduct the necessary studies. Often he cannot, for the money and conditions for experiment may not be available. In making recommendations based on too little information, the psychologist tries to point out his doubts about them.

Studies that psychologists recommend are often not carried out because executives do not think they are worth doing. In specific cases, they may be right. In general, though, executives are too unfamiliar with the point of view, knowledge, methods, and usefulness of the psychologist to make the best use of his abilities. It is part of the psychologist's job to familiarize the executive with how he works and what he can do. It is a vital part of the job of the good executive, however, to familiarize *himself* with these modes of operation. It is also the responsibility of the company to see that its executives do this.

> Management development programs need, I submit, to be oriented toward the future, toward change, toward differences from current forms of practice and behavior. . . . We ought to allocate more of the effort of our programs to making our student a more competent analyst. We ought, in other words, to try to teach them to think a little more like scientists, and to know a good deal more about the culture and methods of scientists (Leavitt, 1961).

REFERENCES

Adams, J. S., & Rosenbaum, W. B. The relationship of worker productivity to cognitive dissonance about wage inequities. *J. Appl. Psychol.*, 1962, **46**, 161–164.

AFL-CIO. Wage incentive plans. *Collective Bargaining Rep.*, 1957, **2**, No. 12.

Albrecht, P. A., Glaser, E. M., & Marks, J. Validation of a multiple-assessment procedure for managerial personnel. *J. Appl. Psychol.*, 1964, **48**, 351–360.

Allport, G. W. The psychology of participation. *Psychol. Rev.*, 1945, **52**, 117–132.

Amir, Y., Kovarsky, Y., & Sharan, S. Peer nominations as a predictor of multistage promotions in a ramified organization. *J. Appl. Psychol.*, 1970, **54**, 462–469.

Argyris, C. *Interpersonal competence and organizational effectiveness.* Homewood, Ill.: Irwin and Dorsey, 1962.

Argyris, C. *Integrating the individual and the organization*. New York: Wiley, 1964.

Armour, J. B. Student attitudes in relation to classroom achievement. Unpublished master's thesis, Michigan State University, 1954.

Ashburn, A. Detroit automation. *Ann. Amer. Acad. Polit. Soc. Sci.*, 1962, **340**, 21–28.

Babchuk, N., & Goode, W. T. Work incentives in a self-determined group. *J. Amer. Soc. Rev.*, 1951, **16**, 679–686.

Bacon, S. D., & Straus, R. *Drinking in college*. New Haven, Conn.: Yale, 1953.

Banfield, E. C. *The moral basis of a backward society*. New York: Free Press, 1958.

Barnard, C. I. *The functions of the executive*. Cambridge, Mass.: Harvard University Press, 1938.

Barnes, L. B. Organization change and field experimental methods. In V. H. Vroom (Ed.), *Methods of organizational research*. Pittsburgh: University of Pittsburgh Press, 1967.

Barnette, W. L. Feedback from bachelor of arts psychology graduates. *Amer. Psychologist*, 1961, **16**, 184–188.

Barrett, G. V., Svetlik, B., & Prien, E. P. Validity of the job-concept interview in an industrial setting. *J. Appl. Psychol.*, 1967, **51**, 233–235.

Bass, B. M. The leaderless group discussion. *Psychol. Bull.*, 1954, **51**, 465–492.

Bass, B. M. *Leadership, psychology, and organizational behavior*. New York: Harper & Row, 1960.

Bass, B. M. Interface between personnel and organizational psychology. *J. Appl. Psychol.*, 1968, **52**, 81–88.

Bass, B. M., & Flint, A. W. Some effects of power, practice and problem difficulty on success as a leader. *Tech. Rep. 18* (Contract N70NR 35609). Baton Rouge, La.: Louisiana State University Press, 1958.

Bass, B. M., & Vaughn, J. A. *Training in industry: the management of learning*. Belmont, Calif.: Wadsworth, 1966.

Bavelas, A. Group decision in setting production goals. In N. R. F. Maier, *Psychology in industry*. Boston: Houghton Mifflin, 1946, 264–266.

Bavelas, A. Role playing and management training. *Sociatry*, 1947, **1**, 183–191.

Baxter, B., Taaffe, A. A., & Hughes, J. Training evaluation study. *Personnel Psychol.*, 1953, **6**, 403–416.

Beer, M., & Kleisath, S. W. The effects of the Management Grid laboratory on organizational and leadership dimensions. In Salkind, S. S. (Chrmn), Research on the impact of using different laboratory methods of interpersonal and organizational change. Symposium presented at the meeting of the APA, Washington, D.C., September, 1967.

Bellows, R. M. *Psychology of personnel in business and industry.* Englewood Cliffs, N.J.: Prentice-Hall, 1954.

Bennis, W. G. *Changing organizations.* New York: McGraw-Hill, 1966.

Bennis, W. G. Organizations of the future. *Personnel Admin.*, 1967, **30**, 6-19.

Bennis, W. G. *Organization development: its nature, origins, and prospects.* Reading, Mass.: Addison-Wesley, 1969.

Bennis, W. G., Burke, R., Cutter, H., Harrington, H., & Hoffman, J. A note on some problems of measurement and prediction in a training group. *Group Psychotherapy*, 1957, **10**, 328-341.

Berkshire, J. R., & Highland, R. W. Forced-choice performance rating: a methodological study. *Personnel Psychol.*, 1953, **6**, 355-358.

Berlew, D. E., & Hall, D. T. The socialization of managers: effects of expectation on performance. *Admin. Sci. Quart.*, 1966, **11**, 207-223.

Berrien, F. K. The effects of noise. *Psychol. Bull.*, 1946, **43**, 141-161.

Biggane, J. F. & Steward, P. A. *Job enlargement: a case study.* State University of Iowa, Bureau of Labor and Management, Research Series No. 25, July, 1963.

Bills, M. A. A day in the life of an industrial psychologist. *Personnel Serv. Bull.*, 1934, **5**.

Blake, R. R., & Mouton, J. S. *The managerial grid.* Houston, Texas: Gulf Publishing, 1964.

Blake, R. R., & Mouton, J. S. *Corporate excellence through grid organizational development.* Houston, Texas: Gulf Publishing, 1968.

Blake, R. R., Mouton, J. S., Barnes, L. B., & Greiner, L. E. Breakthrough in organization development. *Harv. Business Rev.*, 1964, **42**, 133-155.

Bluemel, C. S. *The troubled mind.* Baltimore: Williams & Wilkins, 1938.

Bowen, H. R., & Mangum, G. L. *Automation and economic progress.* Englewood Cliffs, N.J.: Prentice-Hall, 1966.

Bowers, D. G., & Seashore, S. E. Predicting organizational effectiveness with a four factor theory of leadership. *Admin. Sci. Quart.*, 1966, **11**, 238-263.

Bowers, D. G., & Seashore, S. F. Peer leadership within work groups. *Personnel Admin.*, 1967, **30**, 45-50.

Bradley, J. V. Direction-of-knob stereotypes. *J. Appl. Psychol.*, 1959, **43**, 21-24.

Brayfield, A. H., & Rothe, H. F. An index of job satisfaction. *J. Appl. Psychol.*, 1951, **35**, 307-311.

Broadbent, D. E., & Little, E. A. J. Effects of noise reduction in a work situation. *Occup. Psychol.*, 1960, **34**, 133-140.

Bronfenbrenner, U. Some familial antecedents of responsibility and leadership in adolescents. In L. Petrullo & B. M. Bass (Eds.), *Leadership and interpersonal behavior*. New York: Holt, 1961.

Bronfenbrenner, U., & Newcomb, T. M. Improvisations: an application of psychodrama in personality diagnosis. *Sociatry*, 1948, **1**, 367–382.

Brooks, J. The impacted philosophers. *New Yorker*, May 26, 1962.

Brown, G. E. Jr., & Larson, A. F. Current trends in appraisal and development. *Personnel*, 1958, **34**, 51–58.

Buckner, D. N. The predictability of ratings as a function of inter-rater performance. J. *Appl. Psychol.*, 1959, **43**, 60–64.

Burke, R. J., & Wilcox, D. S. Characteristics of effective employee performance review and development interviews. *Personnel Psychol.*, 1969, **22**, 291–305.

Burnham, W. H. Success and failure as conditions of mental health. *Ment. Hyg., N.Y.*, 1919, **3**, 391–392.

Cameron, N. A., & Margaret, A. *Behavior pathology*. Boston: Houghton Mifflin, 1951.

Campbell, D. P. Occupations 10 years later of high school seniors with high scores on the SVIB Life Insurance Salesman Scale. *J. Appl. Psychol.*, 1966, **50**, 369–372.

Campbell, D. T. Reforms as experiments. *Amer. Psychologist*, 1969, **24**, 409–429.

Campbell, J. P., & Dunnette, M. D. Effectiveness of T-group experiences in managerial training and development. *Psychol. Bull.*, 1968, **70**, 73–104.

Campbell, R. J. (Chm.) On becoming a psychologist in industry (A symposium), *Personnel Psychol.*, 1970, **23**, 191–221.

Canter, R. R., Jr. Psychologists in industry. *Personnel Psychol.*, 1948, **1**, 145–161.

Carlucci, C., & Crissy, W. J. E. The readability of employee handbooks. *Personnel Psychol.*, 1951, **4**, 383–395.

Carp, F. M., Vitola, B. M., & McLanathan, F. L. Human relations knowledge and social distance set in supervisors. *J. Appl. Psychol.*, 1963, **41**, 78–80.

Casbergue, J. P. Measuring the benefits of sales training program sponsored by the Indiana Restaurant Association and a survey of training programs in other state associations. Unpublished master's thesis, Michigan State University, 1961.

Cattell, R. B., Blewett, D. B., & Beloff, J. R. The inheritance of personality. *Amer. J. Human Genet.*, 1955, **7**, 122–146.

Chalupsky, A. B. Comparative factor analysis of clerical jobs. *J. Appl. Psychol.*, 1962, **46**, 62–66.

Champion, J. M., & Bridges, F. J. *Critical incidents in management.* New York: Irwin, 1963.

Chapanis, A.   On the allocation of functions between men and machines. *Occupational Psychol.*, 1965, **39**, 1–11.

Chapanis, A., Garner, W. R., & Morgan, C. T. *Applied experimental psychology: human factors in engineering design.* New York: Wiley, 1949.

Coch, L., & French, J. R. P. Jr.   Overcoming resistance to change. *Hum. Rel.*, 1948, **4**, 512–533.

Cozan, L. W.   Forced choice: better than other ratings methods? *Personnel*, 1955, **36**, 80–83.

Craig, R. L., & Bittel L. R.   (Eds.)   *Training and development handbook.* New York: McGraw-Hill, 1967.

Crockett, W. H.   Emergent leadership in small, decision-making groups. *J. Abnorm. Soc. Psychol.*, 1955, **51**, 378–382.

Cronbach, L. J. Processes affecting scores on "understanding of others" and "assumed similarity." *Psychol. Bull.*, 1955, **52**, 177–193.

Dale, E.   Greater productivity through labor-management cooperation. *Amer. Mgmt. Ass. Res. Rep.*, 1949, **14**.

Dalton, M.   The industrial "rate-buster": a characterization. *Appl. Anthrop.*, 1948, **7**, 5–18.

Dalton, M. *Men who manage.* New York: Wiley, 1959.

Daniels, H., & Otis, J.   A method of analyzing employment interviews. *Personnel Psychol.*, 1950, **3**, 425–444.

Danish, S. J., & Kagan, N.   Measurement of affective sensitivity: toward a valid measure of interpersonal perception. *J. Counseling Psychol.*, 1971, **18**, 51–54.

Davenport, R. W.   Enterprise for everyone. *Fortune*, 1950, **40** (Oct.), 65–69, 200–208.

Davis, K. *Human relations in business.*   New York: McGraw-Hill, 1957.

Dearborn, D. C., & Simon, H. W.   Selective perception: the departmental identifications of executives. *Sociometry*, 1958, **21**, no. 2.

Dickson, W. J., & Roethlisberger, F. J. *Counseling in an organization: a sequel to the Hawthorne researches.*   Cambridge Division of Research, Graduate School of Business Administration, Harvard University: Harvard University Press, 1966.

Diebold, J.   The application of information technology. *Ann. Amer. Acad. Polit. Soc. Sci.*, 1962, **340**, 38–45.

Dore, R.   The development and validation of forced-choice scales measuring attitudes toward leadership methods. Unpublished master's thesis, Michigan State University, 1960.

Dreese, M. Guiding principles in the development of an employee counseling program. *Publ. Personnel Rev.*, 1942, **3**, 200–204.

Dunlap, J. W. The management of morale. *Personnel Psychol.*, 1950, **3**, 353–359.

Dunnette, M. D. A modified model for test validation and selection research. *J. Appl. Psychol.*, 1963, **47**, 317–323.

Dunnette, M. D. *Personnel selection and placement.* Belmont, Calif.: Wadsworth, 1966.

Dunnette, M. D., Lawler, E. E., Weick, K. E., & Opsahl, R. L. The role of compensation in managerial motivation. *Organization Behavior and Human Performance*, 1967, **2**, 175–216.

Eddy, W. Dimensions of organizational behavior. Unpublished doctor's thesis, Michigan State University, 1963.

Evans, C. E., & Laseau, L. N. My job contest. *Personnel Psychol. Monogr.*, 1950, no. 1.

Faunce, W. A. Automation and the automobile worker. *Soc. Problems,* 1958, **6**, 68–78.

Ferguson, L. W. The development of industrial psychology. In B. Gilmer (Ed.), *Industrial Psychology.* New York: McGraw-Hill, 1961.

Fiedler, F. E. Leadership and leadership effectiveness traits: a reconceptualization of the leadership trait problem. In L. Petrullo & B. M. Bass (Eds.), *Leadership and interpersonal behavior.* New York: Holt, 1961.

Fiedler, F. E. Leadership experience and leadership performance—another hypothesis shot to hell. *Organizational Behavior and Human Performance*, 1970, **5**, 1–14.

Finkelman, J. M., & Glass, D. C. Reappraisal of the relationship between noise and human performance by means of subsidiary task measure. *J. Appl. Psychol.*, 1970, **54**, 211–213.

Fitts, P. M. (Ed.) Human engineering for an effective air navigation and traffic control system. Washington, D.C.: National Research Council, 1951.

Fitts, P. M. The information capacity of the human motor system in controlling the amplitude of movement. *J. Exp. Psychol.*, 1952, **47**, 381–391.

Fitts, P. M., & Jones, R. W. Psychological aspects of instrument display. I: Analysis of 270 "pilot-error" experiences in reading and interpreting aircraft instruments. Air Matériel Command, Aero Medical Laboratory, Dayton, Ohio. *Rep.* TSEAA-694-12A, 1947.

Flanagan, J. C., & Burns, R. K. The employee performance record. In T. L. Whisler & Shirley F. Harper (Eds.), *Performance appraisal.* New York: Holt, 1957.

Fleishman, E. A. The description of supervisory behavior. *J. Appl. Psychol.*, 1953, **37**, 1–6.

Fleishman, E. A. Dimensional analysis of psychomotor abilities. *J. Exp. Psychol.*, 1954, **48**, 437–454.

Fleishman, E. A., & Berniger, J. One way to reduce office turnover. *Personnel*, 1960, **37**, 63–69.

Fleishman, E. A., Harris, E. E., & Burtt, H. E. Leadership and supervision in industry: an evaluation of a supervisory training program. *Bur. Educ. Res. Monogr.*, 1955, no. 33. Columbus, Ohio: Ohio State University Press.

Flesch, R. A new readability yardstick. *J. Appl. Psychol.*, 1948, **32**, 221–223.

Foreman, W. J. A study of management training techniques used by large corporations. *Public Personnel Rev.,* 1967, **28**(1), 31–35.

Fouriezos, N. T., Hutt, M. L. M., & Guetzkow, H. Measurement of self-oriented needs in discussion groups. *J. Abnorm. Soc. Psychol.*, 1950, **45**, 682–690.

Franco, S. C. Problem drinking and industry: policies and procedures. *Quart. J. Stud. Alcohol.*, 1954, **15**, 453–468.

Fraser, R. *The incidence of neurosis among factory workers.* London: H. M. Stationery Office., Indian Health Res. Board, No. 90, 1947.

French, J. R. P., Jr., Ross, I. C., Kirby, S., Nelson, J. R., & Smyth, P. Employee participation in a program of industrial change. *Personnel*, 1958, **35**, 15–29.

Fryer, D. H., & Edgerton, H. A. Research concerning "off-the-job training." *Personnel Psychol.*, 1950, **3**, 261–284.

Gage, N. L., & Exline, R. V. Social perception and effectiveness in discussion groups. *Human Relations*, 1953, **6**, 381–396.

Gagné, R. M. Military training and principles of learning. *Amer. Psychologist*, 1962, **17**, 83–91.

Gagné, R. M., & Fleishman, E. A. *Psychology and human performance.* New York: Holt, 1959.

Garry, R. Individual differences in ability to fake vocational interests tests. *J. Appl. Psychol.*, 1953, **42**, 267–284.

Ghiselli, E. E. The validity of a personnel interview. *Personnel Psychol.*, 1966, **19**, 389–394.

Ghiselli, E. E., & Barthol, R. P. The validity of personality inventories in the selection of employees. *J. Appl. Psychol.*, 1953, **37**, 18–20.

Ghiselli, E. E., & Brown, C. W. The effectiveness of intelligence tests in the selection of workers. *J. Appl. Psychol.*, 1948, **32**, 575–580.

Gilmer, B. V. H. *Industrial psychology.* New York: McGraw-Hill, 1961

Given, W. B., Jr. *Bottom-up management.* New York: Harper & Row, 1949.

Glanzer, M., & Glaser, R. Techniques for the study of team structure II: empirical studies of the effects of structure in small groups. *Psychol. Bull.*, 1961, **63**, 1-27.

Glaser, E. M. Psychological consultation with executives: a clinical approach. *Amer. Psychologist*, 1958, **13**, 486-489.

Golden, C. S., & Ruttenberg, H. *The dynamics of industrial democracy*. New York: Harper & Row, 1942.

Gooding, J. It pays to wake up the blue-collar worker. *Fortune*, 1970, **80**, 133-168.

Gordon, L. V. Clinical, psychometric, and work sample approaches in the prediction of success in Peace Corps training. *J. Appl. Psychol.*, 1967, **51**, 111-119.

Graham, N. The speed and accuracy of reading horizontal, vertical, and circular scales. *J. Appl. Psychol.*, 1956, **40**, 228-232.

Green, B. F., & Anderson, L. K. The tactual identification of shapes for coding switch handles. *J. Appl. Psychol.*, 1955, **39**, 624-633.

Greene, M. R. The role of employee benefit structures in manufacturing industry. Eugene, Oregon: School of Business Administration, University of Oregon Press, 1964.

Greenly, R. J. Job training. *National Assoc. Manufacturers Labor Relations Bull.*, 1941, no. 35.

Grether, W. F. The effects of variations in indicator design upon speed and accuracy of altitude readings. Air Matériel Command, Aero Medical Laboratory, Dayton, Ohio. *Rep.* TSEAA-694-14, 1947.

Grether, W. F. Engineering psychology in the United States. *Amer. Psychologist*, 1968, **23**, 743-751.

Grinker, R. R., & Spiegel, J. P. *Men under stress*. New York: Blakiston, 1945.

Grossman, B. The measurement and determinants of interpersonal sensitivity. Unpublished master's thesis, Michigan State University, 1963.

Guest, R. H. *Organizational change: the effect of successful leadership*. Homewood, Ill.: Irwin-Dorsey, 1962.

Guilford, J. P. *Personality*. New York: McGraw-Hill, 1959.

Guion, R. M. Some definitions of morale. *Personnel Psychol.*, 1958, **11**, 59-61.

Guion, R. M. *Personnel testing*. New York: McGraw-Hill, 1965.

Guion, R. M., & Gottier, R. F. Validity of personality measures in personnel selection. *Personnel Psychol.*, 1965, **18**, 135-164.

Haire, M. *Psychology in management*. New York: McGraw-Hill, 1956.

Hall, W. B.   Employee self-appraisal for improved performance. *Tools for improved personnel relations: Amer. Mgmt. Assoc. Personnel Ser.*, 1951, no. 140, 29–34.

Hamann, J. R.   Panel discussion. *Amer. Mgmt. Assoc. Gen. Mgmt. Ser.*, 1956, no. 182, 21–23.

Harding, F. D., Madden, J. M., & Colson, K.   Analysis of a job evaluation system. *J. Appl. Psychol.*, 1960, **44**, 354–357.

Havron, M. D., and McGrath, J. E.   The contribution of the leader to the effectiveness of small military groups.   In L. Petrullo & B. M. Bass (Eds.), *Leadership and interpersonal behavior.* New York: Holt, 1961.

Hay, E. N.   Cross-validation of clerical aptitude tests. *J. Appl. Psychol.*, 1950, **34**, 153–158.

Hemphill, J. K., & Westie, C. M.   The measurement of group dimensions. *J. Psychol.*, 1950, **29**, 325–342.

Henry, G. W.   *Essentials of psychiatry* (3d ed.).   Baltimore: Williams & Wilkins, 1938.

Hersey, P., & Blanchard, K. H.   *Management of organizational behavior.* Englewood Cliffs, N.J.: Prentice-Hall, 1969.

Herzberg, F.   *Work and the nature of man.*   Cleveland: World, 1966.

Herzberg, F., Mausner, B., Peterson, R. O., & Capwell, D. F.   *Job attitudes: review of research and opinion.*   Pittsburgh: Psychological Service of Pittsburgh, 1957.

Herzberg, F., Mausner, B., & Snyderman, B.   *The motivation to work.* New York: Wiley, 1959.

Hollander, E. P.   Buddy ratings: military research and industrial implications. *Personnel Psychol.*, 1954, **7**, 385–393.

Hollander, E. P., & Julian, J. W.   Contemporary trends in the analyses of leadership process. *Psychol. Bull.*, 1969, **71**, 387–397.

Hollander, E. P., & Webb, W. B.   Leadership, followership and friendship: an analysis of peer nominations. *J. Abnorm. Soc. Psychol.*, 1955, **50**, 163–167.

House, R. J., & Wigdor, L. A.   Herzberg's dual-factor theory of job satisfaction and motivation: a review of the evidence and a criticism. *Personnel Psychol.*, 1967, **20**, 369–389.

Hovland, C. I.   Two new social science research units in industrial settings. *Amer. Psychologist*, 1961, **16**, 87–91.

Howell, W. C., & Goldstein, I. L.   Engineering psychology today: some observations from the ivory tower. *Organization Behavior and Human Performance.*   1970, **5**, 159–169.

Hughes, J. L., & McNamara, W. J. A comparative study of programmed and conventional instruction in industry. *J. Appl. Psychol.*, 1961, **45**, 225–231.

Hulin, C. L., & Blood, M. R. Job enlargement, individual differences and worker responses. *Psychol. Bull.*, 1968, **69**, 41–55.

Hunt, H. G., & Turner, L. M. The abandonment of wage incentive schemes: two case studies. *Personnel Management*, 1967, **49**, 40–46.

Jacques, E. *Equitable payment.* New York: Wiley, 1961.

Jenkins, J. G. The nominating technique as a method of evaluating air group morale. *J. Aviation Med.,* 1948, **19**, 12–19.

Jerison, H. J. Effects of noise on human performance. *J. Appl. Psychol.,* 1959, **43**, 96–101.

Johnson, D. M., & Smith, H. C. Democratic leadership in the college classroom. *Psychol. Monogr.*, 1953, **67**(11), no. 361.

Jordan, N. Allocation of functions between man and machines in automated systems. *J. Appl. Psychol.*, 1963, **47**, 161–165.

Kahn, R. L. Human relations on the shop floor. In E. M. Hugh-Jones (Ed.), *Human relations and modern management.* Amsterdam: North Holland Publishing Company, 1958.

Kahn, R. L., & Katz, D. Leadership practices in relation to productivity and morale. In D. Cartwright & A. Zander (Eds.), *Group dynamics.* New York: Harper & Row, 1953.

Kaponya, P. G. Salaries for all workers. *Harv. Business Rev.,* 1962, **40**, 49–57.

Karlin, J. E. Human factors evaluation of a new telephone numerical dialing system. In E. A. Fleishman (Ed.), *Studies in personnel and industrial psychology.* Homewood, Ill.: Dorsey, 1961.

Katz, D. The motivational basis of organizational behavior. *Behavioral Science,* 1964, **9**, 131–146.

Katz, D., Maccoby, E., & Morse, N. *Productivity, supervision and morale in an office situation.* Ann Arbor: Institute for Social Research, University of Michigan Press, 1950.

Katzell, R. A. Contrasting systems of work organization. *Amer. Psychologist,* 1962, **17**, 102–108.

Kellogg, M. S. New angles in appraisal. In T. L. Whisler & Shirley F. Harper (Eds.), *Performance appraisal.* New York: Holt, 1962.

Kelly, E. L., & Fiske, D. W. *The prediction of performance in clinical psychology.* Ann Arbor, Mich.: University of Michigan Press, 1951.

Kenagy, H. B., & Yoakum, C. S. *Selection and training of salesmen.* New York: McGraw-Hill, 1925.

Kennedy, J. E. A general device versus more specific devices for selecting car salesmen. *J. Appl. Psychol.*, 1958, **42**, 206-209.

Killingsworth, C. C. (Ed.) Automation. *Ann. Amer. Acad. Political Soc. Sci.*, 1962, 340.

King, M. S., & Kimble, G. A. Job opportunities for undergraduate psychology majors. *Amer. Psychologist*, 1958, **13**, 23-27.

King, N. Clarification and evaluation of the two-factor theory of job satisfaction. *Psychol. Bull.*, 1970, **74**, 18-31.

Korman, A. K. "Consideration," "initiating structure," and organizational criteria: a review. *Personnel Psychol.*, 1966, **49**, 349-361.

Landsberger, H. A. *Hawthorne revisited.* Ithaca, New York: Cornell University Press, 1958.

Lawshe, C. H., Jr., & Cary, W. Verbalization and learning a manipulative task. *J. Appl. Psychol.*, 1952, **36**, 44-46.

Leavitt, H. J. *Managerial psychology.* (2nd ed.) Chicago: University of Chicago Press, 1964.

Leavitt, H. J. Unhuman organizations. Address given at MIT, Cambridge, Mass., April 27, 1961.

Leavitt, H. J. Toward organizational psychology. In B. vH. Gilmer (Ed.), *Walter Van Dyke Bingham Memorial Program.* Pittsburgh, Pa.: Carnegie Institute of Technology Press, 1962.

Lefkowitz, J. Effect of training on the productivity and tenure of sewing machine operators. *J. Appl. Psychol.*, 1970, **54**, 81-86.

Lesieur, F. G. (Ed.) *The Scanlon Plan.* New York: Technology Press and Wiley, 1958.

Lesieur, F. G., & Puckett, E. S. The Scanlon Plan has proved itself. *Harv. Business Rev.*, 1969, **47**, 107-118.

Lewin, K. *A dynamic theory of personality.* New York: McGraw-Hill, 1935.

Likert, R. Measuring organizational performance. *Harv. Business Rev.*, 1958, **36**, 41-50.

Likert, R. *New patterns of management.* New York: McGraw-Hill, 1961.

Likert, R. *The human organization: its management and values.* New York: McGraw-Hill, 1967.

Likert, R., & Katz, D. Supervisory practices and organizational structures as they affect employee productivity and morale. *Amer. Mgmt. Ass. Personnel Ser.*, 1948, no. 120.

Locke, E. A., Bryan, J. F., & Kendall, L. M. Effects of monetary incentives on behavior. *J. Appl. Psychol.*, 1968, **52**, 104-121.

Lohmann, K., Zenger, J. H., & Weschler, I. R. Some perceptual changes during sensitivity training. *J. educ. Psychol.*, 1959, **53**, 28–31.

Lynton, R. P., & Pareek, V. *Training and development.* Homewood, Ill.: Irwin-Dorsey, 1967.

McGehee, W., & Owen, E. B. Authorized and unauthorized rest pauses in clerical work. *J. Appl. Psychol.*, 1940, **24**, 605–614.

McGehee, W., & Thayer, P. W. *Training in business and industry.* New York: Wiley, 1961.

McGregor, D. M. An uneasy look at performance appraisal. *Harv. Business Rev.*, 1957, **35**, 89–94.

McGregor, D. M. *The human side of enterprise.* New York: McGraw-Hill, 1960.

McGregor, D. M. *The professional manager.* New York: McGraw-Hill, 1967.

McKee, J. P., & Sherriffs, A. C. The differential evaluation of males and females. *J. Pers.*, 1957, **25**, 356–371.

Mackworth, N. H. Effects of heat on wireless telegraphy operators hearing and recording Morse messages. *British J. Industr. Med.*, 1946, **3**, 143–158.

McMurry, R. N. Validating one patterned interview. *Personnel*, 1947, **23**, 263–272.

McNair, M. P. Thinking ahead: what price human relations? *Harv. Business Rev.*, 1957, **35**, 15–22.

Mahler, W. R. Effecting a change in individual performance. In H. F. Merrill & Elizabeth Marting (Eds.), *Developing executive skill.* New York: American Management Association, 1958.

Maier, N. R. F. *The appraisal interview: objectives, methods and skills.* New York: Wiley, 1958.

Maier, N. R. F., Hoffman, L. R., & Lansky, L. Human relations training as manifested in an interview situation. *Personnel Psychol.*, 1960, **13**, 11–30.

Maloney, P. W., & Hinrichs, J. R. A new tool for supervisory self-development. *Personnel*, 1959, **36**, 46–53.

Mann, F. C., & Dent, J. *Appraisals of supervisors and attitudes of their employees in an electric power company.* Ann Arbor, Mich.: Institute for Social Research, 1954.

Mann, F. C., & Hoffman, L. R. *Automation and the worker.* New York: Holt, 1960.

Mann, F. C., & Williams, L. K. Organizational impact of white collar automation. *Proc. 11th Annu. Meeting*, Industrial Relations Research Association (Madison, Wis.: IRRA Publication), 1959.

Marrow, A. J., Bowers, D. G., & Seashore, S. E. *Management by participation.* New York: Harper and Row, 1967.

Maslow, A. H. A theory of human motivation. *Psychol. Rev.*, 1943, **50,** 370–396.

Maslow, A. H. Some theoretical consequences of basic need gratification. *J. Pers.*, 1948, **16,** 402–416.

Maslow, A. H. *Motivation and personality.* (2nd ed.) New York: Harper & Row, 1970.

Mayfield, E. C. Management selection: buddy nomination. *Personnel Psychol.*, 1970, **23,** 377–391.

Mayo, E. *The human problems of an industrial civilization.* New York: Macmillan, 1933.

Mayo, E., & Lombard, G. F. F. *Teamwork and labor turnover in the aircraft industry of southern California.* Boston: Harvard University Business Research Bureau, 1944.

Meehl, P. E. *Clinical vs. statistical prediction.* Minneapolis: University of Minnesota Press, 1954.

Meltzer, H. Industrial psychology in *Psychological Abstracts*, 1927–1959. *J. Appl. Psychol.*, 1960, **44,** 111–114.

Menninger, K. A. *The human mind.* New York: Knopf, 1945.

Merenda, P. F. The relative effectiveness of formal school and on-the-job methods of training apprentices in naval occupations. *Personnel Psychol.*, 1958, **11,** 379–382.

Meyer, H. H., Kay, E., & French, J. R. P. Jr. Split roles in performance appraisal. *Harv. Business Rev.*, 1965, **43,** 123–129.

Miller, H. G. Effects of high intensity noise on retention. *J. Appl. Psychol.*, 1957, **41,** 370–372.

Morrison, J. C. Organizational climate, individual background and values, and personal job goals in a sample of Scanlon Plan plants. Unpublished doctor's dissertation, Michigan State University, 1970.

Morsh, J. E. Job analysis in the United States Air Force. *Personnel Psychol.*, 1964, **17,** 7–17.

Mosel, J. N. How to feed back performance results to trainees. In E. A. Fleishman (Ed.), *Studies in personnel and industrial psychology.* Homewood, Ill.: Dorsey, 1958.

Mosel, J. N., & Goheen, H. W. The validity of the employment recommendation questionnaire in personnel selection. *Personnel Psychol.*, 1958, **2,** 481–490.

Myers, J. H. An experimental evaluation of "point" job evaluation systems. *J. Appl. Psychol.*, 1958, **42,** 357–361.

Nadler, L. Management development and the employment scene. *Personnel J.*, 1968, **47,** 32–36.

Nangle, J. E. The effectiveness of communication in preparation for change in an insurance company. Unpublished doctor's dissertation, Michigan State University, 1961.

Nealey, S. M. Determining worker preference among employee benefit programs. *J. Appl. Psychol.*, 1964, **48**, 7–12.

Nelson, C. W. A new approach to leadership: its rationale data, reliability, validity, and application. *Int. Harvester Res. Project.* Chicago: University of Chicago, Industrial Relations Center, 1950.

Opsahl, R. L., & Dunnette, M. D. The role of financial compensation in industrial motivation. *Psychol. Bull.*, 1966, **66**, 94–118.

Oskamp, S. W. Overconfidence in case-study judgments. *J. Consult. Psychol.*, 1965, **29**, 261–265.

Parker, J. W., Taylor, E. K., Barrett, R. S., & Martens, L. Rating scale content: III Relationships between supervisory and self-ratings. *Personnel Psychol.*, 1959, **12**, 49–63.

Parrish, J. A. (Chrmn.) The industrial psychologist: selection and equal employment opportunity (a symposium). *Personnel Psychol.*, 1966, **19**, 1–40.

Pashalian, S., & Crissy, W. J. How readable are corporate annual reports? *J. Appl. Psychol.*, 1950, **34**, 244–248.

Patton, A. How to appraise executive performance. In T. L. Whisler & Shirley F. Harper (Eds.), *Performance appraisal.* New York: Holt, 1962.

Peach, H. Interest and boredom in repetitive work. *Bull. Industr. Psychol. Personnel Pract.*, 1946, **3**, 19–22.

Pelz, D. C. Influence: a key to effective leadership in the first-line supervisor. *Personnel*, 1952, **29**, 209–217.

Porter, A. Effect of organization size on validity of masculinity-femininity score. *J. Appl. Psychol.*, 1962, **46**, 228–229.

Porter, L. W. A study of perceived need satisfactions in bottom and middle management jobs. *J. Appl. Psychol.*, 1961, **45**, 1–11.

Porter, L. W. Job attitudes in management: I Perceived deficiencies in need fulfillment as a function of job level. *J. Appl. Psychol.*, 1962, **46**, 375–384.

Porter, L. W. Job attitudes in management: II. Perceived importance of needs as a function of job level. *J. Appl. Psychol.*, 1963, **47**, 141–148, (a).

Porter, L. W. Job attitudes in management: III. Perceived deficiencies in need fulfillment as a function of line versus staff types of jobs. *J. Appl. Psychol.*, 1963, **47**, 267–275, (b).

Porter, L. W. Job attitudes in management: IV. Perceived deficiencies in need fulfillment as a function of size of company. *J. Appl.. Psychol.*, 1963, **47**, 386–397, (c).

Prien, E. P. Development of a supervisor position description question- naire. *J. Appl. Psychol.*, 1963, **47**, 10–14.

Pritchard, R. D. Equity theory: a review and critique. *Organization Be- havior and Human Performance*, 1969, **4**, 176–211.

Pugh, D. S. Modern organizational theory: a psychological and sociological study. *Psychol. Bull.*, 1966, **66**, 235–251.

Recktenwald, L. N. The drop in undergraduate degrees. *Amer. Psychologist*, 1957, **12**, 229–230.

Reed, J. D. Factors influencing rotary performance. *J. Psychol.*, 1949, **28**, 65–92.

Richardson, M. W. The free-written rating. In M. J. Dooher & V. Marquis (Eds.), *Rating employee and supervisory performance.* New York: Amer- ican Management Association, 1950.

Roadman, H. E. An industrial use of peer ratings. *J. Appl. Psychol.*, 1964, **48**, 211–214.

Roethlisberger, F. J. The foreman: master and victim of double-talk. *Harv. Business Rev.*, 1945, **23**, 283–298.

Roethlisberger, F. J., & Dickson, W. J. *Management and the worker.* Cam- bridge, Mass.: Harvard University Press, 1939.

Ronan, W. W. Relative importance of job characteristics. *J. Appl. Psychol.*, 1970, **54**, 192–200.

Rose, A. M. The social psychology of desertion from combat. *Amer. Soc. Rev.*, 1951, **16**, 614–629.

Rothe, H. F. Matching men to job requirements. *Personnel Psychol.*, 1951, **4**, 291–301.

Ruda, E., & Albright, L. E. Racial differences on selection instruments re- lated to subsequent job performance. *Personnel Psychol.*, 1968, **21**, 31– 42.

Ruh, R. A. Ego need gratification, extra-work socialization, and attitudes toward the job. Unpublished doctor's dissertation, Michigan State Uni- versity, 1970.

Ryan, T. A. *Work and effort: the psychology of production.* New York: Ronald, 1947.

Saltonstall, R. *Human relations in administration.* New York: McGraw- Hill, 1959.

Sanford, F. H. *Authoritarianism and leadership.* Philadelphia: Institute for Research in Human Relations, 1950.

Sargent, D. S. The job-rotation method. In H. F. Merrill & Elizabeth Marting (Eds.), *Developing executive skill.* New York: American Manage- ment Association, 1958.

Sawyer, J. The industrial psychologist: education and employment. *Amer. Psychologist*, 1960, **15**, 670–673.

Schein, E. H. *Organizational psychology*. Englewood Cliffs, N.J.: Prentice-Hall, 1965.

Schipper, L. M., Kraft, C. L., Smode, A. F., & Fitts, P. M. The use of displays showing identity versus no-identity. *Tech. Rep.* Wright Air Development Center, 1957, 21–57.

Schuh, A. J. The predictability of employee tenure: a review of the literature. *Personnel Psychol.*, 1967, **20**, 133–152.

Schutz, W. C. *FIRO: a three-dimensional theory of interpersonal behavior*. New York: Rinehart, 1958.

Scott, W. D., Clothier, R. C., and Spriegel, W. R. *Personnel management* (6th ed.). New York: McGraw-Hill, 1961.

Sears, Roebuck and Company. The Sears experience in the investigation, description and prediction of executive behavior. Unpublished report of Psychological Research and Services Section, 1962.

Severin, D. The predictability of various kinds of criteria. *Personnel Psychol.*, 1952, **5**, 93–105.

Shimmin, S. Concepts of work. *Occupational Psychol.*, 1966, **40**, 195–201.

Shultz, G. P. Worker participation on production problems. *Personnel*, 1951, **28**, 201–211.

Simon, H. A. On the concept of organizational goal. *Admin. Sci. Quart.*, 1964, **9**, 1–22.

Sleight, R. B. The effect of instrumental dial shape on legibility. *J. Appl. Psychol.*, 1948, **32**, 170–188.

Smith, H. C. Music in relation to employee attitudes, piece work production, and industrial accidents. *Appl. Psychol. Monogr.*, 1947, no. 14.

Smith, H. C. Team work in the college class. *J. Educ. Psychol.*, 1955, **45**, 274–286.

Smith, H. C. *Personality adjustment*. New York: McGraw-Hill, 1961.

Smith, H. C., & Dunbar, D. S. The personality and achievement of the classroom participant. *J. Educ. Psychol.*, 1951, **42**, 65–84.

Smith, P. C. The prediction of individual differences in susceptibility to industrial monotony. *J. Appl. Psychol.*, 1955, **39**, 322–329.

Smith, P. C., & Cranny, C. J. Psychology of men at work. *Annual Review of Psychology*, 1968, **19**.

Solem, A. R. An evaluation of two attitudinal approaches to delegation. *J. Appl. Psychol.*, 1958, **42**, 36–39.

Springer, D. Ratings of candidates for promotion by co-workers and supervisors. *J. Appl. Psychol.*, 1953, **37**, 347–351.

Stagner, R. The gullibility of personnel managers. *Personnel Psychol.*, 1958, **11**, 347–352.

Stogdill, R. M. Personal factors associated with leadership: a survey of the literature. *J. Psychol.*, 1948, **25**, 35–71.

Stone, V. W. Measured vocational interest in relation to occupational proficiency. *J. Appl. Psychol.*, 1960, **44**, 78–82.

Strong, E. K. *Vocational interests of men and women.* Stanford, Calif.: Stanford University Press, 1943.

Strong, E. K. Permanence of interest scores over 22 years. *J. Appl. Psychol.*, 1951, **35**, 89–91.

Stroud, P. Evaluating a human relations training program. *Personnel*, 1959, **36**, 52–60.

Tannenbaum, A. S. *Social psychology of the work organization.* Belmont, Calif.: Wadsworth, 1966.

Tannenbaum, R., Weschler, I. R., & Massarik, F. *Leadership and organization.* New York: McGraw-Hill, 1961.

Taylor, H. C., & Russell, J. T. The relationship of validity coefficients to the practical effectiveness of tests in selection: discussion and tables. *J. Appl. Psychol.*, 1939, **23**, 565–578.

Thomas, E. J., & Fink, C. F. Effects of group size. *Psychol. Bull.*, 1963, **60**, 371–384.

Thorndike, R. L. *Personnel selection: test and measurement techniques.* New York: Wiley, 1949.

Tickton, S. G. The magnitude of American higher education in 1980. In A. C. Burich (Ed.), *Campus 1980.* New York: Dell Publishing, 1968.

Tiffin, J., & Phelan, R. F. Use of the Kuder Preference Record to predict turnover in an industrial plant. *Personnel Psychol.*, 1953, **6**, 195–204.

Tinker, M. A. Illumination standards for effective and comfortable vision. *J. Consult. Psychol.*, 1939, **3**, 11–20.

Trier, H. E. Job satisfaction and occupational status. Unpublished master's thesis, Michigan State University, 1954.

Trumbo, D. A. Individual and group correlates of attitudes toward work-related change. *J. Appl. Psychol.*, 1961, **45**, 338–344.

Uhrbrock, R. S. The personnel interview. *Personnel Psychol.*, 1948, **1**, 276.

Ulrich, L., & Trumbo, D. The selection interview since 1949. *Psychol. Bull.*, 1965, **63**, 100–116.

U.S. Department of Labor. Order of Secretary of Labor on Employment Tests by Contractors Subject to Provisions of Executive Order 11246, 1968.

U.S. Government Printing Office. *Task force report on personnel and civil service*. Commission on the Organization of the Executive Branch of the Government, 1955.

Van Zelst, R. H. Sociometrically selected work teams increase production. *Personnel Psychol.*, 1952, **5**, 175–185.

Vincent, N. L. Second annual Division 14 salary survey. *The industrial psychologist*, 1969, **7**, 46–57.

Viteles, M. S. *Industrial psychology*. New York: Norton, 1932.

Viteles, M. S. "Human-relations" and "humanities" in the education of business leaders: evaluation of a program of humanistic studies for executives. *Personnel Psychol.*, 1959, **12**, 1–28.

Vroom, V. H. *Work and motivation*. New York: Wiley, 1964.

Vroom, V. H., & Mann, F. C. Leader authoritarianism and employee attitudes. *Personnel Psychol.*, 1960, **13**, 115–141.

Wakeley, J. H. One way to get more meaningful results from attitude surveys. *Personnel*, 1964, **41**, 43–47.

Wakeley, J. H., & Shaw, M. E. Management training—an integrated approach. *Training Directors J.*, 1965, **19**, 2–13.

Walker, C. R., & Guest, R. H. *The man on the assembly line*. Cambridge, Mass.: Harvard University Press, 1952.

Walker, C. R., Guest, R. H., & Turner, A. N. *The foreman on the assembly line*. Cambridge, Mass.: Harvard University Press, 1956.

Wallace, S. R. Criteria for what? *Amer. Psychologist*, 1965, **20**, 411–418.

Wallin, J. E. W. *Minor maladjustments in normal people*. Durham, N.C.: Duke University Press, 1939.

War Manpower Commission. *Training within industry report*. Washington: GPO, 1945.

Warner, W. L. *The social system of a modern factory*. New Haven, Conn.: Yale University Press, 1947.

Weber, M. The essentials of bureaucratic organization: an ideal type organization. In Merton, R. K., Gray, A. P., Hockey, B., & Selvin, H. C. (Eds.), *Reader in bureaucracy*. Glencoe, Ill.: Free Press, 1952.

Weick, K. E. The concept of equity in the perception of pay. *Admin. Sci. Quart.*, 1966, **11**, 414–439.

Weider, A. J. Some aspects of an industrial mental hygiene program. *J. Appl. Psychol.*, 1951, **34**, 363–366.

Weiss, D. J., & Davis, R. V. An objective validation of factual interview data. *J. Appl. Psychol.*, 1960, **44**, 381–384.

Weitz, J. Job expectancy and survival. *J. Appl. Psychol.*, 1956, **40**, 245–247.

Weitz, J. Selecting supervisors with peer ratings. *Personnel Psychol.*, 1958, **11**, 25–35.

Weitz, J. Criteria for criteria. *Amer. Psychologist*, 1961, **16**, 228–231.

Weldon, R. J., & Peterson, G. M. Effect of design on accuracy and speed of operating dials. *J. Appl. Psychol.*, 1957, **41**, 153–157.

Wherry, R. J., & Fryer, D. H. Buddy ratings: popularity contest or leadership criteria? *Personnel Psychol.*, 1949, **2**, 147–149.

Whisler, T. L., & Shultz, G. P. Automation and the management process. *Ann. Amer. Acad. Political Soc..Sci.*, 1962, **340**, 81–89.

Whitehead, T. *The industrial worker*. Cambridge, Mass.: Harvard University Press, 1938.

Whitla, D. K., & Tirrell, J. E. The validity of ratings of several levels of supervisors. *Personnel Psychol.*, 1954, **6**, 461–466.

Whitsett, D. A., & Winslow, E. K. An analysis of studies critical of the motivator-hygiene theory. *Personnel Psychol.*, 1967, **20**, 391–415.

Whyte, W. F., & Gardner, B. B. The man in the middle: position and problems of the foreman. *Appl. Anthrop.*, 1945, **4**, 1–28.

Whyte, W. H. *The organization man*. New York: Simon and Schuster, 1956.

Wofford, J. C. Behavior styles and performance effectiveness. *Personnel Psychol.*, 1967, **20**, 461–496.

Wofford, J. C. Factor analysis of managerial behavior variables. *J. Appl. Psychol.*, 1970, **54**, 168–173.

Woodson, W. E. *Human engineering guide for equipment designers*. Berkeley, Calif.: University of California Press, 1954.

Wooley, H. T. A dominant personality in the making. *Pedagog. Seminary*, 1925, **32**, 569–598.

Worthy, J. C. Organizational structure and employee morale. *Amer. Sociol. Rev.*, 1950, **15**, 169–179.

Wright, O. R., Jr. Summary of research on the selection interview since 1964. *Personnel Psychol.*, 1969, **22**, 391–413.

Wyatt, S. Boredom in industry. *Personnel J.*, 1929, **8**, 161–171.

Young, M. L., & Odbert, H. S. Government support of psychological research: fiscal year 1959. *Amer. Psychologist*, 1960, **15**, 661–664.

Zavala, A. Development of the forced-choice rating scale technique. *Psychol. Bull.*, 1965, **63**, 117–124.

Zelko, H. P. The lecture. In R. L. Craig & L. R. Bittel (Eds.), *Training and development handbook*. New York: McGraw-Hill, 1967.

Ziller, R. C. Leader acceptance of responsibility for group action under conditions of uncertainty and risk. (Abstract) *Amer. Psychologist*, 1955, **10**, 475–476.

NAME INDEX

Morsh, J. E., 162
Mosel, J. N., 174, 358
Mouton, J. S., 130, 131, 305, 313,
    314, 321, 323
Myers, J. H., 247

Nadler, L., 112
Nangle, J. E., 82
Nealey, S. M., 254, 255
Nelson, C. W., 190
Nelson, J. R., 95, 262
Newcomb, T. M., 215

Odbert, H. S., 339
Opsahl, R. L., 243
Oskamp, S. W., 163
Otis, J., 163
Owen, E. B., 18

Pareek, V., 201, 204
Parker, J. W., 280, 281
Parrish, J. A., 186
Pashalian, S., 145
Patton, A., 279
Peach, H., 260
Pelz, D. C., 116, 154
Peterson, G. M., 69
Peterson, R. O., 255
Phelan, R. F., 179
Porter, A., 113
Porter, L. W., 43, 44
Prien, E. P., 170, 187
Pritchard, R. D., 245
Puckett, E. S., 57, 263
Pugh, D. S., 10

Recktenwald, L. N., 333
Reed, J. D., 66
Richardson, M. W., 269

Roadman, H. E., 194
Roethlisberger, F. J., 8, 74, 88, 89,
    147, 331
Ronan, W. W., 38
Rose, A. M., 88
Rosenbaum, W. B., 245
Ross, I. C., 95, 262
Rothe, H. F., 148, 252
Ruda, E., 185
Ruh, R. A., 55
Russell, J. T., 182
Ruttenberg, H., 53
Ryan, T. A., 75, 79

Saltonstall, R., 209, 210
Sanford, F. H., 116
Safgent, D. S., 221
Sawyer, J., 335
Scanlon, J., 55
Schein, E. H., 4, 88, 89, 91
Schipper, L. M., 66
Schuh, A. J., 173
Schutz, W. C., 350
Scott, W. D., 18, 160, 173, 175, 176,
    204, 208, 250, 329, 330
Seashore, S. E., 116, 134, 317, 320
Severin, D., 231
Sharan, S., 193
Shaw, M. E., 202
Sherriffs, A. C., 120
Shimmin, S., 37
Shultz, G. P., 83
Simon, H. A., 10
Simon, H. W., 58
Skinner, B. F., 222
Sleight, R. B., 69
Smith, H. C., 17, 94, 196, 211, 236,
    289, 340, 345
Smith, P. C., 245, 259
Smode, A. F., 66
Smyth, P., 95, 262

SUBJECT INDEX